RECENTERING
SETH

"Take a seat. Open this book. Settle back and transform into a student of the universe within the outstanding chamber of cosmic truth *Recentering Seth*. Everything we must know about this world and beyond is described within these enlightening pages, from the structure of our energetic system to ways to deal with our emotions. Your guide, a multidimensional being with the originality and authority evocative of Seth, channels through John Friedlander to invite you deeper and further into the divine revelation that is life itself. Radiating profundity throughout, simply put, this is a powerful book about life."

CYNDI DALE, INTUITIVE, HEALER, AND
AUTHOR OF *THE SUBTLE BODY*

"Given the abstract nature of the Etheric and Astral realms, Friedlander has made the numinous remarkably easy to understand. His approach to intuition and channeling is both fluid and confident, rooted in years of teaching. He manages to create a resilient ecosystem of practices that will withstand the test of time, rather than a rigid set of rules liable to quickly fall out of fashion. Friedlander's world is one where psychicism is not a superpower reserved for the elite but a subtle skillset anyone is free to develop. This book is a gift that has the magical ability of reminding the reader that they, too, are a gift."

SOPHIE STRAND, POET, HISTORICAL FICTION WRITER,
AND AUTHOR OF *THE FLOWERING WAND*

"In the mental atmosphere in which our minds are immersed, the psychosphere, there exists useful information for those adventurers with the courage to believe. This Multipersonhood channel source called Seth has, does, and will continue to help us answer fundamental human questions: Who am I? Why am I here? Through John Friedlander's lawyer mind we learn that synchronicities offer clues to how we participate in the creation of our own realities."

BERNARD D. BEITMAN, M.D., AUTHOR OF *CONNECTING WITH COINCIDENCE* AND *MEANINGFUL COINCIDENCES*

"If you have ever suffered and experienced pain, this book is for you. Drink in the pages. Their healing salve illuminates the human psyche with gold. Friedlander's way of literary kintsugi comforts the brutality of illusion with medicine for the soul. Relatable and personal, the universal qualities of his autobiographical offerings sublimely weave a north star into the creases of our lived experience and consciousness."

RACHEL WOLFE, MFA, ARTIST

RECENTERING
SETH

Teachings from a Multidimensional Entity
on Living Gracefully and Skillfully in a
World You Create But Do Not Control

A Sacred Planet Book

JOHN FRIEDLANDER

Bear & Company
Rochester, Vermont

Bear & Company
One Park Street
Rochester, Vermont 05767
www.BearandCompanyBooks.com

Text stock is SFI certified

Bear & Company is a division of Inner Traditions International

Sacred Planet Books are curated by Richard Grossinger, Inner Traditions editorial board member and cofounder and former publisher of North Atlantic Books. The Sacred Planet collection, published under the umbrella of the Inner Traditions family of imprints, is comprised of works on the themes of consciousness, cosmology, alternative medicine, dreams, climate, permaculture, alchemy, shamanic studies, oracles, astrology, crystals, hyperobjects, locutions, and subtle bodies.

Copyright © 2022 by John Friedlander
Foreword © 2022 by Richard Grossinger

Cataloging-in-Publication Data for this title is available from the Library of Congress

ISBN 978-1-59143-437-5 (print)
ISBN 978-1-59143-438-2 (ebook)

Printed and bound in the United States by Lake Book Manufacturing, Inc. The text stock is SFI certified. The Sustainable Forestry Initiative® program promotes sustainable forest management.

10 9 8 7 6 5 4 3 2 1

Text design and layout by Debbie Glogover
This book was typeset in Garamond Premier Pro with Gill Sans MT Pro, and Jazmin used as display typefaces

To send correspondence to the author of this book, mail a first-class letter to the author c/o Inner Traditions • Bear & Company, One Park Street, Rochester, VT 05767, and we will forward the communication, or contact the author directly at **psychicpsychology.org**.

THANK YOU

Richard Grossinger, for your stunning gift of drawing together over two hundred hours of classes into a "second class," an inner class. You have accomplished your stated objective "to distill the heart, meaning, and function of what John was saying—and channeling—to capture both its sense and spirit."

All the professionals at Inner Traditions, for your attention and excellence. Special thanks to my copy editor, Sarah Galbraith, and supervising editor, Renée Heitman. I am thrilled at how you are able to bring a subtle, caring understanding and find the flow of this book.

My students and friends across the years—your own sharing, questions, excitement, and struggles are essential to this material. It is and was always intended to be a group project.

Gloria Hemsher, for sharing our psychic and spiritual adventures, writing and teaching, and for your support, feedback, occasional push-back, healing, and insights. Most of all, thanks for your friendship. Art Giser, my long-time spiritual co-adventurer.

Violeta Viviano, JoAnn Wess, Sara Remke, Brian Greminger, Gilbert Choudury (Gloria's husband), and many others for your decades of support. Brian, for your initiative in making our internet seminars possible.

Pamela, my wife, for forty-five ever better years of love, support, and companionship—my favorite companion.

Contents

PART TWO

A SETHIAN APPROACH TO REALITY AND BEINGNESS

PART THREE

DESIRE, ANGER, NEUTRALITY, AND BELIEFS

PART FOUR

PICTURES

PART FIVE

THE SEVEN PLANES OF CONSCIOUSNESS
AND PERMANENT SEEDS

**Note to the Reader
Regarding a Glossary of Terms
and Sample Exercises**

The author's system of teaching contains specialized terms and exercises. Key terms are defined and detailed in the glossary for your ready reference. The reader will find introductory versions of the in-class exercises available at the back of this book.

The Big Picture

Richard Grossinger

This is a book of John Friedlander's teachings. It was assembled from transcriptions of selected classes that took place between 2010 and 2019. In compiling this material, I have tried to distill the heart, meaning, and function of what John was saying—and channeling—to capture both its sense and spirit.

John says that Jane Roberts's channeling of Seth set up humankind's explorations for the next twenty-five hundred years. That may be hyperbole; I think that John meant it not literally or as prophecy as much as a statement of the radicalness and complexity of the transmission and its context. It will take twenty-five hundred years to get to the bottom of what it is saying and its implications. Even after twenty-five hundred years, it will still be saying new things and changing its energy apropos the universe.

Seth said that only Jane Roberts would channel him in her lifetime. I take that to mean that the entity—the Multipersonhood adopting the name Seth—would only appear as Seth through Jane. Seth was not the energy's name to itself or to others, so by definition Seth *could* only speak through Ms. Roberts. But Seth exists and transmits in other forms, by other names, and through other teachers, beyond time and space, and likely elsewhere in the multiverse.

John was also not channeling a single "personable" entity as much as a transpersonal spectrum of extradimensional intelligence with person-like foci. The beings used names just as other beings coming through other channels have used names like "Seth," "Abraham" and "Michael." In classes, John naturally incorporated his own lessons, insights, and interpretations into those he was receiving. At most junctures it was as impossible as it was unnecessary to know *who* was speaking. The reader of this book won't either. That is not a problem, and "Seth" or recentering "him" is not a problem. You can read this material as Sethian, post-Sethian, para-Sethian, or non-Sethian, and it will still be Sethian, by dint of John's engagement with the Sethian locution.

John has recentered Roberts's system by continuing to channel the greater Multipersonhood while fusing it with (1) traditional theosophy from Helena Blavatsky, Alice Baily, Annie Besant, Charles Webster Leadbeater, *et al.*, (2) the human-development course of Lewis Bostwick at the Berkeley Psychic Institute of the 1970s, and (3) Dzogchen Buddhist teachings—any of which may have been partially downloaded from the same intelligence field. John is also informed by his years of study at Harvard Law School and subsequent legal practice—human jurisprudence is a Physical-plane adaption of cosmic law. He may not have extended the warranty of Jane's system beyond two and a half millennia, but he has begun the twenty-five-hundred-year deciphering project and added his own tensors of complexity.

That doesn't necessarily make the system *more* complex—it was already as complex as it could possibly be, nests of probability states arising and expanding in all directions. What he did was limn the *actual* complexity of the system.

The transmission we are identifying as Sethian addresses humanity's existential crisis at its core, including personal identity, world, climate, and civilization. John is neither fatalist nor apocalyptic regarding the plight of humanity and this planet—quite the opposite, he believes the universe can never be made less than it is, here and elsewhere. John's classes offer unique perspectives for personal healing, transformation, service, and redemption of what is closest to the brink. Maybe we can't fail in the long run, not if the universe is biased on our behalf, as John's guides say; but there are also many probable universes, and it would be nice to steward this one more effectively, and to understand more precisely where we are in the whole of things—the big picture—both morally and cosmologically.

Yes, class notes make for an uneven muddle, but that doesn't undermine the effectiveness or clarity of the material, and I believe that the spoken voice has a certain charm that a more conventional approach wouldn't. Plus, a more conventional approach wasn't available.

I undertook this project after acquiring and participating editorially in the production of a prior book that John co-wrote with his colleague Gloria Hemsher, *Psychic Psychology: Energy Skills for Life and Relationships.* Following its release, I tried to interest John in writing a book of greater Sethian ontology and cosmology. He knew that those elements of his teaching were mostly missing from *Psychic Psychology* and prior books, but he told me that he didn't want to undertake a massive project that would divert time and energy from his ongoing teaching and practice.

Something else had totally eluded me. I didn't realize before I began that much of John's teaching comes from his guides: from wisdom centers like Seth, Mataji, Yukteshwar, and others. He is *channeling.* I knew that intellectually, but I didn't grasp its ramifications. John can't reproduce, or even sometimes remember, his teachings and responses outside the frequency of the workshop.

So, this is only partly a John Friedlander book; it is also a Seth or Mataji book in much the way that the various Jane Roberts transmissions from Seth make them Seth books as well as Jane Roberts books. That the circumstance is not exactly the same is partly a difference of forty or so years in the way that compound intelligences and higher-portal guides have entered our world. They are not entirely separate voices anymore; they are flowing into our voices. It is a characteristic of Multipersonhood that a channeled voice or spirit guide can elicit a facet of John without losing its status as exogenous information. This operates as both an outer knowing and an inner experience of voices—a dance that John does elegantly enough that the presentation is seamless. I am reminded of the role of dark energy, junk DNA, and unconscious regions of the brain and mind in completing information sets that are simultaneously personal and transpersonal, individual and collective.

Knowing all this, John encouraged me to compile a book from his classes. I had been telling him that there was fantastic stuff there, and he hoped I would work on it long enough to catch the big fish.

As soon as I began, I discovered that most of the classes were only available as audio recordings, many with placeholder titles, or labeled with a month and a day but not a year. The seven or eight key classes I was looking for could not easily be identified. In the end, I listened through roughly two hundred hours of audio recordings for what I wanted, transcribing, abridging, synthesizing, and clarifying as I went. I organized and edited the entirety multiple times to make this book.

Though I have left major chunks of classes intact as they occurred, I also brought together transcriptions from widely separated classes and fused them as if a single thread. Will Ives and the mud run are two of my larger weaves. I took their main bodies from at least six different courses.

I purposely didn't revisit *Psychic Psychology* in the process because I wanted to excavate a new text and make a different book. I didn't want to have to eliminate material that was already in John's previous books or spend time sorting and framing against their backdrop, so there is duplication, sometimes word for word. Yet what you have here, in the replicates, is a different emphasis, context, and nuance, not unlike deleted scenes of a movie—a developmental or emergent set of meanings with their own trajectory and story.

I was interested in the universe that John was mapping: *this* universe, how and why it came into being, and how and why it operates the way it does. Unlike in physics or science in general, here we get to ask *why* as well as *how*. Not all of that is explicit in the "Seth material" and its recentering, but it is implicit. The emphasis, no matter who is speaking (John or his guides), is on a mysterious arising, a metaphysical implicate order. It is a cosmogony of as much weight, in my opinion, as astrophysics' Big Bang or biology's genetic code; it is as groundbreaking as Einstein's theory of gravitation, for it includes a way to live life. That sounds like a wild exaggeration or inflation but, after all, the

Big Bang is still seeking a moral order, a why, and an ontological and moral background against which to impose its orthodox version of creation. General relativity, quarks, black holes, and DNA lack all three; they paradigmatically happen—the radical contribution of physics and microbiology—but they cannot be accounted for. Seth's transmission accounts for them, and John recenters that accounting through his *own* relationship to Jane and Seth.

I have tried to preserve or recreate the vibration of class situations, but they are at a depth and veridicality that words cannot easily denote. Four- and five-dimensional logic doesn't translate into a three-dimensional continuum that is made of group energy, a psychic field created by formal exercises and clairvoyant intuitions. In transcribing, I realized that these came and went in a flicker during the classes; they are caught and framed here like butterflies (though not killed and pinned). You get a glimpse as they flutter off.

For instance, what seems, at first, like a playful or circumstantial response to a student's query or a trial-and-error attempt at explaining an exercise becomes a shape-changing crystal once it is pulled and isolated. The beauty of making this book was that an answer without its question often had a power and depth that wasn't evident when John was responding to a student's query. In that sense, I felt a hint of guidance in the transcription and assemblage, as if I was pulling Rosetta stones blindly out of rebuses.

I am reminded of pre-Socratic fragments, though John's are neither fragmentary nor recovered. Their ellipsis represents a different internal difficulty, the transdimensionality of channeling.

At times I fancied myself capturing elements of a second class that John was also teaching for a constituency of invisible admirers on other planes. In that regard, John's teaching reminds us that we are *never* just talking to those who are present or apparent. The formation energy behind our syllables and concepts lies in *the necessity to create them.* The universe for which they were previously unspoken speaks them through people. People, at the same time, speak them for the universe. The universe itself arises from these "dialogues," most of them conducted by "beings" that are not human, terrestrial, or animate. In that sense, they are thoughtforms: intelligences giving rise to formations (atomicities) as atoms and molecules coalesce into the creatures transmitting those thoughts. Cause and effect blend, reverse, and synergize—that's what reality is.

Some of the concepts, like probable and sideways lives or Multipersonhood, may seem not only fantastic but logically impossible. They blow up (in both senses) all our ideas of who we are, the meaning of our lives, and the nature of reality.

These high transmissions could never *not* be spoken at some level, whether John voiced them or not. At the same time, they remain abeyant, in an unmanifested tongue like the Sumari language cited by Seth that was never used by any living group. John doesn't have to speak them for them to exist at large, and his speaking them does not encompass them—it archives them in the Akashic records. There they will continue to exist outside time—along with plays of Shakespeare and graffiti on tenement walls—even when our universe is gone.

My transcriptions mostly elide the remarks of John's co-teacher Gloria Hemsher, but not always. I picked a few places where her voice was essential, notably a key exchange with a student I renamed Vivian. Finding that exchange was my marker for when to end my transcription, for I refused to stop looking—listening—till I found it. It was too amazing to concede and, per emerald tablets in general, it was hidden in a place I least expected to find it. For approximately my last seventy-five hours of transcription I was searching for it. It made the book richer, in itself and by leading me on a merry quest, for I found several other gems after I considered myself otherwise done.

I violated usual rules of book formation regarding repetition and redundancy, including multiple versions of the same material or *almost* the same material. If you read carefully, you will find that there are no pure repeats. They yield new layers of meaning at each repetition. In that sense, the script reads to me somewhat like a chorus of a song: it changes meaning even when it stays identical to its last refrain.

Occasionally I added a phrase, sentence, or, on a few occasions, a paragraph in John's voice to give continuity, clarify a point, or add a dimension. When I voiced my concerns about this to John, telling him that I was jumpy about taking liberties, he responded, "You have always understood not just what I am saying but why. You get the relative weight I always intended."

Thanks, John. Thanks then and thanks now.

The sections and paragraphs in this book could be arranged in many different orders and still provide a viable reading. Each potential organization of them within their own matrix highlights certain aspects of their reality. Likewise, one can pretty much enter *Recentering Seth* at any point but with the proviso that certain ideas pop in without complete explanation. For instance, in my sequencing you hear about making your crown neutral before you know what either the crown or neutrality is. You encounter references to the Seven Planes in explanations of the emotional aspects of the Astral, but the Seven Planes themselves are detailed much later. John adds, "I have used the Seven Planes belief system for fifteen years now actively to help me and my students gain some technical proficiency. Now much of my guides' work no longer fits inside the clear structure of the seven planes." Yet during most of the classes sourced here, the Seven Planes was a guiding construct.

If you find yourself clueless, confused, or lost in transmission, the answer is always to read further, gaining clarity as you go. Alternately, try using this as a book of guideposts, selecting or dipping randomly as one would the I Ching. Everything works pretty much anywhere— starting anywhere and, likewise, concluding anywhere. John is proposing multidimensional realities as well as alternate probabilities, so what ties each concept or meaning to the next could lie in any of a number of those dimensions. Wormholes are implicit.

Remember, there was always an option to get these classes transcribed as they were given and then to run them chronologically or by topic. It would have been an interesting book but encyclopedic. To achieve anything like the honey gathered here would have required a dozen volumes. In this book you receive the distillate of two hundred hours.

John departs from the Buddhist canon, yet he departs from it in recognition that Buddhism, of all organized religions, approaches the truest picture of our reality. In his departure, he is following Seth in a view that human life is neither an accident nor a punishment. We are here not because our soul was stupid or miscreant or took a wrong turn. Life is a divine revelation, an invitation and enticement to experience, and an exquisitely designed format for souls and complexes greater than souls to experience their own paradoxes and ambiguities.

The Buddha premised that life is *dukkha*: dissatisfaction and suffering. If you don't get what you desire, you are unhappy and long for it; if you do, you are in constant peril of losing it and your happiness. The sole way out of suffering is to detach from the entire dynamic, to recognize the essential impermanence of all phenomena, including your own existence and ego. This obliges a neurological awareness of emptiness or nondual awareness, depending upon the school of Buddhism.

John's plan or life formula is the opposite of most Buddhist practice. His prescription is not to extricate ourselves from the pain of *samsara,* the cycle of death and rebirth, in order to enter enlightened consciousness, though that is our ultimate destiny. It is to experience life in all its sacredness, depth, and poignancy, and thereby to have experiences that will be a major source of material and inspiration for the ever changing, ever expanding process that we are—through eternity. We have entered a body to experience an aspect of creation that spirit can't encounter as spirit alone. John's system is, paradoxically, both Buddhist and the antidote to Buddhist practices that leads back into the heart of the Buddha's message.

Any way you look at it, John's basic topic is the reality in which we find ourselves—how it formed, how we happen to be in it, what its uses and orientation are in relation to the greater universe of All That Is, and what our responsibilities to incarnation are. I do not want to imply teleology in a traditional sense, as if this is a *divine* plan or even a kernel of your soul's plan; it is more that things have come to exist in a certain way with particular rules. John comes at this from the standpoint that reality has an inherent sacredness, no matter how painful and temporally ugly, cruel, or random some of its emanations are. Much of his teaching is an attempt to look behind appearances and find switchbacks, alternate views, and counter-intuitions. Many common events can seem triflingly mundane, merciless, or misleading because of spurious values imposed by social norms and habits. Yet some of the most basic aspects of human (and animal) existence are the universe speaking directly, operating as a truth machine. Hopefully this text allows you to appreciate that machine and run it for yourself.

RICHARD GROSSINGER is the curator of Sacred Planet Books, a member of the Inner Traditions editorial board, the founder and former publisher of North Atlantic Books, and a founding copublisher of *Io,* a seminal interdisciplinary literary journal that ran from 1964 to 1993. He attended Amherst College and completed a Ph.D. in ecological anthropology at the University of Michigan. He has written more than thirty widely acclaimed books on alternative medicine, cosmology, embryology, and consciousness, including *Dark Pool of Light: Reality and Consciousness, The Night Sky: Soul and Cosmos, Bottoming Out the Universe: Why There Is Something Rather Than Nothing,* and *Dreamtimes and Thoughtforms: Cosmogenesis from the Big Bang to Octopus and Crow Intelligence to UFOs.* He lives in Bar Harbor, Maine.

Preface

I have a distinct memory—maybe from one of the early Seth books, or from one of the Seth transcripts of classes that took place before I began attending, or from a live class I attended in 1974—of Seth saying that we, students of the Seth material, would be attracted to his material through a misunderstanding of what the material was really about. In Seth's early books, and even more in the classes, Seth exploded the usual understanding of the scope of our creativity and ability to affect our lives.

At the time, and even now, most people's understanding of the spiritual meaning of impediments and difficulties was that, primarily, any difficulties we encounter arise from our past in other lives or our current life. Usually this is explained as *karma*, the reaping of consequences of past actions. Before Seth, the common understanding of karma was that you mostly worked through it by experiencing a set of automatic, hardwired outcomes that had been set in motion by your previous actions. Without some divine intervention of grace, unfortunate karma was something you endured and paid penance for in your suffering, not unlike a prison term. But Seth brought a groundbreaking way of framing some of the deepest mystical understandings and practices that were not widely known or appreciated, placing those insights in a dramatically different context. Through his explanation of simultaneous time and infinite probabilities, Seth was able to explain that, no matter what you had done in the past, you could actively change your life in the present.

The point of power is in the present, Seth said over and over. This gives you a way to commit to actively engaging and learning from your life rather than merely patiently enduring the ill effects of prior mistakes. Over and over in the classes, even more strenuously than in his books, Seth emphasized that each of us has the power to create our lives in this moment. I still believe this. I have seen that power over the decades in my life and others'. What didn't get emphasized is how profoundly the Seth material is best oriented to an active engagement with everyday life—an engagement that is not a set of commands you can issue simply by working on your beliefs, aligning your intent, visualizing, or even working on your dreams. All of those things can help, but they only help reliably if you also actively engage new life in the realm of ordinary human consciousness in the time you live. Only by allowing life to speak back to you, to surprise you, can you find ever-growing meaning and flow and a reliable path to happiness committed to experiencing the ordinary environment of human consciousness.

This commitment to engaging in a conversation with life took decades for me to understand. It seemed to so many of us reading and studying Seth that all we had to do was work on our beliefs and we would get everything that we wanted.

I asked Jane in class one night whether there would be a recession that year, and this story is told in more detail later in this book. In short, she responded, "Not for me," to the laughter and approval of the class. But there was a recession that year and while Jane did prosper, I didn't. Years later, I came to understand and feel my hard times from 1974 to 1977 were, in the long run, one of the great gifts of my life. Those hard times fostered a radical change in attitude and direction when I was forced to engage life as I found it and created it. I and so many others had thought Seth's promise that we could create any reality just by working on our beliefs meant we could substitute a lucidity of mind for the give-and-take of life experience. Even Jane tried to deal with her rheumatoid arthritis without ever practicing yoga or tai-chi or modifying her diet. She also never followed up by diligently working with a psychic healing guide who spontaneously presented itself to her. I who had graduated from Harvard Law School, but couldn't write clearly and who had no common sense and who had no people skills, thought I could waltz into a law firm and make bundles of money just because I knew the secret Sethian knowledge. In fact, I was useless at that time to any law firm. Over the years and decades, I have encountered and continued to encounter friends and students who try to follow their bliss and make money without trying to learn how to do useful tasks or develop their people skills through experience. Instead, many of them try to just work on their beliefs or their intent or their visualization, and then try to use those techniques to win money by gambling or day trading or various other schemes. It isn't just in business that people try to step out of engaging the world that they have created, but also with health and relationships and any other part of their lives.

Even our desires themselves, by the nature of reality, contain tensions and contradictions. A simplified example of the intrinsic tension in our desires is my youthful desire for great riches. When I was young, I wanted to be fabulously rich. But I also, without even particularly raising it to my attention, wanted to be happy. Only through life experience, as I pursued becoming fabulously rich in stupidly naïve and clumsy ways, did I begin to understand that I was lucky I hadn't become fabulously rich because most of the reasons that becoming fabulously rich appealed to me were unrecognized arrogance—at least, I didn't recognize it, although others did—and control issues. Had I become fabulously wealthy, my arrogance and control issues would merely have grown. I would have alienated more people and would, surprisingly, have been less happy. Slowly over decades of experience, not just with friends and family, but in my practice of the law and other ways I tried to make a living, sometimes people would just fade away; sometimes they would expressly invalidate me. As I evaluated and attempted to understand my experience, I read the literature and got help from people like my friend Art Giser, Gloria Hemsher, my coauthor on my last two books and books to come, and most of all from my second wife, Pamela. I came to understand myself and relationships much better and have become happy. I wouldn't turn down being fabulously wealthy now, but the principal motives when I was young simply are not motivating anymore. My principal desires today are to achieve even more happiness by becoming ever more authentically kind and generous and, as is the case for many older people, better health. It's quite good for a seventy-three-year-old, although I wouldn't mind if it were better. But even that no longer has the kind of urgency that my youthful desires had.

So many students of Seth and New Agers in general thought we could avoid the tension, contradiction, and often messiness of life just because we had the secret. I'm certain that neither Seth nor Jane believed this even if Jane, too, narrowed her approach to life. When my then-wife left me, taking our one-month-old child, in March of 1975, I called Jane asking for advice. I had also recently been fired from my first job as a lawyer. She said, "John, you'll have hundreds of worse things happen to you in your life." That probably wasn't meant to be a prediction. My life has greatly and steadily improved over the following forty-six years. I think in a profound way she was educating me in the point this book is trying to present. She was saying life is not a victory march,* that it is important and meaningful and even sacred to engage the life we find ourselves in, *as that life is;* that we can find and create meaning in every moment in ways that fulfill the promise of our lives. Jane must have been in terrifying pain from her own crippling rheumatoid arthritis; and I in my youth and given numerous privileges like my education probably correctly seemed to her to be overdramatizing my loss and the despair of my predicament, real and painful as it was. Jane was signaling to me that, even with her pain, her life had an extraordinary meaningfulness and beauty and was filled with her own thrilling adventures, all of which I think she experienced as a blessing. I know that her life and works are a continuing blessing for society.

Life is set up to give us back more than we can imagine. Just as the Tao sign contains two sections, one light and penetrated by a small spot of darkness and the other dark and penetrated by a small spot of light, so life itself contains a dynamic creative interplay of what you think you understand and what surprises you. When you jump into life, surprises constantly require you to enlarge your point of view.

---

*This sentiment was loosely taken from Leonard Cohen's phrase, "Love is not a victory march, Hallelujah."

I don't remember if Seth said these exact words, but Seth grounded the meaning and adventure of life in the fact that all consciousness expands in all directions. This implies, as we explore in several ways in the book that follows, that there are no dead ends. Even your worst mistake and even bad-faith action inevitably expands into unique and individualized sacred actions. The Buddhists are right that there are no permanent or fundamentally separate essences. But the fact that all consciousness expands in all directions, both inside and outside time as we understand time, leads to the exploration and centering of this book. Seth is not about turning your life into a victory march. It's about a sheer exuberant exploration of your own unique, though interdependent, creativity in the field of everyday consciousness and relationships. This exploration inevitably leads, with an absolute guarantee, though probably with many ups and downs, to your own divine conversation with people, with life, and with consciousness itself. Inevitably you will develop your own subjectivity that expands sacredly in all directions through all time and even beyond time.

WILL

My dear friend, Will, is mentioned often enough in this book that the editor suggested I say a little about him and his impact on me and this book.

In August of 1972, I returned from a summer law firm internship to the yoga ashram where I planned to live the next school year while I finished law school. Within a few minutes I was sitting around the kitchen table when Doug, a devoted yogi getting his doctorate in math from MIT, said with an excited smile I can still see in my mind's eye, "Wait 'til you read the books Will has," and several others joined in urging me to read those books. We were all young, sleeping three or four to a room on one-inch cushions on the floor. Will lent me his two books, *The Seth Material* and *Seth Speaks,* both of which had just been recently published by Prentice-Hall and were written by Jane Roberts. I started reading one of the Seth books that early afternoon and read the two of them straight through that day and the next, stopping only to eat, sleep, and walk down to Harvard square to buy copies of the books for myself. My life, which had been centered on my yoga practice, notwithstanding my studies to be a lawyer, changed that first afternoon. Ever since, it has been centered around engaging all experience from an understanding principally shaped by Jane Roberts's Seth, an understanding that naturally has changed, grown, and become considerably more subtle, and I hope, more kind, generous, and authentic in the almost fifty years since that encounter.

Will was the most notable figure in the ashram. He always had a calm, clear, precisely articulate viewpoint about whatever exciting idea we were discussing or exploring. We were quite close because I respected his ideas, but we weren't as close as we were to become in the Seth classes themselves. After I graduated from law school, I traveled to San Francisco to study with Lewis Bostwick who taught a form of meditation based on developing your ability to read auras, but I did not finish that course before I came to understand I needed more experience in ordinary life.

I decided I could study for the bar and practice law in New York State, while also studying with Jane Roberts and Seth if I moved to Ithaca, New York. I moved in January 1974 and started studying for the bar and attending Jane's classes. Will was already there, having moved there several months earlier. We became very close as both our lives centered on our spiritual journey and in particular on Seth. Eventually I got a job as a lawyer and moved away, but we continued to stay very close. I was married, but this was also the time when I lost my job after only a few months and my wife left me and took our one-month-old baby. So, I moved back to Ithaca and again Will and I spent a lot of time together. Both of us were trying to get jobs and get moving in our lives.

One day, we were sitting by a lovely stream, talking, and Will said to me, "John, if my life were as bad as yours, I would commit suicide." With Will, even to the very end, I never understood how distressed he was, because he always sounded perfectly assured and centered in the elegant way he held himself and his easy, articulate, kind, and insightful speech. Eventually I did get another job, while jobs in his field, teaching, were just not available in that area. We lost touch the last two months of his life; I was still struggling, and I think he knew I wasn't solid enough to help him. He drifted off into other directions. In early February 1976, he committed suicide. Even today, forty-five years later, I cannot talk about Will without tearing up or just crying; and I often get more than a little angry at him, though in the long run, I know he has found peace, meaning, and joy.

Slowly, steadily, my life got better, though there were two more moves for two jobs. I met my current wife in May 1976, finally got a job I didn't get fired from in 1977, eventually built my own law practice, and felt ready to move into full-time coaching, psychic reading, and teaching, when my wife and I moved to Ann Arbor, Michigan in 1989 for her to become a professor at the University of Michigan. I had an idea that Will had moved on into other incarnations, but I really had no idea that I would meet him again and learn as much from him as I have ever learned from anyone.

Around 1992 or 1993, while meditating, I saw this beautiful, helical violet ribbon. The ribbon was conscious, it had an identity. I recognized it as Will, but a wise, calmly joyous Will. It is by interacting with this Will that I came to my current understanding of Seth's all consciousness expanding in all directions, because this "ribbon" is simultaneously, joyfully, and uniquely—or, as Jane would have said, idiosyncratically—participating in numerous realities, some of which I can track and some of which I cannot. One reality he participates in is as my constant companion, most of the time deep in the background of my mind.

PART ONE

A JOURNEY
THROUGH
CORE CONCEPTS

1
How I Teach

As you're taking these courses, you may get very excited about them, but I think it takes years of study and looking at them from different perspectives through those years to really start to get what this system can bring you. It's not going to make you czar of the universe. It's not going to give you everything that you desire. It's not going to make everybody be nice to you. It's not going to make you find a job where everybody is sweet and supportive and brilliant and wonderful and kind.

My approach is more embedded in the rough and tumble of everyday life. It will allow you to see ugly stuff as really ugly but will also allow you to see that, in addition to being ugly, it is beautiful and sacred. That doesn't excuse the ugliness of it, but it will make you more effective in engaging and making the world better in your own way.

I am reminded of a book that was around when I got started called *Three Pillars of Zen*. Someone asked a Zen monk, I guess he had been a monk for about eight years, what he was accomplishing, and he said, "I don't know but when I get up in the morning everything seems beautiful." He didn't say, "I've created a world where I get everything that I want"; he said, "Everything seems beautiful."

What's most important as far as I'm concerned is your ability to live in this world; work toward becoming more authentic, kind, and generous; develop really good communication skills; and to find enough neutrality that you can be open to life as it is.

To me the central part of this is, how can I be a more effective human being? So the focus always brings us back to the very specific experience of being human.

In a paradoxical way, that is enhanced by going really far out.

We get programmed by our parents, our school system, our religions. There is an implicit threat behind that programming: if you find a wrong answer you're going to get punished. And that is a very distorting concept.

I see people get fixated on what happened to them when they were four years old. When they get stuck like that, putting their crown junior to what they think their trauma then was, the story they're telling themselves is, "I'll never really be whole because this stuff happened to me when I was four years old."

We are not caused by the past. If anything, we are caused by the future. But, really, we're not caused by anything. As every moment expands in every direction, a horrible experience that you remember may not even be part of you anymore. And you can learn to help it not be part of you. You can come from resource states that don't *have* to go through the terrible past, that allow more flexibility and more openness to life.

Your personality is composed of sensations, emotions, and thoughts, and you might notice that in some sense they're separate and independent and then, in another sense, they're interpenetrating and interdependent.

You are dealing with stuff that you so much take for granted you might not be able to generate curiosity about it. But just be interested in the fact that you have sensations, you have emotions, and you have thoughts. Whatever experience arises, ask yourself, Is that a sensation, an emotion, a thought, or some blend? And notice how things move from one moment to the next. Now notice how your sensations, emotions, and thoughts are affected by other energies in the room.

I've said, from time to time, I channel these classes. I have a kind of informal channeling that goes on when I teach, actually it goes on throughout my entire life. It's kind of a blend of me and not-me. It's not that I go unconscious when I channel. Rather, I have conversations with my guides and share my opinions while I'm doing it.

I will work on an upcoming workshop, but not in the usual sense of preparing. I walk around and get lit up and my guides sort of drop little things. It comes together however it comes together: "Hey, this looks like it would be cool, who wants to jump in the pool with me and see what happens?" And anyone who wants to join is invited in. This is the way that I teach.

My benefactors, as Castaneda would say, were Lewis Bostwick, who founded the Berkeley Psychic Institute, and Jane Roberts, who channeled Seth; each gave me freedom from the other. They each had their significant blind spots, so I was fortunate to study with both of them. My spiritual project grows out of their work.

Alfred Whitehead said that all Western philosophy is a footnote to Plato. What he meant is that Plato set up twenty-five hundred years of subsequent human exploration. I think that the next twenty-five hundred will be a footnote, or expansion, or exploration of what Jane channeled from Seth. It's that vast and eloquent and mystically radiant.

The Sethian information came in three big waves. Madame Blavatsky and the theosophists were the first wave of a distinctive Western point of view, even though it's not clear whether Madame Blavatsky had any idea what she was doing. But it was profoundly important.

Those old theosophists, they were something else. You know, you read their stuff, it's just drenched in the exhorting Victorian trip-laying energy, because they *were* Victorians—why wouldn't it be like that? But they saw really incredible stuff, and I don't know where they got it from, because there weren't really any real precursors for the left-hand turn they took. They studied with a bunch of Buddhists and Hindus, but they transformed it into a very Western approach, where becoming enlightened was no longer the objective.

Then you have a second wave through Alice Bailey. She couldn't be less Sethian because her writings are a constant harangue against what is uniquely limited and human. She decided she was a "Master," and in some sort of sense, she was. But I would argue that, profoundly important as her work was, it was off. Yet as I look at her now, she not only became an incarnated soul, she went on up from there.

Jane Roberts was the fulfillment. Jane comes along and is completely down to Earth. She's a real character in the best sense of the word. Boy, did she screw some things up! That was also part of her strength. But because she was who she was, she could bring something really incredible. She broke through all kinds of walls, and her limits, as they are for all of us, were part of her strengths. If she hadn't had the kind of belief system of "let's fully explore our independence," I don't think she could have forged the solitary road that she did, breaking through millennia of spiritual approaches that are inconsistent with the coming Aquarian Age. She had to be hyper-individualistic to get to interdependence.

Basically, she didn't understand the creative use of polarities; she would focus on a very willful approach to the world, one where she could impose her point of view on her own life. To her, that is how you improved life itself. Of course, you *want* to engage your point of view as you engage life and you work to push things that you think you want— anything else would make no sense at all—but no matter how good you are at creating your reality, you're not going to get everything you want, and a lot of the stuff you thought you wanted isn't even going to turn out as good as you thought it would.

I love Jane beyond limit. As I said I think that she may be the most important intellectual figure for about the next two thousand years, but I'm going to be harshly critical of her at times because that's the human condition. There are some things that she didn't get, that she just didn't understand, as there are for me and I believe anyone.

One of the remarkable things about Seth's books is that they are literally different now than when I first encountered them forty-five years ago in 1972. The words are the same, but the energy connected to those words has changed. It happened mostly unconsciously.

I feel Seth talking to me through these words with a different energy now. Of course, while he's doing it all at once for him, it's unfolded slowly for me. But I think Seth is also *literally* different now than he was forty-five years ago.

Seth is a big enough being that, in current time, each person engages a Seth book in their own unique way and in different ways at different times. Seth himself operates in multiple time frames. He is not time-limited, nor are the guides who channel this seminar.

Seth is there all the time, and in Seth's experience, to the extent that I can describe it, which I can't, it's all happening at once. It's sort of like the way you could see the Great Plains and the mountains off in the distance. Someone who's walking down on the Great Plains is different each place they are. And the experience in the mountains is different from the experience in the plains. For Seth they're happening simultaneously.

So Seth outside of time broadcasts material *through* time, and at certain places in time his energy connected discretely with his words. They carried a certain meaning and at other places in time they carried another meaning. That may happen to a tiny extent in an ordinary person's words too.

I channel several entities around the Seth project. I used to call it "Seth," but Seth people get very prissy about other people channeling Seth. Seth had said he would only come through Jane in her lifetime, but it's not as though he just goes away. He was almost certainly who was talking to Alice Bailey earlier, though she thought she was talking to a Tibetan. Seth also doesn't have a single memory bank. He uses information in different ways depending on who channels him. He blends with the personality. For instance, the Dalai Lama is an emanation of something much larger, but he is not the *only* emanation of that bodhisattva. Jane Roberts likewise interacts with an emanation of a much larger being and her channeling of it will never be repeated because no one will interact with that being in the same way. Emanations can even disagree with one another, though the entity disagrees with itself skillfully.

I call the being I channel who is mostly "Seth," Yukteshwar, who is Yogananda's guru, infuriating both Yogananda and Seth people. At this time, I more often channel Mataji, a female guide from the Yogananda world. This corresponds with a shift in myself toward female energy at Etheric and Astral levels. Whoever my guide actually is, she sounds a lot more like Seth than Yogananda.

It behooves you, if this stuff is important to you, to practice it regularly. I hesitate to name a number because most people, if they can't spend that long, say, "Oh, I'm a failure," and then they stop doing it altogether. It's like exercise. If twenty seconds a day is what you can spend, spend it. If you want to become really competent at this practice, try to find at least twenty to thirty minutes a day. To do Etheric work, you really need to spend as much time on your personal or Astral aura as on the Etheric because too much concentration on the Etheric without connecting it to the Astral breaks the connection between your body and your emotions.

The practice doesn't have to be in just one or two sessions. If you spend twenty seconds a hundred times a day, that's a pretty good effort. And if you just spend twenty seconds once a day, that's better than spending twenty seconds once a week, which is getting to be pretty lazy. But it's still better than nothing.

Most meditation systems start in the area Lewis Bostwick used to call "mechanical." He set the core of his meditation system in the personal aura. He called that "kindergarten." There were more advanced things he did over time, but everything fed back into the personal aura.

Basically, what we do when we study the personal aura in this system is we work simultaneously on making ever more distinct distinctions, trying to avoid going into resistance to the polarity that is automatically established whenever any distinction is made by anyone.

It is very satisfying and simultaneously amusing when I have people have breakthroughs as we are talking and say to me, "You've been saying this for six years, why didn't I get it before?" You know, this is not rocket science. But you don't get it until you get it. Because this is life. The richness of these things, these concepts, these ways of being—they emerge gradually—and I imagine those same people six years from now will have similar breakthroughs and say, "You've been saying this for twelve years; how it is that I didn't get it?"

Now part of it is that you *think* you know. Once you understand a concept, you think, that's either right or wrong, and you're done with it.

That's just not the way things work.

I don't believe in any sort of conviction that you're "right." That feels like resistance to me.

For instance, you may say, "I really understand female guilt," and then one day you feel this really yucky energy in your space and you look around to see whose energy is making you feel so horrible. All of a sudden you realize it's you. And you also realize, I don't kick this energy out of my space. It *is* me. Then you learn to female-ground it and become senior to it.

People say, "John, I've been listening to you for twenty years, how could it take this long?" Because that's how long it takes sometimes. This is a subtle world we live in. It is not obvious how "this" hooks into "that." For instance, people say, "I am so over this person, and I'm not going to meet them again in this lifetime." They grit their teeth a little harder and say, "*Good-bye!* I'm not going to meet them in another lifetime. I am so over so and so," and they grit harder and harder and resist more and more. That's the perfect way to bring that person back to you. Just because you have announced you were so over doesn't mean you were over at all; in fact, every time I've ever heard someone say, "I am so over" they are announcing, "I'm just so stuck."

Plus, what you resist you become.

You may have an insight seven or eight days from now and not make the connection back to a particular meditation, but it's there. You might also open up to an understanding that you *can't* understand something, like life. John Fulton, this really great teacher in California, said, "Understanding is the booby prize." The real prize is a kind of living that simultaneously cherishes those cognitive processes—what you might call your conscious mind—and understands, or at least opens to the fact, that *you're not meant to get the full picture.* You're meant to focus very sharply on certain contrasting modalities. The full picture comes to you every night in the dream state. You may not bring it back, but it's there, and it comes to your self-understanding at some point after death. It might come very quickly after death if you're pretty aware and not in resistance; it might come after one thousand years more experience, or ten thousand, or ten million, but it comes to everyone, no matter how sacred their life was, no matter how impeccable, horrible, or wicked their life was. Every portion of the universe is ultimately redeemed in something approaching self-identity, but your self-identity does not happen in that part of yourself that has pat answers, it happens in a part that's a little bit bigger, or even a lot bigger, though it's still part of your personal self.

When people have near-death experiences, so many of them report that everything made sense. *Everything made sense.* That's where your identity ultimately lies, in that intersection among all these individual contrasts, everything making sense.

We work with energy. Energy transcends identification or designation. If something works for you, it's real.

If you latch onto a superficial understanding, you may actually be worse off than if you can allow that you don't understand it yet. That being said, a superficial understanding can be useful as long as you don't take it too seriously.

Niels Bohr, one of the founders of quantum physics, said, "In ordinary truths, like scientific truths, things can be right and things can be wrong. But great truths are not true unless their opposite is also true." Love solves all things and love solves nothing. Both of those are *completely,* 100 percent true.

Mistakes are not optional. They're required. As you do things, you'll grow in skill. If they were optional, there wouldn't be the kind of creativity that's the whole deal in human consciousness; this would be a game of tic-tac-toe. Or it would be golf where you got a hole-in-one with every shot. But that assumes that the point of golf is to get the ball in the hole. It isn't; it's to experience playing golf and everything in the countryside around you on the course, your partners, and so on.

Every few years I myself have a reconfiguration, re-understanding of the way things are. As I express things with perfect certainty, which I do, I would hope that every one of you hears, rather than my apparent perfect certainty, merely commitment in the moment. It's important to learn how to be committed to your understanding, recognizing that it is only going to last for a few years anyway. Then you will understand things differently. My friend Art Giser once said, "Wouldn't it be awful to believe the same things two years from now as you do now?"

If you ever get where you permanently know how things work, you're in trouble. No matter how much you know, the universe is always expanding in all directions, so your knowledge, while once true or true from your viewpoint, becomes a lie.

There's a danger to any system that explains everything. Best to take a system as a plausible story for now or a set of working hypotheses for taking your next breath.

No matter how much you grow, you experience and do things that take your breath away at how stupid and self-defeating they are, and that can either depress or excite you. You can come into this as, "I've done all this and I'm still making mistakes like this—I haven't done anything."

In fact, I've listened to that voice myself in just the last week; it said, "I've been doing this for forty-four years and I'm making *this* kind of error. I really haven't accomplished anything." Here's the problem: the goal isn't to *accomplish* something, it's to be alive and engage the world. I checked that voice out and saw that it wasn't my authentic voice, it was punishment. It wasn't true that I hadn't accomplished anything—I've accomplished a lot, but in some areas I have accomplished far less than I think I should have. But some things taking much longer than you expect is just a consequence of just how subtle the world is. None of us work with the focus and speed we would like in every area. That voice, that punishing inauthentic voice itself, is part of the deep subtlety of life and it gets highlighted while I think I am working on other things that are more important and easier. The *Tao Te Ching* says, "What's in the way *is* the way." Clearing and assimilating that punishing voice is actually my next spiritual step.

I often participate in my own classes as much of a student as anyone. I see aspects of my soul, I see things and feel things and I understand things that that I've never done or seen before. I think that's the way it always works.

Most of the work we do is done in very light trance, and staying in *only* a light trance is necessary because we're dealing with everyday life, with emotions, and with communication. You can't be in good communication if you're sitting in a bound lotus position in a deep trance. You don't have to go that deep in a trance state or that deep in the energy field. If you're looking to do certain kinds of dream work, you really only need to go to the Etheric or Astral, you don't need to go to the Buddhic plane.

But some of the stuff that we may want to do requires, at the very least, more focus. That's why we're on a long, slow pace to developing focus. I don't personally want to be able to develop the kind of focus that breaks the relationship between my emotions and my Etheric body, which is what so many focused meditations do. And then they'll flood that emotional space with love from the Buddhic plane and above. And that's wonderful—I just don't think it's what our humanity is about. That kind of love is not an emotion in the sense that it isn't an Astral, or lower-Mental-plane, energy. So that's why we're developing focus slowly and we are doing it in the context of our everyday lives.

Focused meditation very powerfully clears the chakras and activates the powers of chakras, so if you're one of what I call six-strike guys— well-educated, straight, cis male, not an alcoholic, not an artist, and not an engineer—focusing on the chakras is probably the way that you'll become clairvoyant.

If you can focus, you can do a lot of things with this form that you can't do otherwise, and the form itself will be healthier than it would be otherwise.

The object is to try to have a smooth flow that maximizes the amount of learning that you can assimilate and take with you. It would be easy to make this class like an acid trip and you'd walk out of here and say, "Wow!" but you wouldn't get as much out of that as you do with this sort of in-and-out rhythm, so that's why we do it.

Some of these are very abstract concepts, but you play around with them enough they come through. Seth talked about how a lot of the alterations of consciousness that we try to do, we overshoot the mark. The things that we're doing can be very easy to overshoot, easy to go into too deep a trance.

Clairvoyance is really cool and a lot of fun, very powerful; but you know it's not the be-all or end-all, either.

There are some souls who really like to do everything by themselves and there are some souls who like to do everything in collaboration with other beings. I tend to be more *that* kind of soul. So even though I'm male, I will always ask for directions and I'll ask for them ten times between here and there. That's also how I teach.

When I was four or five years old, my cousin got really angry at me. She was two years younger than me, and she said, "You can beat me up now, but in two years I'll be as old as you, and in four years I'm going to come and beat you up." Then her older brother said, "Oh Jill, he'll be two years older and four years older too."

You've been doing this for a long time, but in this lifetime I'm always going to have been doing it for a longer time. Even so I'm still going to be lost.

My certainty reflects only how long I have practiced this system. I have done some of these exercises thousands of times. That gives me context and street cred, but it doesn't prove me right.

The more technical skill you get, the faster your technical skill grows. And you'll only be happy when you enjoy the ride rather than looking excessively and seriously for the destination. There will always be parts that will be hard and challenging, and the hope is that you'll find those parts fun. Other parts will be just automatic. Lewis used to encourage us to have fun and, when we're not having fun, to have fun *not* having fun. What I understand that to mean is, no matter how awful a thing is happening to you, if you pay attention to it and use your tools to learn from it, there's a certain excitement and fun in engaging it with your tools and growing. The underlying experience may still be unpleasant but engaging that unpleasant experience with curiosity and growth is itself pleasant and sometimes enough to transform the whole experience. Even when curiosity isn't enough to transform the whole experience, it still makes it much better.

If your objective is to not be challenged then you're in the wrong planet, wrong universe probably. The more we can learn to be open to the fact that challenges will continually arise, the better off we'll be.

When I give instructions or have you attune to energies, please let the energies come to you rather than you come into my aura to find them because that enmeshes us. It's not good for you, it's not good for me.

Go out and do this stuff and see what happens. I think the future will bear it out. But in the long run it doesn't matter. You do the best you can and let outcomes take care of themselves.

Everything's connected with everything else, but they're connected in their own unique ways. That's the sense I'm hoping people will get. Everything we do is used throughout the universe, and not as a mere intellectual construct.

Everything I say is going to operate in our sense of time and directionality and so consequently it's not going to capture the sheer exuberant simultaneous multidirectional creativity of a gestalt that's doing all kinds of things on all kinds of levels. The universe is incredibly bigger and vaster and much more multidirectional than humans ever have imagined and ever could imagine.

One profound difference, just a mind-boggling difference, between this spiritual system and most others, is that we actually intend to come in and clear the pain out of the body. Now for your regular nondual system, who cares? Just leave all that behind and become nondual and you won't suffer. Well, our reason is that pain that you carry in your body changes your aura and energy and also affects everybody else on the planet. If you gain nondual awareness but haven't cleaned the pain out of your body, your pain will remain in the human realm and other humans will have to deal with it at the physical level. Also, humans will not be able to move to the next step, to Aquarian pre-group and later to group consciousness—where we can we can act as human beings, as material beings, and engage in Multipersonhood—until we have cleaned that emotional pain out of our bodies. And it's hard, if not impossible, to clear that pain if you are not also *in* your body.

In Tibetan meditation, they talk about a Buddhafield with infinite Buddhas. Those Buddhas of the Buddhafield are all out there, but they can't really impact us a lot at the physical level because they don't have physical bodies. High quality channeling also taps directly into the Buddhafield, though in a very different format. The channeled being brings a focus on the particularities of human interaction and intimacy into the channel's body. Therefore, it has a greater impact in the everyday world than meditation can. The presence of the Buddhafield is brought closer into ordinary physicality and is enriched with an emotional life. But not even channeled guides can clear human pain as directly as a fully incarnated human in the physical body. There are depths of clearing that only we can do.

2

Shoulds, Have Tos, and Oughts

Anytime you try to run intimate relationships based upon what you assume is true, you lose genuine meaning and communication, because relationships are not a matter of knowing or conquering, they are a matter of exploring and generating directions.

That sense of wanting to always know is called grasping in Buddhism. And grasping—we're in complete agreement with nondual practitioners here—is problematic and leads to unhappiness.

At another level, Jane Roberts used to say, "Spontaneity knows its own discipline." True enough. But she was stuck on that polarity and didn't understand that discipline knows its own spontaneity too. The Tao gives you both order and chaos. There will be times when your whole life fits into order and there will be times of chaos. Without chaos, there could be no creativity. If you didn't have chaos, you wouldn't have an open-ended universe, you'd have tic-tac-toe.

I was in a line five to ten years ago at a supermarket with Gloria and someone was taking a really long time getting through the checkout. "It's probably not the first time they did this," I thought to myself. "Can't they see there's a long line?" But they continued speaking to the cashier. Then Gloria says, "She's been enjoying the social interaction, and that might be the only social interaction she gets today."

The other day I was on another checkout line thinking, "Could that woman possibly take more time? She has done every single thing she could do to be as slow as possible!" Then I remembered Gloria. I still had a preference that she not be in my line—as if it were *my* line—but it was a preference, not a judgment.

You cannot know what someone else *should* be doing; you can *wish* what they would do. You can think the world would be better off if they would do things differently; you can have a *desire* that they would act differently; you can have a *very strong preference* that they act differently. You still cannot know what they *should, have to,* or *ought to* do. Why does this matter?

Let's say you're in business together and you think the business would be more productive if *they* did something. As soon as you say to yourself that someone *should* do something, you literally jump out of your aura and you no longer take responsibility for yourself. You're not saying, "I wish she would move through that line more quickly," or "I wish this person would collaborate with his co-workers," or "I wish this politician wouldn't steal money," or "I wish this person pointing a gun at me weren't pointing a gun at me." You're saying they *should.* When you say that person pointing the gun, that person is being a real jerk and abusing power, should be different, you're no longer in your aura. When you say "I wish," you're in your aura, you're owning that that is your impression.

Think of something that mildly or moderately annoys you. Think of a specific instance and say to yourself that person should be—whatever—fill in the gap. Say it over and over again. Watch yourself get angrier and angrier.

Where are you when you were saying what this person should be? Are you in the center of your head? What happens to your third chakra?

Now say *and mean,* "I *wish* this person wasn't pointing a gun at me," "I *wish* this person collaborated with co-workers," "I *wish* this person drove more the way I like?" Where is the part of you that you want to be in the center of the head? What happens to your third chakra?

This is a way to work on judgmentalness rather than trying to wash it away in a sea of love.

The formulation for shoulds, have tos, and oughts comes from psychologist Albert Ellis. But it's the underlying energy, not what words Ellis or anyone else uses to describe it. You're having a judgment when you think you know what someone else *should* do.

Ellis pointed out that it isn't things in the external world that make us miserable. They may be painful or unpleasant, but they don't make us miserable. It's our response that takes us into misery. And we generate our response with the stories we tell ourselves about the experience. In particular, we use certain formulations Ellis described as shoulds, have tos, and oughts. We make ourselves angry by telling ourselves that someone *should* treat us with respect or telling ourselves that we *have to* make that next light while it's green, or a co-worker *ought to* be working harder, or the woman at the cashier *should* get done and make the line move closer to us.

Sometimes we don't know how to motivate ourselves or respond to people whose actions we don't like without our shoulds, have tos, and oughts. Then, to us, the most effective way of transforming people seems to be by jumping out of our body into their space.

There's a subtle logical mistake in all of these. What we end up losing when we say shoulds, have tos, and oughts is a certain richness of experience. We end up narrowing down our experience, alienating ourselves from our experience, and working ourselves up into anger, fear, or depression.

While I'm shoulding this person, it's not a minor or private thing. What's it doing to me in some other totally unexpected direction that is diminishing my joy in life as well as other people's enjoyment of me?

What is so remarkable about this particular approach to judgmentalness is it allows you to have preferences. You will still have resentment, anger, and the so-called negative emotions. The difference is you won't stoke them with your many shoulds, have tos, and oughts.

Clearing your shoulds, have tos, and oughts is the way to emotional health.

There's a huge difference between *your* pain and what other people should, have to, or ought to do.

You can start to remove specific anger or resentment dramas. I can imagine the time will come when I can notice people who are moving more slowly through supermarket checkout lines than I wish they were without getting angry. Right now, I get much less angry, but I'm still upset. The woman is costing me a maximum of forty-five seconds, but my story is, I have to get back to my house for a reading at one.

I don't *have to* get back to my house. It might be inconvenient if I'm not back at my house. I'll be ashamed of myself, which is another should, have to, or ought. Life will go on if I'm forty-five seconds late or if I'm five minutes late. It also won't be because of that forty-five seconds max that that lady was taking for her socialization of the day. So if I stop stoking my anger with my conscious or subconscious shoulds, have tos, and oughts I will be more okay with her, especially if I start to ground and blow pictures.

You never gain perfect equanimity, but you gain so much more equanimity this way.

Shoulds, have tos, and oughts are generated by other people's energy. That doesn't mean you're not responsible for your shoulds, have tos, and oughts. Everything that happens in your space you're responsible for, even—and maybe even especially—if it's someone else's energy.

First, ask yourself whose should is that? Once you clear that should out of your space, then you might say something like, "Why do I want to go to work?" And then you might say, "Well, I don't really want to go to the work in the way I want to eat a piece of chocolate cake; however, when I sit and I think through the consequences of not going to work—when I consider all of the alternatives in taking this day off or even dropping this job and meditating full-time or whatever—I think I'll decide to go to work today even though I'm tired and irritated and frustrated." Not I *wish* I could take the day off because you always could, but I wish I felt comfortable.

It's important that you understand every should, have to, and ought work better as a preference, a want.

How do you get up in the morning without a "should" to push

you through your resistance to do something? If you're motivating yourself with shoulds, have tos, and oughts, that may be expedient for the moment, but it is not a good long-term strategy because that's someone else's energy. If it's worth doing, you can take your time, clear your space, and find a way to motivate yourself to do it with your own energy.

Say your kids are not cleaning their room; you have to sit down and decide, based on your wish, what you're going to do about their not cleaning their room. If you're going to deal with this situation, you have to deal with it by not getting angrier and angrier but taking responsibility for your emotions and deciding, "How big is this to me? How skillful am I at communicating this? Is this something I can talk with them about right now? Are they going through a crisis? Or is this the fiftieth crisis they're going through and do I want to talk about it even though they *are* going through a crisis?" You do all these things instead of just raging about how they should do it. If you stop raging about how they *should* do it and you stay in touch with your emotion about how you don't like it when they don't, then your only choice you have to make is to decide, what do I want to do about this?

Create a rose for a should and start to clear the energy out of that should that isn't yours. You can do a gauge: what percentage of that energy in that should is yours? Then start to clear the energy that isn't yours. Ground it down into the Earth, send it back to the people it comes from. If you don't know where it comes from, give it to some guide to redistribute, give it to the Sun. If any energy in that should is yours, create and destroy roses so you can bring a should you may have learned when you were two years old into current time. It will probably change quality to a preference rather than a should. If it doesn't, it's probably some cord or some contract that you haven't tracked that's refilling your should with someone else's energy.

This is not an exercise to finish in a few minutes. It can take weeks or months to clear shoulds, have tos, and oughts.

See what happens when you go to sleep and wake up. You may see a resilience and joy from higher aspects of yourself that come in, not necessarily as words but as energies when you're waking, and in your overall assimilation of the earlier day's experience, the prior day's or week's experience. It will affect profoundly your capacity for life.

Likewise you can remove things—but here's the catch: you can only remove something if you're willing to have it removed and very often you're not, not really. You might want to remove a judgment that you have about certain kinds of people, but you'll still have that judgment if you surreptitiously hold on to your shoulds, have tos, and oughts.

And these unfold. You don't necessarily know every should, have to, and ought that you're carrying.

One of the ways we use our shoulds, have tos, and oughts is in a vain attempt to punish another person. If you find yourself thinking, "Oh my God, things will never change unless humans decide that people *should* do this and they stand up to these terrible people who aren't," that's really a covert form of punishing. It's not obvious why it is, but if you track it when you're should-ing somebody, you'll see that you're really sneakily trying to punish them. You say, "Oh my God, if I stop saying he *should* cooperate with his coworkers, he'll never change." The magical thinking is, "If I grit my teeth and say over and over again, 'He should collaborate, he should collaborate,' that's going to change him." It doesn't work.

Go into one of those situations where you think—you don't really think this but you act like this—"This is so important that I have to sort of bop that person with a should, have to, or ought. I have to punish them—altruistic punishment. For example, if I see somebody do something that I consider to be really dangerous on the road, it didn't affect me, but I'll pound the horn to punish them, to let them know that someone thinks they should have done differently." You have a sense in which altruistic communication in those situations is important, but if you're doing it at a punishment level, you're just feeding into the same sort of stuff that they're doing. Likewise, "I have to kind of punish my spouse so that women on the planet eventually be free." We all do things like that.

If you decide that the business of humanity is to learn how to be kind and generous and then you start demonizing people who aren't kind and generous, you're kind of missing the point. I would suggest that a lot of stories of enlightenment or stories of science or stories of "you create your own reality" easily get into control stories, which increase the polarity and resistance. Not always, but they can.

You think you believe, "May all beings have happiness," but you are saying underneath, "Except him, except him." Well, if I'm truly saying, "May all beings have happiness," that even applies to "him." "May they be free from suffering"—same thing. I might like to punish him, but that isn't really consistent with this thing I know really works if you can do it authentically. "May they find the joy that has never known suffering"—gee, is that going too far for that person? "Maybe. No, I guess it's not."

"May they be free from hatred and attachment"—good idea, except I'll hold onto a little bit of hatred and attachment for him. "Oh well, maybe I'll give that up too."

If you really value human life, you wouldn't say, "May they be free from ignorance" in a shoulds, have tos, and oughts way.

One of the reasons people stay with their shoulds, have tos, and oughts is their belief that that's the only way you can motivate people. That's one reason why society isn't ready to let go of their shoulds, have tos, and oughts. I completely agree with that. This society at large isn't ready to let go of its shoulds, have tos, and oughts. *You* are. We have seen maybe one society that did it successfully on something vitally important, but it required someone with the charisma of Nelson Mandela with his truth commissions rather than punishment. We know societies *can* do it and so we can aspire to that, but we can aspire to that by beginning with ourselves.

So let there be peace on Earth and let it begin with you. No pressure.

3

Polarity, Flow, and the Center of the Head

It's natural for us to try to find a secure place in our emotional-mental awareness, but the moment you try to set up a secure place in the Astral you merely trigger polarities. The Astral body is the most polarized energy field there is.

Polarity is an intrinsic part of consciousness. It's not just *part* of your overall Astral body; every speck of your Astral body generates a polarity. It's an ontological feature of consciousness itself to generate polarity.

Every time you make a distinction you create a polarity. Now that's what we're all about in physical reality. We as humans have specialized in drawing sharp distinctions between polarities that are mutually reciprocal: hot and cold, male and female, and so many more. Any polarity you want to draw requires the other half even to have a meaning. And they flow one into another, so a large part of our current cultural understanding of reality is to try to control and isolate polarities.

We are distinction-making machines and the universe is ecstatic each time we make a distinction. You just don't want to impale yourself on those distinctions.

In the logic of spiritual practice, polarities are really the same event. If you want to win your next tennis match, the part of your aura that is vibrating at that desire generates all sorts of complementary polarities to it. For instance, it also wants to know what it would feel like if you lost.

You might ask, why do that, why not just get all of the blockages out of my Astral body? Well, that's impossible. It's simply impossible. Polarities are intrinsic to awareness in the Astral plane. Even people with nondual awareness have polarities in their aura, especially when they practice from a Buddhist perspective. They experience them but without resistance to them as polarities.

There are some spiritual systems that try to train you *away* from making distinctions. There are Hindu ideologies where you're in bliss all the time but, if you're doing that, you're nowhere near your body. Almost no mature mystical system seeks permanent bliss.

Though each part of the Astral is polarized, that's not a problem when it's flowing, that's an adventure. The polarity of the Astral field is only a problem when it gets stuck. When it's not stuck, it's a great divine creative process. The Tao sign doesn't just stand for the upside or downside of polarity; it means that you have to have chaos to have creativity, at least in any plane I have experience in.

The best you can ever do in the Astral is to have a kind of flow, but the only place you can be in that flow and not get stuck is a perfect nondual awareness that my guides say isn't actually achievable today in physical reality

We're exploring our interdependence and how these huge consciousnesses play into the utter validity of your personal self. Your personal self rides on a sea of chaos, on a sea of other consciousnesses that extend beyond human imagination. Your aura is full of some of your own energy and other people's energy pictures and other people's cords and pictures. You bring as much clarity to it as you can.

You clear cords the way you clear pictures, by using your psychic tools, by dissolving or cutting them or using some other visualization at their frequency. In the case of cords, you have to work a little higher than the chakra in which they're stuck. Not a whole step higher, just a shade higher.

By "sea of chaos," I mean open-ness. There is unpleasant chaos and it is a natural price to pay for the potential of creativity, as we use that term for human beings. I'm intentionally using the word *chaos* to help us open up to experience as it is, hopefully to make us braver.

Ignorance is part of the very nature of reality. No matter how much order you can impose on reality, there's always a creative underbelly of ignorance from which creativity itself emerges.

I don't think anyone on this planet has a perfect nondual awareness. People might claim that the Buddha had a perfect nondual awareness, but I don't think it's possible if you have a physical body. You can have quite a nondual awareness, but it is still not perfect.

So instead of nondual awareness, you can have flow, but people who cultivate nondual awareness do not run that flow in their Astral body. In fact, that's the point: they circumvent their Astral body, and that's *how* they attain that nondual awareness. They neurologically bypass certain areas of the brain, those that engage the Astral body. They *do* have a spontaneousness, and that's a nice model for what we would look for in the Astral body, but it's just a model.

You cannot actually find a perfectly safe place in your Astral body or any other subtle plane. That's why what you shoot for is a flow. And one place that flow arises in our system is from interdependence. The other obvious way that we work on flow in the Astral body is by clearing out energies that aren't ours and exploding pictures. Everywhere there's a picture, there's not a flow in that part of the Astral body. Let me put that differently. Everywhere there's someone else's energy, there's a flow all right, but it's disconnected from other aspects of you. It's a flow, but it *isn't a good flow, it isn't your flow.*

As we move into the Aquarian Age, we will enjoy the exquisite imbalances of polarities without isolating them. There will be more of a flow, more of a dance. There's a kind of neutrality that will come into play when we are capable of bringing group consciousness into this physical world, which Babaji* in my channeling calls "super-neutrality." We're not capable of working out of that now; it's a group process, not a single-person process.

You can't have the dance of life if you're stuck in polarities. Life will appear not to be dancing at all. No one currently incarnated can do the dance, but it's required before you can fully engage group consciousness. I don't know if any of us will ever get there—I mean while we're alive—but that's completely okay. All of us will eventually get there after we die.

A lot of the punishment energy I've been dealing with sets itself up as a demand that the world engage me logically and rationally. And what that works out to is a refusal to see, feel, and hear people as they are. We engage the world with a demand that it be rational. Or how we might address it is by trying to have it reach *its own* highest spiritual aspect. But many of us have a demand that the world be perfect by whatever *our* criterion is—the rest of the world just isn't paying attention to our demands.

---

*Babaji is a well-known figure from Yogananda's classic, *Autobiography of a Yogi*. It's a book that is both fun to read and full of great information. However, from a Sethian point of view, it is full of out-of-date information and misleading interpretations. For example, Yogananda tells several stories about the character known as Babaji, including an actual meeting with Babaji. His understanding of Babaji is of a great yogi who attained enlightenment long ago and decided to stay physically incarnated now for hundreds of years. My understanding is that Babaji is an emanation of a huge being that has guided humankind for thousands of years. Sometimes that larger being incarnates physically and sometimes it just engages us as channeled guides like Seth, or guides on inner planes. Thus, Babaji himself is not really a physical being, but can appear as such for humans either in full force for short times or for longer periods of times through ordinary yogis who channel him, consciously or unconsciously, with whatever skill they have.

Like all emanations, Babaji communicates with us in ways that we are able to understand. There are many people who channel Babaji (it really isn't hard), but different channelings of Babaji can be very different and contradictory. Most of my most important guides are emanations of the huge underlying being for a group of emanations such as Babaji, Seth, Mataji, and others.

Lots of people have met physicalizations of Babaji, including, I am convinced, me in July or August of 1974 near Rishikesh, India. He was the most wonderful and powerful yogi I have ever interacted with, but his message was very different from those in Yogananda's book.

Judgments, in the sense of judgmentalness, always lead to entanglements. So we use the Western intellect, the analytical intellect, to help extricate ourselves by cognitive therapy, looking at our shoulds, have tos, and oughts. This means having to disentangle Astral enmeshments that hold us into repetitive thinking patterns.

Our demand is not actually a legitimate or even an accurate one. The objective is not to impose our will on the Earth so that we get we want or so that everyone behaves by our ethical demands. Our true objective is to engage in a continually expanding, even becoming ecstatic—though sometimes sad and painful—conversation with the world.

Another part of the way we can engage flow in the Astral body is in its interdependence, so when you bring *you* into the center of your head, you're really bringing part of your Causal soul. And it is neutral to all those stops, all those resistances, all those bindings in your Astral body.

Being in the center of your own head allows you to have a flow by which you are senior to various blockages that are in your Astral body. But being in the center of your head is not what you always shoot for. When you're out and about, it might be easier for you to be in your crown, the chakra at the top of your head. Sometimes when there's a lot of chaos, you'll find that it's better to be in your crown. While we don't want to let that be a substitute for being in the center of the head, a lot of times it's easier to read from your crown.

Try to find the center of your head and get a sense of how that gestalt is made up of pieces from unity, from your soul and group soul and from Mother Earth. If you're not in the center of your head, see if you can find yourself. Measure the distance between you and the center of your head. Create and destroy roses so you can free up pieces like little bits of mercury that have gotten stuck someplace so they come back to the big ball of mercury.

To get into the center of your head means dampening the analyzer in the brain. You're not dampening because there's anything wrong with it—after all, some of us can have a certain amount of analytical stuff going and be in the center of the head also—it's just harder.

Feel your consciousness and, if you can, have some sense of it being an interdependent gestalt with roots in unity, with roots in your soul, with roots in other lifetimes, with a presence in just the Mental plane and in emotional and physical realms as well. Ask yourself, how are you here? Why don't you go flying off in some other direction? See if you can feel, hear, or see what it is that makes your *self* engage this self. See if you can get any sense of what it is that allows this self to make choices and to focus its attention.

All of this comes together, and the word *commitment* is probably too serious. I'd like you to come up with your own word, your own sense of the right word, what your yous engagement with you is in everyday life. The objective is to try to find that energy of choices that you are making every moment, that you in the center of your head are making to be a human being, even if it gets lost in places. We're trying to track the moment-to-moment choices that you make, that you have the capacity to make, the choices that let you find your humanity enticing.

Being human can be really, really hard and it can be really agonizing. If you want passion, though, then this is a planet to choose because there's these large ranges of contrast.

Just consider the relationships between parents and their children. I watch how painful this often is, but people choose that.

And when you wake up from this virtual reality machine called human life no matter how passionate and full of contrast it was, 99.99 percent of the time you say, "That was terrible and fantastic and I think I'd like to go on that roller-coaster ride again." Or sometimes you say, "Now that was a little bit more intense than I want to go the next time. I think I'd like to go on the merry-go-round the next time."

That life can be so difficult at times and still be sublime is really quite advanced, so you might not get this, but each of us has a knowingness in the back of our brains and it's coming out the pores of our skin, a yes to life. Try to see if you can track that "yes" to your particular life that's going on in the center of your head.

4

Experience, Pain, and Joy

The sublime and the horrifying aspect of human consciousness is that we lose track of its very nature, which is that consciousness wants to have experience. As humans, we want to have pleasant experience. But consciousness *itself* wants to have experience. Seth talks about the very nature of consciousness being to explore every dimension. Now that is a far more radical statement than you might initially imagine. And humans, even as alienated as we are from the nature of consciousness, want to have experience too; we want to have *all* experience.

You could say, how could anyone have all experience? Doesn't that mean you'd have no experience? Well, set that aside for now.

You exist as a human as a collaboration of four bodies: the Physical, the Astral, the Mental, and the Causal. The Astral gets deeply into the neurological structure of the Physical-Etheric. Let me explain.

Lewis Bostwick was very big on the integrity of the body, which actually vibrates at the Physical *and* Etheric level. But when he said, "Go to the body," he was really going to the lowest two sub-planes of the Astral. They have a lot of connection with the body and they are also its personal and emotional frequency.

It's been over forty years since he said that, and I think it's still important that we go into the Etheric as well as the Astral, as I will explain. Because in the first two years of exploring the Etheric, I too was actually exploring the lowest two sub-planes of the Astral where Lewis had done his work. Now I understand the difference and am teaching it.

The Physical-Etheric body is here to experience sensation and it's open to all sensation, painful and otherwise. The Astral Body is here to experience love and desire; it is naturally open to all emotions, pleasurable or painful, but humans are also exploring resisting their emotions, so most of us are in resistance to a large portion of our experience much of the time.

The Astral Body is the focus of what I call the personal aura. It too is made up of all kinds of consciousnesses. Different elementals and devas hold it together. It gets interwoven with the moon and the Earth and the stars and the sun. The Astral Body is the most individuated portion of a human being and most closely associated with what most humans think of as themselves. It hasn't always been the case. But throughout what we think of as human history, the Astral Body has been the most significant layer or level of personal identity.

The Astral Body explores love and desire through contradiction and identity, contrast and agreement, polarity. These days the contrast is quite extreme and the contradictions are equally extreme. Contradiction, though, is intrinsic. I think it's probably intrinsic in all dimensions, at least all of them relevant to human consciousness.

Our spiritual plan in the Astral or personal aura is to move relatively out of resistance to our experience and into neutrality, which is open-ness to life as it is. This was mostly, if not entirely, the purpose of Lewis's program at the Berkeley Psychic Institute.

Emotion is your body communicating with your Astral body and it's really the core of what it means to be human. No matter how large a consciousness is, it's driven in some way and that drivenness is equivalent to the inevitability of your next breath.

While human beings use pain to punish people, the universe does not. It does not engage in punishment ever. Yes, it engages in pain, and a human may interpret that as punishment. But that's the human interpretation. Even karma is not punishment.

Pain for the universe is a healing, a redirection. The message when you feel pain is, "Try something else." It's not always easy to figure out what that something else is and make the shift. But that is *always* the message. It is never, "You are an evil person and deserve to be punished." It is, "Try something different, okay?"

Pain is a form of healing. Pain is an energy that says, in this aspect you're on a detour and you want to change your direction. Humans use pain for punishment, but the universe uses it for redirection. If your energy is in pain, you get the chance to bring it into current time and redirect yourself. Over time you have less and less pain in your body. There are exceptions, but I'm not going to elaborate on that now.

When people say they've tried everything, they haven't. If you're in an unpleasant experience, then by definition you haven't tried everything. You may have tried everything you can think of. You may have tried everything your local expert can think of. But you haven't tried everything yet.

One way to get some more possibilities is to sit down with your Mental permanent seed and say, "You got any ideas?" It might say, "Do this, and this, and this." But it's more likely to gradually push an energy out and you wake up some morning with a new direction.

John Fulton will be teaching a class and someone will spin out this tale of woe, and he'll often say to them, not entirely without sympathy, "Are you complaining or are you bragging?" Even people who are fairly self-aware can miss how fascinated they are by their pain.

Finally, you need to put your emotion into something the human neurological system can absorb and use. There *are* things ordinary human emotions *can't* process. When that happens, you have a choice: you can keep on trucking through the pain and strip the screws or you can take in and change the quality of emotions through lived experience.

It's usually a bad idea to commit suicide. You can't do something so bad that it cripples you for all time, but if you don't generate experience here, then you're more limited throughout, maybe not eternity, but for the next thousand years or so. You may say, "Damn, I wish I had had those experiences."

Now in that space you eventually get to the fact that all of your experience is sacred. That means your life is not better because you had more pleasure or worse because you had less pleasure. Pleasure is a divine attraction to experience. Pain is a divine healing.

In this system, we define joy as something that's too big to fit in an individual. We use happiness for a sort of personal reliable satisfaction. And we use pleasure for the polarity of pain. Underneath or above fun, there's a kind of joy that animates all life and all experience. You can't really run your body at joy, but it's always and already there.

The Mental plane's primary purpose is affiliation. That's not the way human beings use the Mental plane these days, but as we move into the Aquarian Age, we will learn how to use our minds to engage in group consciousness. The old concept of the Aquarian Age is that individual differences will be blotted out, which utterly misses the point. The true meaning of the Aquarian Age is that individual differences will be embraced and affiliated and understood and integrated by what Seth calls "the spacious intellect." This intellect uses discrimination and difference joyously to affiliate. It uses polarities for unity.

Next is the abstract intellect, which is the Causal body, including the personal soul. The personal soul is big and the very nature of its being is embracing all experience. It craves experience and engages in it in myriad dimensions. One of those dimensions is our human experience.

Being a human being is really, really cool. This is true no matter what happens in your life. When you read about near-death experiences, you often find out that the person realizes that their life made perfect sense, even the stupid things they did. Everything made perfect sense. And that's because the soul throws itself into the limitations we so often experience as being painful, with joy and happiness.

Take some piece of your experience, let's say lunch this afternoon. Notice how you as a personality experience events in linear time: You may have associations with them. They may bring up memories from the past, hopes for the future. They have a kind of structure to them.

Now hand that experience to your soul and watch what happens as time in the structure you know gets stripped away. Your lunch today might be experienced with a thousand other lunches into one big sense of what it means to have lunch and simultaneously be experienced with five thousand other interactions with people, including the people who fixed lunch for you.

Stripped of the conventional structure of time and space, one person is not entirely separate from another. This is a radically different way of experiencing your emotions and other people's emotions and your connection and relationship to them. Actual complexity and interrelationship increase. There is a richness of being simultaneously interconnected with all kinds of things that would never occur to you in the body alone. And each of those things is expanding in all directions. Each expansion is also simultaneously relating to things in multiple areas as part of one big delicious stew of experience. Together these yield a rich and complex pattern of what relationship might mean.

Your lunch remains utterly itself even as it gets ripped apart and related to other things without the playpen structures that keep one thing separate from another.

For the inner self, every decision it will make gets explored in so many ways that the waking conscious mind cannot directly track. That is one reason why no experience is ever a failure. It may be painful, and within the arena that your physical conscious mind explores it can certainly be a failure; but in the part that is most you, all experience grows in all directions. It has no choice, and *you* have no choice. You couldn't stop it if you wanted to.

Let your soul take some experience that terrified or horrified you. Let it get into the energy field where separation no longer exists. The soul knows that experience as you're experiencing it, yet it also experiences it interconnected with many other things in multiple other ways. Causality is no longer the issue—just meaning.

Feel what happens in your body down here in the Physical-Etheric plane as your soul takes in an experience, assimilates it, interconnects it, sees it from a near infinite number of vantage points. Feel how your so-called awful experience increases the power and glory of your soul. If you pay attention, that power and glory in this moment undergird your existence. You have full drawing rights, like you won the lottery. Perhaps you can begin to feel why your soul never shrinks sway from any experience.

Take another experience. Take a hundred experiences. And give each of them to your soul. Let your soul do what a soul does—radically reorganize its appreciation. Share them with the Sun. Share them with Mother Earth. Feel each experience pinging throughout the universe as it goes into every gestalt that you're a part of and the meaning that each of those gestalts makes with the others. Notice how immediately available these are to your body and personality as a wellspring of strength and joy. Interdependence is not static.

Your personal experience is never going to be the same as the experience of your soul, but your soul underpins all of your experience, so the more that you are open to it, the more depth and courage, openness, kindness, and generosity are available to you to use as a personality and to convert into meaningful everyday experiences, which then feed back into the soul.

You know the phrase, "Life is hard and then you die"? There's a certain amount of truth to that. But after you die, everything starts to make sense. Now it might make sense right away; it might make sense ten years from now—of course, time doesn't flow in the same way in the after-death experience. It might make sense in twenty million years on another planet if you've been a particularly terrible person. But for everyone it makes sense.

Now you might say, "What do I care if it makes sense after I die? I'm in pain right now. I'm suffering so much now, what do I care if it's all going to be better forty years from now, four hundred years from now?" The answer is that while we are primarily focused on our waking selves when we are awake and things like our desires are particularly important—our individuality, our egos are the central focus for our waking selves—it is useful to remember that simultaneously you are always and already much more.

God concepts bring with them paradoxes and puzzles that only make things harder. When you're looking at a one-directional God, it's really hard to justify pain. Why would anyone have something horrible happen? You can come up with answers in linear time, and those are somewhat satisfying. But as you move into multidirectional time, the question sort of disappears. The question almost doesn't make sense anymore. Its answer is already present.

The Western concept is stuck in time. It's about a male sky-God who is the Creator and gets tied up with jealousy and competition and stuff like that. There is more an ecstatic, creative, non-timebound entity absolutely committed to each of us individually and to things beyond knowing. It values our experience as conscious individuals, yet it recognizes that it is also embracing a kind of ignorance to focus us into our own personal story-telling. Every single story that you tell yourself as a conscious individual leaves out more than it puts in. In the dream state, you interact and you create your world with the bigger story, and yet you wake up every day and you're back in this smaller story, this still really sacred exciting profoundly compacted thing.

Dream energy is a lot like the energy that people report in near-death experiences where they start to move out of linear time. Even if they don't necessarily understand what it is they're doing, when they say, "My whole life made sense. Everything made sense," they mean, makes sense because it no longer has to be justified.

If people say, "Oh, okay, from the big picture everything is fine, but here I am suffering," they are misunderstanding what the real big picture is.

The cause of pain is intrinsic in the creativity of life, intrinsic in the play of life; it is a play of polarities. You cannot do anything without contradiction being a fundamental part of it. It is contradiction that generates the expansion of life in all directions as you explore your contradictions.

The big picture isn't only after you die. This *is* the big picture too, even if you don't know that.

5

Personality, Soul, and Atman

For a human being, there are four operating systems in your range of consciousness. The Physical-Etheric craves sensation. The Astral craves love and desire. The Mental craves integrated affiliation and appreciation of difference. And the Causal craves the whole thing.

There are two central consciousnesses that initiate, organize, provide the energy for, and sustain your physical incarnation—the Causal Soul and the Hindu Atman. I often call the Causal Soul the Western Soul. That's where the theosophists placed the soul and it is much, much more complicated and huger than people imagine. The theosophical aura exists really from the soul's perspective, not from the personality's perspective. When you work from that perspective, you can do very powerful healing.

The soul brings all sorts of infinities to its point of view as it looks out toward you. They're not in themselves full, but they're part of what the Causal soul *is*. It cannot help but bring its totality, even as it brings itself from infinite dimensions to something huge and excited and joyful and resilient and impeccable and kind and generous and childlike and wise, and full with its fullness. It's just outside both the directly inner creative self of you and the camouflaged you that's normally—and appropriately normally—the area of interest in your human incarnation. Perhaps you can feel it with its entirety, fully engaged with both the direct creative inner you that's not limited by your neurological system and the camouflage you that is limited and ultimately enhanced by its access to a neurological system.

And note, even as this incredible soul is always there in its big form, it also goes through a kind of portal—we're not going to elaborate now—to provide most of the energy, well not most, say 40 to 60 percent of the energy, more than any other consciousness, for the directly creative inner self. So it limits itself, I guess, and narrows itself to form the inner self of this particular incarnation and narrows itself further as it goes through the permanent seeds.

The Causal Soul and the Hindu Atman, through the Physical, Astral, and Mental permanent seeds, provide a good 70 to 80 percent of the energy of your physical incarnation. Entities like the Earth, Sun, and innumerable devas and elementals provide the remainder. So the soul is simultaneously, as the Beatles say, within you and without you. And the part within you—if you want to think of yourself as an energy, or a substance, not just that it's there as an observer—contributes to bones and sinews of your body, the *chi* of your Etheric body, the emotion of your Astral, and the thought and sharing of your Mental blueprint.

Be in the Causal plane as yourself and sort of give a shout-out to your soul. Quite an awesome being! For the moment let yourself kind of melt into the larger consciousness of your soul. Then let it put a narrow focus through filters into you, as you, and let yourself dissolve into the greater soul. You no longer have that separate sense of self. To a powerful extent you *are* the soul. And then let that soul precipitate out a focus of itself out as you the individual. You'll probably be limited by the fact that you have a physical body that doesn't yet know how to hold these multiple focuses simultaneously, but let it be the individual you at this Causal level and simultaneously be the whole personal soul without granting some sort of specialness to one or the other, letting them both be full selves, full personhoods, interdependent, each one enhancing the other.

Take the worst most horrible thing that you ever did or that ever happened to you in this lifetime, hand it to your soul, and, without judging, just notice what the soul does with that. You don't need to argue with it, you don't need to decide whether it's right when it does that; just see what the soul does with that.

Now give it the fifteen most difficult things from this lifetime, give it all at once. Hand them to your soul as roses or whatever you want to do. Just see what the soul does with each of those, and with all of them. You may even notice the other, even larger parts of your self immediately start digesting and assimilating those experiences.

Take those experiences back. You can just explode all but one of them and when you look at that one, see if you can see a time when your soul was not already part of that experience.

When you go on up, past the Causal, past the Buddhic and the Atmic into the Monadic, you encounter a form of consciousness that plays a big part in Hindu mysticism: the Atman. In some ways, the Atman is the foundation of your eternal personality. Sometimes it is called the Jiva. It is incomprehensibly large, existing in infinite directions, and able to track those infinite directions.

As a human being you will encounter this Atman in a way that seems most like what you would imagine your personal soul to be. It is the most important factor, the most important dynamic portion, or the part of the universe that is motivated to experience your humanity in your individuality. And it is the portion that most seems like what you would imagine eternal life to be, if you as an individual had eternal life. Let me change that statement. Somewhere in Seth's writing, and I paraphrase, he said that you do have a continued existence. Of course, it is different from what you can imagine. But, and I don't remember how he said this, I am really paraphrasing, when you get there you will satisfied that you, me, John, or Brian, or Violeta, or whoever, have a continued, meaningful, and even redemptive existence that is the you that you knew as a human being.

We're going to explore the inside of your continued existence. We are going to introduce what Seth called the Inner Ego. But I don't think we've ever really begun to explore what the Inner Ego might be, the Inner Self that is not the soul. It's kind of aligned with the way you would meet the Atman, but it operates at a different energy level, much closer to the human personality. And so, we're going to start off exploring this and try to carry it in deeper and deeper ways. We get a new enlarged, enhanced sense of the soul and how it exists as itself and incarnates as us.

Perhaps you can imagine that the Atman weaves itself together with the personal or Causal soul and comes down and is there as a ground of being and a support and a creative spark for both the direct creative self, which also is not limited by a neurological system, and the ego self, which is profoundly committed to a neurological system in order to narrow and focus and enhance your experience of the creative dynamics you are exploring as a human being. In addition to being outside your directly creative self, and outside your ego self, the Atman intentionally simplifies and funnels its focus so that it can participate as a primary energy (let's say 10 percent) of the directly creative self, and let's say 20 percent—and I think we have our percentages off, but I'm not going to worry about that too much—of the ego self. The ego self, which you can also think of as a "camouflage self," has much smaller percentages of Earth, sun, stars, animal, vegetable, mineral consciousnesses, cetaceans; those are mostly the personal Causal soul and the Atman. So our excitements and joy play into both the inner or directly creative self and the ego self. And as you explore these inner connections, the communication—especially in the dream state, or deeper unconscious parts of your waking state—will be clearer, will operate more fluidly, to everyone's great advantage.

Now, in some ways, each part of you is a separate life. The life of your Physical-Etheric is in some ways complete and alive in and of itself, has agreements with the Earth and the Sun to participate in your life as a human. In some ways it's separate as is your Astral body, which has its own agreements with Sun and the Earth and other consciousnesses, as does your mind in the Mental plane. Take a breath.

Lots of the people think of the soul as eternal, and it is, but that's not the soul's private deal. The same status exists for the personality and the Atman too. It's because nothing is ever lost in the universe. Nothing is ever thrown away. Nothing is ever stripped for spare parts like a car wreck. Your experience is not gobbled up by your soul and you disappear. Everything expands in all directions, including you.

You folks are eternal as yourself as well as a soul, as well as part of the weather, as part of a mountain that you may have loved. All of those dimensions are eternal.

The title of Seth's second book is *Seth Speaks: The Eternal Validity of the Soul.* Hidden in there are all kinds of hints that it isn't just the soul that has eternal validity but the personality, and every subjectivity has eternal validity, and that's why your cat can reincarnate. If you look at it in one way, your cat's dust; but if you look at it through your heart, you know who your cat really is.

I like to joke that death changes people, but it doesn't change you as much as you might think. It doesn't change you so much that you would consider yourself lost or disassembled.

The human personality is seeded into this reality, you could say, to answer questions that the soul cannot answer any other way, to explore and develop a fresh orientation that the soul cannot develop otherwise. You are the soul's question answerer. The soul has all these questions. What will happen if? How do I understand this? How can I be loving with an identity that appears to be in conflict with other people?

These are things that the soul has to explore. These are things that the Earth explores, through you. And the Earth is, of course, doing all sorts of other explorations.

None of the universe's larger beings are worrying about the question, When is this personality going to become enlightened? That is not the purpose of incarnating. The purpose of incarnating is to be yourself.

The core of our journey is the exploration of life-as-it-is through the divine focus of the individual human personality.

Your body's awareness is the thing that most people would say is subject to termination: ashes to ashes, dust to dust. But your body's consciousness is eternal, just as eternal as anything else and everything else in the universe. One of the radical things that you can get out of the Seth material is that everything in the universe is eternal, nothing is ever lost. Everything always changes, but nothing is lost, in time or out of time.

As you start to play with these concepts, you get a sense of the patience and endurance of your body. You don't get that sense when it's tied up with your Astral body, which is innately impatient. Over time you can appreciate the eternal nature of your body and consciousness and that all kinds of other consciousnesses are collaborating to create this personality that is you. As you do so, you might find yourself tapping into a kind of joy and playfulness that are hard to achieve otherwise.

There is nothing to evolve beyond; of course, you will evolve, but not in any sense that is better than the human personality. And once you do, other aspects of yourself will still engage in explorations that arise out of the unique individuated and apparently dual consciousness of the human personality.

Your individuality could not even exist in the way that it does without your being part of innumerable consciousnesses that are not centered in your human personality but nevertheless help make the personality what it is.

Everything is interdependent, even the Atman, but that doesn't keep it from being uniquely and profoundly itself. The Atman is in some sense what keeps you being eternal. When you die, you gather experience until you can sort of come from the Atman in multiple times and multiple spaces and know yourself as yourself. So if you die tomorrow, you won't end, you'll continue exploring as a soul, an individual, and an Atman.

That's one big picture. There are a lot of other big pictures, but that's the one we focus on.

6

Reincarnation, Time, and Will Ives

Time does not flow in the way our bodies force us to experience time. They force us to experience time so that everything won't happen all at once, because no one here is capable of operating in this kind of richness, as a self without time. Time seems to structure our experience and break it up into little bits and a certain sort of logical pattern that we can follow.

Time is a kind of psychological training wheel on your bicycle. It's a device to keep everything from happening at once. Right now we humans need time because we can't understand it if it all happens at once. We can't even understand the concept of it all happening at once outside of time. I know I can't.

We co-create time, so the fact that everything is simultaneous matters. You may not understand this now, but you will—or you will *almost* or *won't* in interesting new ways.

Seth says that time is an energy, which is really kind of mind-boggling. He also says that everything happens at once. And he *also* says that it might be more accurate to say that your future creates your present than that your past creates your present. When you get it, it sort of makes sense.

It seems like you are *in* time, time is a preexisting structure, and you get carried by time. Ask yourself if you can feel the wind of time carrying you forward in your body, and then see if you can find the part of yourself that willingly collaborates with everything else on this planet in this particular frequency.

A human body and human neurological system start with it being impossible to have experience without having time. We humans have one dimension of time and that represents the nature of experience, but there are other types of consciousness like Seth. Part of him is outside of time, not in *multiple dimensions of time,* but outside of time itself. Yet he keeps insisting that he *has* experience. How can you have experience without having time? How can you have something that's analogous to growth without having time? He swears he can do it. I believe him 100 percent, but what that means, I have no idea.

This is one of several aspects of consciousness that you at least brush up against, capture glimpses of. You cannot, in the waking state, fully engage these other times and other spaces while you're engaged here.

By the way, you're only one infinitesimal aspect of consciousness in this planet, and not all of them are in one dimension of time. If you think it's your job to save Mother Earth, that's really funny, because Mother Earth doesn't depend upon whether this particular snapshot of Mother Earth gets polluted and humans lose this opportunity to experience Earth. There are oodles of other Mother Earths right here. And that will be part of her awareness. To Mother Earth, it would be more like the burning of Atlanta in *Gone with the Wind,* that in this one space humans destroyed the movie.

The time when it all makes sense—that is, after you die—only seems a long distance away because you're exploring time in a linear fashion, but that time in the future is always and already present here, underneath your waking consciousness. And that's an important point. Every night you go to sleep and you visit other dimensions. We think of them as other dimensions in a hierarchical way, but they're actually part of you all the time right now; they're just not parts that you can track fully while you are in a physical body—awake.

So how is it that you come to co-create and participate in *this* time?

If you just sort of hook into your body in a conventional way, you will notice that it is carried along by time so that, in each moment, one distinct required pattern follows the next. Notice that while the body gets carried along, your Astral self can kind of dart back or forward through time. You can get a message from you five hundred years from now.

Do that now. Just open up and say hello to some aspect of you five hundred years in the future. And say hello back. Notice how that changes your energy, as your experience resonates throughout your physical self, how it changes your Etheric energy and your Physical energy.

Send an announcement out from your Astral body and ask if there's any future self, either in this lifetime or another, that has something it would like you to consider. You may not be able to put it into words. You might notice that there's actually a constant flow of communication from one or more future selves. Ask to speak to a future self that has resolved some of your concerns.

GLORIA: A reminder, and for the newer folks who may be unfamiliar with the concept, hello is actually at the heart of our system. Saying hello to something is to allow it to be what it is, exactly as we find it or experience it, while cultivating our nonjudgmentalness, just giving it space to be as we find it.

There are many stories and approaches to what happens to your individuality after death. There's the materialist idea that when you're dead, you're dead. Nothing happens, forever. There's the Western monotheistic idea, notably in Islam and Christianity, that there's an afterlife where you continue essentially as the human that you were for eternity. That's usually imagined as a wonderful place without much if any further learning or change. There are many Christians who believe this today: you're raised in your physical body and are given eternal life. You stay pretty much the same before and after death.

Then you have standard ideas of reincarnation that mostly arise or are talked about in Eastern religions. In Hindu systems you have one life at a time. You finish one life and spend some time perhaps in an after-death state, but you can't really make much further progress until you reincarnate. In both Buddhist and Hindu theology, there is a strong sense that you can go backward, very far backward, in a particular life. So you could be on the spiritual path toward enlightenment, make a lot of progress, and fall all the way back in one or a series of lifetimes to a point where you're benighted and not on much of any sort of spiritual path.

The formal Buddhist concept of reincarnation is more problematic and more difficult to understand. Some people talk about incarnation as being various aspects and tendencies and trends coming together in a single person and giving rise to that person. Other folks spend a lot of time saying that a person is not the reincarnation of someone else, even though he or she can be connected to a prior incarnation of someone.

Certain psychics and people with clairvoyance could see what happens after death, but they restrict the term reincarnation to lamas or tulkus who have done a special process that carries a consciousness from one body over into a second body. Only that special process is called reincarnation, for everyone else the lack of continuity is highlighted by calling it an incarnation.

The normal as opposed to the Tibetan-tulku view of incarnation draws from a hootenanny of various aspects including incarnations from the same personal soul, various guides, and various family members. In some of the initiations that Tibetan lamas do, they actually take those apart so that you're not affected as much by other incarnations. You are more solitary, and it's that solitary piece of you that's incarnated in the tulku process. So instead of having the whole hootenanny of aspects, the Dalai Lama will only have, for the most part—and even here you have to have a caveat—the last prior incarnation and the large group consciousness that the Dalai Lama is an emanation from, and even that last incarnation starts to wither away.

Otherwise, incarnation occurs only for those who are subject to delusion. Those who penetrate the illusion and become enlightened move beyond incarnation, but some who have taken the bodhisattva vow choose to reincarnate to help others get through their illusions. One comes back as a service.

So far as I know, it is never the case in Buddhism that one incarnates for the particular beauties of a human incarnation or that the experiences of an incarnate being are of value *in and of themselves*. This is the change that Seth brings to our understanding, though there have certainly been spiritual teachers who preceded Seth who didn't view incarnation solely as a mistake generated by illusion.

Reincarnation is not worthy of the word *reincarnation* in the way we use it because, when you look at it within linear time and space, when Annie dies, the Annie self doesn't just plop into another body, something apparently from Annie's soul incarnates. If you don't know where to look, it looks like Annie disappears. When you open up to the Sethian point of view, there is no objective Annie. We can't take a pen and draw around her aura and say that this is Annie and everything outside is not Annie and everything inside is. Annie is made up of a composite of all kinds of things. You go to the edge of one composition and there's another component that is also part of Annie.

Traditional mystical systems treat that as a problem. Seth looks at that from a multidimensional perspective where Annie is eternal *because* Annie is composite, and because Annie has a subjective sense of herself. That subjectivity, while constantly transforming, moment to moment, is never lost.

It is absolutely true that you have no objective essence, no objective separateness, no objective existence as an essence because you arise interdependently and impermanently. So even your soul is not a separate thing, even the Atman is not a separate thing, but all of those things arise interdependently and are impermanent.

Each gestalt's subjectivity is eternal *because of* its impermanence. Because of impermanence, all consciousnesses change constantly. That very change generates expansion in all directions. Each gestalt's subjectivity expands in all directions and is thus eternal, even though time itself is an illusion, an apparent contradiction.

Because mystics have until now looked only in the one dimension of the physical Earth's time as humans know it today, this eternal change was only observed to lead to the dissolution of all forms. But when you look in all directions, the subjectivity of every gestalt continues meaningfully and identifiably in innumerable directions even though forms come and go. Specifically, each human's personal, individual subjectivity continues forever.

Just as the banyan tree is the center of a whole ecological system, you as an incarnated person are the center of a whole system. All kinds of beneficial interactions are going on within the consciousness that you think of simply as Ed or Judy or Annie, or as, "I have a soul and I want to really be a kind and generous person."

What Seth is inviting you to do is simultaneously to luxuriate in your subjectivity as a human being and understand its full involvement in a whole community of beings. Just as you are the center of a whole community in which other consciousnesses participate and are still in some sense you, you participate in multiple ecological and psychic communities. Saying hello to those will greatly enhance your joy, your emotional resilience, and the skill with which you engage the world and also begin to set up the stage for Aquarian consciousness.

Every bit of consciousness is creative, not just spiritual masters, not just God, not just Seth, but even the most odious person on the planet is engaged in a form of creativity. And there is no one so wrong, bad, or awful that they won't eventually be redeemed because that point will expand in all directions, and one of the directions is in its subjectivity.

You change moment to moment—death's just a bigger change. In either case, your subjectivity as Annie or Ed continues to expand in all directions. And the way I like to say this, and even though death has changed you and you cannot imagine what your subjectivity will be like after you are dead, if I came up to you after death and I said, "Annie, do you feel that your Annie-ness has been maintained, or do you feel kind of cheated because you lost what was unique about what you thought of yourself as Annie?"—you would immediately and enthusiastically say, "I'm quite well; it's different from how I was in linear time with a physical body, but everything I did in body is integrating and making my meaning and I'm doing ever more exciting things. And I can see that that will go on without end."

How can something be without end, if time itself ends? It can because existence happens both inside and outside of time. What does that mean? I don't have a clue. I just know it's true.

This incarnation, this you, has its own eternalness that you can't conceive of right now. A hundred thousand years from now, Ed will be very different from the Ed here. As with Annie, if someone interviewed him then and said, "Ed, do you feel like this fulfills an idea of an eternal existence as Ed continuing to learn and grow?" And he'd say, "Yeah, I'm satisfied. I didn't get short shrifted. I didn't get eaten or gobbled up by my soul and lose my sense of myself."

You do also get gobbled up by your soul. All consciousness expands in all direction so all of Ed's experiences will be taken in by his soul, will be taken in by any number of entities—the Sun, the Earth—and yet eventually Ed will know himself as all these things in addition to being Ed.

As time goes by, if you go into other dimensions and encounter some six-dimensional being and find that Ed and say, "Do you feel cheated? Have you lost Ed here, who was born in the twentieth century and lived well into the twenty-first century?" his answer will be *his recognition of your question.*

My friend Will Ives committed suicide in February of 1977. In the early- to mid-nineties I was meditating and, all of a sudden, I saw a beautiful violet ribbon of light. And I knew it was Will and I was shocked because I also knew that that there had been two subsequent incarnations. But it *was* Will, and it was Will who wasn't in pain and who had become something vast and deep.

I can say hello to Will now, even though there's no circle you can draw around Will. If you knew Will and you met this Will, you'd say, "Okay, that's Will."

The Will individual is now Will as something much more complex and richer and kind and generous and yet knows itself as that—and is centered as that. Over subsequent years since the mid-nineties, I started to notice more details or maybe Will spread out in more detail. When I see Will now, Will is centered in maybe five consciousnesses that I can perceive and have some sense of what they are. They are different personae of Will. Each one of them is as much Will as any other. And each one of them is fully engaged as that consciousness knowing itself simultaneously as each of the others.

Will goes off in maybe a hundred different directions that I can't begin to track.

Each one of these—this is kind of hard to understand—is Will. It is as much Will as any other and is aware of itself as the center of its own existence.

So, there's a Will who says hello to me as Will. Then there's a Will that reminds me of a mini-Seth, a little sports club or psychic football team except that they're a blended consciousness in the sense that these beings came together and formed one consciousness but they each had a specialty that they contributed to that team. I don't think there was a quarterback, but there might have been two or three that were more leaders and two or three who were specialists in healing or two or three who were specialists in gathering information, so that's one way he knows himself. And then there's a Will that's part of something that's so huge that I think of it as a planet but I'm guessing that it's only the soul, maybe the soul on the fourth or fifth level of the Buddhic plane. The soul is so big you can't even imagine—not what we call your per-sonal soul, though even *that* is unimaginably big.

Will the personality knows itself as the soul. It's like a brilliant planet of light, of diamond light. And that's Will; it isn't Will rather than—it is Will as centered in and experiencing himself, itself, as that in vast dimensions. Then there's another Will that is exploring all of the probable Wills. That's one I can hardly track at all. But somehow or other, this Will explores sideways, not through time but what *could* have happened at a particular moment, and in other probabilities *does* happen. All these things are going on simultaneously.

Okay, so there's that ribbon that is Will as an individual, but simul-taneously there's also a Will exploring various probabilities of different lifetimes in a sideways way. It's exploring all the things that didn't but *could* have happened. It's kind of mind-boggling to watch that, but boy when you explore probabilities like that, it really changes your relationship to outcomes. I mean think about how wrapped up we get with outcomes. Outcomes give a certain structure to life, but beyond that structure is only a richness. When you really understand probabilities, you realize that everything that *could* happen *does* happen, so it really makes less sense to get quite so upset about it any particular outcome. Or the joy is in the play of consciousness. I don't think you can really appreciate that till you explore probabilities.

And then there's a Will that is sort of centered in my consciousness and is living as, from my point of view, a collaborator though he's not always speaking in my mind. It's there and gives me access to deep rightness with all consciousness. And, I think, from Will's point of view, he probably looks at my responses as some amazing comedy with an actor who's doing all of these ridiculous things.

Will is deeply joyous and serene right now. What's amazing is that he knows himself as his soul, as all these probabilities, and as this, and as that, simultaneously. He also knows himself as me and experiences all of my experiences through his point of view—knowing himself as me but *his* version of my experience.

Will will live forever. He will continue to grow, but he will never get the experience that he didn't have because he committed suicide rather than accept his despair and move through it. Within a few days of his suicide he was reviewing his life experiences and he came to the very things that had caused him to want to die, and he laughed and laughed. That was a personal experience. It wasn't just his soul's experience; it was Will's experience, the experience of the Will that I know that's right here right now and is so serene and joyful.

In 1977, he thought, "Life is horrible. I've lived a long time now. I'm thirty-three years old." Give me a break, at thirty-three we were still being born. He didn't think, "Stick around a few more years. It will work out." Now he can never get that back, though he can travel through probabilities where he didn't commit suicide and in some sense experience it.

That's part of the reason you come back. You get out, die, and then you say, "Damn there's some stuff that I didn't get and I really, really, really want to get it so I'm going back." Nobody makes you incarnate, as strange as that may seem. You come back to complete your experience, for the universe as well as for yourself.

Everyone finds happiness, even people who commit suicide, but Will missed out on what he could have done here, so while his experience is ecstatic, if you would ask him, I'm sure he would tell you if he had it to do over again, which he doesn't, he'd make a different choice. I mean you can kind of redo things over again and learn things, but the intensity of this virtual experience—this is it. This will be part of your core, essentially for eternity.

I'm not saying that to scare you. One of the things I hope you have is a sense of the infiniteness of existence, and consequently I'm hoping you'll relax and recognize that there is no way *not* to make mistakes. All consciousness expands in all directions; consequently, everything you do is ineradicably sacred. The worst thing you ever did was ineradicably sacred; the best thing you ever do is ineradicably sacred—and you will always do some of both.

7

The Driver

The only motivation of the body—both the Physical body and Etheric body—is the experience of sensation. The body alone has no resistance to pain or pleasure. So what is the apparent resistance? Where does that arise?

It comes basically from two sources. One is programming to survive. If you didn't pay attention to pain, you'd die. Your system has reflex arcs so that, if you're touching a hot stove, it'll pull back, it will respond to pain through those reflex arcs. We'll get to the emotional basis of pain later.

Because of the nature of the human race's exploration of contrast, something in the brain is very powerfully set up to move you away from pain and toward pleasure. I call that "the driver." I see it as about the size of two or three Chiclets in the limbic system, toward the back of it. It's not quite an inch side to side, maybe one-quarter to one-sixteenth of an inch thick, maybe five-eighths to three-quarters of an inch front to back, and is right about level with the top of your ears. Go in through the back top of your ears and you'll find the driver. That's the part of the brain that keeps you resisting your own physical pain. It has a pretty important function. However, if you have chronic pain and you've already got the message, the driver keeps insisting you run away from it, so it brings additional suffering.

As critical as survival is to the body, apparent physical suffering is just sensation. And the body is as cool with pain as it is pleasure. It is no more resistant to either than a granite outcropping is resistant to the weather. The rock in the mountain is experiencing a kind of joyous sensation, a different kind, but a kind.

Back in the days where they were exploring LSD legally, there was an experiment in which they gave it to people with terminal cancer, and at least some people got relief from the pain. One cancer patient was interviewed and said, "You know the pain's there, it hurts just as much, it just doesn't matter anymore." The only reason the pain matters the way it does is our brains are set up to drive us to respond to pain and to try to get out of it, to try to solve pain, and that's part of the overall function.

When the driver gets separate from its ordinary pattern, then you can have a painful experience neutrally. LSD liberated that cancer patient from the part of the brain that is set up to drive you whether you can do anything about it or not.

You have someone like Gandhi who had an appendix removed without any anesthesia. One or more of us, when we get old, will experience serious pain at some point. It would be really nice to say, "Oh well, the body hurts, but it doesn't matter," just bypassing that part of the brain that has the emotional interpretation that this is awful.

For the next exercise I'd like us to look at the body, and in particular the cells in the body, and see if you can start to notice how the body does not mind any sensation intrinsically. When I look at my brain, the driver is the part that feeds into your emotions and says, "This is awful." What I would like you to begin to see is that bodies don't mind any kind of experience, bodies are open to all experience. Every part of the universe except for your personal aura is open to your experience— good, bad, or indifferent. It doesn't flinch from any experience.

We take the position that the personal aura *does* have preferences and even aversions but not as intrinsically a mistake or some sort of cosmic joke. Human beings set this system up to create a certain type of psychological thickness. Every single personality is eventually redeemed into nondual awareness. Having a personal self is really sacred and meaningful, but it is useful to realize that these kinds of revulsions or aversions that we have *only* apply to the personal self. You look at a body that's jerking around in pain, and it has no judgment against that pain. It will naturally move out of pain if it can, but your personality is what has the judgment. That judgment comes from the driver.

See if you can remember some time when you had physical pain, say you hit your funny bone, and see if you can track the fact that the pain receptors in your arm or shoulder are sort of flashing *pain, pain, pain, pain,* and notice that in your arm itself, that's not a problem. If you watch the process of your body being in pain, you may be able to notice two things. One is that before it gets to that part in the brain it's not a problem, it's just information. The body doesn't have a judgment on it.

Maybe it's easier to do it with pleasure. Imagine putting sugar on your tongue and notice that, in your tongue, that's just sensation, and see if you can track where it goes. It'll be a different part of the brain but see if you can track where it goes and that the emotional content is poured on top of sensation.

Imagine your favorite dish, your favorite thing in the world to eat. Imagine that you're eating it, and see if you can track how it starts off as just sensation, and as that sensation goes through your system, probably in the front part of your brain and in the limbic system, an emotional overlay gets put on top of it, and a story gets created about that. Notice what the body does with that before emotions get laid on it and before a story gets told. And as a kind of extra credit, and this is really cool if you can feel it, see if you can home into individual cells. You may notice that each individual cell is always joyfully engaging the sensations that it's experiencing. In other words, the cell has a small but not insignificant consciousness that actually straddles probabilities. See if you can notice that cell's joy of being part of this sensation engine. If you can, imagine the cells in your finger touching something that you love touching. Feel a breeze or feel the sunshine. Notice, if you can, the joy that the individual cells experience just by being part of a body and experiencing sensation.

See if you can become aware that every single cell in your body, healthy or unhealthy, has this joy. Dying cells, cells being born, they all have this; they enjoy being part of the universe, every single cell.

And if you can do that, you may notice that the body also experiences just as much joy if it gets cut with a knife. Now what you think of as "you" doesn't enjoy it that much, because being cut with a knife goes up into the brain and emotions get laid on it, ideas get laid on it. This is not a bad thing. This is part of what generates the richness of the human experience.

This can be a kind of resource state for you because in a similar way your soul has joy in all experience even though it has preferences.

8

Creating Reality and Dying Consciously

The keys are stability and resilience, flexibility and playfulness. The point is not to live as long as you can but to fully engage the life that's meaningful to you—we all have to die sooner or later.

There's no reason to extend your life just for the sake of extending your life. You're here to engage human life for as long as it's meaningful for you in the society as a whole. Seth talks quite beautifully about how there comes a point at which the whole creative thrust of your life can no longer find meaning here. And the only place you can be creative is *there* rather than *here*.

A long-term project I have, and a lot of the people studying with me have, is that when it is time to go, we'll be able to shut down in a conscious way and just leave the body or, ideally, we'll be able to take our bodies with us—our rainbow bodies.

My guides said in the 2030s some humans would stop dying in the way that we understood that concept and start to leave in rainbow bodies in a more public way; it occasionally happens privately now. Instead of dying, you just kind of sit down and pull all of the living cells in your body into energy and you bring all that into an Etheric space. That way, you take your physical body with you. You bring it up in frequency so that it becomes Etheric. Everything gets taken except for fingernails and hair, which are dead. You can take the rest.

You might think of it as something like the electrolyting process. You get something to put the gold on, you put the right energy through it, and the gold goes on the item. In that sense the physical body, cell by cell, atom by atom, emerges from the Etheric in collaboration with your soul, the Earth, the Sun, and all kinds of beings.

That's an enormous benefit because there's always some information that gets lost with the body, a lot of information that gets stuck in the Physical-Etheric if you're not able to take your body with you, even if you're really, really good at taking information with you. Leaving this world in a rainbow body will open the communication between those levels at a time when humanity is ready to take that step. It will make the interactions among the three sub-planes of the Physical and the Etheric smoother. My guides say that will be a great blessing individually and for humanity. It will open up space for humanity. There will be a lot more flexibility.

9

Spacious Intellect

There are infinite universes in which consciousnesses exist. There are infinite relationships between embodiment and consciousness. Our relationship with Mother Earth, really for the last ten thousand years, has been developing a particular kind of structured neurological system, especially for about twenty-six hundred years. But we are moving out of it into a new neurological stage.

Toward the end of the Piscean Age, which is now, we as the human race have developed our concrete intellect, our discriminating intellect, the intellect that chops things up and distinguishes one thing from another. That's a great function, and all sorts of cool stuff has come from it. We as humans attach meaning to everything.

I wouldn't want to live in a world without discriminating intellect. But it can also close us off and alienate us. Underneath it is a kind of naturalness that ebbs and flows just like the rain and the sun and bugs do for a tree.

As an experiment, think of the worst thing that ever happened to you in any lifetime. Now notice that a tree meets that with joy or with a kind of assimilation that then becomes joy.

A long time ago, I asked my guides, "When will human life begin interacting with intelligent life?" The answer was, "When humans develop intelligence." It's because humans do not yet exhibit Seth's "spacious intellect," an integrating intellect that appreciates differences and incorporates them into group consciousness. I don't know that anyone alive now will be around when true group consciousness begins to develop for humans, but we are taking preliminary steps.

The normal place where we analyze our thinking is in the Astral plane. When you think, you think in a cloud of thought with other similar-thinking people. So in a very rudimentary sense, we can begin to take advantage of that to make change.

As we move into the Aquarian Age and as we begin to develop spacious intellect, we will begin to appreciate what is already the case: thoughts are not individuated to the extent that emotions are. They seem to occur in one brain at a time, but actually thoughts crowd together. You cannot think a thought by yourself. You can't think just in the Mental plane, you're thinking with your Astral body, with your emotions, your Causal soul, with the weather probably too.

An appreciation of the interdependent arising generates a kind of compassion for yourself and others. I'm not sure I can articulate why, but every time I see my personality as arising and being supported by my soul, and yet limited and imperfect, I find myself becoming more and more compassionate toward myself and others. The more I see things as aspects of one another and interpenetrating and mutually-supporting, I also become more compassionate because I see how the universe uses the worst, most distasteful thing about myself and loves it, and what an ongoing process that is. It helps me let go of resisting. I'm less insistent that things be the way I want them to be.

After unenmeshing in the Astral plane, you can go to the Mental plane and try to notice all the people you're flocking with there, perhaps a bunch of New Agers who are telling themselves, "You create your own reality, thus you can get what you want. That'll make you happy." They train you to hypnotize yourself into believing you're going to get this, you're going to get that. I think that's a recipe for disaster.

So many New Agers promise you that you'll learn how to dictate to the world, make it stand up and behave. But you won't. Not for any sustained length of time. Maybe even for one lifetime, but not for the full experience of a particular personal self as affiliated with your Atman. Eventually, everyone redeems and works through their issues and reaches some kind of wholeness that's interdependent and ever-changing but meaningfully identified. It's an eternal process. But you don't get to do it at will or by forcing matters. You continue to create, and it happens when it happens.

Exploding pictures back in the Astral plane will help you to hang out with a more fruitful crowd.

We're going to explore how no consciousness is a separate and divisible entity. We do not live in a billiard-ball universe where separate essences bounce off of one another. We live more in, like, a rice-pudding universe where you have apparent centers of consciousness (those would be the raisins) mixed in a sea of interdependence (that would be the rice). Or more like the way cloth is woven. There really is no such thing as the cloth; the cloth is an illusion that arises from the way in which the various threads interact with each other and you get this whole gestalt of the cloth. Every consciousness arises out of a unique and ever-changing interweaving of all the other consciousnesses in infinite universes. This is a core concept of Seth.

You have these centers of gravity, sort of like strange attractors in chaos theory. You can't draw a circle around one and say that everything inside here is X and everything outside of it is Y—that everything inside of here is Ed and everything outside of it is not-Ed.

Everything is interwoven, and yet each of us arises and tracks self-ness in meaningful but impermanent gestalts. And as we track, nothing remains the same.

Once you exist, you're part of your soul, you're part of the Earth, part of the Sun, and always have multiple perspectives where you never get lost, no matter what happens. You change, you grow, you become ever more fluid, but you don't get superseded by your soul. It is true that your soul provides most of the energy that is you, but *you aren't your soul*.

Remember, there is a higher abstract intellect that operates outside of linear time in the Causal soul, and it is always integrated and getting its take on a particular belief.

Your personality is composed of all kinds of small and great gestalts. You exist inside the consciousness of the Earth, inside the consciousness of the Sun. You exist as a part of overall human consciousness. Each human has a number of agreements with Mother Earth, with the animal kingdom, with the plant kingdom, with weather.

The weather is a consciousness. For instance, instead of reincarnating, you can become part of the wind or rain or cloud formation. But if you want to personify the North Wind as a consciousness, you're going to be far more accurate than someone who merely tells you the barometric pressure.

The Sun is a very huge consciousness and it has enormous resources for you; the Sun is always and already you. Your body is never separate from the Sun. The Sun is the physicalization of the consciousness in whom all of us in this solar system live amongst other consciousnesses. *The physicalization of consciousness itself!* As we live inside of and as part of the Sun, it's always part of who we are; it's a part of your body, it's a part of your emotions, it's a part of your mind, and *vice versa,* you're always contributing to it.

Why does the Sun shine on us? In last spring's workshop, we experienced the Sun's pleasure as we breathed. We and the Sun are interdependent, and what is profoundly significant in Seth's work is how fabulous it is to be interdependent. Everything is a collaboration between various consciousnesses. You can't live without bacteria in your gut.

Next time you're out sunbathing and you're just really loving the sun beating down on your skin, see if you can wonder, what's in it for the Sun? What is the Sun getting out of this? You might get an answer; I mean, you might be able to feel it. Nothing in the universe happens except that some form or forms of consciousness wants it. The Sun gets at least as much pleasure shining down on you as you get from it shining down. See if you can feel the Sun's pleasure when it shines on you.

Or the next time you set a grounding cord, see if you can feel Mother Earth's pleasure as you do so.

We're part of other gestalts too. And other consciousnesses also sometimes decide to take human incarnations. It's a much wilder, cooler universe than you can imagine.

10

The Universe Optimizes Experience

Y ou can never do something that makes you less or makes the universe less. You can never make a choice that makes the universe less than it was before you made that choice; no matter how bad your choice is, the universe is always enriched by your experience—good, bad, or horrible. The universe and you, in particular, are always enriched by your experience.

You can do things that make you miserable. And you can do things that put you in a temporary hole that takes you a long time to get out. But even getting into that hole makes you *more*. It makes you everything you were *plus* this new problem. You're always more. So there's nothing you can do that will keep you from growing and keep you from being redeemed. You can't do anything that doesn't add meaning to the universe; no matter how horrible a thing you do. Meaning always expands.

You can, however, miss some opportunities.

Our lives are nested in things that are unimaginably big. No matter who you are or when you are, the whole universe wraps itself around you and re-wraps itself around you each moment. The whole universe changes its address to you each moment. No matter how small a change you make, the whole universe—and all universes—instantly change in a way that it wraps around you. Not just you of course; you as part of the whole universe change and wrap yourself around every other subjectivity in the universe.

How in the world does this miracle work where you're creating your reality according to your conscious beliefs and I'm creating my reality according to my conscious beliefs and yet it's so flexible that, moment to moment, it all coheres? The universe is so creative that when you change, everything immediately adjusts.

Everything that happens to you at any given moment—it's a little more complicated than this, but for starters—every single thing that happens to you is the optimal possibility given your beliefs at that moment. So the worst disaster that ever happened was your optimal outcome at that moment given your beliefs at that moment.

This struck me with some force one night when I was tired and up in the middle of the night and my computer crashed. I thought it was important to fix it and in doing so I was going to miss sleep and not be ready for the next day. I thought, "This isn't what I need." Then I realized that this must in fact be *just what I need*—my optimal outcome—because I got to practice grace under pressure.

You can play self-defeating mind games with yourself, saying, "If I didn't have these beliefs, then I would have a more pleasant outcome." Avoid that because it gets you less than nowhere; it just makes it hard.

Given the beliefs you have, no matter what happens, it is the optimal outcome. It doesn't mean you have to like it, but the universe sorted through all of the possibilities given your beliefs at the moment and chose the one that was the most pleasant, maybe not in the short run but overall. It's all creative, even your mistakes.

Everyone has their own dharma in that sense—in this class, we use dharma in an updated twenty-first-century Hindu sense of your individual or particular path, not the Buddhist sense of *the* path. Even when you resist your dharma, or never address your dharma, then *that* turns out to be your dharma, because every bit of consciousness is always and already enlightened.

This world is so cool that everybody, through their Causal soul and the interplay between them and other beings, has an individualized dharma, depending on what's up for them. And moment by moment, your dharma changes. Yes, moment by moment, your individualized dharma changes. No matter what decision you make and no matter how horrible a decision you make, at *that* moment the universe immediately reconstructs itself to optimize your chance of developing spiritual freedom or spiritual meaningfulness. I'm not saying it makes it easy because you may have made enough bad decisions that it's really pretty hard, but given the context that you have created, the universe always changes *every* aspect of itself to optimize your ability to make meaning in that moment. And if you make great decisions, the universe immediately recalculates and is ready in the next moment. Or if you make a bad decision, it immediately recalculates and is available in the next moment.

The universe is always listening to you; it never goes unconscious. You may be on the phone with me and paying me a hundred dollars for a half-hour session, and I might gather wool for a minute or two, but the universe *never* does that. It always optimizes for you in that moment.

Clearly, some choices are better than others, but all choices are sacred. It behooves us to make the best choices that we can make. Either way, the whole universe immediately adjusts to wrap us in this web of meaning and joy that we may not be able to track, but it's always present, manifesting through the play of polarities. Sometimes we're going to gracefully deal with the play of polarities and that's a kind of effortless growth, and sometimes we're going to stumble on those polarities and find contradiction. Sooner or later, all of us get to places where it's just hard. And part of the reason that it's hard is because there is no way to get there from here because we have so many contradictions. Yet you can never go backward. Your experience can degrade. But all experience makes you more than you were.

A good outcome isn't necessarily winning the lottery. It's learning more about energy as represented by money, whether you win the lottery or not, whether you go bankrupt or not. Through bankruptcy, you may experience a more unpleasant aspect, but you can never know less about money than you do right now, even if you go bankrupt. You will know more about money and what it is to have it and what it is not to have it.

There may be times in your life, let's say, when you're making money hand over fist and then there may be a ten-year period of time where you have a very hard time making money at all. Your experience has degraded and you certainly have less money, but you as an eternal person know more about money, and part of knowing about money is knowing about *lack of money*.

You're not worse off and you're not a victim. You are simply someone who used this awful thing that happened to you to add to your experience. You didn't understand that you were adding to your experience, you certainly did not want that, and you're not an idiot for doing that.

I'm hoping that part of this will allow you to see that you are never stymied, you are always working on what's up even if you're choosing *not* to work on things. That's part of your process of working on things. It's never fundamentally about your goal. Your goal draws you into engaging life, but whether or not you attain your goal, that life experience enriches you and expands your understanding.

There are goals we think we have, and goals the deeper wisdom of the universe is always and already pursuing. We are naively certain we know exactly what will enrich us. It may be that we are all biologically programed to believe we fully understand our desires and all their important ramifications. But life always gives us surprises. Life always adds a "thickening" and subtlety to the meanings we think we know beforehand. For example, my wife and I love our cats as full members of our family. As a psychic and a healer, I could see that my cats were very capable in creating their lives and collaborating with my wife's and my desires. Therefore, I assumed that each of them would live a long and healthy life and then cross over easily, with a minimum of fuss and bother. Our second cat to cross over had cancer at age nineteen. It took months while we learned to hydrate him and coax him to eat. Still, he sustained an elegant graciousness and enjoyed following the sun throughout each day and sleeping with us each night until we perceived he was ready to go. That time with him when he was sick and required strong support deepens our relationship and love for him, and it taught us so much about him, ourselves, and the flow of life. We both became kinder and more generous people. Our sixth cat was so charming the vet said he was therapy for her. That vigorous little guy came down with an aggressive cancer at age six and our hearts are still broken. But each of those events with our cats and other events has made us more than what we were. Each presented us with deeper lessons we didn't know we needed; but deeper portions of ourselves did know, and our conscious selves, just below our conscious awareness, enrolled in those lessons.

That's the power of the Taoist precept that says, "What's in the way *is* the way." Some people say or think that what's in the way means you have to get that out of the way before you can work on what's next, as if what you *really* want to work can't be your project yet because there's something in the way. That's not the way I interpret it. What's in the way *is* your next spiritual step. You might like to say, "This is what's keeping me from my real life." No, this *is* your real life. "What's in the way is your real life." Becoming curious about just what surprises and hidden meanings it has for you is always the fastest way to happiness and fulfillment.

11

Addressing Fierce Aspects of Reality

Very often if you find blocks in the physical body. They have their origin in your emotions, so that's what's *in the way* and *is the way*. If you see a block in your communication at a physical level, you can use any of your tools on it; you can also invent tools. The block that you're seeing has important emotional components; therefore, when you work on that block, it helps you to acknowledge your frustration, give it space, and move to enough neutrality that you can be open to working on the block with all of your tools and all of your approaches and to be resourceful and in communication with it. Try asking, "Why are you there? What's going on?"

Everything is going here, there, and everywhere in this delightfully sacred way. Not just when you do something good but when you do things bad. They happen, maybe not quite as delightfully, but still very sacredly.

If you're freaking out with or shutting down any particularly powerful energy, try hanging with it and not having to fix it fast. Just start to look. Also, instead of fighting the shutting down, observe *how* you're shutting down. Become more interested in how you're shutting down. Have fun *not* having fun.

Once again, we're too quick to try fix things. If something's going wrong or uncomfortable, the first thing you try to do is fix it—that's only logical. But if it doesn't work, then become interested in why fixing it isn't working, rather than worrying about the fact that it's not working.

It isn't making mistakes that hurts you; it's not getting *value* out of your mistakes that hurts you. It isn't getting caught up in a problem that hurts you. It's resisting the problem and not being interested in it that hurts.

Hold as much as you can in your body without stressing to hold it all in your body, because some things *are* too big to contain in your body. Stay yourself and stay *in* yourself, changed by this experience, without trying to hold all of it *in* yourself. Do both. Let it be too big for you to hold. Hold what fits in you there and let the rest spill over. Let that be okay, what you hold, what you don't hold, and the fact that you can't hold it all.

The reason that you want to hold it all inside you is that you want all that joy. You don't know that that's the reason because it's intrinsic, not only the joy but the wanting to hold it. But what can *also* be intrinsic is doing both.

In our system, we do something that would make no sense to most mystics. We don't try to stay in joy—because you cannot stay in all that joy and be personal with the sharp focus that's here. What you *can* do over time is experience the joy at times and be yourself and know that joy is there in the sense that it percolates up without being the center of your awareness.

A lot of systems will try to get you to that place where you are in that joy all the time, to have that joy flood your consciousness. We intentionally *don't* do that because to do it sacrifices too much. Instead, we gather experience as individuals.

At any moment, you are whole and complete, even though future growth is missing and unobserved. You won't have had your present realization in earlier moments, but you were aware of the other experience of that earlier moment and that was full of life for then. You underwent a gradual change in perspective. It is not that you are suddenly "better" and "wiser" and must regret how you were. Rather, you are always whole and complete, and each moment is whole and complete and needs nothing.

It really helps if you can understand you may find certain experiences appallingly painful, but that is not the complete truth. You're not a victim in the sense that, no matter how horrific something is, everything that happens minimizes your overall pain and maximizes your overall gain. It might not feel that way.

No matter how psychic you are, no matter how enlightened you are, you don't have the whole story. The whole story will not fit in the human neurological system—that is, the human waking neurological system. It just won't. You may very well get much larger pieces of the story in deep and protected parts of the dream state. And the work creates percolation points where you can, without full understanding—even without understanding at all—access the overdetermined whole.

Every lifetime, no matter how awful, even if you have done the most heinous things, is still sacred. When you have the full picture, you will know its worth. You may regret some of the things you did, but you will know its worth and sacredness. And that's *part* of the sacredness.

Every experience you have becomes the raw material—not just for the rest of your life, for the rest of eternity.

The best long-term solvent for stuck energy is called life. Life will keep saying hello to your stuck places. In the first book I co-wrote, I think we called it the "grim promise," which means you will succeed. What makes that a grim promise is you don't get to say, "This is too hard, I'm going to stop this, I'm never going to deal with this." Life will keep bringing you back, this lifetime or another, and you *will* succeed. There are no problems that you are capable of *not* succeeding at. If you systematically decided, "I'm going to make the worst decision that I can possibly make every time I have a decision," you would be incapable of carrying it out because your very decisions would change the meaning of your choices, prior and afterward.

As a practical, pragmatic purpose, we each want to make a living, have people that we love, people who love us, to minimize pain, and to maximize pleasure; but, underneath all that, there's a joy that pushes life and is always and already ecstatic. You can't be aware of that with your neurological system in a dualistic state, but it's there and it percolates up all the time.

It will get on your nerves after a while if you come at this as, "I'm broken and I have to be fixed." The reason you come at it as "I'm broken and I have to be fixed" is that pain is senior in your space. Your crown is submerged under that pain. There are two ways to deal with that. One is to go transcendent. The pain stays, but it isn't a problem. And the other is to gain seniority in your crown. You see the pain, and in the process of engaging life as it is, you start to release the tangles that are the pain.

If someone is trying to be senior to her pain, and still finds it really interesting when she encounters someone who isn't, then that's one way she becomes more senior to her pain.

You never release all the pain. The pain is part of the experience. The Buddha is absolutely right that all life in duality, when you're in a dual state, involves dukkha. Maybe not this moment, but intrinsically, there's an unsatisfactoriness. Now if you recognize that, then you can start to be a lot happier. But if you say, "I want to get to that nonpolarity and still be in the Astral plane where I don't have anything significant that bothers me," then you're going to be an unhappy person. Or a trivial person.

Remember, some energies are really fierce. You can always sit in your space, even if you can't get it out on a rose, even if it's owning your crown. You can pull your energy out of it and start to ground some of its energy into the Earth. Attach a rose and ground that rose in the Earth. Work with it for a while. It may take you a long time, but that's okay, because you don't have to get rid of it in the course of the exercise or even today or even this month. You can get rid of a little of it and you can take however long it takes because, if it's that fierce and you're working on it, then it's good news; it's probably been there for more than one lifetime. If it's been there that long and it takes you a year, that's not a long time for something that you have carried around for one hundred or one thousand years.

If it is too controlling in your space, then you can leave your space and work on it from outside by pulling your energy out of it. There are some family thoughtforms I have dealt with that, as I went further, they went further. I finally had to get a position beyond the edge of the universe and work on them and, even then, it was touch and go. But, you know, those were such fruitful thoughtforms to work on. And every little bit of progress that I've made on them is really golden.

So you work on them and if you have to stop because they are too fierce, then you put a grounding cord on them, or on a part of them, or ask your guides to deal with them, or turn your attention as best you can to something else. Even if you keep doing that, even if it is really miserable for a couple of days or years, you'll probably find that it gets a little better and a little better.

During this calendar year I had a situation with something like that that lasted for more than a week—fierce for three days and strong for nine days beyond that and I'm still working on it months later. There's nothing strange about that. It happens.

There's another thing that you can do. Examine your belief that says that you have to get rid of it all at once. See if you can find a way to do what neurolinguistic programmers call "chunking it down." You can get a smaller piece to work on while the remainder of it is grounded and you let that remaider know that you're coming back to it.

Another tool that I like with things that are really, really hard—I don't know if it works as well for other people—is what I call a two-year-old level. I get in a conversation with it and say, "Why are you here?" And it says something like, "You need me." But whatever it says, I say, "Why?" Even when it comes up with something that makes sense, even if the answer makes perfect sense, if I'm not comfortable yet in my body and aura I ask, "Why?"

Very often it will go in a loop through maybe twelve questions and get back to the first question and start to go through the loop again.

Each time you go around the loop, the energy starts to get shaken out of it. If it refuses to answer, you say, "Why are you refusing to answer?" And it may again refuse to answer. At some point I'll say to it, "Look, this is my space. Either answer the question or leave." That usually works for me. It will say, "Oh, well, because I want to kill you." I say, "Well, why do you want to kill me?" "Well, because." So, you stay at two-year-old level. It's not a fast technique. It can take an hour or two or three or longer.

12

Overdetermination

There are always an infinite number of causes, each of which is 100 percent responsible for whatever discomfort you may be experiencing. By 100 percent responsible, I mean that if you somehow wiped out everything else, you would still have the discomfort and you could still develop a causal explanation by simply saying, "This is what caused that." But if you assimilate or clear *any* one of those infinite causes from neutrality, all the other causes will also be assimilated.

So matching pictures always generates an expression of whatever is your next step. Whatever you meet in the world, wherever you have a matching picture light up, that's your next step in clearing your matching picture. Remember, "what's in the way *is* the way."

The reason that "what's in the way *is* the way" works is that everything is overdetermined. You can say, "This is caused 100 percent by this, 100 percent by that," because consciousness is multidirectional. Every dissatisfaction, every weakness is overdetermined. Every weakness you have can be the result of some past life, of something your parents did, of something society did to you, of something you did to yourself, of something that jerk in front of you is doing at this moment. There are an infinite number of causes, each sufficient to generate your dissatisfaction. If you think there is only one answer that's the real cause, you're likely to get enmeshed and caught up in that and really be deeply stuck.

In this system, current time does not mean what it usually does.

Sometimes current time is visiting a past or future lifetime. It's whatever is really up. You never have to go to the cause because it could be caused by any number of things. There are literally an infinite number of causes for your discomfort and any one of them that you deal with profoundly will heal all the causes.

Remembering that what's in the way *is* the way allows you to pick one of those infinite causes of your discomfort that is most accessible to change.

If you can work on something with neutrality, you do not have to find some childhood trauma. Whatever is in the way is a good start. You may have certain ways that you prefer. You might prefer going back to childhood traumas, but that sort of change-work is very, very slow and not very powerful when it's done without neutrality.

In that sense, insight therapy is of very limited effectiveness. People go to ten years of therapy and develop elaborate stories about why they're miserable, as opposed to ten years earlier being miserable without an elaborate story of why. You can be stuck in that insight for ten more years without changing. You have an explanation for why your throat is sore, but to work through it can still take you a long time.

And again, it's multiply caused. You could say it's caused by patriarchy, making you unable to own your own voice. You could say that it was caused by a choking death in the early 1700s. You can have an insight, "Oh, this was caused by my parents when I was young." You could say that it's caused by them thwarting your ability to express yourself. You can work on any one of those and entirely clear it. The difficulty is that those sort of insight approaches are not as effective and quick. Those stories can be real, it's just that working with them doesn't give you a lot of traction for changing. But taking the story and making it energy and working with it does.

If you say, "What is the spiritual energy here?" you work with that spiritual energy. To some of you this might sound straightforward, but I've discovered experienced people, brilliant people, and they clear pictures and then they get back into the story because that's what our society has told us is how you solve pain.

If you learn how to deal with the situation in this way—spiritually, energetically—you will clear pain out of your space. It doesn't matter if you're right. It doesn't matter who should be punished. And yes, of course, you stand up for yourself. But most people think that to stand up for yourself means not letting anyone say anything nasty to you. That's an absurd idea. You can't be spiritual enough, powerful enough, or rich enough to have people be fair to you. The Chinese Communists are not fair to the Dalai Lama. People aren't fair to President Obama and people aren't always fair to Melinda Gates. I have been engaged on a spiritual journey for forty years and after all that time I'm not always fair to my wife. There isn't going to come a time when people are fair to you. Obsessing about whether or not people are fair to you is one quick way to become unhappy and unsuccessful.

Let's go back to a psychic way to pull yourself out of your stories and your shoulds, have tos, and oughts.

13

Matching Your Crown

To become something, you match your crown to it. So if you match your crown to all this stuff you're interacting with, you become that stuff. Now you're listening to me and many of you are matching your crown to what I'm saying, and that allows you to deeply understand what you're doing. But it also means that you're becoming what you're trying to understand rather than being who you are and *looking at* what you want to understand. The downside is if you don't clear after studying what I am saying, then you fail to find your own way of understanding the points I try to make. In the long run in this system, you'll learn other ways of saying hello to the information that's coming so that you won't have to match your crown to it.

The more neutrality you have, the faster, more powerful, and more pleasant any change-work is.

Basically, neutrality in the body is having your crown color be a different color from what you're looking at and then being in the center of your head or crown. You're not going to be able to have that crown at a different color if you've lost your grounding, so grounding is a part of the way you get to neutrality. Sometimes you can be so overwrought that your body is running all these stress hormones and stuff, and you just go out of body. But then you work on it from out of body and try to blow pictures until you can come in body.

Having said that, I don't expect you to necessarily go home and do that right away because it takes some practice.

You can have more sense of objective truth in your crown than is good for you. Something might be someone *else's* idea about a thing or that something's either true or not true, but you are matching it in your crown.

We make nouns of what's really a kind of verb. There's really no such thing as truth; but there is truthing, which is the unfolding, moment by moment, of what is. Truthing encompasses as much distortion as objective reality because in the moment everything is expanding in all directions. What you get in the moment as truth will grow into something else the next moment. And distortions will be part of that process. Seth talks about the profoundly powerful instabilities and imbalances that are required for life to be creative and purposeful.

One night when I was studying with Lewis, he turned to me and looked at me and said, "You're smart," and I thought, "Hmmm, people are noticing." Then he said, "I knew a psychic once who was smart." I thought, "Wait, this is an insult."

Essentially, what he meant was that it's harder to have a revved-up analyzer and be psychic, though there's some useful stuff to the analyzer too.

The reason you don't create space is because you get locked into a picture or a cloud of energy, someone else's is energy, so for the first exercise I'm going to ask each person to take a moment and just become aware of their aura. And notice the differences in it.

Take a look over by your liver; think of an instant that you were angry and notice that you can step into that anger and that becomes your reality, that becomes who you are. Match your crown to the color of that anger or the feeling of that anger.

Okay, change your crown color back up to violet or gold. Notice that that you are probably less angry, but that potential for anger is still sitting there in your aura.

Now go to your heart. Notice a time that you demanded certain things from a loved one and notice what that feels like. Match your crown to the color of that demand. And notice when you're matching your crown to it, that's who you are.

Now stay in the heart area. Find a time when you just kind of lost yourself in a pleasurable activity. Same heart, very different experience. Match your crown to that pleasurable engagement. Again, notice that that's who you are.

Now, on your own, explore your aura either by feel or by color, or you could do it by sound, you could use any of your senses. Find two or three different energies in your aura. Notice that you can dive into one of them. Match your crown to it and that becomes who you are and that becomes what is real for you. Now go into another one. Match your crown to it, and that becomes real for you. That is now who you are at that particular moment.

14

Life Is Meaningful Rather Than Real

We never fully understand our experience because experience doesn't exist as a simple isolated component that can be controlled. Experience is meaningful and meaning grows in all directions, so the meaning of it continues to change as your experience changes.

We're going to introduce a concept from a direction that I don't think we've ever looked at before. This starts as an attempt to help you find the ability to meditate when chaos is going on all around you.

Now when we have a group like this, it's pretty easy to meditate because everybody's meditating on one thing, and the pain in your space that would keep you from meditating gets kind of shunted aside. This also is intended to help loosen each of us up from treating what we're focusing on as being objective truth, what exists. Everything has multiple meanings that continue to change and grow even if the event seems to have ended. Treating our current subjective sense of what is going on or what has happened as objective truth makes us less able to find the painful energy causes and change them.

Our system is based upon contradiction. If you look at the Tao symbol, it's based on the creative play of the tensions of polarities, and the whole universe arises in this ecstatically creative dynamic between order and chaos, yin and yang, you name the polarity. One polarity that arises very powerfully in our system is that we are committed to daily life as meaningful in its own terms and for its own purposes. Most spiritual systems, and all energy systems including ours, recognize that our experience with its palpability, with its seeming concreteness, is an illusion, that it's a group agreement, and that illusion as we engage it can often be painful. It's simultaneously ecstatic and often can be pleasurable, but our brains are set up more to avoid pain than they are to seek pleasure, which is understandable. Life can seem deeply problematic, and one answer to that problematicness is the Buddha's answer, which is that there's a certain inescapable suffering in experience as long as you perceive reality in what's called a dualistic way. The object then becomes to stop the suffering.

The Dalai Lama still experiences pain, but the Dalai Lama does not experience suffering because his consciousness is deeply nondual. That heroic solution to the problem of suffering has been a great benefit to humanity for twenty-five hundred years or so.

The Buddha purposefully did not consider what happens to people after death and did not interact with other dimensions as part of his solution to the problem of suffering. What he did do is teach a path to generating an enormous neurological shift that allowed people to step out of the illusion that there's an inside and outside to their world. Technically that's not the same as unity consciousness; it's something more subtle and profound.

That *is* a solution to the problem of suffering; the solution is to blast through the illusion. Blasting through the illusion makes a lot of sense if you think the illusion is just a matter of ignorance, that it isn't serving a positive purpose. Seth and my guides have argued that the illusion *does* serve a positive purpose. In the same way, the sense of continuous movement, as in a movie or a television—that really isn't a person talking there, those are moving pictures—is just an illusion, but it's a profound illusion and it serves important purposes. However if you ascribe great purpose to this illusion that we're in, that will inevitably generate suffering. Once you start ascribing meaning to the illusion, it is almost impossible to avoid ascribing that meaning to how "successful" you are in manifesting your desires. And you start treating this illusion as too real and you miss the point.

The point is not the person with the most toys or the most money wins, or whatever that phrase was in the sixties or seventies. The purpose is to engage life, to engage this drama, to engage this conversation. Many systems treat the experiences of everyday life as if they were real and argue that if you are in pain, you just simply haven't figured out the right technique.

That's not the way things work. The Dalai Lama didn't get exiled from Tibet because he didn't understand creative visualization; he got exiled because life is rich and complex and deeply meaningful. Even horrors like the Chinese invasion and control of Tibet are rich and complex and deeply meaningful.

Those of us who attribute meaningfulness to this illusion in physical reality overly reify it. Everything we do is a concept; we're exploring concepts by being incarnated as human beings. I like to say this life is unreal but deeply meaningful. What happens is that we latch onto a particular feeling as being the reality of our experience in such a way that we get stuck in pain. Once you learn psychic techniques, you will still get stuck in pain sometimes because sometimes life is tough. But as you start to learn these techniques—I mean you've already done most of them, but you haven't done them with this frame around them—I believe you will have an easier time being fascinated by your experience and understanding. Hopefully this will create much more flexibility and playfulness in how you use your attention.

Some of you say, "I've done so much work on this, how can I still have an issue with this? How can issues still be coming up?" Imagine you're climbing a mountain. One hundred feet up is hard. Two hundred feet up is hard. Three hundred feet up is hard. The only thing that changes is your view gets better, but you're still climbing a mountain, which you volunteered to do. That's the joy of being out there.

You may be part of a gridlock. Imagine New York City being gridlocked for about thirty blocks in all directions. You're on Broadway and you're just trying to get across the street to see a play, but you can't do that because there's that gridlock and it's not going to break up until you go back thirty blocks and start trying to free up the cars there.

You might say to yourself, "This gridlock is in the way of getting to the play," but the real play of your life is not *to get to that play*. The real play of your life is to clear the gridlock, even if you miss the night's play. To clear that gridlock, you may have to go thirty blocks west and thirty blocks north, and it may take you years. You may say, "But the play's right there. Why do I have to clear all that gridlock?"

Because the gridlock is a much richer experience.

Children don't learn to walk because they need to know how to walk when they're thirty-five years old. They learn to walk because they have a pure joy of walking.

Sad is not a problem as long as you're in current time with sad. When you're not in current time with sad, it becomes depression. We've all, when we're young, had these goals for ourselves. Most of us don't reach them. I think, if you've engaged your life with any modicum of attention, when you look back on it, you see that what you got was much richer than your young imagination of all these triumphs. I'm not saying it is better than the triumphs. I'm just saying if all you got in your life was your young idea of what a triumph is, your life would have been impoverished. Our lives are so much richer than we can imagine when we're young. When we're young we think of it in terms of one success after another, because why wouldn't we? But I don't know anyone who goes through life, one success after another. I think everyone who attends to their life, if they open their vision, will say, "Boy, this was painful at times but richer than I could have imagined."

Real life—real engaged life—draws richness from things that seem to have nothing to do with the main event. It's worth saying over again because it is so pivotal. There are things we want to do, books we want to write, things we think are important to say, but we can trust life. Ordinary events like going to work or trying to rent or sell a house may not be fun, but they *are* incredible. If we write a book, those things will be there. And if we don't, those things will still be there. All life expands in all directions.

If you let it, you can be more receptive to a slowly increasing, percolating-up-from-the-universe joy, and that will help you be resourceful in your life. And it's not that you don't know how to do these things or some other part of you does—you really do know how to do these things. It just doesn't occur to you to male- or female-ground, open your third chakra, own your crown, and stop treating the outside world as if *it* were the problem. The outside world is an information bank; it's part of a conversation you have. You may be in pain, but the problem is not situated outside you. If you start to treat the outside world as information and feedback, you will learn from it much better and be more resourceful when you engage it.

You create your own reality. But another way to say this is: you engage the outside world because it *is* you, not because it will make you happy. When you engage the outside world with authenticity, kindness, and generosity, and a rigorous working on your own attitude, it will make you happy, not because you're going to get what you want but because life is incredibly sacred.

Treating the world as information and feedback is a divinely, sparklingly—even if sometimes bitterly creative—feedback. It gives you back more than you give it by its very nature. And it's these divine instabilities and imbalances that generate that fact: the world *always* gives you back more than you give it. When you treat it as unreal but deeply meaningful, then it becomes one of your resource states. Because for any blindness you have, any spiritual blindness, treating it as not real but meaningful will help you see, sooner or later, no matter how much you resist it.

Not only is resistance futile, but it is, like all other vices, inevitable. As long as you have a personal life, you will have some resistance, you will have some anger, you will have some selfishness.

You'd probably laugh at a lot of us in Jane's Seth class. We were young and full of ourselves.

Everyone I knew, including me, initially misunderstood what creating your own reality meant. I interpreted it to mean that I was going to become a god and be able to make myself happy by manifesting basically everything I want. More than a few of us stressed about what we were going to do with all the money we were going to make just by changing our beliefs, and other people wouldn't have as much and would we give them stuff? Because it was going to be so easy; All you had to do was get smart and realize that you create your own reality according to your beliefs.

I think the Abraham work is probably more sophisticated than that, but I'm constantly meeting people who read it and say, "Oh, all I have to do is fix my intent and I'll get love and riches and perfect health and duh-duh-duh-duh." It doesn't work that way because pulling energy together is a skill that takes time.

But that's sort of the way I was. I thought that within less than five years I would have multiple homes, a mansion with horses—I didn't even ride horses, but my soon-to-be ex did, so that's why the horses were there. What I didn't understand was the sacredness of dealing with those tensions and learning from them. So I learned how to be a lawyer and, in learning how to be a lawyer, I learned how to be a human being. It requires that kind of focus.

It wasn't important for me to learn how to be a lawyer—well, it was—I had to earn a living. What *was fundamentally* important was for me to learn lessons about arrogance and alienation and communication and compassion that I learned while being a lawyer.

People who misunderstand what Seth meant by saying "you create your own reality" start to treat life as real but meaningless. What I mean is, they feel like any part of their life that isn't what they want it to be is somehow an assault and insult, a refutation of their being. That's what I mean by treating life as meaningless. It's as though the only thing that matters or could matter is what they want or don't want. They treat life as if there couldn't possibly be something valuable in this thing that's happening to them.

We get so fixated on what we're entitled to, what we deserve, what we need, and who should be doing what. We treat that only as it appears, rather than as some sort of divine engagement. We treat it as meaningless because it's not what we want, it's what we *don't* want.

It would be much more useful, paradoxically, to treat it as unreal. Then you can say, "That's not my favorite emotional sparring partner," or, "That's me engaging me through this polarity with its own creativity," or, "That's me engaging with something that is not literally only external to me." If you treat it as unreal in the sense of not the sole objective reality outside of you, it can become something subjective and deeply meaningful—a much more resourceful place to be.

That's how modern science has it backward. Scientists explore objective nature—the world of atoms and molecules—as if it were real and the only real thing. Because of the way they view it, making themselves and it objective to each other—they decide that it's meaningless. It has no intrinsic meaning, it just happens.

But they have it backward. It *isn't* real. It only seems real because they are limiting themselves to that seeming reality. It *is* meaningful— incredibly meaningful.

15

Probabilities

For the universe to work in the way it does requires a very confusing concept called probabilities: anything that can happen, does happen, as the major decision points in your life branch out into different directions. I have already mentioned it, but I have not given it its due or let you in on how complex and elusive its meaning or function is.

The idea of multiple versions of yourself makes it easier for you to cherish each version of yourself because it doesn't seem so confining and you can see how one version leads to another version. That just isn't there if you think the universe only has one version of you. If you think of it from your soul's point of view, why just do one version, why not explore lots of different versions? You see some choices now that you didn't see at the time.

Remember in *Close Encounters of the Third Kind,* a spaceship lands and it has these little lights blinking. Souls experience moments like lights that are blinking and they're all available and they can be linked with an instant when you were two and when you're forty-two and when you're eighty-two. They each make different kinds of noises, have different pictures, and have different resonances for the soul. It's processing a myriad of tastes and smells. It takes our lives, which we can only imagine experiencing in different apparent realities, and it explores them and enriches itself, and through our personality's own deeper knowing and intuitions, enriches us, the personality.

Probabilities split and reconnect all the time, so at times it might be two separate probabilities of you and then, a month later, those have rejoined. How can they be? If you let go of your simple idea of causality and consecutive moments, it starts to make sense. We often talk as if the soul's doing this and the personality's doing this; but remember, the soul *is* the personality and the personality *is* the soul, and yet they're not the same thing and that's part of what makes it so glorious.

That's where Multipersonhood will start to emerge. When you say, oh, the soul is this and the personality is this, you lose so much; and then you see only the march of time and you don't understand the eternity and the richness of your personal soul.

Everybody, create and destroy roses. Please be in the center of your head; cut off your grounding cord and make a new female or male grounding cord. Say hello to your belly-button chakra, to your body consciousness. Another way of doing that is to say hello to the consciousness in each cell in your body as it contributes to the overall consciousness of your body.

While you as a waking human being may not be able to track all your probabilities, the cells in your body have consciousness too, and their consciousnesses are not localized in time nor probability the way your waking ego consciousness is. You might get a sense of how they track alternative yous, future yous, and alternatives that you can choose in the future. They try to maintain a certain kind of resonance and stable resilience and life. And that supports the body. As the body and the cells in the body stretch out perceptually through other yous, they also process and interact with other people, with animals, with the air, with stones—that is part of why crystals work so well—with devas, with elementals, with the Sun, with All That Is, and especially with Mother Earth.

Begin to get a sense of how they rise out of Mother Earth and how Mother Earth luxuriates in their unique experience. Feel this happening simultaneously. Moment by moment your cells arise out of the Earth, out of the energy system that is Mother Earth, and she stretches out through those cells into a tiny, tiny portion of her consciousness and yet she's utterly and completely fully present in each cell. Notice that, in her, the body consciousness is eternal and expands in all directions. Even when you are buried in the earth, and the cells turn into dirt themselves—ashes to ashes, dust to dust—even then your consciousness, in through time and outside of time, interacts with other consciousnesses as itself and yet much more distributed and spread out. It doesn't need to hold itself the way our ego consciousness does, the way it did when *it* was ego; it stays itself even as it loses itself, loses itself to the way our ego consciousness would think of it.

Feel the Sun encompassing and giving rise to the Earth, giving rise to your body, and taking your body. Long after what you think of as you leaves the body and comes to know itself in Multipersonhood, long after that body has become dirt in the Earth, there is profound interconnection. No interconnection is ever lost. Those interconnections continue to grow, without limit, without bound.

Even as you luxuriate the ecstatic arising and expanding of the body in and through the Earth right now, say hello in the heart area to your personality. It's a little bigger than the ego, it's more you and all your relationships. Notice how beautifully relationships are enhanced by and enhance individuality, and imagine that as the Sun shines *into* your body, there's an especially subtle prana that comes through the back of the heart chakra. In every plane and dimension of consciousness that the Sun enters into your heart, shining light molten gold, it provides the energy for your personality. Not just your personality moment by moment but simultaneously throughout all eternity and inside and outside of time as we know it. This is more than a fullness; this is ineffable, inexpressible. Through that motive energy, you explore both within and outside of time through all dimensions as you expand in all directions, in ways that "you" even now understand and in ways that are utterly unlike the way you think of you now.

One of the most interesting things about the Sun providing this motive power is the unstoppableness of you. Any question, any issue you move toward unstoppably. It may take you a day, it may take you a year, it may take you a lifetime, a lifetime of the Earth, or more, but can you feel this unstoppable expansive energy, this utterly secure energy that is the primal motive for your curiosity and divine play? No matter how stuck you are, that energy is always and already there, and one way or another you will learn and grow and answer that question, and then the questions that that question's answer engenders.

I feel the Sun's motive power very differently than I feel Mother Earth. Mother Earth is such a tender joyously nurturing energy. This Sun's energy is an objective unquenchable lust for experience. It's nice to know and maybe even feel that you cannot be stopped. You may encounter obstructions, but you cannot be stopped.

It is because you are eternal that you can be fine with the fact that as long as you have a consciousness there will be suffering, there will be dukkha, because it allows you to create a particular kind of meaning that you can only attain with a of myriad experiences. And each experience changes everything.

The word *dukkha* is most often translated as suffering. Unsatisfactory is probably closer but there are no English words. Unsatisfactory captures the sense that, even if you're getting everything that you want, it passes. Your experiences are impermanent, so there is a loss. They're also interdependent so that you cannot control them.

The Sethian as opposed to the Buddhist takeaway is that you have incarnated into ignorance on purpose. And when you are dead, you will gradually emerge from that ignorance through experiences that occur afterward.

One of the kinds of experiences that you can have is participating in further incarnations. So, on death you might go up and talk to your soul, talk with your guides, and say, "Gee, to fill out my experience, I would like to be a little girl between four and eight years old. On the other hand, I would also like to be a lawyer in a wealthy situation between the ages of eighteen and forty-four. I don't care what gender; I just want to be a lawyer and be wealthy and explore this life as an adult in that environment." Maybe there are four or five others.

You don't suddenly re-manifest or walk in to other bodies or get born as an infant with that destiny. It's far cooler. What you do is you get together other incarnations from your soul and you experience a little girl, you become part of her unconscious from ages four to eight. You feel what it's like to be her. And you also have some impact on her because your feelings become part of her unconscious. Yet she is the center of her own experience and—this is kind of hard to understand—you are the center of your experience too. So while it's her incarnation, it's your exploration as part of the gestalt that includes little girl.

Let's say she clears so much karma that it changes the nature of it. She could do that unconsciously so that the setup is no longer what your co-personality was expecting. You might be surprised how much your co-personality would get out of that because, remember, it participates too. So the odds are, it will learn enough in a year and a quarter that it would be ready to move on to what's next.

Of course, no subjectivity *has* to grow with another subjectivity. Different parts of the gestalt can dig in their heels in and say, "I'm not done holding this or that resentment. I'm entitled to my resentment. I was treated wrong and I don't want to live in a universe where I don't get to do revenge." People have a right to stay at that place.

But you'd be surprised at how often parts *do* change. And it could also happen that one part of the gestalt outstrips the other; one of the co-personalities learns their lesson more quickly.

The universe is so enormously creative. Probabilities are not any harder than the concept of synchronicity, which is an acausal all-things-happening-at-once, even though one thing doesn't cause another.

The standard scientific model is not adequate to the true nature of time and probabilities and what earlier hominids were like. Some ten thousand years ago, your neurological system was not wired in the same way as it is now *vis a vis* time and identity. Seth talks about a mother being able to go off hunting and watch her children, who she left under a tree—watch them *as* the tree as well as in her consciousness as a hunter-gatherer.

In that consciousness you don't have the starkness of the contradictions that you have now. You have a vividness of experience and clarity of focus that you did not have ten thousand years ago, which, in addition to having fabulous rewards, has more pain in it than we've had before or will have in the future. In some ways, the consciousness that human beings have developed over thousands of years is reaching a peak in this particular pain direction.

And as you move forward, you'll be able to take that vividness and join with other groups of consciousness so that within a thousand to two thousand years from now, you will be able to engage direct creativity even as you engage the intense clarity of your camouflage reality.

For now, though, you must inevitably experience reality as full of contradictions and a certain amount of pain.

In 1974 I was talking to a channeled being. I said something—not quite this crass—to the effect of, "Why doesn't the rest of the world catch up to me and become peaceful?"

I was told, "If everybody in the world had your beliefs, there'd still be war."

I said, "If everybody had the same beliefs as the Dalai Lama, would there be war?" and he said, "Yes."

What he's saying is that everyone on this planet creates reality according to their beliefs, so if the Dalai Lama is on this planet—and he is—then he plays some part in the movement to world peace. But there are aspects in his aura that match—not in the normal English sense of the word *match* but in the psychic sense—that get lit up in the same way as terrorists because there couldn't be terrorists if he didn't have some match. It's not like if, all of a sudden, he cleared that match, all terrorists would disappear from this Earth. *He* would disappear from this probability.

Past lives seem to fit within a linear time frame even though they don't actually happen that way. For human beings at this time in human history, a very strong circuit connects certain pasts with certain futures. We live in a single probability even as others are branching off. That's more what's happening than sequential lives.

The particular way in which we experience the universe with sequential and linear time seems to make our choices higher stakes than they really are. There are indications in physics that time may be more playful than the rigid movement we experience as humans, and there are others ways of experiencing time, even on the Earth.

Humans are probably the only animal on the planet that experiences time in such a linear way. Yes, animals that hunt have to experience a certain amount of linearity to be able to leap and track where their prey will be. But even animals that hunt experience a more flexible time than humans do.

Each of our decision points has a kind of life to it and expands in its own terms. The story of the life you lived expands into other stories that you *didn't* live. It doesn't just go down the track that you lived now. And if you look at these stories, they expand back into this track and change the way that you experience this reality.

This isn't just a mental construct. If you perceive this, you will begin to see the energy of the life you are actually living changing as a result of those other probabilities. They've kind of expanded back into this one, as this one has expanded into theirs.

Seth also talked about simultaneous time. Prior to him, there had been people who taught interaction between various times—how you might have a Revolutionary War incarnation coexist with a twenty-first-century incarnation. The Tibetan Buddhists have seen pretty much all things, simultaneous time included. Sethian versions of incarnation would not be news to Tibetan lamas, they've just made different meanings out of them.

When I was studying with Seth, I had a couple of dreams where I interacted with past incarnations of mine, one with a Revolutionary soldier, a Hessian in the British army. He and I met in the dream state and I was truly affected by his suffering as a soldier.

This wasn't something that happened a long time ago. I was meeting someone who lived in a regular three-dimensional—or maybe you would call it four-dimensional—world, in a different time period. He was interacting with me and communicating to me from the dream state across the centuries.

In a more dramatic dream, I was walking down a corridor with many doors and I opened one. There was this woman, somewhere around Baltimore 1890. When I opened the door, she saw me and put her hand up to her mouth in shock like "Aah," the way people do. I woke up shortly after this, knowing that I'd gone to sleep with her as a past incarnation of mine, she'd gone to sleep as a past incarnation of me and, when we met in the dream state, she and I were both changed by our encounter. We each went to sleep one night—different nights, of course, and different centuries—and woke up the next day changed by our encounter. My past self, when I awoke after that dream, was a different past self than she was before I went to sleep the night before. She was more in touch with her greater or bigger or inner self that included both masculine and feminine elements. She saw a masculine part of herself. I saw a feminine part of myself.

These kinds of interchanges go on all the time, especially in deep dream states, but we don't normally track them. We stick to linear time and sequential lives and miss what's happening.

We think of the choices we make as culminating in the thing that happens, but choices generate other branches of consciousness every bit as real as we are, and those probabilities are constantly interacting with one another. We are also probabilities of each other.

There's a fifteen-year-old me that I can kind of remember who didn't grow up to be me. He grew in two other directions. One of them became a lawyer who's successful in Atlanta and didn't really get involved in spirituality until the nineties and he's sort of playing around with Buddhism now. His relationship with my parents, even his childhood as he remembers it, is different from mine. Even his life before birth is different. Everything is different. And yet we intersect in that fifteen-year-old me.

Another direction that he went in is as a professor of mathematics at the University of Chicago. He has his life, he's an atheist. Again, he has a very different childhood than I do. Everything is changed. It didn't just change going forward, it changed going backward too.

When he left or when I left, not only my future but my past changed.

Let's take this a step further. My two-year-old self didn't come only from my one-year-old self but from my twenty-five-year-old self.

Here's an exercise. Put your life on a timeline and just go down that timeline and find a "you" that grew in a different direction—a you that never became this you.

Now, this may or may not be a very vivid experience, but just become curious about what happened to that you. When you get done with that one, find another place on the timeline that diverges. Even though it diverges and goes in a different direction, that information becomes part of a bigger you on the Buddhic plane. It broadens out the experience that you have, incomparably so.

Now I'm looking at a five-year-old me who died and was quickly reborn as a daughter of the African-American lady who raised me. And that me is alive and closing in on sixty and doing very well. She broadens out my experience as a sixty-five-year-old guy and casts it in a different light.

As I was waking up one morning, another me that was kind of above me, said, "Oh, I see, now." And that me went off into its own life and I woke up. It was a me that had married a woman named Paula. That me at this point is dead, died at about age forty-three. It married Paula and went to bed one night as he and Paula were in the throes of the dissolution of their marriage, thinking, "What could I have done to avoid this?" And *I* was the answer.

Float around in a time where you made some key decisions and, as you do so, open up your heart chakra, which is where probabilities spread from, so instead of looking at just that one time, open your inner feeling, seeing, what other probabilities of yours were doing. You don't have to make it a literal thing. Sort of look around there. Just a little bit wonder what the me who didn't get married did, or wonder if I had married that person in a different way with different intentions.

Your life, in effect, expands sideways into the things you *could* have done rather than what you *did* do. You have lifetimes where you're happily married to people you never married, and where you're happily married to someone in another probability whom you unhappily married in this probability. Some of those lifetimes are just as physical and as real as this, which is mind-boggling.

Enjoy the incredible generosity of life that holds all of those probabilities in place and in relationship, that permits them to be sacred, that luxuriates in all of them, not just the so-called good ones. Perhaps you get a sense of the integrity of each of those probable selves and how each one of them is now in some sense eternal and active and living out its life someplace and feeding back and in and out of this reality and amongst themselves. The whole is greater than the parts.

Hopefully, this will help you loosen up your sense of responsibility. The purpose is to be liberating, to free you from punishing yourself, from second-guessing yourself. Because you go in so many directions, you don't need to hundred-guess yourself. There's really no reason to compete with yourself. There are always an infinite number of yous that did better, there are an infinite number of yous that did worse. Wherever you are in infinity is always in the middle.

Now, if you're deeply puzzled by this, you're on the right track. As you start to think about it, you get a sense of how much more multi-directional and creative everything is than you ever suspected.

In the Seth classes about in mid- to late-February of 1974, Jane was talking about some dreamwork regarding a book she was writing with Seth. In the dream, Seth was taking the book she was writing and switching pages out of it, doing this and that, and she balked. She told us it was all too much. We had an extended conversation about the implications of probabilities and most, if not all of us, seemed to agree it was just too confusing. The concept of probabilities was one of the reasons we were so excited by Seth; yet when we dug into probabilities, it was just too much. Seth came in and promised us that when we were ready, probabilities would be an adventure.

Part of the difficulty is neurological. Over time, if you keep encountering these probabilities, your neurology will shift and some of the things that I'm saying will start to make sense. You can do that in ways that retain the kind of linear thinking you do really well and increase its capacity too.

I myself wasn't ready to deal with probabilities until the late '90s or early 2000s, when it began to dawn on me that these were not some sort of magical portals where you could move to a lifetime in which you got more of the things you wanted. Probabilities were not just a neat way of getting out of the mess you're in, that you shift probabilities and suddenly you now have money and good looks and love: "Okay, I'll just jump from this probability to another probability." That can happen—not very often, but it can happen. But it missed the point of probabilities altogether.

I began to understand that probability is a different way of valuing and engaging experience. It will help you profoundly if you stop telling yourself, "I had this past and it's made me the way I am."

You can start to reimagine that you had different pasts. You can nourish yourself in such a way that you can bring a different you to the table. You may be in the same existential situation, but you'll look at it differently.

Over time as I got more technically skilled and was able to interact consciously and intentionally with other probabilities, mostly through the heart chakra, I came to understand that you can't appreciate your humanity without appreciating your probable selves, because in the particular locked focus we have without probabilities, there seems to be only one you and it seems like outcomes are so important, so vital to the story. The outcomes that happen become too much a question of right or wrong, good or bad.

Probabilities free you in two ways. They make it impossible for you to beat yourself up by measuring yourself against choices you didn't make because there is nothing to measure yourself against. You simply enter one probability without excising multiple others. As you begin to get probabilities, you see all the different things, all of the mistakes, all of the successes, but you can see their sacredness and begin to engage the world through it.

It does kind of blow everything up for everyday life here, for to be engaged in a personal way requires a linear focus. That's why at this time in human history we don't have full access to probabilities and we don't explore them with neutrality. That's how we designed this reality. You mainly access other probabilities in the dream state or, if in the waking state, subconsciously and unconsciously.

Once you start exploring probabilities and you look at all the different ones, you'll start to notice that each probability is sacred. Remember, whatever choice you make, the whole universe readjusts and resets itself so that you remain the center of it for your consciousness. It supports you, it doesn't drive you; it supports your ability to make the most meaning out of that experience that you could. That's how the universe continues to optimize and re-optimize. It doesn't set itself up as, "Oh, this is a second-rate probability and I'm not really going to throw myself into it." Every probability is centered on the choices you made to get to that point.

The best example I have is when I was in college and driving home for vacation with two friends from school. I was entering a merging highway at high speed. I wasn't able to see the other traffic—there was a concrete wall between us. I was rounding a curve at a rate of speed at which I thought I would just fade over to the other road so that I wouldn't have to brake and also wouldn't be at risk of going too fast for my turn radius. Then I just got this—almost like an idea, almost a sound in my head—that said, "Your friends wouldn't respect your driving if you drifted over into the other lane." It had no force of urgency, but I listened to it anyway. You don't always recognize that a major probability is arising, but I stayed in my lane and was shocked as soon as I got to where the roads actually merged. If I had been drifting into the merging road, I would have had a horrible car crash.

Somehow, I know that I would have survived that without too much damage, but my two friends, at least one of them would have been horribly injured. He would have had to deal with that and I would have had to deal with all my guilt.

For decades I was haunted by that and feared looking at that probability. Finally, once I was able to engage across probabilities, I explored that outcome. I saw that he handled it. He had a hard time, but after years he handled it.

The same thing for another probability in my earlier life. I could have gotten busted for marijuana in a small North Carolina town and ended up in jail. I would have had a hard life for a long time, but a deeply meaningful one.

By the way, this is one reason why you can't explode all your pictures. No matter how many you explode there are other probable selves that are feeding more in.

What I found in myself and others, when you explore the better probabilities and the worse probabilities, is that you begin to get a sense of why and how they're all sacred. The better ones aren't that much better and the worst ones aren't that much worse. You adjust within those probabilities and you deal with things. Even dying is a probability and you deal with that.

Once you get a sense of how all of the yous in all those probabilities are alive and meaningful, it starts to help you grok that outcomes of pleasure and pain are not really the primary determinant of the ecstatic sacredness of life. You begin to get a much more Sethian perspective on life, not to become enlightened, not to extricate yourself from an illusion—it's for the sheer experience of it.

There are some people who resonate more with probabilities, with the concept that all life expands in all directions. A lot of people just don't have that kind of flexibility neurologically. But as we talk about it and as we work with these energies, they will change. It may even be that a week from now, after this workshop because we are tinkering with the Etheric plane, that you will begin to get some sort of a glimmer of it because, somehow or other, this hooks into the Etheric body. I have a clear sense of that. Yet I don't expect people to walk out of here understanding that fully because it's not a learnable cognition or idea. It's more that, as you gain flexibility in your Etheric body and start to have a different intellectual, analytical understanding of it, it will open you up neurologically to these kinds of concepts. Your Etheric body naturally has an easier time with concepts like probabilities.

If you shine Atmic energy down and bring the probable life you didn't live from the Astral into the Causal soul and let that combined energy shine down into the Etheric of the world, you may feel a different probability being birthed into its own Earth, its own Physical Earth. You may get some sense that it is just as "real" as the real life you are living. And then you may get a splash back into this lifetime so that a healing takes place. Not quite as dramatically as if I had done it in *this* probability back then.

I don't think you can really understand meaning without understanding probabilities. Because when you start to see from the soul's point of view, you explore this and this and this and this. You did the same thing, but you did it fifteen, forty, one hundred, one thousand different ways, and each little package you look at has a different energy gestalt to it. I think you begin to understand why the soul can joyfully live any of its lives.

Part of the reason why we focus on one probability at a time is to learn what it's like to totally commit to something, and that's part of what it means to be a human, and this is good. As human consciousness grows, though, we will be able to commit and explore multiple probabilities. First, our neurological systems will have to change.

16

The Dream State

You can go into that place where time is built, and in that place, before the structure of time is built, people chose to enter time to explore intense contrasts in ways that you cannot when you're your soul or the Sun. That's an intentional choice that is set up by certain structures that you participate in on purpose, but underneath them is something that's going in all different directions and has a different level of sense to it. If you go into that energy of all different directions, it will dramatically change your experience. That inner part of you is more real and eternal than your conscious waking part. It's a player in your inner self—that you're creating something wonderful as part of something much bigger, not yet bigger to your soul but bigger to you.

I hope people get glimpses of this, but I expect people from time to time to say, "I can't find the words or words can't express this," because if you find a word, then you may be saying something important but you're not talking about this bigger part because there are no words that will really describe that. That part of you is not going to be the foreground of your consciousness, but by tapping into it you start to find an inner glue that will help you hold your body together.

That inner being is the ground of being of your waking conscious self. By its very nature, it experiences and knows itself in ways much bigger and freer than you, the personality, experience and know yourself. You don't have to share that deeper self's freedom and vastness consciously. You can't really, and still embrace the full encounter with

what is uniquely the human experience. But you can bring it in slowly—
you just sit with it, let it come through the back of your mind. And over
time you'll start to fold its depth and breadth into your life, perhaps
consciously, or perhaps unconsciously, but in a way that makes you more
secure and capable, warm and wise. This gradual conscious or unconscious incorporation is one way of taking in information that's too big
to understand.

If you don't know whether something is just a dream or real perception, turn that around and start thinking, "Did you go to sleep and
become you?" The answer is usually yes. Where you are sleeping and
becoming you, there'll be many, many dreams that come together to
form you.

Each moment in time the body is being created and destroyed.
Time matters. Time materializes. Time takes that other self that falls
asleep and becomes you and creates you as a material person.

Even if you can't track what you did when you fell asleep, sleep holds
this very powerful connector between the world where you're in time
and everything is linear and the world that is multidimensional and
part of you is out of time. That is like a shuttle that takes your waking experience into what we call the dream state, but for other parts
of us is their waking state. You take your waking life—which is itself
really a kind of dream—and bring your waking experience and information with you as you lift into your dream state. What you see as your
dream-self integrates you, which it sees as a dream, into it. To you, it is
a dream; to it, you are a dream. When you come back from your dream
(as it is to you), if you let yourself, you'll come back more integrated.
This is because your waking experience has been processed through this
bigger point of view of your dream self. That's why naps can be so powerful, even a ten-minute nap.

Create a rose for everything that's happened to you since you last fell
asleep, hand it into some bigger part of yourself, let go of it, and ask it to
process it through its point of view, to let that come back to you not as
words but as an energy, in your bones, in your ears, in your Astral body.

You can experience a whole field of energy that just hasn't really been processed. You can blow some pictures, but that's not the whole process because that just brings them into current time with your waking self; it hasn't put them in this larger multidimensional context.

When you ground yourself, ask yourself that all of your emotional experience gets uploaded as you're falling asleep rather than just the emotional experience that you have suitably addressed. The portions of your emotional experience that you haven't integrated and owned, if you're grounding well, are not meeting your criteria of being grounded.

When you go to sleep, instead of bringing all of your emotional energy out and into this dream state, you may be only bringing the emotional energy that is sufficiently grounded that it meets your approval. There will always be stuff that doesn't get grounded, so I'm going to encourage you to say, "Okay let's get nice and thoroughly grounded." Just really validate how good your grounding is, and then say to yourself, "Everything can come up and get addressed by my guides and my inner self."

I had a client for about a year who was planning to go to the Himalayas. I spoke to her once a month, and she must have asked me six, eight, ten times: "I'm planning on going to the Himalayas, but I'm afraid I'm going to die and you know I really have people who depend upon me and do you think I'm going to die when I'm there?" I really started getting annoyed at her because I kept looking and I saw her going to the Himalayas and coming back and she wasn't going to die when she was there. Well, she came back and died the next day.

What I learned from that is if someone's concerned, don't just look at the question that they asked you but try to figure out why they're concerned. Now I don't feel guilty about that, even though I clearly blew it. When I miss things like that, I'm comfortable with that. I mean is it pretty clear to me that she knew she was going to die and she was choosing to die and that she was going to the Himalayas before she died. I think in a strange sort of way she found comfort, and in some way I was validating that.

If you have a category in your mind, it can be too tight. It would be better if other things were part of that. There are portions of your emotional experience that aren't in your question, "Who am I?" When you ground yourself, there's an implicit questions: "Who am I? What is there to ground?" So, when you ask yourself, "Who am I?" there are portions of yourself that you don't include in that question; you unconsciously don't include them because you don't recognize certain portions of you. Certain portions of you that you don't recognize are *not ready* to be addressed; certain portions of you that you don't recognize, I believe, *are* ready to be addressed. I'm suggesting that before you fall asleep you say to yourself, "I would like all the emotional parts of me that are ready to be addressed to go on out, whether I've grounded them or not." You can dream them into the next phase.

One of the most amazing aspects of human consciousness is the neurological structures that force us to experience time as consecutive moments where the past seems to drop off of a cliff and no longer be accessible and the future simply doesn't exist yet. It is not only inaccessible. It doesn't even exist. This is the way humans have experienced time for several thousand years because it is hardwired into human consciousness.

I often say that time is what keeps everything from happening all at once. That's the kind of accounting system our neurological structures set up, where all that exists is this moment. It allows for a particular type of consciousness. This particular type of consciousness is in some ways a fact of the physical universe, but not in all ways.

In reality, one piece of time hooks up with another in a way quite unlike what you experience in your physical body. Even though there are all of these probabilities going in all these different directions, each of us has a circuit board hooking us to one past for each moment. But we can change that circuit board and that will change our overall aura.

Part of the reason that you can change the past is that alternatives are out there. Your official past is not official because it is the true past; it's official because you have a circuit going into that. That's all. And if you change the circuit, then something else becomes your past. That can be very upsetting to a few people; it really re-orients ideas of causality.

17

Change History

Probabilities are not just hypothetical or unconscious or available in the dream state. Any time you have an encounter in which you're not happy with the resourcefulness you brought to it, you can actually go back and re-do that encounter and improvise until you're happy with your behavior. When you are finally pleased, the other person can, at an unconscious level, choose, "Oh, I kinda like that one better than the one we did originally." They can hook the circuit board up so that you were behaving resourcefully and it replaces the one where you were behaving unresourcefully. I find time after time after time, when I go back and change history, the next time I see that person they respond to me more as if I had been resourceful in the initial instance. It is not because I'm forcing the other person to change but because they prefer the replacement option.

I can see the other people involved accepting the change to some extent. They don't have to know that you're engaging other probabilities—in fact, they almost never know or suspect it—but they are also experiencing other probabilities, probably unconsciously, so they experience the change in yourself as a change in *their* selves, both because they receive the energy of you changing and because they are engaging probabilities too.

It's very important that you *invite* the other person to join you in this new probable past rather than demand that they join you. If you manipulate the other person as you're changing history, you're not doing it correctly and you can create karma and violate boundaries. If you're taking your time about this and careful not to violate boundaries, you're even lessening the amount of violation that was already there.

There are two advantages to changing history. One is that you get to practice something until you get it right and therefore you're more likely to behave resourcefully when you meet a similar situation in the future. You could do it better right away or by practicing it to get better at doing it. By working on your energy as you're practicing, you're giving yourself a way to install a different energy system, a different set of behaviors when you encounter certain situations.

The second is a very magical level. Any time you interact with somebody and you wish you had interacted more resourcefully, and then go back and change history, you change the wiring of that circuit in time and the circuitry of time itself. From my perspective, you are literally changing history in the sense that you are changing the electrodynamics of that circuit that makes that particular event your history, and that it is a real structural change in time.

Part of what makes it hard to understand is we think that everybody has the same past, that there is a real past and any other past that someone remembers is not real.

My past is not the same past as yours. I can change my past with you and you can completely stay in the past that happened before I changed my past. We can be in the same world with two entirely different pasts. And that's not uncommon. A lot of fights that go on in a marriage literally take place because the parties have two different pasts.

One of the reasons people will argue with what happened in the past is because each person's circuit lines up with a slightly different past. Even with a person you know well, the past circuit that covers your shared past together is not the same past circuit as his or hers. Both pasts happened. But your circuit board has one past, and their circuit board has a different past. As a result, the overall electricity of each of your lives is drawing on different pasts and affects what flows into each of your auras.

You can't really begin to understand how creative the universe is and just how much your power is in the present. It may be useful to go back to the past as a symbol of how you got here, but if you really think you're like you are now because of what happened in the past I think it undercuts your confidence.

Now I have people go the other way and they say, "There's no such thing as past incarnations and everything happens in the present." But just because you say you're not paying attention to the past doesn't mean you aren't.

By creating ourselves in our dreams, we answer some serious questions for ourselves and we become much more independent and mystical than we would have been had we not had a dream where we answered a question by seeding a different version of our self, which is you.

Since time is in this playful interchange with timelessness, you have so many more chances to work on it. So when you do something you're unhappy with, you could just ignore it or get angry about it in and work it out in a future lifetime; but since it's all happening now, one of the best things you can do is sit down go back in time and do it again until you like your behavior, you like who you are in that past interaction.

If you have an interaction you don't like, as soon as you get a chance, put yourself back in that interaction in an improvisational theater of the mind, change your behavior, and work your energy and respond to the new responses your imagination tells you the other would do now that you are changing your energy. Keep practicing in your imagination until you like who you are.

I was telling someone about change history and I gave as an example: "Say you're being you and you're driving and you're behind a slow driver and you start getting more and more aggravated and maybe you honk your horn angrily—so how would you do a change history for that?" And he said, "Well, I would go back in my mind's eye and I would remove that driver." That's missing the point; the point is not to rearrange things to your benefit or taste. The point is not whether you get there on time. The point is to work on your energy so that you behave the way you want, because there is no real world where you're *not* behind drivers that drive in ways different than you would prefer that they drive. The purpose of change history is to change yourself. I know it can feel like drudgery at times; it's still at an opportunity.

The clear drop of light that you step into in change history is to inform you that you're always and already there, so it changes the context in which you deal with your frustrations and it helps you understand the *meaning* of those frustrations.

Find a moment where you were growing and reaching out. Maybe you thought you knew what you were doing. Probably a teenage or early adult time would be a good place to look. Your current self can look back on that younger self with all its newness and openness and excitement and fear and bring the relative wisdom and knowledge that you have now. Link up in some way or another with that earlier you. Don't try to control it; try to be in the back seat observing it. Maybe give it a little bit of wisdom. While your body is here in current time, let his or her body be every bit as alive in its own time. Let it be cupped in time, just as today, your body is cupped in time. Let the whole universe feed into him or her and his or her current time, which for him or her, is happening in a now that is every bit as rich and real as the present one.

Observe his or her nowness, his or her openness or closed-downness, whatever his or her experience was in that moment. As you stay with her or him, gradually let go of your conceit, that you know where he or she is going. You know where he or she went in *your* reality, but as he or she is alive in his or her moment, there are still infinite possibilities. Yes, there are limitations of experience and belief—that's always true—and yet the very next decision that he or she makes will be hers or his, not yours, for you are in a different time.

Bit by bit, release your hold, release your conviction that you know who he or she is, what he or she will do, and watch the energy bubbling up in that young person. Notice that you are always there for her or him from this time—from your current time and place—and yet there are an infinite number of subtly different yous, now as well as then. He or she finds their own vitality that goes off in a direction that is not identical to the one that you took when you were that age. It might be close or it might be very different.

Now, wave goodbye to her or him and yet know that later tonight or some night in the dream state, you will meet him or her as he or she will meet you, and you will share the excitement of your individual and yet interconnected adventure.

Now start with some attitude, a physical aspect, or life situation, maybe an adverse one because of bad decisions you made, or bad decisions other people made, or your genetics, or whatever seems to have happened in the past. But for now, reference just your past, not other people's pasts. Let your actions, even your other lifetimes, be a million moments strung in linear sequential time.

In your old view of time, they're done and over, you no longer have any agency, any choice, in them. They've fallen off of a cliff and disappeared. Now realize they are every bit as alive and every bit as reaching out to their own past and future and alternatives too. As they reach out in their own time, open your heart in a way that doesn't constrain them but lets them be what they really are, which is consciousness expanding in all directions from every central moment. As they do that, you may feel an impulse coming from above your crown, gathering up your story in the fifth chakra, breaking it into a million directions in the fourth dimension, and giving you a new power to appreciate the past as you remember it and yet to set it free. Perhaps you can feel, as it is free, you are also freer than you were.

Now please be in the center of your head and again observe, as you have freed up those million moments of your past, you have freed yourself from the hypnotism that they radiate—giving you more and more freedom in your present to explore each moment as it arises more graciously, creatively, with kindness and generosity and authenticity.

Consider the current crises in the Middle East. As you pull energy out of other lifetimes and probabilities in the Middle East, you can feel that energy changing, changing you, feeding back into them, feeding back into the Middle East, changing people there. You're dealing with your probabilities here, there, reciprocating, altering, dealing with past lives, changing your relationship to the Middle East in, say, 1535, as all these things are going on, and everyone is affecting every *other* one; and instead of sort of dampening down, it actually causes them to grow. It may not be enough for you to see the change in present times, but that doesn't mean change is not happening. We're used to linear time and mechanical processes, but that can blind us to how things are changing when they actually do.

If you want peace in the Middle East, instead of just sending light, which can be sort of invalidating, change yourself, change your relationship to it. That becomes more effective, with the added benefit that you're changing yourself and you get to keep those changes too.

You can't change the universe, but you *can* change yourself and, when you do, sometimes the universe miraculously changes too.

Now, can you also make it so that you're in a probability where Kennedy didn't get shot? That's a different sort of change. Very few people can do that. Robert Monroe who wrote *Journeys out of the Body* had a few trips where he went into a kind of alternate universe that was more than just the kind of probabilities that we have been looking at. In that alternate universe, some of the technology was different, significantly different. So it can be done, but that's not likely to happen, and certainly not on any permanent basis with just one person working on it.

I can imagine years from now we might go into the dream state as a society and all of a sudden 9/11 didn't happen. But that would take a lot of people working very skillfully. And that's kind of a silly example because, if they could do that, they would have a totally different experience of time anyway as well as reality itself.

18

Cats and Dogs

Do cats and dogs reincarnate? The usual answer is no. If you don't understand the Multipersonhood of a cat or dog, which cats and dogs understand, then that thing that human beings identify as the cat or the dog does *not* reincarnate, but that's an example of human limitations as we think of ourselves as the highest beings in the universe.

If you look at just that piece, the standard explanation is that piece—the cat itself as that little cat being—doesn't have enough individuality to incarnate again, maintaining any sort of individuality. And that's true. It doesn't, but that's because we require a certain kind of separateness to consider a reincarnation.

Another understanding, the theosophical one, is that a large number of cats, a large number of dogs, a large number of trees are overseen by a larger deva. Not *diva,* Miss Piggy is a diva. A deva is a parallel consciousness to humans. It's about the same consciousness as a human being but a very distinct and different kind of consciousness. Some devas, in fact, are much bigger than any human. But the little cat, he's so small. That's a category error. A cat can be a spirit being who takes a cat form for a particular purpose, but that cat form has many dimensions to itself, one of which is an ordinary Earth cat, others of which are spirits of trees and brooks and thunderstorms, one of which is a spirit guide. Some very powerful guides can take the parts of cats. Guide cats have another being that's participating, though not in linear time.

The cat knows itself in all these dimensions. It knows the deva and it co-participates with humans in their incarnations.

Your cat insists upon eating what a cat insists on eating, and yet your cat is not locked into its catness. When it comes time for a cat to die, the cat leaves the body and just moves smoothly into other forms without any painfulness or resistance. When a cat is dying, it will usually leave its body and allow the body to go through its stuff. The cat doesn't suffer because it doesn't think of itself as that body. It doesn't think in our sort of cognitive ways. What you see the cat's body going through is not what the cat is going through.

Bodies don't mind sensation; bodies don't stick values on sensations.

Most mystics looking at cats read them as having dual consciousness. But that's a category that, because we have bodies set up at a human level, we impose on other consciousnesses. So cats, as we *cat*egorize them, are in fact dual consciousnesses, but they don't have to hold the category. I know, I keep playing with the word *cat,* but I do love cats and any jokes we make about them.

When we look at a cat and ask if it can reincarnate, the standard sophisticated answer is no, it has a group consciousness, it doesn't have its own individual consciousness. But that is a category we have imposed upon the cat. The cat knows itself as multiple, innumerable consciousnesses that flow gracefully.

When your cat is out sleeping on a rock in the sun, it has a different kind of relationship to that rock than you do. And it has a different relationship to its body than you do. It's not so hardwired into thinking it *is* that body. It knows itself as the storm that's happening or the sunshine that's happening and as the emotional aspect of the family it lives with, and as part of the Earth, as beings on the moons of Jupiter, as All That Is, as the star system. It *always* knows itself as all of these things. And not with the sort of cognitive schema that humans use but as itself. It grasps them in absolute unity with its individual identity.

It doesn't remember that in its brain because that's not how the cat brain works. It knows its larger self in its Multipersonhood. It never thinks,

"Oh, I'm a cat, I'll have to incarnate over thousands of years before I can individuate and become a human, and then I can become enlightened."

In very meaningful ways a cat can reincarnate as a cat or something else through one of its many aspects. It experiences itself as fluid and simultaneous. Part of that experience is in its more limited sense of a cat. It chooses that aspect for the sheer joy of cat experience.

When you hear people say a cat can't reincarnate because they don't have a separate individual self, they're not really getting what a cat is. The cat knows itself flexibly, so it goes out of body easily and tracks that journey and its shifting identity.

Cats don't need enlightenment. Humans, because of the way we categorize the world, make enlightenment an important concept. But cats and dogs and rocks and roses and suns, they're already enlightened.

If a cat knows itself as a planet, it's really kind of silly to call yourself a higher form of consciousness.

Seth talked in one of his books about taking a vacation and becoming a tree for 150 years. Now he's trying to talk to us in terms of what we would understand, but Seth doesn't live in linear time so he doesn't go on a vacation and become a tree instead of being Seth, and yet there's some sense in which becoming a tree for 150 years, in whatever multiple time, is a wonderful vacation.

So if, as you get more psychic, you walk outside and a tree literally talks to you, it might be Seth in addition to being a tree in addition to being a deva in addition to being the planet. The only people who reincarnate like humans are humans because they're the only people who don't realize that they're already all those things—cats know it, dogs know it—I'm sounding like Cole Porter. But only people are as separate as we are. So yes, cats can and do reincarnate; dogs reincarnate, because that little rich subjectivity that you interact with in various ways as your dog comes to inhabit, not overpower, but be part of another dog that you get after it dies—and that relationship is as real as the 12th Dalai Lama to the 13th Dalai Lama to the 14th Dalai Lama.

19

Camouflage Self and Multipersonhood

For your culture, at this time, it usually takes the equivalent—and of course there's no direct equivalence because once you no longer have a physical body, the nature of time changes dramatically—of three hundred to a thousand years of experience before you learn how to operate in your own uniqueness in direct creativity, unmediated by the camouflage that your human neurology provides you. By that I simply mean that you perceive the world through your senses, through neural pathways, and that becomes your official reality, even if you are open to telepathy and clairvoyance.

Remember, this is a good thing. This is not a mistake.

The criteria of your inner self, your directly creative self, and your camouflage ego self that you normally and reasonably think of as your self, is that your inner self does not experience tension as contradiction. Another way of saying it is, it does not experience tension as invalidation. Your neurological self does.

It is impossible though, within your camouflage reality, to engage that camouflage fully as a native of that reality, as someone who genuinely engages the Astral plane without bumping up against the tensions that your body reads as contradictions throughout every day. Just sitting in your chair listening to me, the mere act of breathing creates a kind of contradiction because, as you're breathing in, your body is already pushing the air out with certain tensions that have grown through your emotional armor. Plus, you're meant to experience your emotions vividly at this time in human experience.

Now we're going to make a rose for that, take that rose and hand it over to the inner self and the inner self's direct creativity. We're going to help you go to that inner self whether you're conscious of it or not. And as you hand that rose to your direct creativity, it utilizes everything that's in that rose including the apparent contradictions. And it observes a much greater reality. It's not limited in time the way your camouflaged self is. It's not limited to your own identity with the kind of rigidity that your camouflaged self has, so it takes every bit of that rose that your camouflaged self was and was not aware of and it spins it through numerous dimensions. That takes place in the pure delight and necessity of creativity—or maybe it would be better to say, the pure delight and inevitability of creativity—because whatever is imagined, consciously or unconsciously, in this realm of the unobstructive and direct creativity of the inner self is spun out into relationship. And whether the camouflaged self recognizes it or not, every atom of every goal is expressed and explored in relationship to this incarnation throughout times and throughout relationships with humans and other consciousnesses, recognized or unrecognized.

See if you can notice how in the Causal plane, your sense of space and time is very different from your personality. Even so, it can say hello to you in the moment in ways that you understand. See if you can let your experience of the soul expand, loosening your assumptions of time and space, of should, have to, and ought. Imagine that it's almost as if you go through the looking glass, letting go of many of your personal assumptions and presumptions, and begin spreading out as you start to see somewhat through the vision of your soul. You can visit your birth and death from the soul's point of view.

Begin to see your life from its point of view. Feel how the personal soul coordinates two qualities that you might have expected to be contradictory. It has a passionate desire, direction, and intent. In its own realm this intent is to experience everything that could possibly happen. One of the things that it experiences, out of that intent, is the specific experience of you as a human being where something seems to happen or doesn't happen. You either married this person or you didn't. See if you can feel that drop in octave or octave-and-a-half where the soul in its own plane passionately explores everything. And another of those everythings is the camouflage reality of your personal self.

Now, here's the tricky part: Can you feel the soul dropping down into the sixth and seventh sub-planes of the Astral and where it manifests as a large portion of the fluid in the center of your head? It isn't the whole because nothing is made up of just one thing. Even though that fluid is neutral and open to whatever is, simultaneously and to what might seem like a contradictory degree, it passionately embraces whatever particular experience you have in time and space. You might even be able to feel a little bit of that portion of the neutral fluid that's composed of the energy of the Causal soul as it drops down in the more limited dimension of the Astral. There, the soul simultaneously engages the particular, the limited, the doing-one-thing self that means you can't do another that's the opposite. And, at the same time, it is completely and utterly passionately open to whatever is.

When you look in multidimensional time, you may be twenty or forty or sixty or seventy. You may think of yourself as starting at birth. But you, as you—as a fully autonomous though interdependent being, before you were born and as you, not your soul—decided, "Okay, I will take this on. I will take on being Ann, I will take on being Ed, I will take on being Noel." And what's more, you actually decide that again each moment now, not just as Noel, or Ann or Ed, but as the you before you were born. Because that decision didn't happen twenty years ago or forty years ago or seventy years ago. That decision happened outside of time as you understand it and happens at every moment in time.

Now, it's hard to remember this when you're here in linear time in a body and often suffering and at times suffering horribly. But the truth is, for very good reasons, each moment you affirm that choice. And there is a kind of a curve ball that, if you think you understand, then you're not getting it. Here goes the curve: If you really choose not to be Ed, you could be something else in the next moment. We might not be able to track you because we have physical bodies. But you, Ed, could be something entirely different. And that choice is made each instant, whether you know it or not.

Let's begin playing with a concept that Seth called Multipersonhood. I don't remember where I saw that quite frankly, but I'm convinced I saw it multiple times in the later books. But he never defined it because it probably can't really be defined.

In some of his early books he talked about Jane as in some sense being a past incarnation of his, but we were not to think of him and Jane as the same being because when Jane got to where he was, she wouldn't be what he is. Maybe in six lifetimes she'll be where Seth was, but Seth will be someplace else. Even though she's in the same kind of spatial location in four dimensions, she's not identical to the Seth that was talking to us back in 1974.

To make it more crazy making—and crazy making is progress because we're trying to shake up your understanding of identity—Seth, Rob, and Jane had a lifetime he described where he was a captain of a boat, of a merchant ship, and they knew each other; so how can Jane be a past life of Seth when they all knew each other?

You're just not in the kind of consciousness that you understand yourself to be. There's a Buddhist concept called interdependent origination, and the Buddhists use interdependent origination to mean there are no essences, there are no billiard-ball essences where one billiard ball can bump up against another but both are separate. There is no Ed that's separate from Judy that's separate from Emily. They appear to be separate and that's the dance that we're exploring as human beings.

If you go back several thousand years in human consciousness, humans had a much more liquid notion of identity. If you go several thousand years forward—you won't even have to go that far—human beings will again have a much more liquid notion of identity. It is only in this period of twenty-five hundred to three thousand years that human beings seem so solid and not blending into each other. The Buddhists point out that you *do* blend into one another and you are not self-arising; you do not come from yourself, you come from a weaving of other consciousnesses. They use this observation together with the other called impermanence to extricate themselves from holding on too strongly to their separateness. And they engage, as do any nondual practitioners, in a set of practices to alter your neurological system so that your perception changes and you recognize directly that you arise interdependently, that what seems to be external to you is only an appearance not a fact.

A major part of what Seth came here for is to change the way we understand interdependence. Interdependence from the nondual perspective establishes the basic ground of suffering, so any human being, as long as they perceive themselves as being separate to any extent, suffers. This is true. This is true in *our* system; this is true in *their* system. Remember, the Buddha who formulated this most eloquently and elegantly refused to talk about what happens after you die. He said, "You're suffering now. I'm giving you some understanding that can remove your suffering now. What difference does it make what happens after you die?"

That was the focus of humanity and that was right and appropriate for that time and, for some people, it may go on for another three or four hundred years.

The times are changing, so when Seth comes in, he starts introducing an almost inverted interdependence. The Buddhists and other nondual practitioners use interdependence to say you have no eternal self because it's always changing. Seth, by implication—he never said this explicitly—is saying because you are interwoven with everything and because everything expands in all directions, both within and outside of time, and with every subjectivity, even though it is always changing, your existence is eternal because it's growing.

I don't know of any nondual practitioners who care about this. But if you understand that not only your soul is eternal but what you think of most as you is also eternal, there will be a continuity. It is eternal in the sense that if you knock on Ed's door five hundred years from now and say, "Ed" he will say, "Here I am!" That Ed will be very, very different from this Ed, but he can tell you, "I'm the same old Ed."

I don't think this can be understood or appreciated without luxuriating in your interdependence, in the fact that Seth and Jane were different and the same. Seth was trying to explain this to us in ways that we could understand. Now it's time to get kind of a deeper understanding of what it is.

Take the story about my friend Will who committed suicide. I can see him clairvoyantly and I can see him understanding himself as Will, my friend who committed suicide in 1977 but is now much wiser and happier. Will understands himself to be Will my friend and Will also knows himself *now* to be an integral part of a consciousness that's so big, when I looked at it, that it seemed to me to be the equivalent of a planet.

In his time, if he's in time, he was also exploring a moment across probable lives so that he could fully experience the richness of a moment by having lived through it taking all kinds of different entries into that point, making all kinds of different decisions in that point. I don't think you can fully appreciate an emotion when it's a response to apparently one framework, yours, one time. In fact, since there are probable yous, you experienced that same moment an infinite number of times from an infinite number of directions. If you realize that, you can start to really appreciate a moment, and you don't respond to the so-called bad decisions with as much pain and you don't respond to the so-called good decisions with as much self-satisfaction and self-congratulation.

Our neurological systems can't handle Multipersonhood, but I don't think you can appreciate your emotions without at least being open to those parts of you that do live in Multipersonhood. I as a human being can't be Multipersonhood because my neurological focus as a waking conscious person intentionally focuses me down to one apparently separate being, but my soul is engaged in Multipersonhood. It knows itself as this huge being and it knows itself as me. It doesn't experience time the same way I do, so in some sense I can add to its consciousness. But of course it *is* me and it knows itself as me, differently than I know myself as me.

The Sun knows itself as me even as, within its solar system, it supports the life of planets and people and who knows what else through infinite dimensions.

PART TWO

A SETHIAN APPROACH
TO REALITY
AND BEINGNESS

20

Nondual Awareness, Duality, Enlightenment, and Suffering

In both Buddhist and Hindu theology you reincarnate out of ignorance. One story is of individualities evolving up from or through mere physicality like rocks, into the plant kingdom, then the animal kingdom, then becoming a human soul and eventually growing out of illusion and into enlightenment. The Eastern point of view is from the bottom up: the theosophical likewise. Only after you start as a rock do you move up through the mineral, vegetable, and animal kingdoms, and then you achieve a human birth. That's the pinnacle.

In all these systems, it was thought that humans were the only beings who could attain enlightenment—and enlightenment was the only authentic goal of consciousness of any kind. Since the only way you *could* become enlightened was from a human birth, and enlightenment was the sole authentic goal, there was an implication that the consciousness of the Earth or consciousness of the Sun was second-rate to being a human being, which of course is nonsense. It's not that enlightenment is only *achievable* in a human incarnation, it's only *relevant* in a human incarnation. My guides joke, "Humans are not the only beings able to achieve enlightenment, they are the only beings *needing* to achieve enlightenment." It's not that you can only become enlightened from a human incarnation—only humans would *try* to become enlightened. Only humans have the category.

It's the self-reflective ego that thinks only human beings can become enlightened, when in fact it's actually the other way. Everything else is already enlightened.

Trees are enlightened, so they don't have the category. Dogs and cats don't need it, and larger beings certainly don't need it. The angelic chain of beings and the Cetaceans don't need it.

At the base of all consciousness is what's referred to as nondual awareness, sometimes called Oneness. I think nondual is a more evocative descriptor because the universe is a divine play of phenomena. As humans, we have the experience that there's a me and a not-me, and those phenomena seem to be separate. But that's an illusion. Everything is always and already nondual. Everything is interdependent with everything else; everything arises in Oneness and every apparent discrete package is merely that, *apparently* discrete.

In older mysticism, the Hindu approach first, you moved to have progressively more unified consciousness, higher and higher, and to do that you eliminated everything that was lower. There's sort of a debate between Hindus and Buddhists. The Hindus think, "Go up and up and up," and at some point in the process you move out of going up and up and up and you hit this nondual awareness. At its core, this is exactly the same as the nondual awareness cultivated by Buddhism, though part of its presentation will involve a higher energy than is usually cultivated in Buddhism.

Buddhism is a more sophisticated intellectual approach. The Tibetans *intentionally* stopped going higher, and they moved to a different kind of practice, Dzogchen—a basis of being and clarity outside of time, a compassion and spontaneous immanence. It's a very effective practice for transformation, though they don't conceptualize it that way, and I don't think they even see it that way.

Let's set the big context. I'm going to use the Buddha as a baseline for all Eastern mystical systems even though there are technical differences among the various Buddhisms. By the way, Seth said that of all the religions, Buddhism was the one that came closest to being a description of the nature of reality.

The Buddha was right when he said all experience that we have as human beings is ultimately unsatisfactory, dukkha. He not only analyzed the unsatisfactoriness of life, but he set up a program that can answer it and can move on to what's called "no self" or nondual awareness. In nondual awareness, ordinary suffering or unsatisfactoriness disappears. That's often called enlightenment.

It's a very compelling case because if you really attain nondual awareness, life's kind of suffering disappears.

People spend their lifetime trying to attain nondual awareness. What makes that so arduous is they're trying to do it in such a way that their neurological system becomes permanently transformed. Their awareness itself is of being nondual in the same way that for the rest of us, our fundamental awareness is dual. It's a neurological realignment.

While my guides discourage people from doing that, that's really quite a magnificent accomplishment.

Nonduality itself is something you can only point at; you can't really articulate it. I think you *can* see it clairvoyantly. When I go to Amma,* I have this sense that it's like this warp in space and time. You just have this zone for a hundred-foot radius where there is a kind of white hole, not a black hole, that pulls you toward nondual awareness. It really is quite spectacular.

Amma doesn't *suffer* from sadness, but she does experience sadness.

---

*Mata Amritanandamayi, usually just called Amma, is known as the hugging saint. She has hugged, over decades, thousands of people for seconds at a time. I have watched her clairvoyantly many days; each of those thousands of hugs involves an instantaneous awareness of who that individual uniquely is, so that the energy she imparts in that moment is uniquely addressed to and healing for them. Her charitable organization operates worldwide and is highly effective.

Sadness passes through her, pain passes through her. She said once at a seminar, "When I experience sadness, I do this." Meaning she handled it.

Pain doesn't disappear because it can't if you have any connection to your body or its experience. If you have a body, emotions and pain are generated. But the suffering disappears or turns into a kind of non-suffering. Your resistance to a painful experience disappears. For the nondual practitioner, emotions and pain simply don't become part of their story. They are not trapped there; they are left and sort of go out into the planet.

You move to utterly no resistance to experience, but some things are lost in your story-making, in your meaning-making, and in the sort of transformation that happens to your experience. It becomes a different kind of meaning-making. And a level of pain that is not addressed does not get healed.

Nondual practitioners cease to suffer, in a sense, because they no longer have conscious Astral duality. As they get deeper and deeper into an enlightened state, they engage the play of appearances as itself without getting caught up in stories about it.

They're occupied in non-conceptual thought, which doesn't go through the same circuits in the brain that concepts do for those of us engaged in dual thought. As a consequence, those constraints that place you in the Astral plane are no longer there.

If you asked the Dalai Lama, "Tell me a story about when you were fifteen," he can tell you a story obviously, but in doing so, he will not go through the part of the brain that experiences the distance between his experience and his response to that experience. This is exactly what people who are pursuing nondual awareness want. And that was the spiritual game up until now.

It doesn't mean that nondual practitioners are not structured by their social conditioning; for instance, Mother Meera was homophobic.

I imagine that proponents of the idea that one could not be in non-dual awareness and yet misbehave egregiously will assert that it is not nondual awareness if it doesn't extend to all the various identities collected around the physical body. But it is never the case that a human being's nondual awareness extends to all that collectivity.

Arguably the two greatest nondual practitioners on our planet today, the Dalai Lama and Amma, have vital portions of their personalities they do not track, which arise in the semi-physical sixth and seventh sub-planes of the Astral. While my respect for those two great saints is limitless, and the blessings they pour onto our planet are also limitless, their inability to see—indeed, their total unawareness of—what goes on in the sixth and seventh sub-planes of the Astral, where it is transitional to the Physical, is its own hurdle for humanity's move into the Aquarian Age. It's a hurdle they will not themselves overcome.

When Ken Wilber says he has emotions and they are even more intense, they're just always joyful, I would agree with him that he has something that's analogous to emotions, but it doesn't vibrate in the Astral plane. It vibrates in the Buddhic plane. And as such, there's a lot of human experience that does not get addressed. There are certain kinds of pain that simply cannot be cleared unless you come into the Astral.

I think there's a good chance to develop clarity now that we are dealing with the Astral body—I don't know anyone up until now who has had *authentic* emotions and thoughts as a principal waking mystical focus. Now you might say, "Aren't the Dalai Lama's emotions authentic?" That's not emotions when you're this sea of transcendent love. The Astral body isn't moving in that. Those are *higher* energies.

When Amma is blessing the entire planet with her love, that's really cool, but that's not an emotion. That's something else.

Can we use these transcendent energies *and* the personal energies to be really healthy, and maybe even, rather than dying, leave in a rainbow body? Absolutely! But I am cautioning that transcendent energies can mask and interfere with your awareness of your personal emotions. So, while we are exploring transcendent energies, we should maintain some assumptions and processes so that we do not lose contact with what is idiosyncratic and untamable. We don't become merely an ocean of love.

Those outcomes are not what will make someone happy, but they're interesting dances to engage to learn how to use energy.

Humans, upon attaining a deep nondual awareness, do not detect their own change and expansion. They are like Moses, seeing but not entering, the next stage of humanity. Beings such as Seth, who are truly Multipersons, track themselves in an entirely different way.

When I first met Lewis Bostwick, he told me about a spiritual training that he had. He put three people in a row and set a readee out in front of them. The reader will start matching and blowing pictures with the readee as he or she is doing the reader. This allows them, the reader, to clear pain out of their own space that is dug in there. Lewis said to me, "What we've found is that we can clear pain that we couldn't get to in any form of mere meditation."

Now, this is the pain that the nondualists have transcended. It is the pain that gets left in the body and continues to affect humanity. It is the pain that, unaddressed, would make group consciousness impossible.

In the theology of some Eastern traditions, life is an ecstatic dance, but even the tantric practitioners are still, as far as I can tell, primarily focused on transcending the illusions that brought them into humanity. Mystics developed a deep calm at an Etheric level and pretty much abandoned the Astral plane because the Astral plane is really chaotic. It is not possible to be in the Astral plane without some degree of suffering. So mystics have circumvented that level and below. When they are engaging their emotions, they're really not engaging them in the same kind of personal way as those of us ensconced in the Astral do. They do it in a more transcendent way, using the Buddhic plane and above.

The kind of rich churning of the Astral body doesn't take place when emotions resonate only at the Buddhic level. Instead, these mystics are doing a biological work-around on some of the circuits in the brain that insert a pause and another interpretation between your experience and your interpretation of that experience. Certain language-processing and story-telling aspects of the brain simply are no longer engaged. They have a much more direct experience—and that has the outcome they seek of avoiding a kind of suffering.

Yet the physical body will inevitably trigger Astral energies. It isn't so much then that those energies necessarily harm humanity, as that the blessings of nondual states have less beneficial impact than they would if the nondual practitioners were not bypassing the Astral.

Why would you prefer to engage the Astral plane and to have an inevitable amount of suffering when you could instead become enlightened and stop suffering? From the old mystical perception, you incarnate as a dual consciousness, subject to suffering because you are ignorant. That is the normal Buddhist/Eastern idea. But Seth teaches that the reason we incarnate is *not* because we are ignorant. It is that we *assume* ignorance so that we can explore what is unique about the human frame of incarnation in this time and place.

You also did not incarnate as a human being because your soul was benighted or too stupid to engage in nondual consciousness. It is engaging through you in incarnation because it is gathering a kind of experience that is not accessible to it in its "own" realm. It engages in dual consciousness *even though* that involves suffering.

The Sethian story is that we voluntarily take on ignorance and suspend disbelief and engage our humanity as if it were worthy of the fullness of our being rather than something that we are peripherally exploring. We take on ignorance so that we go more profoundly and intensely into the experience of our humanity, because there are certain kinds of experiences that can only occur in the duality of human consciousness.

You are intentionally limiting yourself when you are consciously physical and dualistic. I would suggest that you are doing that not because you simply haven't evolved enough to become enlightened but because enlightened parts of you choose to explore everyday life and develop a particular ecological niche in the infinite universes of consciousness that only humanlike consciousnesses can develop.

You have incarnated as you—our soul incarnated as us— in large part because of the *limitations* of being human, in order to get an otherwise unachievable focus that you generate *through* ignorance. Ignorance is not a bad thing; we are always going to be ignorant of something. These limitations then provide a very specific kind of context in which we develop stories. Our stories are what the universe gets out of us. It's our particularly human characteristic. They don't make us better than other entities, just human.

My teachers propose that we're here to explore this incredibly fabulous life as a human being—and in the waking state. The goal of the human race, as they would put it, for the last thousand years is to develop the ability to engage the Astral plane in an individuated but ultimately kind and flowing and generous way. I would express that as each of our principal consciousness-mind goals.

As a human, we are apparently a particular form. Todd is male, Patty is female; Todd's body is not Patty's body, Patty's body is not Todd's body. These are merely forms in which these consciousnesses hang out, forms that they inhabit. Our humanity is also a form that we inhabit and explore.

Other consciousnesses go much more smoothly between forms and their identification with a single form is not so profound or strong. In much earlier history, humanity also didn't so strongly identify for so long with a particular form. Humans would hunt animals, but they didn't take it personally either way. They knew they might kill the animal, or they might be killed by the animal—this was just part of a flow. They didn't have the kind of resistance to death that we have. In cultures practicing in the old ways, this is still the case.

An Englishmen reported attending the hunting of a bear with Native Americans in the 1700s. The hunters shot the bear but didn't kill it and the bear was crying out in pain. One of the group walked up to the bear and berated it thusly, "Be courageous, bear. Your tribe and my tribe engage in this. Had you killed me I would have showed courage and withstood the pain and given honor to my tribe. You should stop yelling and show honor to your tribe."

Early humans could change affiliation. If an early human was killed by a storm, it changed its affiliation and became part of that storm. If a human eats an animal with a sense of sacred participation, part of that animal changes affiliation and becomes part of the human. Its life continues in part through her or him.

Eons ago humans moved smoothly in and out of their human form; they would not identify with it as strongly as we do. They might flow into a river and go down that river for a couple of miles to see what was happening there and whether that was a place they might want to move to. Was there game? What was the weather like? When there was a storm, they became that storm. They still knew themselves as that particular human, but they didn't have this hard-and-fast consciousness that's located within the body; they would feel themselves parts of all kinds of consciousnesses.

This kind of flowing in and out was natural. It is a different way of relating to form. In a funny sort of way, I don't think you can fully enjoy this form that you're in if you really take it quite so literally as we do.

Now that gets distorted. Humanity intentionally started to develop self-reflective ego consciousness, hardened those boundaries. The process took thousands of years. It would have been impossible suddenly to have this illusion that you're not an energy, you're a physical being—that your apparent sense of separation is how things really are. You couldn't have had that all at once and you couldn't have had it if large spirit beings were still talking to you. If you're easily and constantly talking to beings without bodies, how could you think all beings, including yourself, are just bodies?

Unless we have strenuously cultivated nondual awareness, everyone now alive in modern society has a strong sense when they're awake that there's this *them* that either stops at their skin or stops at the edge of their aura or stops wherever they've left their energy and that everything that isn't *that* is not them. You experience things as happening *to* you; the outside world happens *to* you. This is really quite glorious; it allows a kind of intensity of focus, a stage into a new kind of being.

The reason our guides discourage the cultivation of nondual awareness as a permanent state, even though it is the truth, is that to attain nondual awareness you have to essentially change your psychic biology so that you're no longer a player in this drama, this exquisitely subtle reality, that humanity worked so many thousands of years to set up.

We already have very huge nondual aspects of ourselves, for instance the Western soul. Because we have been so human centric for the last twenty-five hundred years or more, when we do deep meditations and pass through our soul levels, we don't notice our soul is always and already consciously nondual. Yet it is intentionally incarnating in this world as us because it is the very nature of consciousness to explore every dimension, including this dimension of human duality. A nondual soul *chooses* dual existence. It is not a slip-up or mistake. Even the youngest soul on the planet chooses to enter a dualistic perception because it's profound and really cool. There are no end goals here.

From a Sethian perspective, you joyfully, ecstatically jump into the ignorance of your dual consciousness because that ignorance allows you to experience a gap between your experience and your interpretation of that experience. And that gap cannot be experienced by a nondual soul in its own realm. So it comes into human physicality to engage that kind of richness, to experience where stories emerge.

Despite profound contradictions and contrast and often painful episodes, we incarnate because of the unique experiences that are possible as a human being rather treating them as some illusion that we're supposed to step out of by gaining nondual awareness or enlightenment. If the latter is your purpose, you don't even really have to clear pain out of your body. They're not going to keep you from becoming enlightened in the long run.

21

Seth

I think we really misunderstood Seth. It's now forty years—wow!—since I was introduced. Our understanding then in the 1970s and '80s was, "Here's this Seth, he was this very large being; he went through his human incarnations he had shared with Jane and Rob Butts and now he's finished and he was coming back and teaching all of us." In his last incarnation he was some sort of ship captain and got high smoking oregano. I tried oregano in the sixties. It's harsh, but it works and it's legal.

It was this linear story of progress. But that's not really who or what Seth is. That's just one story line that fit very well with Jane and Rob. When you go back and re-read the Seth books, that's not who he was at all. That was a particular form that he adopted.

There's a whole other part of Seth that appeared more directly in the books after *The Nature of Personal Reality,* which many people feel are incomprehensible. But that's an important part that we're going to be exploring for the rest of our lives. And, with the kind of technical skills that we are developing, it doesn't have to be so incomprehensible.

The Buddhist terminology of an emanation most captures what the Seth personality was. Instead of thinking of him as someone who lived in physical reality and finished his incarnations and had graduated several steps and was now coming back—though that's true too, in one sense that *is* who Seth was but does injustice to him—think of him as an emanation of this huge consciousness that was operating as part of a process of thousands of years of developing the self-reflective ego that has worked with humankind in many, many ways and has beamed emanations of itself into conversations in the dream state nightly in different forms and different attitudes and beamed other emanations of itself into physical incarnations, one of which, according to my guides, was Yukteshwar Ananda, Yogananda's guru whom he described in *Autobiography of a Yogi*. That's also a description of who Seth was.

There are other places in the books where Seth says, "I was part of a group to put your Earth together." He says that he and a few others created the Earth. Well, that's another layer of Seth.

Still elsewhere he said, "I incarnated as a dog in preparation to learn more about this state so that I can talk to you folks." He talked about—and again this is also a gross simplification of something almost too complex to understand—that he might spend a hundred years as a tree as a kind of a vacation. And prior to being Seth, he had a minor portion of himself incarnate as a guy he called Frank Withers living in Elmira, New York—he's dead now—so that he would understand our society better. I don't know if this guy's ever been identified, but whoever he was, he started coming through Jane.

The truth is that Seth is simultaneously all kinds of things, as is your own soul.

I see these as beams of light—so this particular beam shines and works with Rob and Jane in the dream state and puts together a personality that is believable, a magnificent vibrant reality.

In another sense, even that isn't right. It's as much a history of coming through time and then proceeding in the way that most of us understood who Seth was in the seventies—that's real, and all of what I just said is also real—but it's also just as much this sort of made-up phenomenon, drawing from energies and speaking to us. But made-up doesn't mean unreal, because Seth was as real as any of us.

There are literally an infinite number of descriptions. It is so creative that it has its own changing life.

Seth knows himself to be all these different selves simultaneously. And he was all those things and mind-bogglingly more, and so are you right now.

It is not the case that you will grow and grow and grow until you become enlightened and then you'll grow and grow and grow until you eventually become a group consciousness and then you'll grow and grow and grow until you become a planet and then you'll grow and grow and grow until you become a galaxy, and then you'll grow and grow and grow and be a Seth—you're all those things right now. And so is Seth.

The difference between Seth and us is that Seth can track more directions at one time. When you're committed to your humanity in your waking state, that's kind of hard.

So, once again, humankind isolated themselves as this part of a big project. The nature of the game changed, as the nature of human consciousness changed. There used to be guides like Seth that worked with humankind for a long time a long time ago, but at some point, probably in the period from about 1000 BCE to about 400 BCE, they stepped back and let humans develop. They ceased to be in constant contact with humans who were conscious of that contact. If Seth had popped up then in some sort of form or was channeled, it would have been harder to believe that you're born as only yourself, that you are your body, that you have your experience separate from everyone else, and then you die. If beings were popping in and out with bodies of various sorts, the process wouldn't have worked very well. Withdrawal forced humanity to develop a kind of self-reliance.

This was set up for very rich and powerful purposes. It helped humans turn in on themselves and create this narrow focus we call the self-reflective ego, to answer questions of the Earth, the Sun, the stars, laws of gravity and motion, our souls, and all kinds of things. With the development of the self-reflective ego, humans lost a former sense of identification with nature and its playfulness. That wasn't a mistake. We worked for thousands of years at inner and outer levels—our souls and great large thoughtforms, the Earth itself—to develop this particular different kind of human consciousness.

Humans now are not higher or lower than this, that, or the other thing; it's merely a matter of focusing on a very narrow band of consciousness, which we have been doing intentionally, though this narrow focus makes us think we're fundamentally only that narrow focus. But as we move into the Aquarian Age, we will be able to track our current small intense focus on our individual narrow unique viewpoint even as we identify with large events. We will each be able to do both and meld different ranges of awareness.

There is a lot of ideology that humans are the top of evolution, which is really a very silly idea and very limiting. We miss a whole lot, but it has the paradoxical outcome of making our humanity more valid because if you're not a part of these big things as well as being individual—if you're not eternal—then there really is very little reason to engage your humanity, unless you are on the top of evolution.

The guides started coming back, I think, with Madame Blavatsky in 1875, with the theosophists. She said that she was talking to entities who were great yogis or spiritual masters, located somewhere in the East. That was probably her best understanding and maybe they even appeared to her like that. She did not understand that she was channeling. I personally think that she was hooking into beings who don't have bodies, who were like Seth. I think her guides were beyond that kind of human incarnational system.

Beginning with the founders of the Theosophical Society, these larger beings began communicating to humans, breaking the game open again. Of course guides had come through a little in every culture, but this was the beginning an emerging systematic relationship that will become common.

Everything we get is a simplification. It has to be. It's only a partial picture and, if you're in touch with yourself, you will constantly have your understanding changing and growing. It's impossible to step entirely out of your society, out of your time. So Madame Blavatsky's masters were not unlike the Romantic poets or Goethe or any of the Romantic artists, yet they were also these mysterious masters of the Orient who were giving her this information.

You go forward fifty years and you have Alice Bailey. She was very important in this chain, more down to earth and putting more stress on engaging this life. She also did not understand that she was channeling. She thought she was talking to a person called The Tibetan who literally had a physical body. No, it was just a Sethian-type being. In fact, it *was* Seth.

Alice Bailey wrote these absolutely unreadable books unless you really understand her code. They were, in a sense, deliberately unreadable.

What was current then was the idea that science and clear thinking would solve all our problems. In a sense, science was still magic. So when you read Alice Bailey, it is so aping of that time, of the objective intellect. And you're supposed to arise above all personal emotion. But there's really good material in there if you can wade through all of that stuff.

Then you have the third in that line, Jane Roberts, channeling this vibrant being who was coming into our world. I think that utterly changes the game. Jane's married name was Butts, so it's the three B's— not Bach, Beethoven, and Brahms, but Blavatsky, Bailey, and Butts. It sounds like a triple play or a law firm.

Part of the Sethian message was the personality that came through Jane. Jane wanted to be a poet, and so what you get in the Seth material is of its time: Hemingway, existentialism, the Beat poets, a touch of the sixties. Seth becomes, sort of, in praise of self-expression and individuality. All these things are important parts of the overall message and movement, but they have to be taken with a grain of salt also. They were filtered through Jane.

In some sense even the most tantric of Tibetan practitioners and the most down-to-earth Zen practitioner is stepping out of their ordinary humanity to get out into higher consciousness. Here higher consciousness is coming into this world; that is what changes the game of spirituality. As we open back up to guides coming back into communication with us, we open back up to the penetration of our experience by larger experience. We go out into those larger areas, and that's sacred. And they come into ours, and that's sacred too.

Instead of penetrating the illusion of form in the Tibetan or Zen way, higher consciousness flooding into our lives re-centers the spiritual venture. Not this life instead of other things, not this life after you die or become enlightened or both, but this life while you're awake and alive.

There's a kind of particularity to our experience that is only attainable in this sort of life. That should not be scary because you will not get everything that could be gotten and you can't *not* get something utterly sacred. You can't screw up so bad that it isn't glorious, and you can't get everything that is because there's always more available than could be gotten. That's part of what makes it peculiarly human.

There's a kind of valuing of personal dual experience that I don't think was possible until Jane channeled Seth. The Seth channelings galvanized hundreds of thousands in the seventies with Seth's message that we create our own reality according to our conscious beliefs. I even moved to Elmira, New York, to study more deeply with Jane and Seth. Today, there's nothing I do, feel, or think that is not penetrated through and through with their information, kindness, generosity, and aliveness. Over the decades, however, I've come to understand and appreciate them differently than I and my friends did then.

Most of us, when we learn that we create our reality, think, "I have the keys to the kingdom here; I'm going to create happiness by creating stuff that eliminates all these horrible tensions out of my life." We thought that since we create our own reality according to our beliefs, we would just work on our beliefs, get what we want and thus, through the satisfaction of our desires, find fulfillment. Now, four decades after encountering Seth, I see Seth as teaching a much more realistic and deeper message.

There are basically two approaches that embrace our humanity. One is a kind of misunderstanding of what Seth says, that if you work on your beliefs, every important thing will work out fine. In 1974 all I understood Seth to be saying by, "You create your own reality," was, "If you do it right, you'll get what you want," and that really wasn't at all what he was saying. That's what we *thought* he was saying.

I really think that was what Jane thought that she was teaching too, and I think it was her blind spot. As I was getting ready to leave the class, a week or two beforehand—I don't remember how it came up—I asked, "I wonder if there's going to be a recession next year?"

Jane said—and she got a big laugh out of the group and I cringe when I think about it because it's such a misunderstanding of the Seth material—she said, "Not for me." She didn't say it in a mean way, though it may sound mean. And everybody laughed because, Why not? You create your own reality, and so she's working on her beliefs. There won't be a recession for her.

Well, there's some truth to that, but it totally misunderstands how profoundly imbedded in life and interactive we are. And yeah, there are people who can make a billion dollars as the economy is tanking, but the truth is that we're all in this together. If there are people starving in Africa, that pain is part of your body. You may not track it, you may be Donald Trump* and think, "Oh well, this is great, you know. I'm rich because I'm so smart and creative. And who cares about those people in Africa or Afghanistan."

Well, you create your own reality, but you don't create it unilaterally because there's no such thing as a separate you. You're interdependent, but I think it's really more accurate to say that you become conscious co-creators not just with God, but with everything and everyone.

We are all co-creating this world; so, one half of Jane's statement, "not for me," utterly misunderstands how interdependent we are. Because of interdependence, we cannot control the outcome of anything—we co-create. That distinction is kind of subtle because, nevertheless, we do entirely create our own reality. It's just that reality has an intrinsic creative vitality to it that gives us back more than we put in. If we could control it, it would give us back *exactly* what we put in and there would be no reason to do it.

The other part that is so wrong about her statement is, she was right, the next year she did fine economically. But ten years later she and her husband were suffering economically and, more to the point, because of her limitations and genetics, her rheumatoid arthritis started getting much worse in that next year when she did okay financially. She did okay financially, but not so well overall. So, it's not quite so simple as saying, "Not for me."

Creating your reality is different from controlling your reality. I

---

*This was said years before the Trump presidency.

don't think that Jane understood that. And I don't think that most of the people who engage the Seth material understand that. Life is ineradicably creative and surprising.

Jane also said, "Never do anything you don't want to do." I think that simple formulation is a mistake. Only with a Sethian clarity will it have a chance of working. I would say, "Look at what you don't want to do that you're doing and richly investigate your life. See whose energy is driving you, what sorts of things are going on for you now."

At least a couple of times when I was in the class, someone challenged the formulation to never do anything you don't want. Seth answered, "Well, you know, if you'd been following my suggestion all along, you wouldn't be locked in this conflict." He didn't say, but I'll add, "The truth is you *haven't* been doing that all along, you *are* in that conflict, and how do you engage that conflict right now gracefully?"

It's not as simple as not doing anything you don't want. The fundamental point is profound, important, and practical. If you are doing things you don't want to be doing, it's time for you to think about that, think about why you're doing that. Whose energy is there? What is your energy saying when you take the time and try to be creative? The truth may be that you *do* enjoy your work in addition to being irritated and aggravated, but you enjoy it maybe sixty percent of the amount you could enjoy it without your shoulds, have tos, and oughts.

What Jane did mostly get is that all of life is sacred and that there's something special about a human life. Not more special than dolphin life or cat life or life on Mars or anything else, but nonetheless really special.

She would talk about how amazing our experience is and how mystical and magical, even amongst the pain, which is an intrinsic part of all experience. It was an important redirection that made a different sort of inner world possible. She did this notwithstanding the fact that she was crippled with arthritis. Yet she ran these classes and we'd sit around and we'd talk. She was emotionally and spiritually very generous. I would sit there week in and week out and she would often go on about things and it began to seep in. I began to understand Seth even though I was about to embark upon a catastrophically bad two years where everything went wrong in my life. Her words let me understand and grow from that.

You each create your own reality in accordance with your beliefs, even your conscious beliefs, but not in ways you can fully understand. There are no exceptions to that rule. The Dalai Lama, created, according to *his* conscious beliefs, the outcome where the Chinese Communists invaded and have done awful things to Tibet and have attempted to do awful things to its culture. It's important to realize that there's a difference in culpability. The Dalai Lama is a global treasure. Mao and his confederates were a working out of many of the worst inclinations of human beings in the 1950s and '60s. It's a little shocking and perhaps hard to get used to the idea that a saint creates a reality in which really awful people play a significant role. Now the Dalai Lama is part of a deep game, but it would be an error to think that *all* that he is doing is bringing about healing.

There is no exception to the rule that each of us creates our own reality, we're co-creators, we create with other people. That creation happens in a space that is not limited by direct causality but moves by simultaneity, by synchronicity. We can each be *merely* co-creators and yet in a profoundly true sense completely and utterly the creator of the world that we experience and engage or fail to engage.

We create our own reality, but apparent outcomes are not as important as the work we do before, during, and after. Now we do that by throwing ourselves into trying to create a particular outcome, but our attempt to create that outcome will work best if that attempt is our secondary goal, and our primary goal is in the attempt to cultivate authentic kindness, generosity, compassion, intelligence. And we will never be perfect at it. But these consequential events that we try to create, they're never causative, they are measuring points; they're never final either. Whether we get what we want or don't get what we want, it's important that we keep working our process and what our resistances are, and deal with them.

In this system, we don't, for the most part, try to impact people by directly acting on their aura in the way that people who are sending love, for example, or divine peace often do. Instead of sending out waves of what we think the world needs into the auras of the people who we think need it, we do two things instead. We explode our matching pictures and we communicate to anyone who has the space for our message, not because we're right but because what else would we do? It's like putting a billboard, not an obnoxious billboard that they have to look at, but a picture outside their aura that they have a choice of attending to or not, and that picture has two components. It has a component that recognizes them in their full agency to make decisions, which are always divine even if they're unskillful because, since all consciousness expands in all directions, everything ultimately is sacred, even your worst actions, even other people's worst actions. They may be lamentable, but they are sacred.

22

Story-Telling

When you've read a book for a while and lose yourself in it, you feel that's a really great book. What humanity's done is they've taken that process one step further. They've made a storyline out of dual existence.

Imagine that you're reading *War and Peace*. You could lose yourself for the whole book and temporarily become Prince Andrei or Natasha. Imagine that someone had a machine that you could pay money and for four days you would have forgotten yourself and you would be a character in *War and Peace*. People would pay a lot of money for that. You might be in the midst of the French sacking Moscow and it might be horrible, but when the four days were up, you'd come up and it would still be you. And you'd say, "Boy that was really intense and amazing!" And you might wait six months again, but if you have the money, you'd probably pay to take another trip on that virtual-reality machine.

I suppose it could be a reasonable thing to do if you want to go on one of those virtual-reality trips, to work really hard at realizing that it's not really real, but that's not what you paid for, and the virtual reality of it *is* deeply meaningful.

Why develop nondual awareness if you paid all this money to take this trip on *this* virtual-reality machine?

For everyone except the nondually aware, sensation goes up and is processed by the story-making part of the brain—the inborn virtual-reality machine—and values are placed on our experience.

People who attain nondual awareness stop taking sensation through that part of the brain and they no longer tell themselves those stories. So they have a direct and unmediated experience, and that's really cool.

I'm not being ironic, I'm just saying that humanity is in the process of learning how to weave those stories into larger interpenetrating ones. It is still important to not over-believe the stories you tell. Also, you can't really start appreciating those stories if you think there's only one going on and that you have nothing to do with it.

For most people it would be helpful to treat this life as unreal but meaningful. *War and Peace* is unreal—there never was a Prince Andrei—but it's deeply meaningful.

Part of the way we're going to break the grip of those stories is we're going to hopefully break the grip that you are Kathy and you are Steve and that's all you are—that as long as you're human, everything else is kind of irrelevant, there's just this one track going on.

I mean, as soon as you go to sleep you open up into territories where you become something entirely different. So Kathy and Steve are forms that you inhabit while you're awake and they are deeply rich and meaningful, but they're not who you are and they're not *not* who you are. They're a form that you are committing to and appreciating because everything that form does *is* deeply and eternally meaningful.

The story-making process in the brain creates stories about everything, and those stories, which can operate very unconsciously, are automatically an interpretation of what's going on. There's this huge mistaken sense that the story you tell yourself is a *true* story. And that mistake is the source of pain in your life.

While making stories is your divine contribution both to yourself and every part of All That Is, belief that your story is the correct story is the source of immense pain as a human being.

The traditional nondual approach has been to bypass that story-making mechanism entirely. A nondual practitioner literally changes his or her physiology so that the sensations that they experience do not go into that automatic story-making part of the brain. That is the traditional esoteric approach too, to bypass that part of the brain.

The coming Aquarian approach will be to *use* that story-making process and reassert your joint authorship so that you can rewrite the stories that are causing you pain, causing you to be unhappy, obnoxious, or whatever. That's a *different* concept of becoming enlightened.

What do I mean by an automatic interpretation of what's going on? It's not automatic in an objective way. What the brain does is take all of your emotions and beliefs, including lots of them that you didn't even know that you have, and it weaves the most consistent story that it can. And there will have to be multiple inconsistencies because each of us is always inconsistent. That's because of the nature of the universe; its creativity is generated by the play of polarities, the play of order and chaos.

What we're learning to do in this system is to play skillfully with that automatic story-making process. At the Aesclepian Institute they have this wonderful little saying that they put on lots if not all of their newsletters: "Don't believe everything you think." That's the high road to happiness. Because your stories are made up of all sorts of junk floating in your aura and every time you lose your neutrality to a piece of that junk—and another word for the junk is your fondest delusions and aspirations—then it gets cycled into the story that you tell yourself about the world.

Growing your psychic perception allows you to look under the covers of the stories. There are many reasons to do this, but one is that it is impossible to have complete information about anything because there is always going to be more. The more you know, the more of the universe that you're touching. The more of the universe that you're touching, the more that you don't know. So, in some very real respect, the more you know, the more you *don't* know. The more you *know* you don't know . . . .

The objective is not to get to some purely objective point of view. That misses the point of being human. Your humanity is profoundly subjective, and the story or stories that you land on are your contribution. It's just that being psychic will allow you to explore your stories more skillfully and not lose yourself in a story.

When a story arises, you can use your conscious awareness and skill to look under the covers of that story and say, "Where is that story working for me and where is that story not working for me? Oh, I have this should and it's not working. I'm miserable and I'm about to cause a fight." The tool that I use most to regain some input into the story I'm telling myself is one I call Whose Energy Is It?

A movie is an illusion. There are a whole lot of still photos that go into making a movie, but you have the illusion of continuous action because it zips by faster than your perception can track the separate events. As human beings those of us who engage in what is called conceptual thought run our experience through the story-making part of our brain, and we weave stories out of our experience. And in doing so, we add a richness, a subjectivity, something that is uniquely our contribution to the universe and to experience. Later I'll talk more about why the universe is interested in our contribution.

Now those stories that we tell ourselves are also the source of enormous pain and suffering, so in the psychic system that we teach, you learn how to cultivate playfulness and a sense of neutrality and amusement. You learn how to not get owned by a story, which is itself an effect of conditioning and other people's energy in your space. You start to own your own energy more, start to clear conditioning, so that you start to realize that the story you're telling yourself is just that. It isn't the only story that you could tell yourself, and you learn to engage that story with an openness that can bring happiness to you.

As we move into the Aquarian Age, we will learn to create our individual story lines in duality, while in our group consciousness, we participate in something much bigger emerging from our interdependence with the group, similar to playing a violin in a string quartet. It's really hard to be happy as a human being if you buy into the story line that you are only this individual. It can be done, but it's hard. And you miss a lot of the excitement. But creating, embracing, and exploring our individual story while simultaneously playing a part in the larger interpenetrating group stories is in fact where we're moving as the human race, as we move into the Aquarian Age.

Last night we were talking about losing your crown in your emotions or ideas. Emotions are a particular story. That is all an emotion is. It is a story that you tell yourself. That doesn't mean that emotions don't count, just that they are intrinsically a subjective story, not some divine fact.

It's very useful if you can explore life in a way that you realize that it is, in a sense, unreal, much as *War and Peace* is unreal, or a great movie is unreal, or *Hamlet* is unreal. Unreal, but deeply, deeply meaningful. And the excess value that you bring to life is your skill as a storyteller to yourself. So, your goal is a meaningful story; not a true story or real story, because there is no ultimately real or true story.

When you lose your crown, you lose any say as to what your story is going to be.

Otherwise, you might have a little bit of a sense of humor and a little bit of that sense that you might be in *War and Peace,* but it really is a very passionate experience that you will literally cherish for the rest of eternity.

As you meditate or simply contemplate your existence, you will find lots of aspects of yourself, lots of ways of your being, some of which you will dislike or disagree with. I'm hoping you get some amusement and play-fulness about that and start to understand that this is why a lot of mystics abandon the whole project of their humanity. They start seeing all these multiple identities and they say, "Well, that means there's nothing there, there's nothing real about that." I would agree with them that there's nothing *real* about that; what I would disagree with is whether it's fruitful to engage those identities.

This is probably difficult for a lot of people to understand. Most of us work so hard to get a central core identity that is the real us. Now it's nice to have a central core identity that you can make reference to, but to lose yourself as if that's *who* you are hardens your relationship with the world.

Each self, whether you are aware of its existence or not, is as real and meaningful as anything else. These other selves show up because they exist, because anything that could happen *does* happen. There are forms of your consciousness that travel through all of these possibilities.

In the consciousness that we usually focus in, we work really hard to make certain things happen and other things *not* happen, and there's a lot of really meaningful living experience you get from that. Yet other portions of your consciousness play through and deeply experience everything that could happen, and there's a kind of richness that is unimaginable in that too.

All of reality is enlarged by this interplay between selves.

In our system we don't rigidly focus our consciousness at one time and one reality. Sometimes it's important to be able to do that. If you're driving down a snowy hill, then you want reality narrowly focused. You want one story only.

This is a focused meditation seminar, so you learn how to focus in a particular direction, but we're going to use it almost opposite from the way a lot of mystical traditions do. We're going to use it like Seth did when coming into Jane's identity, enjoying a conversation and hanging out in the warm boundaries of human consciousness. Imagine yourself dropping into your life as Mike or Susan and enjoying the conversation and having a cognac and in that waking experience utterly commit to what it is even if Moscow is burning down. You commit to it, understanding that it's unreal but meaningful.

It's part of the normal human experience to resist parts of life and say, "That is not us," but experience itself couldn't really exist without everything that could happen happening in some sense.

Try this. Drift on out, on over, so that you become the co-personality looking back at what you thought of as you. Commit more fully and yet simultaneously more gracefully and playfully to this waking you. Loosen the kind of desperateness with which you grasp the story that you tell yourself about who you are and who you aren't. It's kind of shocking, but the more open you are to who you aren't, the more capacity you will have to be who you are, and again because who you aren't *is also who you are.*

Anything that isn't implies everything that is and exists only in relationship to all of those things. And the very fact that it is in relationship to all those things means that everything that isn't *is*. Everything that doesn't exist by virtue of it not existing exists. This is the kind of thing that makes people very frustrated about mysticism, because it sounds like gobbledygook, and it is in a way. But I don't mean it in the sense that Medieval philosophers did; I mean it in the utter creativity of All That Is: Everything is and isn't. Everything is contained in everything else.

You can commit even more passionately to this identity because in some sense you are choosing it, but you commit in a way that leaves you flexible and playful rather than rigid.

These aspects of ourselves that we don't include in our self-definition get projected out and we see them in the external world and that's how we engage those parts of ourselves that we alienate from ourselves.

Co-personalities are the way in which past incarnations continue their exploration through future incarnation without getting lost. Most of us at one time thought of reincarnation as if Kaye died and then she was reborn as Joe. Then Kaye would be done and over, but Kaye actually goes on forever and she participates in Joe as the center of her own experience. Every portion of consciousness is the center of its own experience. Since all consciousness expands in all directions, every portion of consciousness is the center of All That Is.

Anarchy is part of the ineradicable, passionate dance of existence; the yin-yang sign gives you order and chaos. The more order you create, the more chaos spontaneously emerges because whatever order you created comes from what you know, and the more that you know, the wider your perspective and the more that you don't know.

You couldn't have surprises if you didn't have chaos.

Now obviously when you see the chaos, you will want to tame some of it. The chaos and the pictures that are stuck and other people's energy and the nasty cords and everything—of course you want to clear those. And as your skill grows, there are ways in which your aura will become somewhat more organized, but the chaos will always be there.

Those stuck pictures and nasty cords and general chaos are also in their own way a source of the inexhaustible creativity of the universe. You can always have both experiences simultaneously. You can be distressed at how much chaos you find, and you can admire the sheer unabashed, rowdy creativity of it all.

The response that traditionally has been taken in many mystic approaches is to say, "This is untamable; therefore, I'm going to buy out of the delusion." What I'm hoping you'll do is see, "This *is* untamable. I'm going to stop beating myself up because I failed to tame it. I'm going stop beating myself up because of this mistake, that mistake, or the other mistake." You abandon yourself and to some extent open up to what it is.

Who knows in multiple directions what sort of creativity will be engendered by all that chaos? So a certain incidental aspect may not bubble up for a week or two or a month or a year, but at some point I think it'll bubble up in the back of your mind and, even if you don't consciously articulate it, you'll start to have a sense that even it, the unpleasant event, is a resource.

In most of our waking state it's still really important to have clear personal boundaries. What we've been doing so far is exploring the fact that those clear personal boundaries are in some sense a convention, a kind of virtual reality. It's important to have those clear boundaries when you're engaging personal reality like driving on that snowy road, but they float on a kind of interpenetration.

When you're doing everyday activity, you want to be open to chaos, not resistant to it, but you want a certain amount of clarity and comfort with it, and that's a skill that you develop in life. You learn how to focus and how to carve out some clarity, and life will always continue answering you back, giving you the opportunity to keep getting more and more clarity.

It's interesting, you'd think that as you get more and more clarity, then everything would become clear. But it doesn't. As you get more and more clarity, then you also begin seeing more and more of the unknown, and where you start to become comfortable, it isn't by being pure clarity, it's by being comfortable with the play of life. So as you become more and more clear, you could call it pure clarity, but I wouldn't. I'd call it more compassion for the ins and outs of life—so that when things are disrupted, you don't have to resist that, you can engage that. You engage even your lack of clarity with a kind of clarity, with a kind of compassion for yourself and for the complexity of life.

Around 1974, Seth said that humans are learning to become conscious co-creators with God. That doesn't mean that we're learning to have godlike powers; that's *not* what he was saying. What he was saying is we're learning how to use creativity. As humans, we're learning how to use creativity in the waking state in that particular form called being a human. So we become even more creative as Cynthia or as John—that is, if we have clear boundaries when we go through this incarnational system and its chaotic freedoms. What we are learning is how to use creativity, we are learning how to chop wood and fetch water, we are learning how to build a thoughtform and explore its manifestation and its life cycle.

Zen people say that enlightenment is chopping wood and fetching water. In our system, reality is chopping wood and fetching water *and* learning how to chop wood and fetch water. In other words, the skills that we build in this reality are in some ways cumulative and meaningful.

You are ready to leave this incarnational system not when you're perfect, not when you're perfectly loving, not when you have nondual awareness—there are a lot of people who have nondual awareness on Earth or are so-called enlightened who have not finished their last human incarnation and a lot of people who *do* finish their human incarnation whom no one would confuse for being enlightened—you are ready when you're ready.

That's why we have time. When you've learned being human well enough—and it *does* require the cultivation of kindness and generosity—when you've learned how to create within the narrower context of a single personality, then you are ready to learn how to create in broader contexts going in multiple directions with an incredible rambunctiousness. You won't need the particular kind of boundaries that you have here. The reason you won't need them is you have learned a kind of clarity that allows you to have boundaries without their being geographic boundaries.

What you're exploring is the truth that your literal boundaries float in a sea of interpenetration and you couldn't be the individual you are without that sea.

As we move into the Aquarian Age and become sufficiently aware of our boundaries, then we'll be able to explore interpenetrating boundaries. But you'll find that cells in your body have been doing that all the time.

To reference Marshall McLuhan, the medium is *really* the message. And the message is that this life that we experience here has a vitality and a creativity and a meaningfulness in and of itself. I don't see any other mystical system validating that. If you're in a rush to get permanently into nondual awareness—if you view the stories that you tell yourself as mere obscurations of the underlying nondual luminosity of awareness, which is absolutely true; if you view your experience and your sense of separateness as a mere obscuration—you lose something important.

Ken Wilber says, if you have dual awareness, it's like trying to rearrange the deck chairs on the *Titanic*. You're in a catastrophe, whether you know it or not. But it's more like rearranging the deck chairs in the movie *Titanic,* which is itself a very rich and valuable and exciting experience, or the movie *Some Like it Hot....* It can be a drama, a comedy, a romantic comedy. All those story lines are possible as a human being. All of them are rich. And they add to the universe.

The sea captain who smoked oregano was only a portion of Seth's experience, but that portion was *so* exciting and *so* warm and loving and *so* brilliant and *so* funny, and this was a mystical validation of ordinary humanity in a way that goes way past what the Buddhists mean by the concept of thusness or suchness. Something that helped create the Earth itself could later sail one of its seas and smoke oregano without diminishment. And not later, because time is an illusion. Seth validated all of our lives in the story lines that we create.

Seth's concept of grace was not what I expected it to be. Before Seth, I thought grace was when your life was working perfectly well, when you're in a state of highest wisdom and love. Seth's concept of grace was—he said it better than I will but I can't remember exactly what he said—when you're moving within your own life reasonably well, not perfectly, not something that comes from on high. If you can begin to understand reasonably flowing, I think you begin to understand an important component of Aquarian consciousness.

In the Aquarian Age, we move from the Piscean alienated isolated consciousness to group consciousness. If you read Alice Bailey, as you move toward group consciousness you drop anything that is particularly unique to *your* personality. That's what she believed, and she reflected longstanding belief systems. No one then that I know of questioned her on the complete dropping of uniqueness.

Seth turns that *completely* upside-down. What you bring to the group consciousness *is* everything that is unique and particular to your personality. But you have to bring it with a kind of playfulness and gracefulness that most of us don't—that none of us have quite frankly, but we're working on it. That's what neutrality is for. Neutrality is not the same thing as nondual awareness. Neutrality is, you're inside the illusion of separateness but you have a sense of humor about it. You're open to life-as-it-is. You recognize that it *is* a story. And neutrality will be easier to cultivate as you begin to cultivate this multilayered consciousness.

Why would anyone ever backpack when they can be at home, eating exactly what they want, taking a shower in air-conditioning? Because there is some unique experience in backpacking that you can't have being at home, and there's some downsides to it.

Being human is a field trip. You deal with the mosquitos and the dirt, but you do go back home and you have all these great snapshots of what you did and you have this memory of the gritty reality of your human adventure that enhances the larger you back at home in a way that not having gone on the field trip doesn't. You can't carry all that joy all the time on this field trip, but you can do the field trip, know the joy is there, visit it occasionally and, when it's time, integrate it all. Mostly that will be after death.

The amount of that joy that you can feel steadily percolating up will grow year by year but in a way that doesn't blot out the exquisite though often painful separateness of the self-reflective ego.

I've often compared the human experience to going on a mud run. There are people who will actually pay money to get up very early in the morning, like five o'clock, in forty degrees, and run through an obstacle course filled with these mud pits of wet mud and slush. And they enjoy it, or most of them do.

You don't have to slosh through the mud. You can go to a thing called a motel room and take a hot shower and watch television on which you might even see the other suckers running through the mud and going under wires and ropes and stuff like that. In some of the mud runs, the wires will shock you if you don't get low enough. So you really have to get down in the mud. And people do this on purpose.

Or you can sit in an RV and listen to Bach. But then you wouldn't have the experience of a mud run. You'd be missing something. You'd have a different experience, but it wouldn't be that challenge of the mud run. Maybe if one's entire life was an obstacle, you'd be insane to go on a mud run. But the mud run isn't your entire life, so many people gladly jump into a mud run, or into other sorts of things.

Not every soul is going to choose to go on a mud run, okay? This soul (John) is not going on a mud run this lifetime. But I sure went on a metaphoric mud run for two years just after the Seth classes.

Even though this soul is not going on a mud run this lifetime, it's obvious to me what a cool experience it is for someone for whom that is fun.

In another sense, though, this life is a mud run, a mud run for the soul that it chose willingly. Your multidimensional self says, "I think I'm going to explore time and space. And I'm going to set these rules for myself. I can't fly and things have to happen one after another. Won't that be interesting?"

Nonduality is sort of like doing everything in the mud run except running through the mud. In other words, you're missing something quite profound.

When you're done with the mud run, it becomes part of the richness of your life. The mud run may be over, but it's part of a story you tell twenty years from now.

What I'm saying is, "Welcome to Planet Earth. It is a mud run. You signed up for it." You may not have understood that you were signing up for it. But at the edges of your competence it's a mud run, shocking as that may be.

Maybe you'll read a book that's put you into crying and you feel awful and you put two days into reading this book and you're going to read another book in a month that makes you feel absolutely awful because of the intensity. Or you'll go to a movie or something like that. Because you long for the emotional intensity. You wouldn't do it if that was all it was, but it isn't all that is. You live and you have a large number of experiences; you can choose and make meaning out of them.

And as long as you have dual consciousness, every one of those experiences, while you are incarnated, will be impermanent, interdependent.

So human incarnation is a mud run. There's a portion of you that comes in from higher levels that are completely joyful and perfectly beyond human enlightenment that voluntarily goes on this adventure called the mud run where there is in fact suffering in addition to pain and pleasure that you could have without suffering. There's a certain kind of suffering, but your soul not only voluntarily incarnates as you but it went with gusto into the incarnation that is you.

Souls incarnate because they know that while some of it will involve suffering, maybe even a lot of it in particular lifetimes, maybe even *all of it* in particular lifetimes, they do it because they experience incarnating as an important contribution to All That Is and they know that somewhere you know that when you chose to enter into this incarnation as a baby being, you had a choice, your soul didn't force this incarnation on what you may think of as you, the personality. You may not be able to believe it, but you, the little personal you, also chose this incarnation before you were even born. And you did so, knowing that life as a human being isn't some mistake. It's a grand, sometimes painful adventure.

Each of you gets to that place where you can engage everything without suffering, maybe pain but no suffering eventually, usually after death. You're at that place of no suffering, though, with a kind of richness that you would never have without human dualistic experience. If instead of engaging the richness of your human suffering, you become enlightened, you've missed something.

Yet if my friends' entire existence was a mud run, my guess is they would not have gone on it. If they had been born at six o'clock that morning and someone said, "Okay you're an adult now. You going to have a life of four hours that involve getting up, driving across the state, freezing your butt off as you run through this," my guess is they would have said, "I think I'll pass on that." But as an episode in a life, they've decided to come back and do it this year, just like you will probably decide to come back and get involved not in exactly the same way but in other incarnations.

Here is another view: When I was in the eighth grade, we had our first summer football practice. It was 102 degrees. Now if that were my entire life—I was born at two o'clock that afternoon and I died at five o'clock that afternoon—then football practice would make no sense at all.

Each of us and each of our souls is learning something here and learning how to integrate energies, learning how to deal with the inevitable tensions that arise when you allow newness. The only way you can allow a newness and creativity is to have the option for chaos. If you can control everything, there isn't the potential for this human kind of newness. It's only because the world is uncontrollable, not just by you but by your soul. You might say, if my soul was there with me, I'm angry with it because it didn't keep these bad things from happening. Well, that's called life as a human being. That *is* the deal. When the soul plunges into life as a human being, it's plunging into the conditions where contradictions and harsh contrasts *do* appear. If it already knew how to do all this and could control the outcome, then why would it do it?

It's sort of like the Harlem Globetrotters versus the Generals; they played eighty thousand games and the Globetrotters have won all eighty thousand. There's a secret there, which is the Generals aren't allowed to win, and it isn't really a game, it's an exhibition. But in this life the reason it pays the soul to invest in the incarnation and the reason it pays you the personality to invest in this incarnation is it is open-ended. That is a really unusual and hard concept.

When you read a lot of New Age or straight mystical literature, there's all this emphasis on mastery. It's just in your bones. You think that if Christ came here, he'd make no mistakes, or the Buddha, they don't make mistakes. Forget about that. They didn't know that much. They were oceans of compassion and galvanizing figures who changed all of humanity, but this idea of perfection is really insidious because it makes you reactive against your life. It makes you less resilient. It makes you run around trying to find someone who has an answer so that you don't have to deal with the tension that's intrinsic in a human life.

I think this is what Trungpa meant when he wrote about spiritual materialism, how people run around trying to find the master so that they don't suffer. Now exactly who is that? Is the Dalai Lama not a sufficient master for you? If he is, why does he let the Tibetan people suffer? Because he's mean? Because he doesn't care? It's because he doesn't control those things. That's the experience of being human.

Do we think it just hasn't occurred to him to sit down and visualize world peace? He *is* world peace and you still have the Tibetan people getting messed over by the Chinese government.

So when I say your soul is there at every point, what I mean is, in its own way, the soul is there suffering with you at every point, but its suffering is somewhat different from yours because it has a kind of courage and fearlessness and openness to life as it is. When you give it your experience, even the worst, it will just imbibe your experience, it'll just assimilate that. Karma is any experience that it cannot assimilate, and so that bounces back and you experience it until you *can* assimilate it. And in a very real sense it *is* you. So be angry at your soul all you want to, but you can only be angry at your soul if you really think you are *not* your soul. And that's the way people normally think about it, that I'm just some sort of puppet that was put here by my soul. No, your soul is in the foxhole with you. It *is* you and you *are* it, though you each are yourselves, just interdependent selves.

The reason we're going through all of this is that soul's courage and resilience is you also. People will say, "Well I can't handle what's happening to me, so the soul ought to take this away from me." But it's really more you can't handle it *without* your soul. When you recognize you *are* your soul, you *will* be able to handle it. You may not like it, but you will be able to handle it.

You know if complaining and resisting worked, I would urge you to complain and resist louder and louder. I'm being facetious, but it's not entirely facetious. Some people are in so much pain that complaining and resisting is their defense against that pain. So if that's you, just go ahead and complain and resist, but eventually happiness will come when you stop blaming your soul and realize *you* are your soul. You're also *not* your soul, and your soul has some resources for you, but none of those resources are plucking you out of the situation. All of the resources are more resilient, more patient, more courageous, and often more skillful than you, and they may help you find a way to let go of your resistance and find ways out that wouldn't otherwise occur to you. But it's not like winning the lottery.

It's a little hard for you to recognize that, but the more you do these kinds of exercises and work on difficult conversations, life as it is, not prioritizing your shoulds, have tos, and oughts, the more access to that courage and resilience you have.

One of the things that separates a child from an adult shows up when I'm feeding my cats. I have this young cat; he doesn't get enough exercise, so I feed him by throwing his kibbles down into the basement, making him run down and get the kibble. Then he has to run right back up and get another kibble. Back and forth. The basement is carpeted, and sometimes the kibble bounces around and will get lost. So he will run down there and, after he's done a certain amount of effort, he'll look at me as if to say, "Where's the kibble?" And I'll throw another kibble down, and he'll think, "There's the kibble!" He eats the kibble and he comes back upstairs.

Well, when you're a child, your parents sort of do that also. The reward is dependent upon your effort, not the outcome. As a child if you make a good effort, your parents say "Oh, okay, you didn't find the kibble, but here's the kibble." As an adult, it's not like that. You're working for an employer. When it doesn't work out, the employer doesn't say, "Well you know you were working really hard, here's a kibble." I mean some will, but you get other outcomes, and it only seems unfair from a child's point of view. The truth is, you are learning how to use energy, and some of the situations you're learning how to use energy in are really tough.

I love Roger Federer, who may be the greatest tennis player of all time, and for a while he was winning everything. Then Rafael Nadal came along and may not be the best tennis player of all time, but he surely was the best clay-court tennis player of all time, and he thwarted Federer. So after all this time Federer is playing in the Australian Open, and now Nadal is not only beating him on clay, but he's beating him at Wimbledon and in the Australian Open, and Federer cries. Well, that's part of the energy he's learning to deal with. He is a great champion and he's learning to deal with victory and he's learning to deal with defeat. He's learning to deal with getting older. That's a very rich life.

Sometimes you set up a life where it's all romantic comedies, but don't worry, people who do that are doing it because they've just finished a life or they're getting ready to set up a life where there's no romance. It's all wars and bombings of cities and concentration camps or whatever—we set up our lives the way we set them up; it's not our soul's fault. You chose this lifetime. You chose it together with your soul and you chose it together with your Atman, but in a way that's incomprehensible. You the personality that in some sense didn't even exist nevertheless chose this lifetime with your strengths, with your weaknesses, with your karma. And you may think you made an awful choice, but you'll be shocked. Each and every one of you will eventually come to validate each and every experience you ever had.

23

The Origin of Individuality

There *is* something new about the New Age. It is true that there are certain fundamental truths that have been known for thousands of years and those don't change. For instance, each of us is unified with All That Is. Our apparent individuality rides on what is called nondual awareness, that is always and already present. These and other eternal truths have always been true and aren't changing, and yet the human race is changing, and the form of our particular consciousness is changing.

What's new is that, as we move into the Aquarian Age, our relationship to form and consequently to All That Is is changing; we're developing new forms of awareness. We are moving into a new way of understanding consciousness—not a way of growing toward enlightenment, or getting everything that you want, or even conventional ideas of group consciousness. As we move into the Aquarian Age, we're going to understand in a radically different way how all consciousness expands in all directions.

Well, what difference does that make?

You can't really understand what is so sacred about your individual dual consciousness without understanding this larger experience. While that larger experience at this time cannot be the primary part of your waking consciousness, it nevertheless is a central part of the meaning of your life.

In this spiritual journey, one of the things that we explore is this looking at the world from outside the way we have earlier understood our humanity in conventional mystical terms.

Mystical approaches—the justifiably respected approaches of Hinduism and Buddhism—the very core of what they're struggling for is nondual awareness and the enlightenments that come with the cultivation of that. That's their singular priority.

Well over a decade ago when we were looking for a parking space, I said to my friend Lama Surya Das, "I'll ask my guide," and he asked, "Why would you use a spiritual resource like that for something as trivial as a parking space?" That question is obvious if you view this life as an obscuration to the real meal that is nondual awareness, but part of what we are learning to do is coordinate energy so that we can become, as Seth would say, conscious co-creators with God.

When you achieve nondual awareness, you see through the apparent sense of self and other; you see that it's an illusion. There's a lot to be said for that. It brings a level of openness to life as it is that's really incredibly joyful. But, from our perspective, something very important is lost. What is lost is the illusion. What is lost is the *basis* of co-creation.

When I tell this to sophisticated Hindu and Buddhist practitioners, they assume first, and maybe second and third, that I have no idea what I'm talking about. And that's a reasonable assumption because I'm disagreeing with a history that goes at least as far back as the Buddha. These people have well-earned and valid social capital.

Most Eastern practitioners usually assume that I just don't understand the basic concepts here, my argument simply misunderstands that the laws of the universe generate the "fact" that nondual awareness retains all the advantages of human dual consciousness minus only the suffering.

Some advanced Buddhists recognize that there's nothing in my argument that violates the Buddha or disagrees with subsequent Buddhist ontology or its understanding of interdependence and impermanence. I am talking about an interdependent, impermanent process, not a *thing*. I am saying that everyone eventually finds that nondual process. I am saying that you incarnate to light up certain storylines that were unavailable in nondual awareness. I am saying that it makes sense to dive in with a sure and certain promise that you will be able to wrap all the alienation of your dual consciousness into your already present nondual awareness in a way that your nondual self will treasure.

The self-reflective ego is part of our Etheric bodies. The nature of our perceptions—our eyes, ears, smell, taste, touch—can be used to set up a sense of separation. People who are achieving nondual awareness and what they call nonconceptual thought are literally changing their neurological structure, they're literally altering their Etheric selves. The Buddhist Heart Sutra literally says it: *No eyes, no ears, no nose, no tongue, no body, no mind, no color, no sound, no smell, no taste, no touch, no object of mind.* It's also sort of as if you went to a movie but you changed your perception so you no longer saw it as continuous event, but you saw each frame as being separate.

It's a very sophisticated process to transform the Etheric body so that the nature of your neurological perception changes and you no longer see your self-reflective ego. It's not nothing or even duck soup. I mean, it just gets shattered. You know who you are, but you no longer have that sense of separation that the rest of us have. Information goes through different parts of the brain. They call this nonconceptual thinking, and clairvoyantly you can see that it's quite different from the way the rest of our brains process information.

In all those situations you're trying to get rid of the obscurations of what is really the true nature of reality. Now I don't want to suggest that these great masters of the East and some of the West aren't making a big contribution to humanity, they're making a huge one. To become an ocean of compassion is a great gift to the Earth. And we have needed those people in the Piscean Age because we didn't have openness and were locked into a rigid point of view and humanity.

The normal story in the Piscean Age, and even before, is that humans would do better to become something other than really human. It was important in the overall human ecology that there be people that became enlightened because humanity needed bridges to the much larger universe even as most humans intentionally narrowed the focus.

Guides like Seth stepped away and didn't play a significant direct part in human consciousness.

People also can be very happy in a nondual state, and that can be their dharma. Some people might have a bunch of fruitful lives where they leave their bodies emotionally. They may even contribute to humanity but have no emotions.

There are many dharmas.

My guides discourage nondual mystical development while you are alive as a human being. They discourage the kind of dramatic neurological transformations that generate the permanent shattering of the self-reflective ego and the loss of that virtual reality of there is an inside of you and an outside of you—the development of what's called nondual awareness. While my guides discourage *that* level of nondual awareness, nevertheless when you get a peek at nondual awareness, it's very moving and helpful.

The reason that they discourage permanent nondual awareness is because they are looking at a much bigger category of experience than the Buddha and similar people. Buddhists intentionally restrict themselves in their vision to one's life as a human being and shortly thereafter in the bardo state. They don't seem to track long sweeps of growth after death that become so important for Seth with Multipersonhood.

The Buddha quite purposefully refused to answer questions about what happens after your death. He said, "I'm not paying attention to that. I'm showing you a way to free yourself from suffering while you are alive and human. And as far as I'm concerned what's after is not relevant. We're not going there."

Within the time frame that human beings have looked at, that's a very reasonable approach. That was, shall we say, the appropriate approach for mystics in the Piscean Age. Humans intentionally isolated themselves and developed a very human-centric point of view on what the universe was.

We even fought the Revolution in 1776 to establish a kind of new consciousness that had been building for centuries, a mode of individuality that didn't previously exist in this form.

Some scholars credit Augustine with inventing the personality, the individuality. In many ways, our contemporary individuality is a by-product of Christian theology. As the centuries passed, you went to either heaven or hell as an individual, so your individuality took on a significance that it had never had before. It may have arisen in a Christian context, but it reached its high point in modern culture.

Huge consciousnesses also set this up for profound reasons. They collaborated so that from one point of view each soul can have the experience of being human.

The kind of individuality we have now, where every moment has a polarity, is the appropriate adventure for humanity, but it is in itself an exception in the universe. We'll eventually use it to develop a *new* kind of group consciousness that retains the sort of individuality that we wouldn't have had without going through this process. Right now, the kind of individuality we have is intrinsically off-center; it's dynamically, intentionally, off-balance. It gets frightened at the thought of becoming part of larger structures. We will inhabit that individuality more gracefully as we move into pre-group and eventually group consciousness.

In the meantime, we've been through a Copernican revolution, a Darwinian revolution and all these changes and shifts on what it is to be human. Prior to about 1915—that's very rough—it was not at all clear that there were any stars beyond our galaxy. Sometimes in the nineteen hundreds, they proved that Andromeda was also its own galaxy and it was way far away, and of course that's the closest one.

The universe just keeps getting bigger, and now there's a chance that there are infinite universes.

But spiritually we still are sort of hooked into this human-centric point of view that paradoxically devalues our human experience because all you can see is the illusion of it. When you start to develop this much larger point of view, you realize that you have a center of consciousness as a human being but that is not your whole being.

The mystical story is that you incarnate until you get it; you incarnate because you *don't* get it. Once Seth and other guides returned, the story changed: you incarnate because one of the dimensions that consciousness explores is what is it like to be a human being now. As a human being, there's a certain kind of intrinsic ignorance that is built into your neurological system that keeps you from fully recognizing your safety and creativity. When you have pain, that isn't suffering to be avoided; it is part of a creative dance that, if you were more open, you would feel directly. It wouldn't be even a theoretical concern. It wouldn't be a lingering problem. It would be part of your awareness as if you were having a waking dream, a lucid dream. Recognizing yourself as you explored the creativity of the dream, you would be secure inside and outside of that dream.

Rather than incarnating because we are ignorant, we incarnate because the ignorance of that incarnation allows us to engage in creative exploration in the same way that we voluntarily, when we read a mystery story, suspend disbelief and throw ourselves into the story (or the movie) and experience the delight of not knowing. We could also just jump ahead and miss everything in between. There are some people— and occasionally I might be one of them—who will jump ahead to the end of the mystery story and find out who did it. But if you do that you cannot have the same experience that you have when you voluntarily assume the ignorance while you read the book. If it's a good mystery, you would have missed quite a lot.

This spiritual journey is centered in your everyday personal reality. Now there are other spiritual journeys that may be centered in everyday experience like Tantra and Zen, but I'm not aware of another spiritual journey that is centered in your everyday spiritual reality; both Jane and Lewis in their own way did that, and I think they may have been the first.

The human race intentionally set up this field of Illusion called Human Experience; we worked really hard at it; we weren't stupid. It wasn't the only way we could have gone; there are other versions of the human race that have gone in other directions.

So human beings intentionally set up this experience where we have a self-reflective ego. At least in this reality our spiritual journey is centered in our humanity and our dual awareness and even in our illusion in the same way that you might read a book or see a movie and get totally caught up in it for a while. Well, this is a movie that you get so caught up in that you lose track that it's a movie for a whole lifetime. And again, the human race worked very hard to cultivate that.

It does behoove you to realize that this is an illusion, but it's a very deeply meaningful illusion. Ultimately each and every personality—and this is what is really radical, not just the soul is eternal—each and every personality is eternal in multidimensional time and each and every personality is ultimately redeemed into a nondual awareness and into the ground of being, but taking a certain kind of thickness, emotional and spiritual thickness, richness, that are especially developed in our human experience. An angel has just as meaningful an existence, but it doesn't have the particular kind of thickness of a human one.

While we're centered in that long-term, I have the hope and expectation that we will explore aspects of our humanity that lie outside the personal or to some extent. I wonder just how healthy we can be when we're in our seventies and eighties and nineties. Eternal life is completely not the purpose of being human, but it would be nice to be healthy and limber until it's time to go. Using the techniques that we will increasingly learn and adding something that I don't think has ever been available before, which is an intense encounter with the personal, the emotional life can be thought of not as something to be transcended, but as something to be fully engaged and assimilated in its own terms and in the natural neurological environment of current human emotions. It seems to me that, if you're doing that, then it might be permissible to use some of these higher energies and lower energies to do really powerful healings.

Take someone like Ramakrishna in the nineteenth century, a very important spiritual teacher: when he had cancer his disciples begged him to heal himself. Now his answer was that I've tried and I work so hard to be—I'm paraphrasing—to transcend those things, why would I bring my energy back down and heal the body? I think that's a partial explanation, but I think it's also the case that there's something not right about healing the body from merely a transcendent level, because the illness has been generated by personal pain and until you can say hello to that personal pain and heal it at the level of personality or unless it's karmically set up to be healed from transcendence, I don't think is permissible

One of the slow things that I'm playing with—and I expect to be playing with it for the next ten to fifteen years or more—is in this new level, having access to the transcendent and the personal, just how healthy can we be. It behooves us to not tie happiness to even physical health. You come on this journey because you want to explore the journey not because you're frightened to death of illness and pain. What you resist you become, so part of this would be in developing that equanimity in the face of things that you don't like. I think it would be kind of an abomination if you developed perfect health out of fear of illness. Words are so slippery. Obviously, most of us will fear illness, but I'm talking about a huge resistance to it.

I think that would be a kind of abomination. You would generate a kind of karma, but if you're doing a little bit of fear but not a resisting fear and instead cultivating a playfulness, then who knows?

It may strongly seem to each of us in our subjective experience that we can do something that makes things worse in an absolute sense, but the evilest action that ever was created leaves more consciousness than there was before. That's why Seth says that evil is an illusion. Evil is real in manifestation, and people pay the price for committing evil—it's not in their own self-interest in the long term—but the evilest thing you can do cannot make less sacredness. It can make less of a clear, easy connection to sacredness and manifestation; but since all experience makes more sacredness, not even evil actions can make less sacredness. Maybe you could say that good action creates more sacredness than bad action, but all action creates sacredness.

When I say that all life expands in all directions sacredly, I'm saying that you can certainly do things that make things worse from a narrow perspective, and that's significant and important, and it's a really, really bad idea to make things worse. But in an absolute sense you *cannot* make things worse. Everything you do adds, and it doesn't add in some sort of abstract theoretical sense, but when you perceive the sacredness of it, you immediately understand the yes to everything.

I had some very bright Buddhist tell me about a friend of his who said that all life is "a meaning-saturated field of existence" and that's exactly what Seth would say. But I just don't see how someone who is saying that it's important for you to break this trance that you're in can truly accept that your life as a human being is a meaning-saturated event. *Every* moment, wise or benighted, is *saturated* with meaning.

People have these near-death experiences during which they often experience the rightness of everything even if particular events seemed horrible. It's not a rightness that cancels out the horribleness of something, but it's a rightness that redeems it.

When you begin to get more of a sense that you are your soul right now, that your soul is you right now and yet you're meaningfully different, there's a kind of value and a kind of sacredness that I don't think was part of mysticism prior to Seth. I don't want to exaggerate that. Again, people have had near-death experience and they've never heard of Seth. The fullness of that experience becomes, "Aha, of course, now I see."

I can promise you that sooner or later each of us will have that "aha" for every single bit of experience we've ever had.

Here's a smaller instance. When I was in high school, I was in a choir and we were singing this Bach chorale. We practiced it for a month and a half. We only heard the vocal parts. I think it may have been "Jesu Joy of Man's Desiring." We got so tired of that music; it seemed so stupid and so repetitive and so boring, but it was going to go into our concert. The week before, we heard it with the instrumental accompaniments; now we heard and understood how beautiful the full piece was, we had been aware of just a part of the whole. We understood, that's why people have been so moved by "Jesu Joy of Man's Desiring" for three hundred years.

It is by engaging all of life, including the horrible tensions, that a you that never existed before is created. That you will eventually itself find a kind of fullness in nondual awareness and a divine playfulness.

When you focus on the things that come up, many of them seem like just a bother, at least as bad as a bother. Sometimes being human can be profoundly difficult and horrible, and sometimes it can be just so wonderful. I mean I can sit here right now and look at flowers and the sky, and it's just mind-boggling. This is such an incredibly beautiful world. Now it doesn't blot out the hardship and the pain, but the hardship and the pain are part of the same wonderfulness. You don't have to go to the Grand Canyon or to some mountains or to the beach for it to be beautiful. You can go to someplace that's ugly and, if you really look at it, it's probably beautiful. I mean this whole planet is incredibly beautiful. It's often difficult too, so it's kind of hard to notice it.

This is what our work is about: learning how to commit to your waking existence as a human being without over-deluding yourself that this is real.

24

Multipersonhood

All consciousness expands in all directions. Mystics have said that for generations, but I don't think they meant it the way Seth meant it. He started putting out that there is Multi-Self: Multipersonhood. Seth didn't experience *him*self as just one story line.

This is important, and I hope people get a sense of it more and more. Your individuality, not even dual awareness *per se,* could not exist in the way that it does without your being part of innumerable consciousnesses that are not centered in your human personality, but nevertheless help make the personality what it is.

So, it is important to spend some time looking at these other ways of engaging the world.

One of the things that we'll probably do—I never know exactly what we'll do in these classes—but one of the things that we'll probably do in this class is explore animal consciousness. Take your pet, for example: How are you, in a sense, part of them and how are they part of you? Not in the trivial sense of everything is part of everything, but in a more specific sense of how the consciousness of my cat Tesh is as big a consciousness as any other consciousness. When you start to look at and explore that consciousness in a non-human centric way without the ideology of evolution or the rush toward enlightenment, you start to see that something unique grows out of what I find special about him, and that goes for all animals, not just my beloved cat.

Spiritual journeys—mystical spiritual journeys, even the most tantric esoteric spiritual journeys—really have had, as far as I can tell, this sense that your primary business is to evolve beyond this narrow focus of being a human being, at least until Jane and Lewis. Those older spiritual journeys taught you how to break that spell that you're in as a human being where there seems to be such a dramatic difference between what's inside and what's outside of you by becoming enlightened. And it's a profound and wonderful journey. And it was *the* way at least since the Buddha.

Prior to Seth I can't find any spiritual approach that fully embraces our humanity in its own terms and for its own purposes.

But we're changing now. Seth's teachings, in subtle ways, refocused the ancient wisdom toward a multiperspectival, multidimensional awareness that is not Unity, nor the nondual awareness that has been cultivated until now, but something that he began to refer to in the later books as Multipersonhood.

The nondual approach, in the hands of certain practitioners such as Tibetan tantrics and Zen practitioners, is also very engaged in everyday life, and that does, in a sense, eradicate suffering. It has been a key spiritual journey since the time of the Buddha. But as we move out of a linear understanding of time, as we move out of our artificial isolation from beings who are much bigger than us in terms of interdependence and Multipersonhood, nondual awareness has serious drawbacks.

As someone with nondual awareness you can engage everyday life fully and joyously, but you cannot do it in its own terms and for its own purpose. In other words, to generate nondual awareness it is necessary to turn off certain parts of the brain—the story-making parts. Those stories are what generate human activity in the Astral plane. And the Astral plane is our ecological niche.

Each human personality is always and already a vital part of many Multipersonhoods, but it is not possible to perceive your own Multipersonhood directly in a human body at this time. Human Multipersonhood will only become directly knowable in a human body as group consciousness emerges in the Aquarian Age between three and five hundred years from now. Over the coming decades and centuries neurological changes to the human body will allow each of us to track simultaneously and separately our individual personality and other interdependent gestalts, and this will lead to group consciousness. Even though we cannot now know our Multipersonhood while embodied, each of our personalities, with further training after death, will know ourselves to be both nondual and multiply centered gestalts that are simultaneously conscious in multiple perspectives.

Around 2060 presumably, some folks will be moving on into a more Aquarian consciousness. It will integrate a deep engagement with the Astral with nondual awareness in a group consciousness that has a profound individuality relating to and engaging in group consciousness.

Humans will be able to be consciously nondual in their group consciousness even as they continue to be dual in their individual consciousness, or something like that. I can't possibly understand it, and the actual path of humans hasn't fully been decided. That new human development will allow humans to follow their individuality as a Multipersonhood and each of them to directly experience himself or herself as not just an individualized self, which will continue to exist, but a direct awareness of self as a group, every bit as palpable as an awareness of self as an individual. They will be able to follow both simultaneously.

I don't claim to know exactly what the world is going to be like then, but I begin to see what a precursor to a new kind of consciousness looks like. Just to experience the sheer gracefulness of this consciousness that's larger than a star while being intimately involved in the act of sipping your tea.

Though that larger and varied consciousness is not going to happen in our lifetimes, some of us just might begin to experience how thoughts are shared and this will allow us to appreciate how meanings are created. Meanings are not just created inside of your head. Meanings are always created in relationship. As we move into awareness of the Mental-Causal plane, you will perceive that more directly.

We are increasing our flexibility. Hopefully, if we do it the right way, we're increasing our kindness and generosity. We're changing ourselves profoundly. It isn't that we're so much changing from one thing to another as adding neurological possibilities. And that's another difference between Sethian Multipersonhood and a nondual approach. The nondual approach changes the neurological status without adding neurological possibilities.

Life in an ego is more difficult than it needs to be. It's rich and it's wonderful, and it's the center of waking human experience, but it is often damn hard. But, if you merely get a sense of your greater self as *transcending* your ego—your singleness, your individuality, your personality—then you lose some of the exquisite focus as an individual particular personality and the spacious generosity of life.

Our work will always be engaged in a conversation between our unique individuality and a commitment to a particular form in a particular time in a particular culture, and the true safety, security, and meaning of that life in the larger context. Our work is for you to become more comfortable with the idea that you can be a thunderstorm and a banker without losing yourself, without losing either, and for you to bring more to both. And at least for some time that won't be necessarily so much a function of consciously experiencing it as it will be a function of *unconsciously* experiencing it and being open to what this can mean. That's a challenge: contacting and working with unconscious meanings without being able to know them. But that's the basis of these classes.

It isn't that group consciousness doesn't yet exist. It isn't just waiting for the Aquarian Age. Group consciousness is everywhere. We have parts of ourselves that are busy doing other stuff all the time. That's easiest to see in the dream state where your conscious mind travels. Every night each of us takes a part in group consciousness. Parts of us just go off and join other consciousnesses. You're already, in deep parts of the dream state, in nondual awareness. Then if your conscious mind joins that part of you, it will bring your dual awareness to it.

No human can experience Multipersonhood with any sort of vividness at this point. We just don't have the Etheric or nervous system flexibility. But that is probably what we're moving toward as we enter the Aquarian Age. Flexibility is required as an entry into group consciousness in our waking life. Group consciousness cannot currently manifest in physicality because humans simply do not have a neurological range to participate in such a state of consciousness and still be engaged in our humanity. That's what we're developing. And to do that we need to clear personal and group pain out of our bodies so that they will be able to develop the kind of flexibility necessary for conscious group awareness as physical beings.

What Lewis Bostwick understood, and Jane didn't, is that you don't clear the pain out without specific contextualization. In everyday life you encounter your pain in a context where it can be engaged. That doesn't mean to get obsessed about pain. That can be just as much a dead-end as anything else. The objective is to engage everyday life fully but not obsessively.

One way of understanding Multipersonhood is in terms of an inversion of two of Buddhism's profound recognitions that are usually referred to as interdependent origination, or interdependence, and impermanence. Buddhists teach that there are no objective independent essences. Every phenomenon arises interdependently; that is, ultimately, despite appearances, you can never completely separate any one identity from other identities. Nothing can exist all by itself. Buddhists also teach that all phenomena change and shift. They use their understanding of interdependent origination and impermanence to facilitate attaining nondual awareness.

Seth doesn't actually use those terms. However, through the years he spoke to and pointed to a different way of embracing impermanence and interdependence. For Seth, while no self has objective independent existence,* there are infinite numbers and kinds of consciousness with subjective and necessarily fuzzy boundaries. He calls these "gestalts." The power of the concept of the gestalt is that it's fuzzy. That allows you to deal with subjectivity. The fuzziness is such that I can be a gestalt even though some of the components of my gestalt are the Earth and the Moon, my cats, and my wife, and you folks, and my past lives and future lives, and the soul, and the Monad. And I would have no existence as John without all these things.

Though we experience ourselves like billiard-ball people bumping into other billiard balls, there is no you that you can draw a line around like the cops do if someone has been shot and is lying on the concrete.

When you try to draw a bright line around John and say, "This is John and that's the Earth," or if you say, "This is John and that's Kathy," your analysis would be insufficient. You can't draw a bright line around John. But you can draw a fuzzy line around him.

In a similar way, words don't have a meaning that you can draw a bright line around.

Wittgenstein noticed that words have no fixed meaning or use but arise in practice as people use language, so the human individual has no fixed meaning or identity but emerges and grows out of a conversation between and among numerous gestalts.

You can't self-define any word in a language. The meaning of any word is dependent upon other words you're saying with it and the context of those words and the long history of those words, their etymology. You can never draw a circle around a particular word and say that this is what it objectively means. There's no such thing. Every word arises from all sorts of experiences that you've had, that other people have had, from well before you were born as well as from the present context, and even novel meanings often arise from familiar words. The meaning of a word is in the use of the word as people who understand

_____

*This is because all phenomena arise in mutual dependence in and on everything else.

that language put it in context. And yet words do have meaning, have meaningful self-existence, *subjectively*.

It's a nice way to think about what it means to be Tom. Tom is a personality game. It's a form of life. It's a set of conventions that we arranged on this planet at this time, where you have cool things like gravity, you have night and day—and you have apparently individual selves. This is only a form of life and that form is intrinsically creative and it contributes to All That Is in a way that no other types of beings can. Other beings contribute in their own way.

Human existence is fuzzy and subjective. It is in conversation with the Atman or original spark, with the soul as that concept is understood in theosophy, as well as with plants, animals, Mother Earth, the Sun, and most of all, with other humans. Each of these gestalts takes part in and gives rise to an individual human gestalt. All of these constituent gestalts themselves arise interdependently, but each single gestalt—you, the Earth, your soul, and so on, interdependent though it is—is nevertheless sacred and meaningful in its own terms and for its own self, though always and also for others and always in conversation with everything that is. Selfhood and interdependence are *themselves* interdependent. A paradox: you'll be able to recognize your self better when you start to recognize that there are all kinds of other things that are just as much you as this you.

You arise out of everything else and everything else arises out of you. Everything interpenetrates. In a sense you *would* actually be dead if you could really draw a line around yourself, but you don't exist like that.

Multipersonhood allows the cherishing of everyday dualistic experience in its own terms for its own purposes. When one takes a more Sethian attitude, relishing the impermanence and interdependence of all phenomena, one gets a clue to a different kind of arrangement in which Buddhist interdependence might point *to* Multipersonhood.

From the Sethian analysis, it is the changing of the self that makes it eternal both inside and outside of time. Inside of time, that changing does inevitably bring suffering. But every single person, good, bad, horrible, eventually achieves nondual awareness that is permanent. And here words break down; it might make sense to talk about something being permanent in time, but it hardly makes sense to talk about something outside of time, but it's the best I can do. Sorry.

In the system I teach, we don't have any well-defined goals as a place to arrive in the sense that you can say, "I've arrived." Seth taught that all life expands in all directions. There is no portion of the universe, meaning even All That Is, that is done expanding in all directions. There's no endpoint in this system. If even Seth or Babaji are continuing to grow in all directions, then we can too, though entities such as Seth are outside of time and hence outside our concept of expansion.

In many of Seth's classes and in the later books especially, if you track the energy, there's a graciousness, a gracious acceptance and embrace of life in its own terms. I have found that nowhere else. And I feel like the near forty years now since I first experienced it, that it's starting to come into my bones.

The real meaning of probability is not that this is a tricky way to do a healing of something I couldn't do otherwise, though it may be; the real meaning of probabilities when you understand it, like the real meaning of all life expanding in all directions, is the utter sacredness of every moment in a way that is palpably different from the sacredness of every moment that you so often encounter looking down the one track of reality toward a nondual horizon and vanishing point.

Now some people who are deeply engaging the utter sacredness of every moment unconsciously are doing it in the way of all life expanding in all directions, even if they are looking down the one track of linear time. But if you understand all life expanding in all directions, you will begin to understand more deeply the sacredness of every moment— every moment that is less enlightened just like every moment that is more enlightened. Neither moment is more or less enlightened if there is no track of reality toward some apotheosis.

Why is this important? It's really important and it's also really hard. It's really hard because what you would call modern societies have spent hundreds of years narrowing your neurological flexibility—making the track. One of the ways we do that is with clock time, like wristwatch time. We measure time so precisely that it only marches in one direction. And we use it as a commodity—time is money. These have bound up our neurological system, and most of what each of us do is really tied into time.

We can quite easily reach the level of our soul or Atman or many other nondual consciousnesses in meditation. Contacting them brings a rich and productive benefit to engaging everyday life. Contacting higher consciousnesses will only bring permanent nondual awareness if that contact reorganizes our physical neurological system.

Now one of the things Seth tried to teach was psychological time. In psychological time something that happened to you forty years ago may be part of or cause what happens five minutes from now. You might say, "So what?" But in all things expanding in all directions, it will work the other way also. What's about to happen five minutes from now can change what happened to you forty years ago.

If you treat *this* as the explanation of *that,* you will limit its effect. One small aspect of that is that you're constantly reinterpreting the past, and those reinterpretations have profound effects on your biology. Let's say that someone had some experience that was utterly traumatic for them at age thirteen, and that festered in their aura and their hormonal system and it's about to cause cancer. And they have an experience that causes them to reappraise their initial reaction to it. It changes their biology. Now you might think that's really not changing the past, but when you understand time, it *really* does change the past, not just changes the past *now* but changes the past *then.*

That's a sense of what all life expanding in all directions means.

Now the Buddhists powerfully deconstruct our making ourselves objective creatures, our sense that I'm John and this is Judy and that's Ed. Those seem to be objective designations, but I'm only John as you know me, and each person here knows me differently and my cat knows me differently. And those are, in important ways, different beings.

Furthermore, John couldn't exist, John's soul couldn't exist, without the unity mode of the Monad. John couldn't exist without the Earth. I don't actually have an existence as John without some interpenetration with the Earth. This body wouldn't exist if there weren't Earth energy in this body, so part of John is the Earth—and *vice versa*.

None of us could exist without our hooking into the Buddhic plane. Our emotions couldn't exist without the Buddhic level and its interdependent origination or interdependence. It doesn't hurt to repeat, "Nothing exists by itself."

Buddhists don't even believe that the soul, or the Atman, exists. It isn't that they don't hit those energies, it is that they point out that they are not objectively separate, they have no separate essences. The concept of nothingness is nicely explained by separating the two parts of the word, no and things. It's not that nothingness is some kind of nonexistence; it's no things and no thing arises independently. Everything arises interdependently and no thing is permanent.

Jane also addresses this with what she called her aspect psychology where nothing is just itself, even Seth. It was in some way meaningful to say that Seth was a future incarnation of Jane, but it was also meaningful to say that Seth was a future incarnation of Rob—I don't think they ever said that; I don't think that they could have handled that concept, but it perfectly matched the system. Though Seth was a future incarnation of Jane, in a meaningful way when Jane gets into that future, she will be herself, she'll be her own Seth and not the one who talked to us. This was more or less what Seth kept pointing out—and it doesn't fit within Western logic. In Western logic something either is or isn't.

Ultimately, though, there is no way to understand it intellectually.

Because of Seth's flip, impermanence subverts your objective existence, but it supports your eternal subjective existence. So, the gestalt that you think of as you will eternally expand in all directions.

In multi-consciousness, the center of your focus as a waking human being is in what I call, evoking the terminology from Alice Bailey, the personality. The personality is the way you tie together your experience and name yourself. It primarily involves your physical sensations, your emotions, and your intellect and how you pull all that together with a story. That's your personality.

There are various other layers of you that are, even while you're awake and busy with your personality, engaging that same personality. You are also your dreaming self, and it doesn't stop when you wake up, but your this-lifetime personality is less directed toward it then.

You are meaningfully self-organizing, and that meaningful self-organizing is a subjective reality. If it were objective, it would just collapse it, it *would* die. But because you are a subjective reality, you can expand infinitely in all directions, and because of that you are eternal, no matter what form you're in.

When you start to follow this, you see that every personality, even someone atrocious, eventually attains nondual awareness, enriched by its humanity, its humanity in duality. If someone's really evil and does torture and murder like Hitler or the jihadists of the Islamic State in Iraq and Syria, it might take them twenty million years and they might be on another planet before they've worked through all of their stuff, but everyone works through their stuff and attains nondual awareness.

In this way Seth has turned impermanence on its head. Impermanence is what generates growth in all directions. In generating growth in all directions, subjectivity is always changing, but it's eternal because it's always growing. If you track it in only one direction, that subjectivity is obliterated, but if you track it in every direction, it's eternal, always growing and ever more sublime.

Since every personality, every subjectivity grows in all directions, no subjectivity is ever lost.

A cat's subjectivity is never lost even though it dies and merges into the deva that structures, supports, and oversees its group consciousness, but that cat subjectivity is much more playfully engaged, so it's not that big a deal for the cat when it dies. For humans, whose subjectivity is more important to them, death is a very big deal, but its *being* a big deal serves functions too.

You know, cats don't bring stories in the way that we do, as interpretations to the universe. They bring something else. Likewise, bigger consciousnesses than us bring something so dramatically larger that you can't really call them stories like us and that's cool too.

In our approach we don't stop trying to tell ourselves stories. If anything, we try to proliferate stories and more and more stories, more skillful and more playful fun stories. That's part of the meaning that humans bring to the planet—our capacity to tell ourselves stories. Even the pretty miserable stories we tell ourselves are part of the meaning.

To quote Walt Whitman, everyone's life is a verse to a powerful play, and every one of those verses, no matter how ridiculous or cool or sublime, whether you're Nelson Mandela or Donald Trump,* adds to the whole, and you the individual get to keep and work on your own verse. And everyone, not just humans but everyone in every dimension, is enhanced by every one of the verses.

I like to think that humans have a particular way of writing their verses because, if you're not nondual, we have this gap between our experience and our interpretation of the experience. In that gap we put a little wobble, a little idiosyncrasy—our own idiosyncratic twist. In *Beowulf*, the medieval poem about a battle between a human tribe and a beast, characters talk about telling their tales in mead halls. I have this image of humans going around the universe, stepping up to whatever kind of beer hall there is, perhaps in the Monadic plane like the bar on Tatooine in *Star Wars* with all those creatures from many worlds, and saying, "I have a story for you!" And that's a kind of story that no one other than human beings can tell, braggadocio stories, stories about the dragons they were killing.

And people gather round, saying, "Wow what an amazing story you human beings have, full of horrors and wonders!"

Stories in the human journey are the way we make meaning. There are other ways of making meaning, but what's peculiar about humans in this part of human evolution is that we're specialists in stories and we enter duality to specialize in stories.

If you begin to understand it that way, you wouldn't wish that no one was ignorant because if there were no ignorance, there could be no

---

*This was said long before he entered the presidential race. I have used him as an example of a nasty, self-aggrandizing person since the late seventies.

creativity particular to humans. You may not like the particular form that person's ignorance takes, but I do not think if you understood it that you would will it away.

People say there's nothing new about the New Age, that these are ancient techniques and they've been around forever, and the fundamental reality is that reality is nondual. Now that is true, there's nothing new about that. Fundamental reality is nondual; it doesn't even make sense to say, "It always has been," because everything is always and already in some ways existent. But what is new, Seth is constantly asserting, is that even though everything always and already exists, every moment is utterly new and changeable and spontaneously creative.

For example, he talks about how all time is simultaneous, so in one sense you can know what's going to happen a hundred years down the road; but—and I think more importantly—you don't know until you actually get there because it can spontaneously change. Now that is illogical; understand that it does not fit within any sort of logical system because time itself is unimaginable. Because of our bodies, we experience time in a sort of linear way, but that's not the way time actually works.

It's fine if you don't understand it. If you *think* you understand it, you can be sure you *don't* understand it. Because it's not understandable. But you can get something evocative that's important. The fact that beings like Seth are now coming into our reality somehow allows us to re-center spirituality in the moment, and people will say, wow, that's a fundamental part of nondual awareness.

Start with the notion that everything happens at once. People often say, "Well, that means that I can know exactly what will happen in the future." If everything is happening at once, if you stand outside that system, how *wouldn't* you be able to know exactly what happened in the future and exactly what happened in the past? But you don't. Much like the uncertainty principle in physics, if you dip into that system to see what happens to you ten years in the future, only then will you know what *actually* happened. Then if you go out of the system and dip back into the same space, you may or may not get the same experience. *All consciousness expands in all directions,* so the future is constantly expanding in all directions. At this very moment it is expanding in all directions. So you can never step into the same moment twice, because it has expanded. If time is merely an energy, I don't have to know what it means to know that it expands in all directions and that makes every moment creative.

All consciousness expands in all directions, but if everything already is, and time is just an energy, then how can All That Is become more and what does that even mean? The answer is, yes it can become more, and there's no way to explain how and why it becomes more. I have no idea what it means, but it's vitally important because it makes every moment and every center, which is everything, utterly sacred. You are generating newness at each moment that expands in all directions. This is not just in three dimensions but all directions. So everything you do is something new to the Earth, it's something new to the Sun, it's something new to your soul, it's something new to you, something new to your friend down the street, something new to your dog or cat—and it's new in all those directions and they respond back.

If you circle back and re-experience this time, you create new newness, more newness. When you think of the future, you create new newness in that future. When you get to that future, you create more new newness. Seth really stressed—I never really realized how much he was stressing it because it's really a radical concept—that Jane could be Seth, a past incarnation of Seth, and Seth a future incarnation of Jane, while Seth is not merely Jane's future and Jane is not merely Seth's past. Each is utterly the center of an ever-expanding world. When Seth talks to Jane, Jane is new even though she's his past. In the moment he's talking to her, newness is being born, but how could newness be born out of his past?

Getting that is what makes everything sacred.

I don't find the idea inspiring that we're all here to somehow become enlightened beings or gain nondual awareness—I don't find that inspiring at all quite frankly—because it means that everything is an illusion, except after you become enlightened, so everything as it falls away is sort of thrown into the dustbin of time. But Seth doesn't throw *any-thing* away, even evil doesn't get thrown away. *Every*thing is sacred, which is not to say that you can't do evil things—and it is a really, really, really bad idea to do evil things—but that doesn't keep them from being sacred.

It just makes chills go to down my back when I really begin to get a sense of the idea that all life expands in all directions. The stupidest, meanest thing you ever did, even it expands in all directions, sacredly so.

Sooner or later each of you will begin to understand that your existence is a collaboration of consciousnesses, that you could not exist as a physical body without nature spirits. If you check in on yourself, many of you will find that nature spirits were involved in that experience where you brought the Atmic energy down into the Astral story, then back up into the Causal where your individual soul resides, and finally back down into the Etheric. You create this triangle that manifests into the Etheric. It can only do that because there are collaborating nature spirits.

By the way, the nature spirits *are* extraterrestrials; they exist simultaneously on other planets. They're a kind of weaving of the solar system and beyond.

There is a whole separate range of consciousness, a chain of evolution right here on Earth that is not physical, called the Angelic Realm. It is about the same consciousness as humans but does not suffer. Its beings are called devas, though in Western occultism they're called angels. Elementals and devas don't have the kinds of concerns that humans have. They just naturally flow toward whatever their next step is without any obstructions. They help create all physical forms and events.

Mother Earth experiences these beings at roughly the same evolutionary level that we are, but without a self-reflective ego. Their awareness never was and never will be dualistic the way a human's is.

Actually, Wim Wenders's movie *City of Angels* with Nicolas Cage and Meg Ryan is a pretty good representation of that angelic experience. Those beings in that chain of evolution naturally and spontaneously go toward the good the way a plant heads toward the sun.

It's really cool to think how interdependent we are. Elementals are very small beings, for the most part, and they just hold a form, and there's really close to zero judgment. Nature spirits are all around, and we couldn't have plants without nature spirits. I suppose you could call huge devas like Pelee a nature spirit if you want to, but we don't normally call Pelee a nature spirit, we call her a deva, or a goddess, so it's a matter of degree.

Nature spirits are happy all the time with this kind of giggly, bubbly enthusiasm. It's hard to describe how simultaneously collaborative and neutral a deva is, how well-intended, and really open to life as it is. Oceans of love like Amma are great, but a deva is just like, "Okay, you're here. Maybe I'll bring some other devas in."

We couldn't even have a form without these neutral, kind, playful beings. I imagine they get a lot out of interacting with us. I don't know what it is, but I imagine they do.

Nature spirits, elementals, devas, fairies, goblins, all these sorts of things are their own stream of evolution. What we can see physically—all the animals and humans—is another stream of evolution. Angels are a different evolutionary line and sometimes, in fact, can and do decide that they would like to become humans. So they voluntarily give up being in a permanently ecstatic experience range to suffer, to have just the kind of experience that humans have.

There are a few humans who get so upset with suffering they go the other way, but a lot more devas who move into being humans than humans who go into being devas because in the long term, every one of us gets to a place where it all makes sense, suffering included. Devas can want contrast too, and they don't get it in their line, so they decide to become human. Not worse or better, just different in the infinite variety of creation.

Angels in a sense go naturally to the good as a plant goes to the sun. That's just as meaningful as human experience, but it's a different game than human experience. Humans choose. Once you have the potential to choose, it can't actually be a choice unless it can also go wrong. But even when it goes wrong, it always generates more than there was before.

The ability of all consciousness to expand in all directions requires a sea of potentiality.

The body is programmed to care a whole lot about the survival of that physical body. There is an illusion there, though, that is really important as you lose loved ones, beloved pets, or your physicality as an alive human being. Just because the body is jerking around or even going into pain doesn't mean that the body has emotion going on there. When you see an animal's body writhing in pain, it's inevitable that you will put your own experience on top of that and that you will start to interpret nature as being, at best, uncaring. But what you see as that body writhing in pain is not what that animal is experiencing. That animal is experiencing the glory of this great cosmic dance, and the body consciousness itself luxuriates in the struggle, luxuriates in the sensation. Part of the dance, part of the drama *is* that body consciousness's move toward survival. But there is a part of that animal that simply and gracefully changes affiliation. Your pets will often leave the body long before they experience pain. And very often with people you love, the most important part of them will have left the body long before. They may seem to be going through a lot of emotion. That's not emotion. That's thoughtforms manifesting through the body. But they themselves are long gone. If you understand that, you will be more skillful in interacting in those situations. If you're interacting with someone who's passing over, if you can learn to say hello to those parts of them that have already passed, you and they will have a much easier time.

With dementia, that passing over can take ten years. And it has its own beauty. Our culture is so afraid of death that we've vilified this in-between state of dementia. If we were much more conscious, people might stretch out death, but do it much more consciously. They would know the body's still working through its karma, but I'm pretty much done, or I'm going back and forth. I'm doing stuff here. I'm doing stuff there. I'm starting to see probable realities. There's a mismatch between what the body is doing and what the person understands and recognizes.

In Eastern spirituality and in Western science we talk about evolution as if everything in the universe is trying to become as evolved as human beings. Human beings are this marvelous development and focus, but cats and dogs and trees are not waiting to become human beings. Their consciousness expands in all directions and is every bit as rich and diverse. It's just not located in the narrow category and range that human beings are.

A tree doesn't think of itself as a tree. It's an interdependent symphony. Every aspect of its experience is specific in the way it is for a tree. It isn't specific for a human being. If you think that tree out there is relating to you as if it were some sort of junior person, it isn't. We have the category of *a* tree; *it* doesn't have that category. It's closer to the weather. And yet if you talk to the trees, they do listen to you, and their response can be very personal. It's not the wood responding to you. It's a larger sense of its Multipersonhood. It experiences itself not in the narrow focus that human beings developed eons ago as their particular focus of life.

I can do a little shift to see that joy and it may be that, when I'm feeling the joy of a tree, I'm feeling it at a Buddhic level.

A tree can't read a book, but trees aren't waiting till they can become human and can read a book; they're living as a tree and doing all kinds of cool stuff. The tree's consciousness is sufficiently fluid that it can see itself as a tree and see itself as a deva. It's our category that separates that, and it's an interesting separation, but the degree to which we make that separate is peculiar to human beings.

When we think of evolution, we under-represent the real richness of all consciousness. A rock has its own rich consciousness. It's not better than a human's or worse than a human's, but it's incomprehensibly larger than a human can imagine, even a human that imagines it has a consciousness.

We have no idea of a consciousness of a leaf. We only think in this one direction. I'm not setting the consciousness of a leaf over against ours, but the consciousness of a leaf expands in all directions. The little nature spirits that are tending to that tree are part of the leaf's consciousness and *vice versa*.

You might wonder what's in it for the nature spirit. A whole lot! It's not a consciousness based upon difference and exclusion the way human consciousness is. Humans develop myths that place themselves at the top of creation—the crown of creation. As Seth says, we think of ourselves as top dog, so we limit our experience of our own psyche.

Again, life in any form is not some great cosmic mistake. It's not some horrible thing that humans bungled into. Our current human focus is divinely rich and meaningful for its own sake, and it is preparation for something much bigger, for Multipersonhood. We limit our human awareness for a particularly intense focus that both serves its own purpose and also serves, long term, the human race's purposes.

Likewise, the idea that humans ought to be enlightened is a category error that arises from limiting your time perspective and not seeing that every single human being, no matter how evil or wise and saintly, eventually finds that place in the Monadic plane where they become what I identify as the Hindu Atman, though with Sethian aspects. It might take someone millions of years and many incarnations in different forms on different planets and in different dimensions and probabilities, but everyone gets there.

We're going to understand in a radically different way how all life expands in all directions sacredly and every consciousness arises from all directions. You can't really understand what is sacred about your individual dual consciousness without understanding this larger experience that, though it cannot be the primary part of your waking consciousness at this time, is nevertheless a central part of the meaning of your life.

In a universe where consciousness expands in all directions, contradiction is an intrinsic part of expansion. So, the best that you can ever have is an answer in current time. Your answer is your next breath. And by implication it is only good for *that* next breath. And it isn't really an answer in the sense that we have all been trained to think of answers. There is no such answer in that sense.

Those people who are working to evolve in the mystical traditions and otherwise might say, "Well, we recognize the sacredness of every moment." And they recognize it in large part because it's an opportunity to evolve, rather than recognize it as sacred in terms of ordinary dualistic consciousness.

Now you may experience your life expanding with your children, or with the people you work with, but you don't necessarily see how those things expand continually in all directions. They expand in so many ways you don't imagine, for instance into the lives of nature spirits.

I used the ideal that all life expands in all directions once in a discussion with a Buddhist scholar, and she said, "I completely agree with that."

She doesn't agree with it at all. She's seeing life expanding down this one linear train track called the road to enlightenment. But all life expands in *all* directions. Everything you do expands in an infinite number of directions.

Not only that, but each piece of life *arises from* all directions. The Buddhists treat interdependent origination as undermining the objective reality of any sense of separate essences, which is objectively true, but the Sethian take on it is delight, not you have a problem or you need to develop nondual awareness to match and, in a sense, neutralize the danger of interdependence.

You arise from all directions; you expand into all directions. You are interdependent but your subjectivity is eternal. This is really important, so I will keep coming back to it. *You are interdependent, but your subjectivity is eternal.*

It's like in chaos theory you have these calculations, and they all attract around a data point or two. They're called strange attractors, but you can't ever draw a line and say, "This is where everything is going to fall," because something's always going to fall outside it.

It's subjectively true that there is no separate personality, there is no separate soul. So when the Buddhists talk of Anatman , they are saying there's no such thing as a separate soul; but what Anatman means is the interdependence of all things transcends and engulfs the very nature of the soul. Therefore, it cannot exist as objectively separate. But that doesn't mean there's no such thing as a soul, there's just no such thing *objectively* as an *objectively separate* soul. The soul is a real gestalt with no hard boundaries, it is itself made up of multitudes.

When Buddhists say that the soul is dual, they mean your *experience* of the soul is dual because you're still dual, and you're identifying yourself as the soul. But that's not sufficiently glorying in the interdependence of all things. Soul is its own consciousness and completely nondual in a way far beyond what any human being at any awakened level can be, regardless of how enlightened he or she is.

In some ways I think Multipersonhood is a hard concept to understand, but you know, it's an important one. Again, I don't think it's very easy to be happy without a sense of your Multipersonhood or multiple layers or multiple aspects. So again, older mysticism was focused on removing the obscurations to pure consciousness, and in some sense that's an eternal process. In Multipersonhood, it still behooves you to get over your illusions when they are painful, but we don't aim to get over the whole category of illusions of separateness. Your play or dance in those illusions is utterly idiosyncratic and adds something new to the universe.

I think there are a lot of sophisticated Buddhists and Hindus who would argue and say that their concepts—and I'm not going to try to explain them, what's called thusness or suchness—are equivalent to what I'm calling your idiosyncratic creativity. I suppose in some sense maybe they are equivalent, but I think there's a profound subjective sense in which they are not equivalent, even if in no other way the brain chemistry of enlightened consciousness makes the divine idiosyncratic stories of duality impossible to fully engage. There is something that goes on when you have a self-reflective ego in the brain that adds thickness and texture to your experience within duality itself, within the natural ecology of human awareness in this century.

Central to most of our experience in life is our experience of our individuality in its seeming isolation from the external world. Understanding the interdependence of our individuality and the group consciousnesses we are a part of is tricky. It may take years of experience and exploration to understand it maturely. We don't notice that the existence of our individuality is impossible without interactions within and among innumerable other consciousnesses such as your soul, the Earth and Sun, groups of humans, plants, animals, and so on. You cannot understand or appreciate your life fully without being open to how these larger consciousnesses are a part of your individuality.

Perhaps you already know your mood is affected by the ionization of the air you breathe, even though humans do not directly sense the air's ionization. In the same way we do not notice the psychic atmosphere created in the dance of our interdependence with larger consciousnesses. We do not notice how directly, though without our waking conscious perception, that atmosphere influences every detail of our daily lives and influences our appreciation and enjoyment of those lives. Our individual personalities are confusingly set to overlook this interdependent atmosphere. Worse, for most people, our happiness appears to depend solely on what we recognize and understand with our waking conscious mind. In our desperation to grasp happiness within the limitations of individuality alone, we wall off and resist the dancing joy that bubbles through the atmosphere established in the interplay of the polarity of individual personalities and group consciousnesses.

When you die, you don't get gobbled up by the soul. This personality is eternal. We will not disappear into the soul or get consumed for our energy by the soul, or by the moon, or a supernatural eagle as Don Juan told Castaneda. You continue to exist through all of eternity. It is true that your soul takes all of your information and uses it for its own purposes, but information is infinitely expandable so even as it does that, and even as you participate in the soul, you also continue to participate as Mike or Kaye or whomever. Not only is the personality's experience furthered and embraced by the soul, the personality itself continues to grow after death, as itself, recognizable to itself as a continuation of itself, in the embrace of the soul and in the embrace of even larger consciousnesses than the soul, even as it also grows in ways marvelously different from the embodied human consciousness or ego consciousness that we all personally know.

Our soul does in some sense take nourishment from each of our experiences, but *we* individually continue, and sooner or later each of us will have that "aha" for each moment of all our life experience. That's why I think it's important to distinguish the Sethian perspective from the normal mystical perspective where mistakes just kind of stay mistakes. Your worst mistake or delusion is also sacred. That's not to say your worst delusion is pleasurable. All things being equal, pleasure is more fun than displeasure, but pleasure is not equivalent to happiness, and happiness, as I use it, is not equivalent to joy. Pleasure comes and goes. Happiness is basically a cognitive strategy for engaging the world—reliable happiness. The happiness that comes and goes isn't really what I'm talking about as happiness; that's pleasure. But happiness is basically openness to life as it is.

Joy is eternal whether you're aware of it or not at a conscious level. Everything you do is suffused with joy, and you *will* come to know that personally for each and everything that you have done.

I know that this completely disagrees with mysticism for the last twenty-five hundred years, but they were only looking in linear time. In linear time, the soul does gobble you up. It spits out the bones and they form the next lifetime. But in Multipersonhood, multidirectionality, you're eternal. You go through changes. Yes, death changes people, but you are very recognizably yourself. Eventually you move into Multipersonhood.

Likewise, there is no separate thing functioning as your personality, and yet you kind of know it when you see it. It's subjective, and that subjectivity is eternal because it continues to grow and change. If it didn't continue to grow and change, it wouldn't be eternal. If you try to say, "This is exactly what your personality is and no more," that dies. In fact, that *is* what dies. One direction your personality—your subjective experience of yourself—grows into, is your soul. And that's only one direction. The personality also grows through probabilities and infinite other directions.

It is also true that as vital as your personality is, it's really only part of the story. It's the part that you track while you're here and awake. And if you were to track too multidimensional a perspective and too fast while you're here and awake, you would lose the exquisite focusedness of your personality.

Your personality *is* eventually completely assimilated by your soul, though without undercutting your simultaneous continuation as your independent, idiosyncratic personality. Every bit of your soul gets every bit of your experience. Your experience is not merely taken in by your soul but utilized in one hundred thousand different ways more than you were able to utilize it as a physical being. We can't track that just yet, but that's part of where the beauty comes from. Even as that happens, nothing is lost by you, and in fact as you hand your experience over to your soul, something inevitably comes back to you that makes you the individual more than you ever could have recognized while alive and awake. As we go through the years, you will start to have more and more of those resonances of those other directions of yourself. Not necessarily consciously tracking them, you find that they add a kind of richness to your experience. And that's where the joy can grow over time. I love that. That's the kind of thing that we're shooting to enhance that is already going on but we don't recognize.

We're already part of group consciousnesses but not conscious of it in our waking life—not directly conscious. We don't have any waking conscious experience of it. In a physical body, we can't.

So, in this seminar, what I've been doing is sort of starting in our personhood, the one that we know—that is John Friedlander as a human being, Ed as a human being, Anne as a human being—the waking consciousness that we know, each of our personhoods. Each person experiences the same event from its own perspective and *is* the event, but only from his or her own perspective, except in the bigger sense.

You can think of yourself as part of a choir, a part that has stepped out and is taking a solo,

Multipersonhood starts from there and is about this play in change of form: the solo that happens to simultaneously be a duet and polyphonic; it goes out in all directions.

It's about being somewhat more comfortable with the flow of your awareness and more able to value both your uniqueness with its pleasure and the fact that you are bigger experiences too with *their* pleasure and pain—that there are parts of you that are too big to fit inside one person.

Now nonduality is *not* a unity state. A human who experiences unity consciousnesses with dual awareness will always experience that duality as the first and final story of the universe. From the agenda of developing a nondual perspective, a cat is less advanced, for nothing is more advanced than a fully-enlightened human being. Yet all consciousness participates in Multipersonhood, so a cat is more aware of its selves than a human.

That dichotomy of dual/nondual wouldn't even be recognizable if you were experiencing your Multipersonhood, because in that awareness, there is no evolution, just experience.

Life can be so miserable at times and sometimes for a long time, so why would anyone choose to incarnate? Yet we do. It isn't something your soul forces on you. There's a whole bunch of things that incarnate into you—your soul, the Sun, all other things, but there is something that in this tradition we call a baby being. It's newly created; there's a new one for each incarnation, and that is the part that is most what you would consider to be you.

Each of us will come to know ourselves as the Sun, in some sense identifiably different from ourselves as our soul, but we'll know ourselves as our soul and we'll know ourselves as the rocks that compose the world. All those things are necessary to make a human being.

We will not actually move into the Aquarian Age until we develop a new kind of consciousness that requires that we pay attention to a bigger frame than just what happens while you are alive as a human being, though it still centers on what happens while you are alive.

Consciousness wants to experience all of it. When you look at your soul, imagine a whole planet of consciousnesses. So your soul isn't just incarnating as a human being. It's incarnating all over the place. It's like June is bursting out all over. It's incarnating in places with four dimensions of time and two dimensions of space. It's incarnating as a star system that is much bigger than the soul in a conventional physical sense. It's incarnating as rocks.

There are humanlike consciousnesses that may be dependent on smell rather than vision. Or they have four dimensions of time rather than one.

And one of the places your soul is incarnating is as a human being where it can have an experience of ignorance that it can't have any other place.

Cetaceans are more advanced than humans are, not necessarily what we see in the water—that's just their dream state—but they're able to track themselves in multiple directions, and that's where the human race is moving toward. The physical bodies we see are a minor part of whales' or dolphins' consciousness. Most of their awareness is focused in directions humans cannot follow.

Someone like a Cetacean, or someone even bigger like Seth, has more overall clarity because they can track themselves in multiple directions than we have. We are learning a skill.

The downside of the concept of evolution is that it makes you think it's important to evolve. It isn't. It's also impossible to *not* evolve. Trying to evolve is sort of like trying to breathe and it gets you out of the natural flow. When you take that concept seriously, you lose your ability to fully commit to the sacredness of your own life in its own terms.

It also tends to make higher consciousness somehow better or more real or more meaningful than so-called lower consciousness. It polarizes your view. There's a sense that your cat or dog is somehow less than a human. It *is* true that a cat or a dog or other animal doesn't have the kind of choices that human beings do and they don't engage consciousness in the same way that human beings have. But their consciousness is far richer and more varied than human beings can imagine because we're hypnotized by the particular kinds of choices and relationships we have to think that's the only kind of consciousness.

Now, when you look at this from a human-centric point of view, you get up to the soul level, you notice that there is still some separation between you and the nondual perspective. But that's an illusion too. That only arises because of your human waking-consciousness-centric point of view. The soul is nondual. There is no separation in the soul's perspective. That's not new or surprising. When humans encounter the soul, which is much larger than they are, they project their category and don't understand the soul to be nondual, but it is.

Multipersonhood values both your soul and your personality in a way that *is* radically new. Your soul is this profound, powerful thing—even the youngest soul on the planet is profoundly powerful—and yet it chooses to enter a dualistic perception. This is a profound shift in attitude and understanding.

You start to realize that your soul is not something that you merely own, which is the conventional Western point of view. Nor are you merely something that your soul owns, which is the conventional Western *esoteric* point of view. Yet people try to turn their entire life over to the soul. That's not your nor the soul's purpose.

Now it behooves you to communicate to the soul because the soul has a perspective and wisdom that you may not, but it utterly defeats the purpose of their being a "you" to entirely turn over your existence to the soul and to try to become a soul, which is what Alice Bailey sought to convince people to do.

In Multipersonhood you are yourself and you are also your soul. It's both/and, and not just you and your soul, but as a small group soul where other individual souls and you explore the nature of the century from different points of view, and other gestalts, each with their own exciting adventure. There's a certain kind of joy that is enhanced if you realize that you are made up of all these beings who just *love* being part of you.

For example, you might suffer now as you set up a fulfillment later in this life or another. If you excessively focus on the apparent isolation of your individual personality, you will miss the eternal flow of joy and comfort from that later fulfillment that is always and already present. You might actually resent your soul for giving that later life pleasure and denying pleasure to you. The later life seems to reap the benefit of your sacrifice. But remember, you will experience that later life's pleasure from your own continued subjectivity, participating in its adventure as part of its subconscious, but as the center of your own experience. That later life is both itself and an intimate fulfillment of your growth in whatever way works best for you, personally, as this self you experience yourself to be.

I'd like to focus on the Atman-Monad here as a more traditional mystical way to arrive at Multipersonhood. Atman has climbed back into my system of adapting Seth's stuff as a matter of observation. The ancient Hindu Atman is not the same as the Monad or theosophical soul or Sethian Multipersonhood, but it is an earlier perspective that we are taking into interdependence. These concepts go backward and forward in time simultaneously to arrive at a larger view that includes the Atman-Monad and Multipersonhood as both Seth and my guides, which may include Seth too, define it. I'd like you to think of the Atman-Monad as Multipersonhood, but Multipersonhood long before the concept of Multipersonhood arose, or re-arose and evolved with Seth. That allows you to conceptualize an incomprehensible vastness and multiplicity from different perspectives and using older and newer terminologies.

The word *Monad* is, I assume, chosen from a term used by Leibniz, the great philosopher and mathematician who developed his whole description of reality in terms of these Monads that are self-contained and yet hold within them the reflective collection of everything else. That's kind of a cool description of Atman too; they are subjectively self-contained and yet they hold within them everything else.

Nothing arises by itself purely *from* itself. Everything arises in an interdependent relationship with everything else, and some of those everything elses are more important to you as an individual. Three of those everythings are your personality, your soul, and your Atman or your highest spirit from the unity level, the spark that gives rise to you. Hopefully, as you become aware of that interdependence, you will actually become more comfortable with the dance of your personality. You will feel how it already has these vast supports, and it'll be easier to understand how every moment is sacred. Hopefully you'll start to have more and more fun.

You can't exist without a soul and without an Atman. I suppose there's some sense in which they can exist without you—and you are always and already your soul. One hears people saying, "I want to align with my soul and I want to become nothing but a soul." Well, you're already nothing but a soul and it incarnated into this reality as you to get a unique personality understanding of its issues and your issues here, now. The Atman is much the same thing. You can think of yourself as what happens when you mix a little bit of soul, a little bit of Atman, and a little bit of the Earth-being you know as your body.

These are the three major partner players in your incarnation: the personality that doesn't yet exist but chose to be born as you; the soul that has been around practically forever and will go on forever and choose to be born as you; and your original spark, the animating spark. The animating spark is usually identified with the soul, but when you start looking in a multidirectional way, you see that this spark is at the source of your personality too, which is why your personality is eternal. It expands in all directions, but there is something that's identifiable as you even though it changes profoundly throughout time. That spark *is* you. This is the Sethian perspective on the Atman.

Your Atman relishes the difference between it and your personality even as your personality could not exist in any moment without the Atman providing all of what it is. In a sense, your soul provides *all* of your personality, and in another sense your personality is self-generating, but they each are interdependent and interconnected.

Before you're born, those three things get together, even though you could argue, "Well how do I have a personality if I haven't been born yet?" But you do—they get together with a bunch of other consciousnesses and set the parameters for this incarnation. And at any time in that process, you the personality can say, "Hey, wait, this doesn't look like a good idea."

Throughout your life these are the three most important parts of your identity. These are the three things that are most vitally involved in your consciousness; these are the things that, as you learn to say hello to them, you will find yourself becoming more playful, more resourceful, more resilient, more courageous, and more skillful. Now of course your body is in some ways equally important. There's a sense in which it is both *your* body and something else. The body is also more a separate consciousness from your personality than is your soul or your Atman. Six months from now I might say the opposite, it depends on your point of view, upon just what analysis you are following. So there is an argument that the body is closer to the personality than the theosophical soul or Hindu Atman.

As human beings, the focus of our waking life is in the personality, in the individual, and in the illusion that there is a self and other, that there's an outside to you and an inside to you. But none of that theater can go on without your soul and without the Atman.

Normally when earlier mystics did these meditations, the reason it was so hard is they were trying to transform their consciousness from an ordinary consciousness into purely soul and then purely Atman or purely nondual—technically it's a different kind of move to become purely nondual. The reason it's relatively easy for us to get to nondual states that are supposed to be so hard is that we're not trying to change our consciousness into the Atman rather than the personality, but we are adding an awareness that we are already the Atman, in addition to being the individual personality. We are not trying to reorganize our nervous system to eradicate the personality's dualistic nature.

You don't have to transform your body in the same sort of way or you don't have to bracket your body *out* the way those in deep trance meditation do. Those mystics who practice those deep trance meditations and have those mystical states, they have much more dramatic experiences, but they're not more important, they're just more dramatic. So if you spend twenty years meditating twenty hours a day, you're going to get to the Atman. But I actually think there are some ways in which your experience of finding the Atman in the next twenty minutes is a preferable way to know it.

That spark, which is eternal, always was and always will be, and yet gave birth to you as an individual, and it's always with you even as it is unified with All That Is. It *is* All That Is. It underlies your individuality but is itself and is All That Is as All That Is homes in on you. Notice how the word *eternal* hardly describes this. We ordinarily think of eternal as sort of not aging—somehow we're at the holding off of aging—but aging isn't even an issue for this. It is each moment new and old and forty-seven other different directions.

And yet in its sparkness, its nature as a spark, it is what you would not exist without, and yet there's no chance of it ever leaving, and its mood is something beyond even the concept of joy, not in magnitude but beyond in quality. It's a kind of quiet, serene *yes.*

This Atman hardly differentiates experience enough to take in a particular experience as a particular experience from one point of view. It relishes All That Is in all directions without the need for time, and yet before you were born when you got together with your soul and your personality—and your personality would not exist without your soul or your Atman—this Atman takes in All That Is without the need of time. Nevertheless, the Atman is there as you, the personality, are making the choice to be born in this century in this country with these parents. Somehow or other in a very particular personal way, it says yes as you say yes. That is why it is at least as good to find it now as to take twenty years finding it. It is not in time, as time itself is not.

Feel this Atman as perpetually a part not only of All That Is but of each particular aspect of you. There's a very real sense in which *you* come from *it,* not derivatively from it but you *are* it, polarized and filtered so that you appear to be different from it, and that appearance is meaningful but it isn't intrinsic.

Ice may appear to be different from water; it isn't something intrinsically ice, it's still water under certain conditions and filters. And similarly, you are the Atman, it is you. Recognize that that Atman is always there as Atman, always there as soul, always there as you, and staring you back in the face when you look at your neighbor. It's there as your

neighbor also. Everything is it, and yet it's meaningfully uniquely individuated as you.

The Western mystical or theosophical concept of the soul is different
in important ways at a surface level from the Atman. When I look, I
see a kind of individualized unit, so you have to talk in paradox about
these kinds of things. One of the principal concepts in Buddhism is
Antman—no Atman; an advanced Buddhist practitioner friend of mine
said, "Just because there isn't a separate thing that is the Atman doesn't
mean that the Atman isn't important."

When I look at the soul at times, it seems like what I think a planetary consciousness would look like, and of course it is, because it knows
itself as a planetary consciousness in addition to knowing itself as the
soul—and it knows itself as me, so it knows itself in all these different directions. That's what makes it so huge. When I look, I don't see
the soul as the underpinning of the eternal validity of the personality.
The personality will play and dance in that greater being of the soul,
as it also plays and dances in other dimensions. The underpinning of
the eternal being of the personality is its identity as Atman. Akin to
but different from the Hindu version of Atman is Multipersonhood
whereby Atman knows itself as this and Atman knows itself as that.
Atman knows itself as all, but it also knows itself as individual, and as
each individual both inside and outside of time.

You're not going to become Atman today, but you can begin to get
a sense—just a tingle of the fact—that Atman is there and that your
personality is eternal within and outside of time, and that consciousness
is bigger than your cognitive self. Your consciousness, the Atman, is the
place where it all makes sense—not intellectually, but perceptually.

Even when the universe itself disappears, you will not. Because you
are outside of time as well as inside of time.

The nondual practitioner seeks to realize that he/she is, at a human level,
always and already nondual, that the duality presented to his/her senses

was always an illusion. However, the exploration of Multipersonhood leaves the apparent duality of that part of the Multipersonhood, which is your conscious awake human self, in place and opens to the fact that each person is always and already flourishing at multiple levels in his/her Multipersonhood. Many of those levels are always and already aware of their nondual nature. Your soul, your Atman, and other self-organizing consciousnesses *are* you, and you are them in a different meaningful sense than the fact that you are one with everything. The Atman is at once unified with everything and yet particularly me. And by me I mean this particular incarnation—my own utterly special and unique life—but much more than that. It knows itself as lots of different things simultaneously and yet it has a unique affinity from this incarnation's point of view to this incarnation. It's kind of the core that makes each incarnation eternal whether or not it's your last incarnation. It dives into all of your experiences as a human being and in particular operates through this neutral fluid at the center of the head, at the sixth and seventh sub-planes of the Astral, which it contributes to creating along with the soul.

These two are prime movers that enjoy and contribute and give a direction to the neutral fluid that, seemingly paradoxically, has a passionate direction and yet no resistance to whatever happens. Instead, it passionately embraces everything as it happens.

Since we are already multilevel, multidirectional beings, and because each of those other levels and directions is always and already fruitfully engaged, Multipersonhood (as well as the soul and Atman) opens us to make our primary waking business the engaging of our ordinary humanity in its own terms and for its own purposes. This is always, we hope, with kindness, generosity, and authenticity. When we sleep, we participate in our Multipersonhood in different ways.

Those consciousnesses we engage while asleep are nondual in their own centered gestalts. They are also aware of their and our human intrinsic nondual nature. For example, your soul already knows itself nondually as: (1) itself, (2) you, (3) something much bigger than itself, and (4) consciousnesses moving sideways and in innumerable other directions. Your soul follows and individualizes simultaneously in multiple directions, as itself and as each of these other selves, individually and separately yet interdependently.

This is only a part of Multipersonhood and it is hard to track. As an analogy, imagine some superhuman who can simultaneously listen to ten different kinds of music, watch several movies, go to five different parties, work many jobs, live in many centuries with different identities, and participate in all these activities while keeping each clearly and exquisitely separate, yet simultaneously enjoying the resonances between and interdependence of them all. This is how not just your Theosophical soul but your Atman and numerous other consciousnesses function as part of your Multipersonhood.

This is essential for your full beingness. There are emotions and bigger things than emotions that feel like emotions and healings and just ways of being that solely having an assumption that you are a separate individual close out, and they don't just close them out consciously, they close out your ability to take advantage of them in the dream state.

Another way to understand Multipersonhood is to talk again about my friend Will Ives who committed suicide in February of 1976. I can find Will on the Monadic plane. The Monadic plane is the Unity plane; it's the plane where I find the Hindu concept of the Atman, equivalent to the talmudic Jewish mystical concept of sparks. Each of us has a spark that comes off of All That Is. I perceive the Atman as very much like a spark that comes off of All That Is, and that spark is what gives rise to you.

What I see when I look at my friend Will Ives, who committed suicide in 1976, is that, by the early- to mid-nineties, he had found a kind of eternal dance where he had been through various subsequent incarnations, so he was wiser and more wonderful and more at ease and exploring multiple directions simultaneously without losing his Will-ness. As I've become more psychic, I can communicate with Will directly any time I want. Death changes people. He's changed, but he's still Will in all his beauty and uniqueness. Before he died, he'd tell you how miserable he was, but he did it with such panache that it never was believable. He made his complaints a work of art.

I first saw Will in this way sometime in the nineties. I was shocked to see him because I knew that he had already reincarnated, but when I saw this beautiful purple ribbon, it was Will on the Monadic plane, a kind of curved ribbon of light but definitely Will. It was the Will that I had known but really, really calm and happy. He had gone through this depth, and the Will that I had known had become wise and serene and joyful. But also, because of his experiences that were so stressful and hard, he had committed suicide. All of that was integrated into Will now, part of what made him uniquely Will.

And, just as an aside, the reason experiencing your life as a human being is so important is that it's a large part of your eternal dowry. You never have a chance to be *this* physical again. And no matter how good or awful your experience is, the more of it that you've engaged courageously, the more you there is for eternity—and all of it will eventually be in that serene joy. People want to know, Why do I have to work off past-life debts? I didn't do them. This is a little hard to track but, before you're born, you get to choose whether you will even exist. It's another one of these things that doesn't fit in Western logic. So, before Will was born, he got to choose whether he would be Will. This spark on the Monadic plane got to choose to be Will and it *chose* to be Will. It was a good choice in some ways.

Each of us has chosen to be ourselves with the karma that we have. I don't mean our souls—our souls choose also—but our personalities choose to be ourselves because we decide that would be a cool jumping-off place for eternity. You may not believe it right here and now, but it is.

As time has gone on, over the last fifteen or twenty years, I've come to see that purple ribbon change somewhat. That's consistent with the Buddhist sense of impermanence. It's not exactly the same Atman that I saw twenty or fifteen years ago, but there's a family resemblance and I recognize it. I'm sure I'm also not the person I was thirty years ago, but some people might recognize me as is, as being the same person. There's a sense in which, as a subjective gestalt, I *am* the same person.

My friend Will knows himself as the soul, but it's not what you think of as the soul or the Causal soul, but a whole solar system. There's a consciousness there that is mind-boggling. In the same way, the cells in my body each have their own life and yet, somehow or other together as a gestalt, they generate this emergent consciousness that is subjectively John. Every one of those cells contribute uniquely to John's consciousness. If they were somehow or other all identical, there would be no John. It's their uniqueness that generates something that's at least sometimes interesting as John. And Will's consciousness, along with unfathomable numbers of other such consciousnesses, bigger and smaller, generates some emergent consciousness that is the planet-like being that I see when I explore Will.

You don't see Will in any place either, he's just the whole thing; but when you look at one of his teams that's going around doing stuff—I can't track exactly what it is they're doing—you can see that his team sort of hangs together and you can see his individual beingnesses as part of a team. So, they're all these different consciousnesses. There's Will as stretched across probabilities and somehow or other exploring them. There's Will as an individual. There's Will as this huge, huge thing you can't see. I don't see anything that is just Will; but somehow or other it's *all* Will, but it's not Will rather than someone else. It's also someone else.

There are at least two sparks here, one of which is participating very fully in my life as John but not interfering in any significant way with those choices. This is at a level not in the person, not really in the personal aura. So if I find Will's personal energy in my space, I would clear it out. But this Will-as-Atman participating in my experience is giving me some insights into nondual awareness and Multipersonhood. I don't clear out Will-as-Atman, but do clear out Will's personal energy from this life and any others. Will-as-Atman participating in my life is taking place with Will being permanently in a nondual awareness. There's some sense in which, when he's participating with me, he's nondually aware and dually aware. He gets to piggyback on my dual consciousness and enjoy that duality too.

Are these Wills all happening in the Monadic? Well, that's part of what's so cool about how interpenetrating this is. That huge being goes beyond the concepts of the seven planes. Yet there is a sense of it, since it's all Multipersonhood, in which you can access it from the Monadic alone. The team of Wills also looks like it's running around in the Atmic. I'm sure there are other teams that are running around in the Buddhic and can obviously access the one running around in the Mental and Physical—I don't know how much emotional Astral connection there is yet. And it's all happening at once and you can go to any one of those and they are the center, so it's not like you have the individual Will as being the only center of consciousness. It's just as real that the Will that's part of me is the center and simultaneously is experiencing all these other things. So there's no center and yet everything is the center, as Will or as me. That is, as me knowing Will or Will knowing me, or me knowing Will knowing me, which is the same as Will knowing me knowing Will.

Each of you is doing that too, but since you have a dual consciousness and that self-reflective sense of separation, you're not usually aware of it. It behooves us to become more aware. It's not *trying* to be a soul rather than a personality. We're trying to extend our awareness that we already are a soul *and* a personality.

Multipersonhood is going on whether you're neutral or not, but you won't be able to participate in your Multipersonhood without cultivating your neutrality, because it does require neutrality to be able to open to your being something other than your waking self.

This brings us to one of the major uses of your uniqueness. Your experience is useful in and of itself. What I mean is, it doesn't need any other justification, it's always what it is. Additionally, it's a basis for what comes next. So for example, a two-year-old is precious in and of him or herself, and yet part of the two-year-old is setting the basis for a twenty-year-old and a fifty-year-old and so on and so forth.

Because you are part of your soul, your experience isn't important only because it is yours, it is also important to numerous other aspects of your Multipersonhood; but your individual experience that you will have eternally *is* enough to make it important. It also isn't important merely because it takes you to what's next, but it *is* important because it takes you to what's next. But it's also important in that your soul and all human souls are developing a more elaborate and fascinating interdependent relationship with the Earth. So as the Earth produces the elements that generate your body and participates consciously in your life every moment, and as your soul produces the foundations for your personality and participates in each and every moment of your life as a human being, and as your Monad or Atman produces a spark that generates a dance in all directions but from a unique idiosyncratic point of view, all of those things mix and all of their huge consciousnesses develop interrelationships. And to take it further, at least some significant portion of Mother Earth's relationship with the other planets in the solar system and the Sun itself is mediated through humans' responses to their daily lives.

Certain mystics talk about human emotions as being food for the gods, food for larger consciousness. If we hear that, we tend to think of that in terms of death, but we are food for the Earth, our souls, the solar system and huge consciousnesses, and star systems beyond us, *now*. In nourishing them we participate in them; we don't nourish them at our expense in the way that we eat food at the expense of animals. But even eating animals doesn't have to be at their expense. You can eat in a conscious way where they become part of your consciousness. Similarly, our emotions being planet and star food is much more for ourselves as well as for them. Everything you do and know becomes a morsel of larger consciousnesses' interrelationship. We are someone's Valentine present. Earth gives our emotions to Jupiter or some other great consciousness in hopes of getting lucky.

When you reciprocate, someone gives you something and you give something back. In this way, reciprocating is a kind of continuous interactive cycle that makes each of them better. You can think of nature spirits as not-you, and it's a relationship. But a more functional way of thinking about it, though very abstract and wild, is imagining it as a phase in an interactive cycle. In one phase you are the human, and in another phase you are in the deva kingdom. This flashing on and off is so fast that the phase is really like a point of view. So, from this point of view, I'm the nature spirit, and from this other point of view I'm the human.

Your body presently cuts out that phase or point of view where you're the nature spirit and all you see is this kind of smooth continuity of your humanity. But if we were neurologically set up, we'd actually see ourselves sort of twinkling on and off. And when we twinkle off here, we twinkle on as a nature spirit.

Imagine that, in one moment, you are a human in an isolated physical body. And in the next moment you are a tree or flower. Imagine that tree as the nature spirit that's tending the tree together with the tree's consciousness. And imagine that that's ticking on and off, tick-tock, tick-tock, or slower. If it gets faster, it's becomes the way a movie shows you different frames but they all become one continuous flow. It's like right now you see a movie, but you see only every third or fourth frame. There's one movie in that. If you were looking at a different set of frames, there'd be a different movie. There are three movies in the same reel, depending upon which set of images you look at.

That's just something to play with. I don't personally experience that with the kind of clarity I might someday as I build up that neurological flexibility. If you get many people doing this, and then some other people might pick it up in the dream state, thinking "Ah, that's a good idea," and pretty soon you have two thousand people doing it, or three thousand. That's enough to change the world.

You simply cannot gracefully understand and value yourself and your experience without beginning to perceive and embrace the larger drama in which you are an integral part. With each new understanding of your Multipersonhood, you will appreciate more directly the commitment of the entire universe to your seemingly alienated and vulnerable subjective uniqueness. In the larger drama, not only the most sublime but also the most trivial, not only the most generous but also the most unskillful acts you ever perform are inextricably woven out of divinity. Thus as we explore the powers of Multipersonhood, we also grow in our capacity to experience evermore directly an exquisite meaningfulness throughout each event in our life.

Your personal self—Judy, Annie, Ed, not just your soul—is eternal. In Multipersonhood, your personality is eternal. Death may change people, but it does not eradicate or destroy your subjectivity.

Personal identity *and* the soul are real and survive. When a personality dissolves at death, it breaks into fragments, each redistributed according to its karma. At least one of those fragments continues to track the life from which it came—and not just track it but know it as itself.

Duality is not a problem. In fact, it's more than not a problem. *It's the whole point.* It's who we are. The soul survives *and* the personality survives. The broader your perspective, the more you see that this is how the universe operates and why we're presently in this dual phase and also why we don't see it. The fact that we can't presently see beyond a dualistic mode is the way in which we are seeing it and the reason we exist.

The innumerable constituent parts that we ordinary human beings lump together, such as bodies and auric energies, themselves continue, within and outside time, to grow and expand subjectively in all directions, together and separately, forever. Language fails, as time itself is only a form of consciousness. In a universe where no single consciousness arises by itself, it is nevertheless true that every subjectivity, from subatomic particles to universes and thus to the human personality, expands in all directions and thus retains an eternal, though ever-changing and interdependent subjectivity that is divinely meaningful.

Again, language fails, because our concepts of eternality rely on time, which is itself an energy construct. It's a particular form of consciousness that is just one of many others that are incomprehensible to embodied humans. In this multidimensional world that ecstatically breaks outside human experience, our human experience of duality is something to be treasured, even though it involves suffering that can be avoided. It is humans' gift to other dimensions of ourselves; it's a gift that they and we human personalities can luxuriate in and continue transforming forever.

Your ideas of evolution and reincarnation make your lives much more painful than they really are, even in the midst of your dual consciousness. Your ideas of growth are joyless and trigger an obsession with fairness, fault, and punishment. But each moment is sacred. Each life is sacred. Each subjectivity is sacred and eternal, in that each subjectivity decidedly explores all directions.

Your sense of growth and evolution, by focusing only in one direction, makes it seem like your subjectivity is extinguished and has no meaning for you but only for your future or for God or for your soul. You do the work and they reap the rewards.

This focus on time and growth was an evolutionary path intentionally taken, bringing with it the fruits of your current ego development. But it is becoming time to learn to track your consciousness in multiple directions. Only in multiple directions can you see God or the universe or All That Is, moment by moment, and bring its entire consciousness to the aid and fulfillment of your subjectivity. Only in Multipersonhood can you understand the play of desire and the fact that each and every desire is already fulfilled in its richest form.

We can't understand this in our lifetime, but at least we can get started.

In certain kinds of nondual unity consciousness, a mystic experiences the whole universe, or universes, as one union with infinite particulars, everywhere present, centered in every aspect. This is, it would seem, a much bigger and more enlightened version of Multipersonhood. But it's not. Let me see if I can explain.

Remember, the truth is that you are nondual right now, but you don't experience that as a fully existential phenomenon. How can that be?

First of all, your soul doesn't incarnate into you and then twiddle its thumbs while you are incarnated. A piece of it gets lost in you intentionally. Other pieces don't get lost, and they communicate and collaborate elsewhere. Your soul is doing these other things too. It might be being a tree; it might be being a dog.

There's not a progression, or rather, there are progressions but it's not limited to linear progression. A person is not better than a tree. No consciousness exists as a separate entity. No consciousness—not ours, not Seth's, not a rose bush—exists entirely as a separate essence. We are each collaborations of innumerable and important separate consciousnesses like the Earth and the Sun. Insofar as our human identity arises out of the Hindu Atman and Western Causal soul, we will continue to explore and deepen our understanding of the Atman's and soul's participation in our eternal subjective identity.

Every consciousness is made up of every other consciousness in differing proportions. Every consciousness is threaded through every other consciousness. And yet the unique way you thread into other consciousnesses, and how other consciousnesses thread and weave themselves into you, creates an ever-changing subjectivity that is expanding with its own eternal joy. Even the more limited experiences of being human add to this eternal and ever-expanding joy.

Because of Multipersonhood, no human being is thrown into the dump of history. No human being, no matter how awful, is ever lost and left unredeemed. Every single human being eventually learns the lessons of humanity. All human beings are fulfilled and redeemed in a way that sustains and validates and enhances their sense of uniqueness.

To recapitulate, one's basic job as a waking human being is the cultivation of that personal aura range centered mostly in the emotional or Astral plane but including our thoughts. This merely astral range, together with our thoughts, is subject to much scorn in mystical literature. Seth made a radical move, and this is what's new about the New Age. In cultivating the personal aura, one is enriching one's own experience moment by moment—that's one value. In some ways, our everyday emotions and thoughts are prosaic and drab compared to mystical illumination, but when we understand the larger picture in which those everyday emotions explore experiences unavailable to the soul in its nondual realm, we understand what is unique and sacred about ordinary human experience.

Another value of the merely astral range of emotional life is one is preparing oneself for certain kinds of growth and, in particular, for growth into Aquarian consciousness where you can bring that particularity that you cultivated into an emergent larger consciousness that is qualitatively different from your individuated consciousness. And in that larger consciousness you will have full awareness of its intrinsic nondual awareness.

This isn't just trivial because every person's personality, no matter how broken or evil, no matter how selfish or cruel, will eventually take part consciously in nondual awareness. That is part of why we don't try to cultivate nondual awareness in your waking self.

The folding back on itself and richness created in the virtual reality of dual awareness is what you bring to the party. It's kind of like what you bring to the party in the Monadic plane—as in, hello everyone, here's a nice bottle of wine. That Monadic awareness is in a different state of being that is always and already going on. In the nondual mystical stories, nondual awareness is also always and already present, but the personality will never experience that always and already unless it, the personality, somehow achieves nondual awareness in that present lifetime.

We're saying something very different, which is that *every* personality will find itself eventually consciously aware of its always-and-already nondual awareness, whether it achieves it in this lifetime or not.

Multipersonhood may not be consciously accessible at our phase of humanity. But what *is* consciously accessible is shaped by our Multipersonhood, and we would be neither conscious nor accessible without it. Practitioners who have nondual awareness point out that you always and already have nondual awareness. We don't cultivate nondual awareness in our waking personalities, but we have personhoods of ourselves that that are currently a part of our Multipersonhood, like your soul and your Atman in their own space, and they operate in nondual awareness.

You always and already participate in Multipersonhood and it enriches your experience. You may or may not become aware of it while you are living, but you the personality will *eventually* become aware of it. Absolutely!

There's no grand enlightenment. There's no transcendence of your ordinary humanity. If you really understand Multipersonhood, you wouldn't want to become enlightened because your soul has questions and it created you to answer those.

PART THREE

DESIRE, ANGER,
NEUTRALITY, AND
BELIEFS

25

Desire and Difficult Conversations

You *can* become enlightened in one lifetime; in other words, you can get nondual awareness, you can become an ocean of compassion and love. But you cannot finish a reincarnational cycle in one lifetime. Amongst other things—and there are plenty of other nontrivial things—is the matter of learning how to coordinate energy. Learning how to deal with boundaries is a very subtle and deep energy process. Learning how to have a difficult conversation requires you to learn to do several things simultaneously, and well. So the major thing I'm personally interested in exactly that: how to have good boundaries and be authentically kind and generous; in other words, how to have a difficult conversation. When I'm dead and gone, I'm sure I won't be finished with that.

You can't learn the particular human lessons of coordinating energy without addressing emotions, the so-called negative and positive emotions. There's no such thing as a negative emotion, although there are definitely unskillful ways of dealing with emotions.

As we move into this new phase of bringing our kinds of tools to our emotions and thoughts, I think it's possible that we *will* be able to use a lot of them to be healthier than we have been. There are lots of things involved, though. There's your own personal karma, there are group karmas, and everything else.

But that's what becoming a conscious co-creator with God is, not that you become godlike but that you begin to understand that the richness of the order and chaos of your humanity has creative effects both within your aura and outside your aura and you create your own reality. You don't create it unilaterally because there's no such thing as a separate you. I think it's really more accurate to say you become conscious co-creators not just with God but with everything and everyone.

A lot of sophisticated advanced spiritual seekers will say that they still have emotions but no negative emotions. What they're calling emotions are neurologically and energetically different from the full energy experience that your soul signed up for. At an energy level they operate in the Buddhic plane, not the Astral. Now as long as you have a body, there still will be emotions, so people who transcend negative emotions will still have little ripples, and those will affect everyone else. They can get pushed away so that they don't even appear in the normal aura, they get displaced into something like the dream state.

They go into the mechanical level of the Etheric, and it's so smooth and nice, and you might even improve your behavior, but you won't be in touch with your so-called negative emotions, your aura will get more and more clogged with unaddressed pictures, or you will just repress them and drive your Astral aura away.

In our spiritual practice we're constantly doing energy work and cognitive work around the places where we have so-called negative emotions—anger and resentment are two of the biggest—and that energy work and cognitive work makes us less reactive to particular external circumstances and more resilient and resourceful in those circumstances. This means we have fewer and fewer things that trigger those so-called negative emotions and we're more and more resilient and resourceful and responsive in the ones we still have. But we never transcend anger. The only way to transcend anger is to vacate the Astral portion of your life. Certain spiritual systems practice that, but they're not doing it as successfully as they claim. There are countless instances of enlightened people getting really angry.

Some of these people who say they are enlightened and never get angry—if you look behind that ideology, you'll see this Dorian Gray type of Astral body that's been put in a box and jammed, literally driven, into another dimension. That would be a choice, but I think it would be a poor choice. And it can really become addictive.

Let's say you had such a chocolate high that you didn't want to brush your teeth or take a shower. At some point you might become aware that you really might like to brush your teeth and take a shower. Yet at that point you could double down your strategy and eat twice as much chocolate. Well, there are meditations that can bring you bliss and blot out painful emotions. That can become just as addictive as chocolate.

Nondual awareness may give the illusion that you never get angry, but if you have a personal aura, it *will* generate anger from time to time—that's just mechanical. Anger is whenever one of your personal pictures gets pushed. When it gets pushed, your aura tends to collapse. And that, by definition, is anger. Whether you yell or scream or repress it, if your personal aura collapses, that's a moment of anger. We talk about the aura, but there are many different fields of spiritual energy that can be called the aura, and many perspectives from which to look at each different field. When I refer to the aura, I am almost always referring to what I usually call the personal aura or, what is almost the exact same thing, the Astral aura. This is the aura of our personal emotions and thoughts. This personal aura, when healthy, is naturally about one to five feet in radius, depending upon each individual's personality and life's purposes. Bigger is not better. People often have their aura vibrating at less than or more than their own natural radius during any particular moment; when one of your personal pictures gets pushed, the aura will at least flutter. If you become quite upset, it will collapse for at least a moment. You are naturally set up to get angry when your aura collapses. Energy then runs through your third chakra, prompting you to take action. If you take action skillfully, you will learn more about yourself and others and make the situation as healthy and meaningful as you can. Unfortunately, most of us respond to our anger in unskillful ways and make the situation worse. Learning how to experience and respond to anger is humanity's most important task.

Now, these great masters will push their personal aura back behind them or out where you can't even see it in the natural personal aura space, into side warehouses and stuff. That's one direction humankind could go, but I don't think that's the direction *we're* going. I'm not saying that they're not learning how to use transcendent energies too, because obviously if you've become an ocean of compassion, you've learned how to use energy, you've learned how to use energies within the human scale of things.

But if you're paying attention in the system that we use, you will never get to a point where you say, as does happen in some other systems, "I never get angry." Now when we look at people who say they never get angry, sometimes their Astral bodies look just horrible. At the very least they're pushed back and away and have no real connection. They may in fact be an ocean of love, but they've still left that pain in the Astral body, a pain that the human race will have to deal with. We will continue to have war until enough of us have dealt with the kinds of conflicts that inevitably arise in our own Astral bodies.

Hopefully we are not clearing it in the superficial way either. We're clearing it as a chosen dance of humankind. Our health, our ability to have difficult conversations, these are important things to have at a personal level. Hopefully we understand that we can't dominate and just make everything work fine; but as we engage inevitable tensions, a richness emerges that is sacred, eternal, and always situated in joy. And it may help us do that to realize it all arises in a luminosity that is always and already there, no matter what *apparently* is going on.

It's interesting how much of what we think is us isn't. Right now, we're focusing on how permeable our sense of self and other is and how the other is already inside our self. Before we can allow our self to have an emotion, most of us to some degree or another feel that we have to argue that our emotion is justified. Part of the downside of that is that

we can't even let ourselves have our own emotions. We go around trying to prove to the world that our emotions are justified. We assume
that the world sees, that everyone sees things the way we do if they're
sensible, and they're just being obnoxious for not admitting it.

Ideally as you cultivate more neutrality, you have the emotions you
have, you choose your behavior skillfully, and you don't justify or not
justify an emotion, you just process it cognitively or as an energy. Most
of the work we've done in this system at the personal level has focused
on a false but an important coherence, which is sorting out what's *your*
energy and what *isn't*. The idea that some energies in the Astral are
yours and some are not is a powerful schema, but it's also true that we
are unified with everything; so from that point of view, it's all one.
That oneness is not what we are exploring. The dance of subjective separateness is an exploration that humans are playing with in their waking
state right now in preparation to understand uniqueness inside complete interdependence. Even for that dance you'll get more skillful as
you start to notice how much of what you think are your own emotions
are in a contentious dialogue with other energies in the room or from
your past.

What we're doing tonight is problematizing the concept of desire,
because when we take it for granted, we let it drive us in ways that are
not really warranted. We let ourselves be happy or unhappy by whether
or not we think we're getting our desire.

Desires feel so urgent, physically and sociologically, because so much
of our desire is part of a strategy to love and be loved, and the energy
of desire automatically seems to generate other desires. But desires may
have no real connection to their goals; they're often just learned strategies. As we begin to see how dependent and contingent desire is, hopefully this will be a powerful tool in learning how to embrace desire as,
yes, a motivation to engage the world, but at the same time becoming
less obsessed with the inevitable thwarting of some or even many of our
desires. This is not to say that part of what we learn in this spiritual
venture isn't becoming more skillful at pursuing our desires. But part of

that becoming more skillful is to become less grasping and consequently more flowing and more balanced as we pursue desires.

Your desires are divine enticement into experience, but there is a risk to confuse what your desires are there for: Your desires are not there so that you have a rulebook about how to become happy, because each of us is in a kind of perpetual adolescence with respect to our desires.

Desires by definition are something that we don't yet have and we haven't yet understood. There's a song I heard some guy singing, it was written probably twenty or thirty years ago, and in it he was a young man and he said that he would give ten years of his life if he could have one more kiss with his girlfriend or something like that. Well, when he was twenty years old, he might think that, but the truth is that would not be a good exchange and it would probably not make him happy.

There's nothing wrong with desires; desires are there to motivate us to engage the world. But the world is there to give us back more than we expect. So engage these desires with commitment, but be open to what comes.

Desires are a core part of our humanity because they draw us deeply into engaging life. Desire itself has such a wild and subtle creativity that when you engage it with courage and unconditional responsibility, it leads you from the surface of your longing to the depths of meaning. But you can get your desire and be very unhappy and you can fail to get what you think you desire and still be quite happy.

We welcome desire as a divine attraction to experience. Desires are utterly central to your waking existence. Desires bring you into engagement. Desires are what get you up in the morning and carry you through the day. They may not even be accurate desires, but then what you learn in the journey like this is to sort out what is your desire and what is generated by someone else's energy.

Desires carry you into life as an apparently separate human being, but they don't determine whether you're going to experience pleasure or happiness or joy. The mistake is to conflate—where you bring two separate things and treat them as if they're the same—like money and happiness. If you conflate money and happiness, you think you will be happy if and only if you have money. So if you conflate getting your desires with being happy—I will be happy if I get this desire—you will have no reliable happiness. You will be tossed along like a feather in the wind. You'll be unhappy when you *don't* get your desires. And very often when you get your desires, they won't turn out to be as attractive as you thought and you are going to be unhappy then. And if you get your desires and they make you happy, then you're going to be stressed because the happiness can be taken away from you.

Now, you're biologically programmed to go away from pain and to go toward pleasure. All of us desire pleasure and wish to avoid pain. That's the setup, and the setup has a divine purpose. But getting your desires is not what brings you reliable happiness; in fact, often it can bring you deep *un*happiness. You're biologically programmed to expect pleasure if your desires are fulfilled and pain if they're not, though there's no one-to-one relationship to either. Everyone has had more than adequate experience with both sides of that. You get what you want and it turns out to be not as pleasant as you anticipated or maybe even distinctly unpleasant, or you don't get what you want and it turns out to be great.

Most people think freedom is getting what you want, but it isn't. Freedom is a kind of flexibility to engage the world in evermore open ways. This is because your desires often arise from programing and delusion. Also, desires arise in a realm of imperfect understanding. That's a major purpose of experience, to allow us to actually feel and understand the consequences, the emotions, sensations and thoughts of taking action in the world, in the vast spontaneity of our society's and our own responses. Therefore, merely getting what you think you want, at times, leads to becoming more bound up in various delusions. For example, some young people want fame and fortune, but so many poor rock stars found it not so satisfying or healthy. But an increase in your skill, resilience, and flexibility increase your freedom to engage whatever arises more pleasurably and skillfully.

Life and love are not censored; they become richer because you are human and have a whole complex of emotions. They include a multitude of experience, including joy and hurt.

In the original *Twilight Zone* there was an episode where this petty gangster was killed and he was met and told that he was going into heaven. He said, "That's a little strange." He was given this great apartment and these beautiful girls and all the money he wanted and he said, "I don't know that I really deserve this, but okay."

He really gets into it for a few days, but he's getting everything exactly that he asked for. After a few days he finds the guy who put him there. "Look," he says, "I shouldn't have been in heaven in the first place. This is too boring. I only get what I want. There is no give and take in this life. I want to go to the other place."

And the guy said, "You *are* in the other place."

We don't want to control reality or order it by our desires because then there would be no separation, no creativity, and no reason for life.

Grounding is really re-grounding the body to allow it to collaborate with the thrashing around of the Astral. You have this body that vibrates very slowly, changes very slowly, and then there's this quicksilver Astral self that participates and collaborates with the body, and it's enough to drive the body crazy. It's like you're trying to play chess and you have a two-year-old demanding attention. The grounding cord allows you to be stable in that interaction and even to enjoy the mercurial aspects of the emotions and thoughts.

In a more profound way, the vitality and sacredness of emotions can't be enjoyed without a kind of spiritual grounding in your larger self, and that can get lost because sometimes we state what we're doing in opposition to those transcending sorts of spiritual journeys, spiritual journeys that are excessively skeptical of desires. For all its earnestness, that's its own counter-problem.

While the desires that are generated and experienced as a separate human being are important to your engaging life, a full enjoyment of your emotions is not possible without an inner understanding, either consciously or unconsciously, that you float in a sea of consciousness. What's going on in your private personal self is really only a small part of whether you experience pleasure, happiness, or joy. And I think I'd go so far as to say a *very* small part. If you were truly receptive every night and every time you fall asleep, or every time your mind wanders a bit—the mind can wander unproductively but the mind can also wander productively—or every time you're kind of drifting and being supported by those levels of you that know more and are happy and joyful, you experience the sea of consciousness. That is, unless you are committed to the idea that the only thing that matters is your awareness of your experience as a separate human being.

You may not always be able to guarantee that you have pleasure, but you *will* be able to assure that, as a human being, you have a vividness of life. If you look behind that vividness, I think that you will find joy. These things become part of a neurological flexibility that allows you, at least subconsciously, to feel more supported. And it gives you a resource, whether you use it or not. In the long term this is part of the human race developing neurological flexibility so that we can once again have a kind of graceful sharing of consciousness.

Let me make this a little more concrete. I have people say all the time, "Why would I care what my next life does? I'm in this one." Well, the short answer is, "You aren't just in this one. If you restrict and tighten your psychic flow so that you are just in this one, it's impossible to fully engage the richness of your emotions."

How we currently view time really locks us into evaluating our lives in terms of accomplishment and success. When you are dead, you look back on the very same things from a very different time perspective. That is why the things that you saw as awful are suddenly rich and wonderful and transcendent.

I think we get about one-twentieth enjoyment out of life that is there to be had. Playing with time will get us a larger percentage of what is there.

You can't see that other incarnation that gets the value of what you learned and worked in this lifetime any more than you can perceptually see the ionization of the air that gives you joy on a cold, crisp autumn day. But it's there.

It may be true that the only thing that matters is what's happening to you as you understand yourself right now. But that's only true if the opposite is also true: none of what matters in your current understanding matters as much as other understandings you will come to embrace in which the full meaning of even the worst experience you ever had is understood to be an exquisite part of the whole—not only the whole of your life but of the universe. You don't have to wait till you die and merge at the Buddhic level to get inklings of that. Doing Etheric exercises and neurological stretching makes that more part of your awareness. Every night when you go to sleep, some part of you at a deeper level experiences these sorts of things very directly, and this allows you to support those portions very directly.

If we take into account multiple directions, none of us has ever had an unfulfilled desire, not one. True, many can seem like it. And this isn't the specious saying, "Well, you really always get what you want."

You never have an unfulfilled desire because it may be fulfilled in some place that you're not tracking. But it never ever goes unfulfilled.

And that's not irrelevant for two reasons. One is, if you're open to the mystery of life, fulfillment comes even if you're not tracking it. It's not the same as an ice cream sundae with a chocolate brownie and there's no doubt about it. It's this wave or waft of energy from somewhere that knows where your desires are getting fulfilled. Even if you're not going to be aware of it, if you're open to the factualness of it, you'll feel better.

Every bad move and every good move is redeemed as you. Not just your soul—your soul's fine with it too. Not just God either, but *you*. I'm asserting, and my guides are guaranteeing, that everything that ever happens to you, in the long run—and not in a meaningless long run, but a meaningful long run—will ultimately feel full and complete and sacred to you. I don't suggest that makes it easy, but the fact that your subjectivity is eternal is important, profoundly important.

Please be in the center of your head. Cut off your grounding cord and create a new male or female grounding. Create roses in front of you, behind you, above, below, and to your right and your left.

Let's take a desire, put the energy of that desire on a rose, set it in its own universe, and study it with the question in your mind: "What in the world is a desire?" For instance, where does it come from? *Who* does it come from? When does it come? What does it do? Whose desire is it that you're looking at? How did it become your or that person's desire or desire itself?

It's not asking, "What am I desiring?" That may be something you look at or explore sometime, but this is about asking, "What *is* a desire?" And if you come up with an answer, ask a little deeper. That could look like: "My desire is my energy, so then, what is my energy *as* a desire?" Stay with the question, get an answer, and challenge that answer with further questions. Start to clear out other people's energy, energy that isn't yours.

If you clear other people's energy out of your space, you'll have an easier time staying alert to your actual desires. You'll have an easier time finding health and joy. You'll be more able to interact creatively and more aligned with your chakras and their true inner nature.

You want to come into current time with your desire so that what you try to manifest is your desire rather than someone else's. Remember, just because you really, really, really want something doesn't mean it's your desire. Intensity of a desire is not an indication of the authenticity of that desire. And in fact, it can often be a counter-indicator because a lot of what we interpret as intensity is resistance: fear and trembling. The trick is learning the difference between running toward and what's running away from your desire. Fundamentally, only experience discloses the validity of anything, and even after experience, more experience may lead to new disclosures of meaning, sometimes meanings quite different than you had initially imagined. You can't know completely whether you have the right strategy or the right desire or anything else. At some point, you do your best, you give it a shot, you enter into dialogue with life. And life will help you understand what's real and what isn't real.

Clarifying the energy in your goal makes it much more likely to manifest. In almost all instances, by clarifying your energy, you will have an easier time manifesting *your* goals rather than someone else's. One of the questions it would behoove you to ask, if you're not getting what you want, is, Whose energy am I using to push this goal? It can be a scary question to ask.

It's pretty easy to say how you become a more effective, authentically kind and generous human being. It's not always easy to do it, but it's pretty easy to say it. It is to learn to be open to life as it is.

I've been working on some big difficulties with my back and hip for about eight years now. I'm making real progress. In the last couple of days, I was looking at a set of pictures that were throwing my hip off. I've looked at them from time to time and am getting deeper in them now. So, there's a picture on this side that's generated, modeled by my mother, that is I have to get what I want, otherwise I won't be special and no one will love me. That is her model, and it's crazy but not unusual. All of us have really crazy pictures.

That is happening on the left side. Now, on the right side, you know how if you hit a golf ball you try to put body English to keep it from going off to the right or to the left? Whether you play golf or not, you see golfers do that. Well, that's sort of what I've been doing with my right hip. I've been trying to raise it, twist it, and put it out to my right so I could keep people from interpreting my actions in a way that is going to bring an adverse response from them. It's not a very good strategy and not that easy to shake, but I'm working at it.

What an incredible way to short-change yourself and your life. You turn away from it being a conversation with life and an interaction, to you being the czar of the universe and telling life and the universe exactly what to do. If you really think about it, my unconscious attempt to control people with a kind of body English like the golfer twisting as the ball is already far into the air is a very bizarre strategy, that you're living your life trying to keep people from having their genuine response to you. There is something off about that. There is something that misses the purpose of being human. I suppose you could set something up where everyone was unreal so you and nobody would ever have a response that felt unpleasant to you, but in the long run that would be emotionally impoverished.

Once you have a goal, there are various ways you can go about manifesting, and one is to hook up with a deva. There's a rich soup of consciousness that you can engage in such a way that it's well disposed toward you. You can do that going to a power spot or you can do that finding some coordinate place in your own home.

Seth has this kind of neat way of finding a coordinate point. You scan the entire area with your crown and with your third eye, and maybe you can feel the place where your energy is pulled. Instead of thinking of it as space crinkling, think of it as consciousness collecting. The consciousness of the Etheric plane collects in these pools and eddies. And it is more conscious and more powerful there.

Keeping to this idea of a conversation, when you're trying to manifest—and other teachers will tell you differently—there are maybe 10 percent of people who work very well by willing things to happen, and that's their natural way. They may have more connection with that devic consciousness than with human consciousness. Some of them may even have come into human incarnation from the devic chain. Remember, there are more consciousnesses that come into human consciousness, with all its pain and suffering, than the other way around, than leave human consciousness. Practically everything I write won't be the right thing for them. But for the rest of us, don't just try to make something happen. Engage life in a communication and be engaged in what life answers. You don't have to like it. You can continue to pursue what you want. Just be interested. Let life give you back more than you put in—more information than you put in, which it always does—but most of us ignore that information.

My guess for most people is that you're finding that you can't really control what your desire does, what it becomes, or what it seems to trigger. We think of ourselves as *having* desires. A more Sethian way to view it is that desires are multidimensional interdependent lives that we participate in.

So again, I'd like us each to take a desire and put it out in a universe, and just sort of ask. Ask questions that occur to you: How could you control it better? Why you are having a hard time controlling it?

When I do this, I eventually get my desire to be quite clear. I put it in the universe, and other energies start popping up as if they were growing out of the universe itself, out of the Astral plane like mushrooms out of a tree trunk. In this instance, the most notable piece came from my father: I asked him how he'd gotten there, and the answer was that it was part of the underlying nature of my being born as his son.

So you're developing a sense, dim or clear, of how much more complicated desire is—desire itself and where it originates. Its fulfillment is no longer an unexamined or assumed preference.

We're going to explore how a desire meaningfully becomes yours, even though it's a small part of the desire field. For instance, if I want good health, I'll want it in a way that's unique to me, but it doesn't seem to be possible to explore it without all kinds of other people exploring that concept from their own point of view. There is something in the nature of reality itself that makes each individual's exploration a joint project.

Create a rose for a desire, start to clear out other people's energy, energy that isn't yours. Now create a rose for the energy of your desire in a universe without any other human beings and see what happens.

When I look at this world without any other human beings, my desire is stillborn and has no impact; it can't become part of a planetary scheme. It seems logical, though I can't articulate why, that one emotion needs other emotions. We can't escape interdependence. That shows the resource of all of humanity's emotions that provides our apparently solitary journeys.

Now identify a desire and let it create a rose of the energy of that desire. This time imagine that desire filled with your consciousness and other consciousnesses. This is a meaningful and skillful part of something much bigger. It's part of something so big and fascinating and secure in its creativity that it can explore the ups and downs of desire itself, in ways and styles that have developed over centuries and millennia, and that now have certain strong similarities and differences for the billions of people on the planet.

Imagine that each of those people's desires twinkle on and off like lights communicating to one another, a bit like the spaceship in *Close Encounters of the Third Kind*. All those desires are communicating with all the other desires in beeps and lights and music, and yet in a certain way a tiny and divine portion of that is your desire. It's large and it includes you.

Feel the vast presence and creativity of this huge consciousness made up of all these beeps and lights and music; yours is a note or two, beeping and lighting and interacting. It's happening whether you're wise or foolish, whether you're kind or nasty, whether you get what you want or don't. Recognize that it's all divine creativity in ways that you wouldn't otherwise notice.

That doesn't mean that, in your own corner of the universe, you can't be disappointed or exploring despair. It just means you're looking at a little bigger pattern and it's still you. It has its own beauty, supported by the essentially infinite creativity of multidimensional creative exploration.

Together we're a cloth that's made up of threads that are enormously bigger than us and of threads that are tiny too. And as we get that understanding of ourselves of riding on this wave of consciousnesses, the first thing to be gained is a sense of how much help we have. The idea of help really worries me a bit because it tends to focus me on outcomes—"Oh, I've got this help"—and kind of doubles back. The adventure is not about outcomes. Outcomes can be pleasant and outcomes can be unpleasant. Naturally, we're highly motivated by whether something is pleasant or unpleasant. But the meaning or value of our life is not accumulating pleasant experiences and avoiding unpleasant ones; it's engaging in this dance in the waking state as human beings. In the same lifetime when we go to sleep, as you know, we're grouped together with other incarnations exploring things; we're parts of small groups, parts of large groups, parts of the land. We might spend time on other planets. In deeper states we might be the planet itself. All those lives interact, and the more comfort we have with that interaction, the more a new kind of support, a new sense of meaning, emerges. You can draw great healing from it.

In this system we heal at least as much because we want to heal, because we enjoy the healing and the adventure of doing healing.

You can also have a healing that hooks into a bigger aspect of an inner dimension of a person no longer alive, a dimension that has more awareness than she did or than she was able to capture in her lifetime. What happens is not in present time as we think of it; the person has passed, the dimension was never manifested in her lifetime or known to her as herself, except maybe unconsciously and in the dream state. She has been changed by death and is no longer present in the spirit or thoughtform with whom the healing is conducted—but it is still a healing and a healing of her where she presently is and knowing herself as herself.

It's possible to do healing at a transcendent level, from the Causal above, without actually healing someone, without it actually fitting together with their personal self. I'm talking about everything that transcends the personal with its apparent separation between what's me and what isn't me, though strictly speaking that apparent separation does get a little fuzzier on both sides of the Astral.

In the Etheric it's a little fuzzier because you don't have *my* Etheric energy versus *your* Etheric energy. If you did, you wouldn't be able to get energy by eating food or breathing air. But in the Astral, it is very clear, there's my energy and there's *not* my energy. Only whatever is my energy is authentic for me. The Astral, in the range we're looking at it, is very unique and is really at the center of why you incarnated as a human being in the first place.

What in fact happens is that those people who can generate transcendental healings choose not to do it. The explanations they give make sense within their ideology, but my understanding is, it's because you have to change within the personal so that you would not be inflicting healing and messing up the personal, the uniqueness, and the clarity that the personal was set up to generate in the first place. You can't override the system you're in without causing more damage than good. What grants you the capacity to heal simultaneously forebears you from using it.

Every single tool we use is about—and only about—opening to life as it is.

The idea is to attend to whatever's up, whenever it is, with an openness to the experience. You can play with time. The principal advantage you get out of that is that it helps you actually respond to the deeper meaningfulness of every moment. Even when we talk about "the meaning of a moment," we are packaging it in linear time and limiting ourselves from really getting the meaningfulness, which is every moment expanding in all directions. So, I think the primary reason to become much more flexible with time, at least psychologically, is that it opens us up for an embracing of meaningfulness that does not fit in linear time—though linear time is part of the playground in which we generate that meaningfulness.

All life is sacred and meaningful and joyous even if it's very hard at times.

A secondary advantage is that creation doesn't really happen in linear time. As Seth says, "Every cell in your body straddles probabilities and is constantly reading past and future probable realities and making decisions underneath your conscious awareness." That's one of the ways in which your reality gets assembled. There are other ways in which your reality gets assembled, and very few of them actually operate in linear time. And as you get more playful with that, you'll have a better time getting out of your own way. But for some reason we want to use our emerging psychic abilities to avoid experience: "How can I get from here to there without making any mistakes, John? Is my soul stupid or something? Why am I even here?"

From one point of view, I can see why people think it ought to be the way they want. But at its extreme I'm seeing people saying, "I don't like my boss. I don't like what's going on. I'm going to work on the laws of attraction or my beliefs or creative visualization, and I'm going to make money by day-trading or betting on the horses or getting on *Oprah,* and then I'll be so wealthy that I'm going to become a philanthropist, and that's how I'm going to create value."

It's sort of like thinking, "With my brains and the universe's money, it's really going to work well." That approach omits the process of cultivating experience in time, with night and day—that's a part of time, night and day. There's a phrase in the Jewish prayerbook: "Thanks for the day and its labor and the night and its rest," or something like that. There is a rhythm to experience during the day and then we explore it during the night. There's a rhythm of, you go out and you do stuff and you have interactions and then you go to sleep, and then you take that experience apart and you explore it outside of the everyday. Then the next morning you do it again. And there's summer, fall, winter, and spring. Those things have rhythms to them. Everything is always and everywhere but also always becoming new in the moment. The implications in our everyday life are profound. They generate fundamental aspects of the meaning of life.

People are looking for jobs, so they call up a psychic and say, "What job should I apply for that I can get and that I'll love?" There's no opportunity for them to learn anything in the process of applying for jobs. But part of the reason you apply for jobs and you go on interviews is to develop your skills as a human being and learn something about what's out there.

Most of us want to jump over the obstacles: "Oh, I hate applying for jobs!"

I asked Seth once, "Should I be a psychologist or a lawyer?" Why not? Seth knows himself to be me and me to be him. But he has such clear boundaries, so he said, "If you knew me better, you wouldn't ask that question." He has boundaries without having the kind of literal boundaries we have.

There's a good reason why you hate applying for jobs; it's a grueling, awful process. We seek to change direction when we encounter pain, so that we can instead seek pleasure. What we miss is that we take into ourselves permanently how courageously we explore and accept life as it is. If you engage things with kindness and generosity for yourself and others, it's not nearly as grueling nor awful, and you generate so much spiritual freedom out of it.

So why can't you just skip that and generate spiritual freedom by working on your beliefs or regulating your intent or creative visualization? Well, all those things are really great, but they are not a substitute for engaging the rhythms and the experience of life.

Most of us, especially in the West, consider our lives in terms of how much we have accomplished, how much we have used our gifts. We tend to trophy-ize even family and relationships and justify what is unjustifiable. The good news is that there is nothing to justify. That is what always and already means.

Every consciousness naturally flows in innumerable directions that will most naturally fulfill it. Drop the goal of pleasant experience and watch as your consciousness, which is itself woven with dozens of consciousnesses, naturally flows into innumerable dimensions. These innumerable dimensions are optimizing your personal growth from a primordial creativity at your core.

I had a client who had ALS and went to live in Brazil to work with a skilled healer. A month or so before he died he told his wife he was the happiest he had ever been. It is *not* the case that the healing usually happens at a physical level, even when working with a healer who is very skilled. The healing of this client did not take place at a physical level, unless you consider that death was a healing in that situation. Also, sometimes this kind of healing work operates in a wormhole in time and space, so it's like you're working in another dimension, and you're taking one body out and putting another in. It's not like you have this car engine and you took it apart really, really quickly and put it back together, but while you weren't looking, the guides took that engine out and they just put a whole other new engine in there with everything brand spanking new. That is what you do in probabilities. Its principal value is not even doing healings. Its principal value is changing your relationship with consciousness itself.

But most of us want to win the lottery rather than go through the experience. We want to have a hike without putting our feet on the ground. Somehow or other, I really think that if we understand time differently, we'd be less likely to want a guarantee that we know the path.

Creativity gets larger and larger and doesn't need the constricted structures that we have. Eventually, we will move into richer, more expansive forms of creativity. Everything we have done in our lives will support that. And basically, all that really counts is, How much did you commit to life, life as it is?

I want to give a sense of how an unpleasant experience is a resource state for you—if you're capable of letting it be. But it's not easy. And I'm not saying you should be able to do this. I'm just saying that, to the extent that you are, life will be better.

Let's say at work something very unfair happens to you. You think, "If I had any dignity, I wouldn't let myself be treated that way." But that is like using a steam shovel to pot a rose. It doesn't work. You can also deal with it gracefully and work with the energies of it and get substantially done with it. People will have great respect for that, and over time it will leave you with more of what's called social capital.

Far more importantly, though, you clear your aura and literally have less pain. The unjust thing that happens is just a manifestation of the pain you are carrying around. A lot of peoples' prescription for being happy is sort of like, "I have a pain in my stomach. If I eat enough ice cream, it will go away." It's conceivable, but a lot of the time ice cream is not the right prescription; other things are better.

If something unfair happens to you, do your best to get what you want from the situation. But what you want has nothing to do with what you're entitled to. "Being entitled" is just a description you use for, "I'm going to stop listening and demand what I want." You're entitled to go after the thing that you want, whether it's ridiculous or not. If you think that you want it, go after it. But go after it with skill. Go after it listening as well as asserting.

You don't have to be entitled to get something, and you can be perfectly entitled and not get something in those terms. What does entitled have to do with it? What did I do to be entitled to breathe air or to have sunlight? If we were required to be entitled, then none of us would be alive. And you can be perfectly entitled and have things not work out because life is a truth detector. What you create is the truth of what's going on at an inner level. What you get is who you are; then you work to change yourself to get more of what you want.

I never, ever tell anyone to stand up for themselves or say, "Oh, you're entitled to this or to that." Entitled is an un-useful concept for this spiritual journey. No one deserves really nasty things happening to them, not even really bad people. But not one of us has done anything to deserve air. When did you put in the work to deserve air?

Many people say, "I want your job. I want to do something spiritual for a lot of people." You know it's easy to stand up and do what I do, making obviously spiritual statements. It's entirely another thing to be in the corporate business world and to be able to work on your neutrality in a world that's not as hospitable toward you as you would like. You'll see a lot of healers—and I'm not necessarily meaning conscious healers—doing things where they interact with the public like being a grocery cashier. That's doing something spiritual for a lot of people.

Assimilating an experience, in the sense that we use the word, is equivalent to letting go of your resistance to the experience. By assimilating the experience, we accept that it's ready to be taken in by the soul as assimilated and utilized. It no longer is stuck in your personal aura or Etheric body diverting the flow of energy and experience. Your aura is freer to respond to the universe. At least that piece of your experience is not blocking it and you from being open to the universe as it is.

But as long as you have a physical body, as long as you engage and stay committed to your life as an individual human being, there will be resistances. You'll never be perfectly open or without resistances.

Understand that being open to the universe as it is doesn't mean not having preferences and even strong preferences plus strategies and tactics to get what you want. It just means that you're open to the fact that you're not going to get everything you want. Sometimes too, of course, you're going to get what you want and find it's not as much fun as you thought it was going to be. Life happens—and it's rich and it's wonderful in all its forms. That's what we're trying to open ourselves to be.

We don't cultivate sainthood in this system. We don't cultivate selfless-ness. But we don't cultivate selfishness either. We cultivate desires as a divine inducement to engage the world. We cultivate engagement and conversation with the world.

If you pursue your enlightened self-interest, you will cultivate clear boundaries with kindness and generosity and unconditional respect. For instance, when you find yourself thinking a person isn't worthy of respect, you can own that opinion and dig deep into what you think the nature of respect is and what being worthy has to do with it. That's the path to kindness, not faking kindness or beating yourself up for not being kind enough.

An exercise like this doesn't guarantee that you'll like the outcome. It just increases the likelihood that the exercise and an open, willing aware-ness of available probabilities will enhance your appreciation for life.

What we're cultivating is an enhanced perception of what is meant by the concept that all consciousness expands in all directions. Your cells' consciousness expands in all directions; Mother Earth's conscious-ness expands in all directions. Your yesterday expands in all directions. Your today expands in all directions.

More and more I understand that to expand in all directions means, in part, to add a sense of serenity and sacredness to things. It doesn't mean I lose a sense of dissatisfaction, don't argue with my wife, or anything like that, but it helps to know both intellectually and directly that all things expand in all directions.

Spiritual freedom is very real, and these problems that are there, these unexplained pains that are there, are real. You may think, these are the soul's pains, what did I have to do with this? Well, this doesn't fit in Western logic, but before you were born, before you existed in terms of time, you had a choice of who you are going to become. So each of us, before we existed as a personality, chose the major themes we would be dealing with as a personality. Time feeds back on itself in that way. Time is not linear.

When you engage events, it may feel like you're layering pain on top of pain on top of pain. The truth is, there's nothing you can do that will keep you from expanding in all directions. Even the most vicious thing you ever did does not change the fact that you are expanding in all directions. You are growing spiritually and you are generating more spiritual freedom. It just may not appear that way.

If you go bankrupt or lose money, you don't have as much freedom with money as you did; but you know more about money as a soul, because now you know more about not having money and understand that absence of money is part of understanding money in this society. You definitely have more spiritual freedom, though it may take you a while to understand your spiritual freedom consciously.

Going after what you want is a very good idea. Demanding what you want is not a very skillful strategy. And, in addition, there's shockingly little correlation between happiness and getting what you want.

People think that life is about getting it right. When I talked to my friend Yvonne, she said she felt she really fucked up. This morning, my friend Larry said, "I've wasted my whole life." This was in response to realizing he had been pursuing the important, things, rather than merely engaging what he found and exploring without the artificial category of being important.

While for some particularly young soul, dying with the most toys might be a success, other people *set up* lives to encounter all kinds of hurdles. And unless you understand this, you'll be in resistance to finding your mistakes.

You set up certain challenges. You don't set up your life as some fantasy about having it all.

Life is about becoming more and more open to engaging life and people as they are; it's about pursuing your desires without grasping your desires or deluding yourself that getting your desires will necessarily make you happy. Or that you can't be happy unless and until you gain some particular desire.

Seth said once, when I channeled him, "The purpose of life is to live it." Take some time with that. I believe it was Kierkegaard who said, "Life is not a problem to be solved, but a reality to be experienced." He probably wasn't channeling Seth, or maybe he was.

When you become more open to life as it is, you become more graceful and playful in the stories you tell yourself about your life, and it is those stories themselves that continue to expand in all directions and become the carriers of meaning throughout the universe.

Treating our stories as ever-changing interpretations of our experience is what lets them become creators and carriers of meaning.

Meaning is not something you find. It's something that emerges out of your creative response to throwing yourself into life.

What's important to understand is this: In some other probabilities you have dramatically different lifetimes, some far more conventionally successful, and those are no less and no more profoundly sacred and meaningful.

When you mention Seth, most people who've read Seth respond with sort of, "Yeah, Seth. He was good back in the day." But I don't think people really know what Seth is because he would say things that were the opposite of what we thought he was going to say when we first got excited by him, things like, "Your world is formed out of the vast unpredictability of consciousness."

Now does that sound like the same guy who said you create your own reality according to your conscious beliefs and really, really stressed that you have access to it all consciously? Both are true, your world *is* formed out of the vast unpredictability of consciousness, because if it were predictable, it wouldn't be creative consciousness. From it you form your own ideas of significance. Since you create your own reality, things wouldn't be any better if everyone were like you

This is why people have ignored the later Seth. What does it mean to say, "You must stop thinking in terms of ordinary progression"? It means you can't buy happiness. I'm being a little cute here. When I say you can't buy happiness, what I'm saying is, we all have this project that says, "All I'll have to do is visualize and work through my beliefs and do this or do that and I'm going to get essentially everything I want. And, consequently, I'll be happy. And I don't have to put up with obnoxious people. And I'll never grow old." It says things like that. But that was never true. You must stop thinking in terms of ordinary progression. That means all life expands in all directions, and everything you do, think, and say is meaningful and sacred.

You form your own ideas of significance. You're exploring significance. You're not exploring getting what you want, you're not exploring being king of the world, you're not even exploring getting what you need. You're exploring significance. And the significance of what you're exploring becomes apparent in that interplay between what you think is the case and what the world answers back is the case. The world is a truth machine or a significance machine. So all of you, including what you don't recognize as you, are invested into the world, and the world expresses back to you what the significance of that is. And it's all sacred. Not only does it reply back to you what the significance is, it always gives you back more information than you put into the system.

The funny thing about change-work is that it requires that *you* change. There's so much of a drive to try to change the external world so that it stops bugging you. Now, what you need to try to change is yourself. Does that mean you don't try to change the external world? Of course, you try to change the external world, but not without taking responsibility for having created it and understanding that you're only engaging the external world to change it but that it will only work to the extent that you change yourself.

People say, "I want to do change work." What they mean is, "I want to change the external world without any significant change internally." Change-work requires that you change internally. You don't have to specify what this is, but part of it is to be open to *your* changes. So miracles can happen, but miracles don't happen without some kind of internal change. That sometimes means giving up your fondest delusions.

The self-reflective ego is made up of the stories you tell yourself. To make a change that is authentic requires that you align your self-reflective ego with the change, and the only way you can do that is to change the stories you tell yourself. Now usually that happens imperceptibly and without your conscious focusing on the fact that you are changing your story; but changing your story is one more way to help yourself understand the nature of change as a human being. Any change you make that does not impact your interpretation of the world is not going to be an authentic or integrated change.

So, when you're blowing pictures, one way you can know if you're actually integrating the shift is that you can look and see if your body has willingly accepted that change. Another is to look at that part of your aura and see if it's flowing more smoothly. And another is to look at your story you're telling yourself and see if that new story is more comfortable and more responsive to the world as it is.

One of the things that I encourage people to be careful of, or to be wary about, is only changing your story in a direction that makes you feel better about yourself. What do I mean by that? You may buy into what I'm suggesting, but then every time you change your story, you'll want to feel better about yourself; but it may also be because you found something that you're not very happy about and you say, "Oh okay, I get to work conscientiously on that."

When you shy away from the so-called negative words, you're actually charging the word *mistake*. It is important to understand that we are all fallible as is everyone else. So when you change your story, just as a cautionary note, you want to be sure that you're changing your story not at someone else's expense and also in such a way that it covers more information and leaves you more comfortable with information, ideas, and energies that you might have resisted.

I probably go too far in the direction of talking about mistakes. Everything's a polarity. But I do want to encourage people to be comfortable with the idea that you are a *fallible* person. You'll find things in your aura that you don't like and it's really great to be comfortable, but if by loving yourself it means that you never say, "Oh geez, I don't like this about myself," then you're impoverishing yourself. And that doesn't strike me as a very practical love. If you can't dislike things in yourself, then you're much more likely to be resistant when you encounter things in other people that you don't like, and you certainly can't get in touch with your body and your Astral aura if you can't allow yourself to say, "Oh, I dislike this, and I dislike that." It may be that it's appropriate for you to do some cognitive work and change. There may be all kinds of good reasons why it's unskillful to dislike it, but it's important to *be able* to dislike it.

26

Anger

Anger is *the* human issue for us to learn how to deal with, yet so many people don't strike themselves as particularly angry people. It's understandable that they might not be tracking that because it's not presenting itself in the way that anger usually presents. It is easy to transcend all anger as you understand anger and have lots of another kind of anger in your space as well as no awareness that you're angry. Some people, especially people who follow certain mystical systems, will push anger so far away that it doesn't even show up in their personal aura anymore. But that doesn't mean it isn't there and isn't a part of them.

If you have a human body, you have anger. If you have some real connection to your body, you will feel that anger. You may be able to successfully cover it up from yourself. And I've seen people so committed to transcending anger that you can't even find that anger in their aura. They've stuck it off in an annex somewhere in other dimensions. But their anger still affects humanity.

Anger is humanity's biggest issue. Even though every instance of anger is a delusion, every instance of anger is also an immeasurably important experience and information.

Anger technically arises every time one of your preferences isn't fulfilled. There will be a wavering of your aura. When you're angry, your aura wavers or, more often, goes all the way to some level of collapse.

Anger is shot from the third chakra as an energy that re-inflates your aura, usually way past the level at which it started. That's why it can become inappropriate aggression rather than just owning your space. Ideally, it would re-inflate your space and prod you to action. Then action can be taken that is more effective than losing yourself in a sense of victimization or moving into illicit aggression. I don't mean even necessarily criminal aggression, I just mean jumping into someone else's space, not honoring their boundaries, or, conversely, repressing yourself.

I'll use common words that everyone knows, but people won't recognize my meaning because we're working at an inner level. I'll tell someone that they have a lot of anger in their space and they won't understand what I'm talking about. I'm talking about something a lot more subtle than what people normally mean. You can take a Nobel-prize-winning physicist and he'll think that his intellect is very neutral, but it's not even close to what we mean as neutral. As a result, it blocks all kinds of energy, energy that is essential to have if you want to follow our sort of spiritual path.

One of the hardest things about this is that you have a lot of emotions that you don't track. This is not the Freudian unconscious. When I'm doing readings, I encounter anger. Many people don't count it as anger if it's justified. It only counts as anger if it isn't someone else's fault. Think about it for a moment. How many times have you gotten angry when you didn't think it was someone else's fault? That's the way you make yourself angry. You tell yourself it's someone else's fault and they shouldn't be doing what they're doing.

But anger is a specific psychic energy and whether you're coding it to yourself as anger or not is important. Learning to track what energies are going on is also important.

If you don't like what someone else is doing and you're about to have a difficult conversation, the key to your skill and your happiness is to make a paradoxical shift. It's to shift from the idea that they are making you unhappy and you are going to try as hard as you can to change them so that they stop making you unhappy, to an encounter with yourself in the context of that emotion. You give up trying to convince or change them until they feel heard and, more important, until you have worked on yourself so that you have an attitude adjustment. Then, if you still want, you can inform the other person, hopefully skillfully, what your complaints and desires are. You can do all this in the context of a conversation.

You turn your attention to clearing yourself as you're engaging them. Sometimes that's too much to do at one time and you might have to come back and do change history later on, but the underlying issue becomes the same. You will become more powerful and more skillful if you realize that if all you do is change them, you may get a little more pleasure out of that interaction, but it's not going to do very much for you. You put all that effort into making them better. It's much more resourceful to put lots of that effort into making you better as you engage them.

If you have a situation that doesn't work for you, then you're the one to fix it. Sometimes, if you're skillful, you can fix it by asking the other person to change, but that can only succeed if you change also. It doesn't matter how wrong or negligent the other person's actions are and how entitled you are to get them to change. It is perfectly appropriate to find some skillful way to ask for them to change, but it isn't going to work unless you change also because you create your reality. Even something that you think is obvious is probably not going to change until you change yourself, consciously or unconsciously. What's obvious to you may seem like a bad idea to someone else, and that works both ways. There are intrinsic tensions between people.

But when you start treating your pain as someone else's problem, you are making yourself powerless and you are giving them all the power in the relationship.

Now you may not have to think about changing. Simply by the act of asking, you may have unconsciously changed, but success is more likely if you're aware that the way to get someone else to change is by changing. It may not be a huge change, or it *may* be a huge change.

If you just try to meditate on not being angry, letting go of this and that, you don't really get to the to the heart of the issue. It's probably impossible never to have any particular emotion. You name it, you probably have had it. That's part of why we do this psychic work. We generally do not track our emotions, but when you can see the energies, it's harder *not* to track them—though even when you can see the energies, you can fool yourself. I have observed instances of that for ten years or more.

For instance, if your crown doesn't match an emotion, that doesn't mean it's not in your space. Your crown certainly knows how to match any emotion: anger, humiliation, resentment. Once you realize this, you start to have fun doing all the detective work.

That's how we work in the personal aura.

The truth is, if you could get to the heart of every issue, you probably wouldn't even reincarnate. You reincarnate to experience life. You get to the heart of the issue by taking on real life situations. By working with specific instances, you get much deeper into a profound clearing. That's a really, really important point. Most spiritual systems have as their ideal that you rise above anger, and you might think that we would too. However, it is positively not an aspiration of this system to rise above all anger. Instead, our goal is find ourselves getting angry less and dealing with it more skillfully.

The reason we do not try to rise above all anger is because we are ideologically committed to engaging the personal, the Astral, on its own terms and for its own purposes, and to engaging the stories that we human beings tell ourselves. The only way to rise above anger doesn't actually work. I think people who rise above anger are simply not experiencing their anger, but it gets expelled out into the spiritual atmosphere and other people have to deal with it. As long as you have a personal self, you will get angry because the personal self will always have lots of pictures, lots of expectations, lots of "I want," and those pictures will get tied in with how you set your boundary.

If you're talking to me in a private consultation and you've had an inter-action with a particular odious person, I'll commiserate with you for about fifteen seconds, and then we move onto how we can improve your life. Fixing that other person is not really going to improve your life. I'm not sure you want to spend a hundred dollars per half hour on mak-ing *them* better. You're spending your money, so you want to get your money's worth out of it and make *yourself* better, and then you are likely to find ways of asking for what you really want and to set boundaries without violating boundaries.

Make *your* pain the energy exploration, not *their* behavior. And you don't transcend it by becoming perfectly loving and saying it doesn't matter. You engage them in a way that you will always win regardless of the outcome, because at the very least, you will have grown. You'll do much better and get better outcomes more often.

Think of a relationship that hasn't been very satisfactory, look at how much more there is to that relationship than you've been tracking, and see how it may even travel through other people and your relationships with them. It may be a vital ingredient in an Astral stew. An Astral stew is pungent and flavorful, bold and challenging. Just consider that there is always more going on that really is part of who you are than you can track, and let that be okay. Let that be a possibility of the richness that's always there.

A picture is an instruction set. Every picture, in a sense, is its own aura. It contains structures and a set of beliefs. The picture structures a cer-tain amount of energy and space. A bunch of pictures together, or one major picture, will really have a profound impact on where you set your aura and how you keep your boundary where it is.

The third chakra will be responsive to certain sorts of master pic-tures in your space, such as what you like and what you don't like. Since you will have preferences and life will inevitably involve times when you don't get your preference, those pictures that are hooked into your third chakra first will get shaken, and that's what I call frustration. Your aura doesn't collapse, but it goes in a couple of inches and then goes back out, and that's frustration. Every picture will have some resistance in it because it's set up to structure space in a certain way. So if you have an experience that lights up that picture—that the picture is in resistance to—it will flutter a little bit and your aura will flutter a little bit. That's if it's not a major picture.

But if it crosses a certain threshold, your aura collapses. And that's what anger is. When your aura collapses, your third chakra is set up to re-inflate your aura. There's an automatic process in your third chakra. When it quickly re-expands your aura, that's anger. When you respond to your anger with an interpretation that you have been victimized, that results in either repression or aggression.

Energy motivates us to change things. Now, most of us have one or both of two unfortunate responses. One is to have our aura expand all the way out so that it literally jumps into the other person's space and starts inflicting pain and demands on them. That is why anger gets such a bad reputation, and this is not a good outcome in the overall scheme of things. The other thing we do, sometimes simultaneously, is suppress a lot of vitality. If you do that, you end up reducing your personal vitality and having this energy that hasn't been addressed and hasn't been assimilated.

So, repression turns your anger inside. Aggression throws your anger into someone else's space as you are trying to coerce them into behaving. In point of fact, you'll probably do both. The repression or aggression may be in the forefront, but the other will almost certainly sneak in there.

Either way, the third chakra will be the mechanism. The solution is eventually going to involve reopening. There may be several steps involved: doing some clearing, finding your grounding, finding your crown. At some point you will re-inflate your third chakra and re-open your space.

You can learn to give your anger its natural space and become aware of what you're thinking and feeling and how you want to respond. It will never be perfect, but if you do that, anger will have the effect of increasing your self-awareness. Any negative emotion that is skillfully used increases your self-awareness. It will motivate you to take some sort of action that may or may not involve responding directly to the thing that lit it up.

If someone hits you in the jaw, there is going to be pain. But if you look at that, probably 90 percent of the pain is the thought, "They shouldn't have hit me in the jaw." So, you find the should, have to, or ought and begin to treat that. You can treat it one of two ways: You can state it in an intellectual way and ask yourself, "Do I really believe in this judgment? Or is it just a preference? Is it something that has to happen or is it a really strong preference?" That's one way you can do it.

This holds even at the extreme. If someone shoots you, it's not a surprise if you're very angry. It *is* a delusion, but it's not a surprise. If someone puts you in a concentration camp, of course you're angry, but the anger is still a delusion.

Another way is just to make your anger an energy, to look at it as an energy. Focus on the energy aspect of it. What percentage of the energy is mine? You clear out the energy that isn't yours. That may take several back-and-forths with your crown. It becomes kind of circular. Clear the energy that isn't yours. Create and destroy roses. For the energy that is left, bring it into current time. You may have a lot of energy behind a thought such as, "My parents shouldn't have treated me like that." Once you clear the energy out, it might be easier to explode your pictures and realize, "I don't know what they should have done, but I can feel that, as an adult, it doesn't need to limit me any longer. Of course, it has affected where I am at this point, but it doesn't control how I respond to new phenomena. It certainly sets up my starting position, but as I clear and become neutral to it, it no longer controls how I respond to the next thing."

If you leave your body in a state of anger or with an active anger event, does it make a lasting impression in the next lifetime?

It depends on how you respond to that event. If you hold onto that anger, it is possible that you'll come into the next life, or a life not too far in the future, seeking revenge. Or you might seek another several lifetimes where you're victimized until you fully understand your contribution to it.

When you have an unskillful emotional response, you don't get to choose from that level of lack of skill how it's going to play out. A lot of people think, "I don't care if revenge karma is unskillful, I'm going to come back into my next life with revenge on my mind. And if that's bad, well then it's bad, but cool."

It doesn't work out that way. You may come back with revenge on your mind and have somebody do revenge against you or against a family member so that you begin to understand the nature of revenge. At a personality level you have the delusion that you can impose revenge on someone without any consequences. It could be that you impose revenge on someone and then are traumatized by seeing the outcome of that. There are other negative results that are not so obvious. A lot of anger in our present time is creating karma that must eventually be addressed—not in the popular sense of karma, but in the sense of energy and its natural balances.

Your soul can make a skillful decision that you're going to understand revenge. Instead of trying to rise above anger altogether, you work with the specificity of the anger, that particular piece of anger. You go and create a much deeper engagement with the world at a personal and Astral level.

Those people who are only loving may or may not be *actually* loving, and they may even be proud of their engagement with the world. It may be profound or it may be joyous. But it probably isn't genuinely engaging the Astral part, by which I mean personal. Consequently, they are not fulfilling the ecological niche that human beings are meant to fill as we move toward the Aquarian Age. I've seen many times, for example, people say, "Okay, when so-and-so dies they will understand what an awful person they were and that I was right."

What that does is it holds you stuck until they die. And they may not change after they die. Death changes people, but sometimes it doesn't change them much.

One of the most powerful techniques you can do is turn a rhetorical question that you ask yourself into a real question. When you ask, "Why do I have to deal with that?" you almost certainly really mean, "I'm too good a person to have to deal with this, I ought to be experiencing better." In this sense, it is a rhetorical question, not a real one. You can turn it into a real question by becoming deeply curious and saying, "Okay! Why *do* I have to deal with this?" And the answer is never "because that other person is a jerk." They may be a jerk, but that's not why *you have* to deal with it. Their flaws are *never* the answer to why you have to deal with it. The answer to asking, "Why do I have to deal with this?" always involves something going on in you because that's your only source of power. So if the answer is, "Because that person is a jerk," that's an off-putting answer. If the answer is that or, "Because I don't love myself well enough," or, "Because I don't have enough prosperity pictures," those are all answers that put off the responsibility to the external world. But when you ask a question as a *real* question, "Why do I have to deal with this?" you will learn something about yourself that's skill-building.

GLORIA: For some people, even saying, "Why do I have to deal with this?" is still in resistance, even if it's framed as a question. What I like to do is a reframe that asks, "Why am I exploring this?" Or, "Why am I exploring this again?" And when I keep bringing it back to "Why am *I* exploring this?" then it gives me somewhere to go. Because asking something like, why do I "have to" deal with this can turn into a should. Exploration by reframing it this way always seems to work for me.

JOHN: Right, reframing the words you use will help you actually turn it into a real question. Gloria's reframe takes you out of the rhetorical question. Rhetorical questions are just a way of making yourself angry, and you will know that you're asking a rhetorical question by the fact that if someone actually answers the question as if it were a question, you will get angry at them. Avoid rhetorical questions by becoming present and changing your attitude to one of curiosity.

You can turn your rhetorical questions into real questions.

27

Neutrality

There are lots of concepts about which you can say, "If you really get this, you've got the whole system." You could say that about each of fifteen things: "This is the core of the system." And you'd be right because it transmogrifies into everything. If you make an input, make an intervention at any place, it affects the entire system. That's the definition of a system.

Well, neutrality—understanding neutrality—is the core of this system.

The reason that we cultivate neutrality is so that we can be open to life as it is. We cultivate neutrality not by making our whole aura neutral so that we're never angry or upset or whatever, but just by making a spot in our consciousness—which could be in the center of our head, or the crown, or back in the corner of the room—neutral, a place where you can be open to life as it is. You *have* your emotions rather than *becoming* your emotions.

The center of your head is a place that's stable no matter what else is going on. It doesn't do away with other chaos; it just gives you a place to look at that chaos, or that pleasure, or that joy that has its own space, so that you're letting your experience be what it is without being excessively caught up in identifying with the experience. When you're too upset to be in your body, you can use the space above your crown; you can go out of body and work the energy from out there until you can eventually come back into the body.

At the personality level, we spend a lot of time learning how to own our crown, not get sucked into the stories we tell ourselves. Yet we still have the full range of our non-neutral emotions and ideas. That's because you're cultivating your neutrality and non-neutrality in a harmonious interaction with one another. You're maintaining that part of neutrality that allows you to have experiences without being those experiences.

One of the reasons that you cultivate neutrality and psychic abilities is so that you can become more and more capable of communicating to people. Otherwise, you like somebody if you agree with them on important things and dislike them if you disagree. You think you become more intimate the more your auras are enmeshed instead of basing your relationships on real rapport and appreciation of difference. Through this system you learn how to have an entirely different kind of neutrality and communication leading to intimacy. In the beginning it will almost seem kind of boring because it's subtle. It's sort of the difference between, you know, a meatball sub with lots of fat and salt—there's nothing intrinsically wrong with that—and a soup that has a perfect blend of vegetables and flavor and balance.

It's really cool when you learn how to say hello at this level. You can even do it with people that you really dislike or people that you're way out of rapport with.

But you can't fake it. You have to do it from neutrality and openness to them as they are. You're not fixing them, not improving them, not giving up your opinions about them, but it's that one little touch, that new kind of intimacy where you say hello to them. You will see their own power sort of surge, their power to be a human being. Not their power to conquer Germany or something like that, but their power to be a human being. You'll recognize that when you can have relationships on a hello level. You just see this light go on. Boom! That's what intimacy is. Not enmeshment, not saying things like, "We were meant for each other till the end of time."

At the deeper level this is why the interdependence of the universe is so cool, because that's intimacy.

Look across space to a person that you're saying hello to. Become aware of some energy or energies in their space. Have whatever feelings you have about those and let those be your personal opinions. Just acknowledge, with neutrality, the existence of what you see. You might be seeing it wrong, but you acknowledge what it is you think you see without a lot extraneous interpretation. And just send a little beam toward that person, to that energy or energies that you perceive. Leave your energy outside their aura, more like a billboard showing them your hello than inserting your hello.

Use less than featherweight. You'll often find that you come in there with a lot more than a featherweight, you might even come in there with a sledgehammer. That's a clear indication that you're really not in neutrality. And as you say hello to this energy or energies, notice what happens to their aura and what happens to yours.

Create and destroy roses for any and all pictures that light up throughout your body and aura. This will also light you up in addition to enlightening you.

Now pick someone, not necessarily in the room, that you have difficulty communicating with, perhaps someone who's unfair to you or is disapproving of you. You'll have to work especially hard to keep your grounding and your third chakra open but playful. Have a rose at the edge of your aura to mark the end of the personal you and the beginning of the outside world. Set your crown at a different color than what you're saying hello to. Have your opinions without them being in your hello. Let a neutral beam of acknowledgement form, go out just to the outside of the aura of the person that you're saying hello to, and see what happens to their aura. Also, look at what happens to your aura. If you are skillful, both auras will brighten.

Hello is an invaluable tool for those people that you get along with and for those people that you don't get along with.

It's very hard to actually say hello to someone you are having difficulty with. That is, it's really hard not to put a little bit of a twist on that hello that says, "Helllllooooo, I'm just saying hello to you exactly as you are, you jerk." If someone rejects you at an energy level, that's probably why, and it's a good opportunity to get back to neutrality.

Put them far enough out in front of your aura so that they are outside of your aura and put a rose at the edge of your aura that marks off your personal space from the rest of the world. Male or female ground. Set your crown at a different color than them. Then look at their energy, start to look at what makes you angry, and catch yourself pronouncing what they should do, what they have to do, what they ought to do. Blow pictures and remove cords and deconstruct your judgment. Remind yourself that just because there is no good reason that you can come up with for them behaving as they are and you have a strong preference that they not, they are still doing it, they are either stubborn or oblivious. Ask yourself, "Is it really a law of the universe that they change right now on my schedule and in exactly the way I want them to?"

Sometimes it's helpful to look at what their defense mechanisms are, what pain drives them. But you don't have to go to that. You can just work on your own should and keep blowing pictures and removing cords. Very often you can deconstruct your should by saying, "Oh, I don't need to say 'should.' This is a preference, not a law of the universe."

If you have a lot of energy tied up in your should, to really clear it requires blowing pictures and removing cords and karma, clearing contracts, pulling your energy out of the person, and sending their energy back to them. Really create and destroy roses and become as neutral as you can as you let go of your shoulds.

There is a you that you might call your witness consciousness—that's a term used in other systems. You have this you saying, "Oh, okay, there's that anger. Wow, look at my stress hormones going and, wow, I really don't like this person and, wow, I have all of these judgments and I don't like being angry." You're not going to be perfectly neutral. Perfect neutrality is not possible in any of the energies that we cultivate in this system. You'll never be *perfectly* neutral, but you can be *a lot more* neutral. And that would a profound effect.

In this system, authentic requires that you have your emotions including your negative emotions and they can never be eradicated. Authentic neutrality is that you have those emotions without losing yourself and your crown in an emotion that is unpleasant or pleasant. When you lose yourself in it, there is no you anymore, there is just a smushed-together you and that emotion. Neutrality is having that emotion and giving it its space and having a space where you are observing this without being so detached that you're not related to your body. This is a very, very difficult technical challenge, but whatever skill you can develop at it will pay huge dividends.

Understand that being open to the universe as it is doesn't mean not having preferences and even strong preferences and strategies and tactics to get what you want. It just means that you're open to the fact that often you're not going to get what you want. Or you're going to get what you want and it's not as much fun as you thought it was going to be. Life happens. And it's rich and it's wonderful in all its forms and that's what we're trying to open ourselves to be. Not perfectly open to life because as long as you have a physical body, as long as you engage and stay committed to your life as an individual human being, there will be resistances. You'll never be perfectly without resistances.

What is distinctive about Lewis Bostwick's approach to neutrality is that it is both in-body and embracing one's human personality on its own terms and for its own purposes. Most other spiritual journeys treat human personal consciousness as a kind of tragic mistake, something that is to be evolved beyond. Even practices like tantra or Zen Buddhism that really engage everyday experience do it with the presupposition that dualistic consciousness, your personal consciousness, in addition to being an illusion—which I agree, it is an illusion—is something for you to evolve out of as quickly as possible. I don't see how if you have that attitude, you can fully validate each life as sacred in its own terms. I don't see how you can become truly neutral.

The difference, as Seth said, "is in the very nature of consciousness to want to explore all dimensions as fully as possible." Human consciousness in this period fills a very important spiritual, ecological space.

I think you're ready to imagine having fun when you're not having fun, when you're having an unpleasant experience. Lewis put it this way,

"Have fun and if you're not having fun, have fun not having fun." He isn't saying, "Play like you're not having a miserable time." When you're having a miserable time, you are in fact having a miserable time. But what he *is* saying is there's an aspect of attention when you shift from saying, "It's horrible that I'm having a miserable time," to saying, "I wonder why I'm having this miserable time." You become curious, and that exploration actually starts to become fun. If you have enough neutrality to be open to unpleasantness and engage it and explore it, the exploration is always fun even when the experience you are exploring is not.

The way you let something start to be fun is by letting it be an adventure. If something is really depressing or horrifying, it is justified to be depressed and horrified. Just understand that there is something underneath all that where every moment is sacred, this one included. You cannot fail over the long term even if you want to.

Take as an experiment the thought, "I'm going to fail on this for a hundred years." It's very hard to do. A person might get into several lifetimes of alcoholism or something like that. But at some point, something will change and they will climb out of that.

I'm not saying in every instance, "Oh God, this failure is so great. What an opportunity!" I don't expect people always to be having fun when they're not having fun. When you're having an unpleasant experience, it's going to be unpleasant. That's just the truth of the matter. If you have enough neutrality to be open to the unpleasantness and engage it and explore it, the exploration itself is always fun. What I *am* saying is that you can cultivate a sense of play. And if you can't cultivate playfulness, you can cultivate curiosity. And you may get pulled into the muck for a week or so, but if you're cultivating curiosity, you're like a flower growing up through concrete, eventually you will push up through and will clear that concrete. That's how life gets to be fun most of the time.

Desperation isn't fun, but exploration is always fun.

I often talk to people about problems that are really unpleasant. For the twenty minutes they're discussing it with me and we're exploring, there's this energy and there's that energy. It's shocking how often they're having fun exploring the psychic energy of this thing that's very unpleasant.

If you can get engaged in whatever you're doing, you can have fun. Some things may be beyond your capacity to have fun, like a migraine headache. The brain is set up to put all of your attention in an urgent sort of way to get rid of the pain, so most times people have a hard time having fun when they're having a migraine headache. But if you can turn whatever it is you're experiencing into an interesting puzzle, then you might even start having fun during a migraine. If you're not enjoying it, then enjoy *not enjoying it.*

Exploring why we're doing what we're doing and how we got that way is better than a mud run. Find something that bothers you right now and notice how closed in you feel when you're just sitting in that botheration and then do a shift—you might have to change your crown color to do it and it really helps to be grounded—do a shift and become interested in what's causing it and let go of your shoulds, have tos, and oughts. Once you're letting go of your shoulds, have tos, and oughts, you're becoming interested in it, maybe even becoming interested in how you created those shoulds, have tos, and oughts. Cultivate some curiosity. I'm not saying it will blot out the pain, I'm not saying that it will be unidimensionally fun. If you find yourself losing yourself for a minute at a time in curiosity, those moments are fun and, even if you haven't lost yourself, you've added at least a bit of fun to what's going on.

So, if you have all of the emotions that you have and engage them, that will speed your process up. If you really do it, you will usually understand what fun not having fun can be. You may not have much fun dealing with the situation where you hate someone else's energy, but you will learn how to change that.

Basically, the so-called negative emotions are compensations. Remember, there really isn't such a thing as a negative emotion. All emotion has vital information. But there are unskillful ways of dealing with certain emotions.

Neutrality is your ability to be open to experience as it is. If you think you are neutral, and yet your diaphragm isn't moving and your chest is tight, you're not neutral. You may not feel anything, but not feeling anything is a polarity to neutrality. Delusion is part of experience anywhere in the universe, though perhaps our concept of delusion might not really transfer.

There's no magic formula that I can give as to when it's okay to do a compensation and when it's not. But basically, even if you're doing a compensation, you can also develop skills and resources and move forward. It's not black or white. Basically, if your changed behavior opens up space in your aura, you are not merely compensating. If your changed behavior closes down space in your aura by filling it up, then you are compensating.

When you can play with your aura, you have a way of evaluating whether you're compensating or not. It's not a perfect way because you may be compensating so much for your fear of failure and your aversion to self-punishment elsewhere that you'll convince yourself that you're opening space when you're not. That's just the way it is, the way life is. There are no roads that, if you follow them perfectly, you'll always get a good outcome. And anyone who tells you that they have such a way, I would encourage you to run from that person.

Another way would be just to look in your aura—you might throw purple light in your aura and ask it to light up any defense mechanism that you have. And then look at the energy of your defense mechanisms and see where they come from and how they trigger your compensations. In other words, our compensations are not random, they are triggered by energy structures in our aura and the purple energy we throw at our aura can make those structures easier to see.

Indignation is a great compensation. It is a compensation for feeling small and weak. I think all of us can find some indignation. Everyone will be able to find at least one compensation.

In this system, you can't be neutral without having your feelings or opinions. Because as long as you have a personal aura, you will have opinions about everything. Neutrality is defined as being open to what is, and if you shut down your relationship with your own opinions, you're not neutral.

So, the challenge is to ask, How can you be both angry and neutral?

A lot of people will say emotions are *in* the body. They are talking about a body that is symbiotically engaged with the Astral level. I think there is a kind of expansiveness to the body consciousness, but it doesn't have an emotional reaction at the body level. It does only as it entangles at the Astral. It forms a symbiotic relationship. Yes, the body has lots of authentic programming that we would call non-neutral.

Neutrality is not something that you impose on your entire aura either. You don't want your whole aura neutral. Your first chakra is not neutral about whether you live or die. Its job is to have a strong direction toward your living, with certain exceptions. There are times when the body consciousness wants to die. But if your first chakra is programmed with lots other people's energy and excessive fear, that's not natural lack of neutrality in the first chakra—it's unhealthy. Healthy lack of neutrality naturally moves in alignment with the natural direction of your life.

The second and third chakras are not neutral. We don't try to bring the female reproductive system, or the male reproductive system, into neutrality either.

Neutrality is not making your whole aura neutral. Neutrality is finding your consciousness, and I'm not trying to define what I mean by your consciousness, I'm going to leave it undefined and I don't know when or if ever we'll try to define it. But it's having your consciousness neutral or open to life as it is, even as the rest of your aura is decidedly not neutral. You have this preference, that preference, and the other preference. That's part of the experience of being human, a waking human. That's the setup. That's the intention.

It's really only the sixth, and maybe seventh, chakra that can be neutral. So that begins to explain how you can have your feelings and be neutral. You have your feelings running through most of your aura, first through fifth chakras, without *being* those feelings by not matching your seventh chakra, your crown, to the color of those feelings. Those feelings run through the body and aura the way you want them to so that you can fully experience them, but you don't associate into them by matching your crown.

If you associate into a feeling by matching your crown to the feeling, you actually can only match part of the feeling, just one or two colors. Feelings, especially difficult ones, always involve multiple aspects. It is simply the ontological nature of the Astral plane that no feeling can be purely one-dimensional. You can try this yourself. Create a fresh space, we call them universes, and put the energy of any particular emotion on a rose and put that rose into your new universe. Very quickly, new emotions and thoughts will spring forth, because they were always at least implicit in the original emotions. When you match your crown to an emotion, you really just match a part of it and get stuck in that part. You may feel you are experiencing its intensity, but that intensity is artificial and incomplete. By changing your crown, you can explore the multidimensionality in any emotion.

Then you cultivate neutrality in the center of your head or, if you are walking around, you can do it from slightly above your crown. From that neutrality, you respond to the messages, the strong desires that come at you from the external world, and you make skillful choices.

You can also find a way of being neutral in the center of your head. That's the only place in your aura that is neutral. You can't really find the center of your head without grounding and owning your crown, so you can't really be neutral just by trying to be in the center of your head before grounding and owning your crown.

As you clear your aura, some of your unskillful lack of neutrality gets cleared.

A goal in this system is to be less and less pushed by our own resistance to life, more and more open to life as it is, and to fully embrace the non-neutrality of desire and love from the skillful place of nonresistance to the inevitable contrast and contradiction of desire and love, of pain and pleasure.

Large beings, like fire or Mother Earth, you can call them neutral because they're not in resistance. These beings have desire without resistance. That's what we're seeking. So there is a sense, if you go deep enough into your own chakras, you will hit the level where there is no resistance. You will also have a riotous non-neutrality, and that's part of your authentic life. And from interaction between your neutrality and non-neutrality comes a dance. Fire is a dance. Be fire. Be your own kind of fire.

I recently began realizing that the way we were discussing neutrality was misleading people a bit. And it's easy to misunderstand because neutrality is so centrally important and subtle. I remember saying, you could be angry in a neutral way, but I think that kind of distorted things. Your anger will vibrate non-neutrally.

With any emotion—anger is just an important one, so I'm focusing on it—with any emotion (happiness, sadness, anger, impatience), those emotions are energies and they make a vibration in your aura. Every experience you have is a vibration. Now, those vibrations are not themselves neutral. And their non-neutrality is a vital part of your experience as a human being. When you match your crown to that emotion, then you become that emotion. You lose yourself in that emotion and you may express that emotion in an exaggerated and aggressive way, because you're not actually able to fully experience it. When you have enough neutrality, you do not match the emotion or idea with your crown, you can then have the emotion without becoming the emotion. And paradoxically, perhaps, you can fully experience the emotion, both the energy and its ramifications. If you lose your crown in that emotion, it will stay either stuck on one note, filled with other people's energy so that it never gets to its natural energy. Neutrality is an additional energy, in the center of the head or at the crown, from which you can fully explore emotions that are not themselves neutral.

To fully experience life requires neutrality in a particular space. Neutrality is basically—actually, I'm not going to define it this time. I'm going to leave it as an undefined term, as they say in advanced mathematics. Neutrality is yourself. So, think of yourself as like a ball of mercury. Only it's not silver, so let it be a lot of different colors. Well, sometimes it *will* be silver, actually, for some people—different people will have it as different colors. So, when you find that, you bring it into the center of your head; that's where we bring it when we're meditating and doing readings. When you're walking around, it often is easier to have this ball at or above your crown than in the center of your head. If you lose your grounding, it may be easier to put it in the corner of the ceiling, five hundred feet above your head or at various distances. When I used to have trouble with a particular set of thoughtforms, I would have to go outside the edge of the universe to find some neutrality. There are times when one universe is not enough. You can create as many universes as you need. Then you work to clear energy from however far you have to go till you can get back into your body. Because the body is where you encounter your person.

Okay, so let's take a moment here and find yourself. You may find that you are out of your body or behind it. You may find that you're in five hundred pieces. Please be comfortable. And from the center of your head, see if you can find where you are, and then draw a line from the center of your head to wherever you are. The cool thing about this technique is that it tends to pull you back into the center of your head.

Now, what happens is that you can imagine the you as a bunch of mercury droplets and they tend to get lost in various emotions that you have. Once you put a certain amount of you in this emotion, and a certain amount of you in resisting that emotion, there's no consolidated you anymore; you're in many little pieces. So, with some playfulness as you find you in the center of your head, you might find you getting pulled out of the center of your head. That comes from your crown starting to match the color or energy of non-neutrality; of other people's energy; of something you're resisting; or of any emotions such as anger, boredom, what you think of as love, whatever.

Remember, you can't fully be grounded if you don't own your crown, and you can't own your crown until you're grounded. These are two simultaneous processes. In some ways you ground so that you *can* own your crown. You can own your crown from a resistance level, but it's not really owning your crown and it takes a lot of effort and a lot of huffing and puffing. You really only own your crown in neutrality.

Owning your crown is having your crown vibrate at a different color than what you are looking at, but it's subtler than that. It's much, much easier to do if you vibrate your crown at a *higher* color frequency than what you're looking at. You own your crown by creating and destroying roses and intentionally setting your crown at a higher color frequency than whatever is tugging on it, whatever is transforming it. Gold is the color that most supports neutrality. Gold is always neutral. So if you're having trouble finding neutrality, going to gold will make it easier. But setting your crown to gold all day long is not likely to be very effective. It's not really a place where people are comfortable that long and it's kind of hard to keep your crown gold all the time.

If you want to put it to gold for this exercise, you don't have to get your whole crown vibrating at gold. You can paint the outside in a circle-like halo. It often is a better idea to set your crown to a violet or blue. Other colors are trickier. I almost always run an orange in my crown, often at an orangish-gold because I do a lot of healing. I do it sort of unconsciously. But if you walk around throughout your day with a crown vibrating at orange you might become an out-of-control healer, like the boy scout who drags the old lady across the street that she doesn't want to cross. You'll be in resistance to a lot of people and jump in their space.

When I say color, you don't have to be visual to do this. You can have a feeling or a sound. It can be very kinesthetic, but there will still be a sensation at which you can run your crown. In the long run, color will be the easiest to do.

When you get your crown at gold or a different color, you can either be at the center of your head or in your crown. Find the energy of the emotion or thought or sensation that you are experiencing, put it on a rose, and put that out in front of you and look at it. It might take you five minutes or five months to get where you can be neutral as you look at it. I mean, you might have owned your crown, but as soon as you put the rose for the emotion you are exploring out there, you may just lose your crown separateness and go right to the color of the emotion you're looking at.

You don't have to wait until you are perfectly neutral to look at an emotion. Even if it takes you five months to get neutral you can still go to another stage of asking yourself, "What percentage of this emotion's energy* is my energy?" This is not a thought question. It is not sitting down and analytically evaluating this in a way that you could defend to your thesis committee. It is an instantaneous sort of sense.

Can that sense be wrong? Of course. And the primary way it's wrong is that the answer you get *is itself* someone else's energy. But you work with what you sense and over time you get more accurate. If you get two answers at once, at least one of those is going to be someone else's energy, someone else's answer to your question.

You start off by grounding, male or female grounding. Then you find the energy of the emotion, thought, or sensation. It is always an energy. For instance, a memory is an energy. You put that energy in the rose and you put that rose out in front of you. Then, depending upon what works for you—and I usually do some of one and then back to the other and then back to the first—you can start by owning your crown by getting it to vibrate at a different color than the color of the emotional reaction.

Or, maybe your crown gets stuck and you can't get it to the color. Then you do what's in the way *is* the way. You start breathing your energy out of whatever is sticking in your crown so that you can get the crown back up. You look at what it is, or feel or hear what it is. You ask yourself, "What's the story I'm telling myself about this?" You explore the story and then you find where your shoulds, have tos, and oughts are. If the emotion you're looking at is painful for you, you can be pretty certain that you have shoulds, have tos, and oughts, because that's what generates resistance.

If you're uncomfortable in a situation, treat that discomfort as important information. Don't do this in a self-deceiving way, thinking, "Oh, I don't like this person for such-and-such reason," which is a fault-finding way. Instead, pay attention to how you answer the questions, "Why am I uncomfortable? Why do I not want to go forward with this exercise?" Ask yourself, "Why am I in this situation?"

---

*The energy on the rose.

Here's another exercise: Find something that really lights you up, such as injustice, unkindness, a political figure you don't like, the weather, traffic jams. Put it on a rose, and keep blowing pictures and clearing energies until you can comfortably look at that without losing your crown.

For this next part of this exercise, let your attention be one particular, specific emotion connected to a specific event. And let that emotion expand until it takes as much space as it wants while, again, keeping your crown at a color different from what you're looking at.

Notice that your emotion is vibrating. It's not neutral but you are. That's how you end up giving the emotion space to be whatever it is. Then you can respond to it as skillfully as you can at that time in your life.

The cool thing is that, every time you get lit up, every time you're in the process of losing your crown, if you create and destroy roses you actually start to assimilate your experience and you begin to open yourself to life as it is. You'll also be less reactive to that particular thing the next time you encounter it. Your aura will be more open and flowing, and you'll be releasing pain and resistance. You get to be a happier person.

This is a huge step on the way to becoming as effective as you could be at aiding the authentic transformation of whatever situation you're unhappy with.

Now, there's another part to really engaging this with neutrality. That's clearing the energy that isn't yours out of the emotion. I'm going to make that a separate exploration.

To do this, put an emotion in a rose and explode it. Create and destroy roses for any and all pictures that are lit anywhere throughout your body and aura. Fill your aura with lots of golden suns and just the right amount of Earth energy for your body at this time.

People are much more neutral now than they were thirty minutes ago. Diane was saying that she blew all of these pictures and then toward the end there seemed to be one that was clinging to her chest.

It is probably always the case that if something seems to be clinging to you, you have your energy enmeshed with something or someone else. And so, pull your energy out of whatever is clinging to you, because it can't cling to you if you don't have your energy in it. Send it back to the person whose energy it is, because they're who needs it and can use it. It's great that you can even perceive that. And if you can't figure out whose energy it is, just pull your energy out of the thing that's clinging to you and send the other energies to the Earth or the Sun. Hopefully everybody is getting that. Nothing can cling to *you* unless you're clinging to *it*.

Here is another way of putting it: It can't cling to you without some picture to cling to. So, someone else's energy cannot cling to you without some picture that acts like Velcro. I usually find it easier to pull my energy out of whatever is clinging to me than to find the picture it's clinging to. But either of those ways will work equally well.

GLORIA: That was very helpful to be able to find the scattered pieces about me. And it came back very easily. I noticed that when it came back, the emotion itself brightened. Then whatever the emotions were, there was an assimilation of the meaning of that emotion that happened at a conscious level, but it burst in its own way across my whole being. It was just beautiful and a lovely surprise.

JOHN: It burst across Gloria's being like that because assimilating an experience, in the sense that we use the word, is exactly equivalent to letting go of your resistance to the experience. By assimilating the experience we mean that it's ready to be taken in by the soul as it is and utilized by the soul. And it no longer is stuck in your personal aura or Etheric body as something that diverts the flow of energy and experience. So, your aura is freer to respond to the universe. At least that piece of your experience is not blocking your aura or you from being open to the universe as it is.

28

Whose Energy Is It?

Whenever I'm experiencing an unpleasant emotion or having an unpleasant experience, at least nine out of ten times, I'll put that unpleasant experience on a rose and the first thing I'll look at is, Whose energy is it? The reason is that you can't make someone else's energy behave in your aura. It has its own will. If you're trying to get out of an emotion, and 60 percent of that emotion is generated by someone else's energy, I'd like to suggest that it will be really productive to drain off the other person's energy. Sometimes you can't drain off their energy until you explode some pictures.

All of those voices in your head that you are arguing with all the time are the people who are writing the story of what your life means. They are writing it if you're not paying attention. So, if that voice is your mother, then she's writing the story of what your life means and what you should be doing. And if you are arguing with the voice in your head, you're getting a mixture that is driven by resistance that generates the stories in your head. Not your mom, not you, but a tussle between the two of you as to whose story is going to dominate.

There are lots of ways that you can go about this. The way that I find the easiest and most straightforward and is always going to work—it may take a month or a year or a lifetime or two to work, but eventually it's always going to work—is asking, "Whose energy is this emotion or idea or even sensation that I am experiencing?"

The two main techniques are moving into current time by exploding pictures and identifying your energy, because your energy will have your information, your natural flow.

The energy in your aura generates the reality that you experience. Now, if most of that energy is your mom's, then your mom's energy and your resistance to it are going to be how you create your reality. A boss you don't like could be what you are resisting. What you resist, you become. If you resist the politics that you don't like then that becomes an ever-larger part of your reality creation. And stopping resistance is not trivial. You can't just say, "Oh, I'm going to stop doing this." Basically, the way that you stop resisting is you cultivate neutrality and the capacity to have emotions vibrating in your aura without becoming them.

What's in your aura is what gets created. Those voices in your head, and your resistance to them, are a large part of your life. All of us have voices in our head. And checking and seeing whose voice it is and using neutrality to help us move out of resistance to the voices that aren't ours lets us give the energy of those voices back to whomever they belong to.

Now, it doesn't mean you can't listen to those voices. You just want to listen to them *outside* of you. They can come from your husband or your coworker or a political figure you don't like. But they can come neutrally from them rather than sitting in your space. It doesn't matter how good the energy is, and this applies to all energy in the personal aura that doesn't vibrate at a neutral level. The Sun's energy and the Earth's energy all vibrate in your aura, but those are so big they are neutral to your experience and, consequently, helpful.

All energy is charged to the will of the person whose energy it is. So Judy's energy, from whatever lifetime it is, is charged to Judy's will. There's a piece of Judy's energy right here from fifteen lifetimes ago. It's still charged to her will. It's not enlightened versus non-enlightened. It's who you are, your particular story to bring to the universe.

If it isn't your energy, it isn't authentic. It doesn't matter how glorious it is. It might be the Dalai Lama's, but then you still want to give it back to the Dalai Lama.

Now, Judy's a lovely person and the Dalai Lama is a lovely person, but when their energies are in my space, those energies are not freely responsive to my will.

You can move any energy in your space; that's part of how you can send it back to whomever it belongs to. But, unlike your own energy in your space, other people's energy isn't accurately responsive to your desires. It does what it wants to. It just sort of wobbles around doing what it wants.

It's sort of like trying to play one of these video games with a cursor or joystick that doesn't work. Those projectiles are flying around in your aura, shooting things, and you're not able to get them to stop because it's someone else's energy. That's a significant exaggeration.

Often, when I'm talking to someone, they give me this long explanation of why they're doing something that has very little to do with why they're doing it. Maybe they are doing it because they have all of this person's energy in their space and that's the way it's going.

If someone else's energy seems stuck in your space, you can always just breathe it back. On the out-breath you send it back to them. That will always work sooner or later. But if you find your neutrality, it's going to work sooner rather than later. Some things are just damn hard. And that's okay.

I may start with whose energy it is, but I get halfway through sending that energy back and I bump into one of my shoulds, have tos, and oughts. Before I can send their energy back, I have to sort through my judgments. To think, "My friend should stop being so judgmental," you might notice, is *my* judgment about *his* judgment.

One of the main things we learn how to do is say hello to people without matching their energy, so that you stay yourself and are able to remain authentic, kind, and generous—not perfectly kind and generous but at least B-plus. And let people have their responses to you.

29

Grounding Cord

The California Institute grounding that we do, where we send a grounding cord down to the center of the Earth, is actually an Astral grounding in the low end, the sixth and seventh sub-planes of the Astral. It's only the Etheric roots that are Etheric grounding. But those sixth and seventh sub-planes are transition phases. They're like the gear system where the Astral communicates with the Etheric. That allows Astral information to get geared into the Physical-Etheric and vice versa.

Why do we ground? One reason is to bring yourself into current time. The main reason that Earth energy brings you into present time isn't that it's greater than your energy, it's that Mother Earth is never out of present time whereas you might be.

I want you to think of your grounding cord as something reasonably reliable, which it can only be if you don't think of it as perfect. It's always there and, though it changes moment by moment because everything changes moment by moment, it's kind of like saying, "Okay, I may not know a lot, but I kind of know that." It's only when you ask your grounding cord to be so magical that it gives you everything you want that it stops being reliable because it can't be reliable for that.

It's a place, an energy, a relationship between your individual personality and Mother Earth. And no matter what you're going through, it's at least theoretically accessible. Now it may not be sufficient, but it's still there for you to deal with what you're going through; it's still there, no matter what you're going through. It's still there as an option even if you lose it from time to time.

See if you're in communication with your third chakra and if your third chakra is in communication with your grounding cord. If that communication is going, your third chakra will be more resilient and more resourceful. And in some ways the third chakra is the center of your body consciousness. It also has to do with boundaries. If you're not comfortable with your boundaries, then you're not going to be comfortable in your third chakra.

Please locate in yourself this sense that says, "I have to have this. I have to have that. I have to have self-esteem, then my life will be fine." It doesn't work that way. These resource states help you feel more resilient, more reliable, more alive. They don't do it for you, and there's no particular one you have to have. You can have a complete lack of self-esteem and be fine, depending on what you mean by self-esteem, as long you have confidence in your grounding cord, or if you're in touch with your intellect or your soul.

Try looking at your body consciousness just as a body consciousness, not the fact that it's in relationship to your spirit. Let it, through your third chakra, say hello to your grounding cord. Notice how it lets your body be at least somewhat more comfortable. There may even be pain in our body, or anxiety, or chaos going on in your Astral aura, but some portion of your body will be comfortable being a body, and more so as a result of your having a grounding cord. All sorts of things may be going on, but your body is moving along, doing its stuff, connected with your grounding cord. It's good to have some sort of resource state; otherwise you just get buffeted around.

One of the reasons we learn to be *in* our bodies is because, if you can't be in your body, you can't really do well out of your body. You're not going to have a productive out-of-body or mystical state if you're not able to hold a focus, and being in your body teaches you how to have a particularly profound focus. That's why we put so much attention into being in our bodies and in dealing with everyday life.

A grounding cord helps your body stabilize and consequently gives you, as a spirit, a stable place from which to engage the world.

Think of something that you find challenging. For instance, do you find it challenging to listen to someone about politics that you disagree with? Do you find it challenging to see people lose their temper? Do you find it challenging to talk to someone who is being unfair with you?

Cut off your grounding cord and engage the challenge in your mind's eye ungrounded. What you'll probably find is your crown matching just what you don't like about the challenge and becoming enmeshed and junior to it. Now, put the energy of that challenge on a rose out in front of your aura and female or male ground. To the extent that you can ground, you'll probably find yourself being much more open to letting that challenge be exactly what it is and developing skill in dealing with it.

You can add another resource state by putting a rose at the edge of your aura to mark where you end and where the outside world begins. Now set your crown to a different color than the challenge, to a different color than the primary color in that challenge.

When you have four neutrality tools going—grounding, a rose that distinguishes you from the outside world, setting your crown, and exploding your matching pictures—there's a good chance for you to develop neutrality to that challenge. There will be some challenges for which this really doesn't work. There may be more things that you need to do and it may take more time to get to neutrality. You don't have to be in perfect neutrality, just find more openness than you would have had. I would hope when you're in this state that you can more easily find the tools and techniques for unenmeshing yourself from that challenge and will be able to engage it without *being* it.

From this more neutral place, see or feel yourself responding to that challenge more skillfully and with unconditional respect for other people even if you disagree with them. As you're doing that, create and destroy roses for the pictures that are lighting up.

With neutrality, you can heal any underlying issues even if you are sometimes unable to change the external world. The trick is getting neutral about something that really lights you up. You might have to start on easy stuff—and even the easy stuff isn't easy.

30

Clearing Karma and Other Energies

Karma appears in your aura as a disk. The way you clear karma is with psychic homeopathy. You start by taking from your own aura some of the energy of the person with whom you have karma. If you have karma with any person, you will always have some of *their* energy in *your* space—so you don't have to go out and grab it from them, it will be there in your space. You don't need to know the person with whom you have the karma, you may never have met them, they may not even be incarnated now. By feel, you can get a sense of them, and that sense is enough to find their energy. Most of this process is done by feeling or seeing; intellectual understanding may or may not come but is entirely unnecessary.

To have karma with someone, you have to be holding onto some of their energy and have some experience that your soul hasn't assimilated.

You just drop the energy—a little piece of energy of the person with whom you have the karma—into that karma disk like homeopathy. And the disk just breaks it up, it implodes. Now it might not entirely implode, but some of it will implode. If some of the karma remains, you can try again, check if some of the karma is with a different person.

You can keep the disk inside your aura or place it outside. Most psychic clearing works better if you put what you're clearing outside your aura because it's a cleaner space. If it's inside your aura, there are all sorts of other things going on.

Let's start clearing thoughtforms now. You don't have to see them to know they're there. That's why we're using roses.

Use a couple of bouquets of roses. Take one out and say, "This represents a thoughtform." Start clearing karma and contracts. Create an identical rose to it and superimpose it. Don't worry about doing it right or not, just go ahead and do it.

I don't jam the roses together when I superimpose them. I sort of shimmy them together and, as I'm shimmying them, I'm clearing pictures, contracts, and energies that aren't mine. I'm releasing my resistance as I shimmy them together. I hope that, as we gain that awareness, we will be able, in a stressful situation, to just work out of the calmness of the Etheric, noticing what's happening in the Astral, being somewhat in the Astral and senior. If it's a difficult situation and too difficult to interact with the person or situation and clear energy simultaneously, then just try in the moment to behave as the solid, reliable, compassionate person that you want to; then, later on, work on engaging at an Astral level and clarifying and becoming senior and clearing Astral pain out of your space. In other words, act with maturity now and clear later.

The denser you get, the slower the change is. You can make changes really quickly in the Astral compared to the Physical; you can make them even faster in the Mental or Causal. Once you get to the Causal, things happen so fast you can't follow them with your neurological system and they very often happen outside of time as we understand it. If you have a cut, it might take a week to heal in the Physical. If you heal it at the Etheric, it might take a day and a half to heal. In the Astral or Causal, the energy part of the healing is almost instantaneous.

You could consider current time, as opposed to clock time, as how long it takes for a change to actually manifest. If you break your arm, current time physically might be the next eight weeks, whereas it might heal Astrally over the next two days. In the Etheric it might heal in the next two weeks. Of course, if they heal at those levels, the physical healing will be faster too. The point is, changes happen more quickly the further away from energy vibration of the physical body you go. It's set up to take longer the closer to the body we get.

Sometimes you work from the body out. Sometimes you work from the Mental or Astral or Etheric in. And you never know because it's always contextual. Jane Roberts had rheumatoid arthritis, and she was so stuck on this idea of working through things with her beliefs that it never occurred to her to do yoga. I never had a conversation with her about it, but I think it's because exercise didn't seem like working with beliefs to her.

This is the mistake of thinking that you create reality by controlling it. Those people who run around saying, "I'm going to creatively visualize myself becoming rich," are utterly missing the point that you're here to have experience, not to supersede experience, and you're not likely to develop the abilities that are consistent with the energies of being prosperous without working in physical reality. You're not likely to solve rheumatoid arthritis without doing some movements to light up where the pain is, where the energy is.

Even if someone goes to a very skilled healer, and they're healed, they're often not really healed. Maybe their physical challenge healed. They may use that as a result to heal everything else at that time, but more often than not there's still work to be done at a different level than where the healing took place.

31

Moving Pictures between the Astral and the Physical-Etheric

Now we're going to watch the process of an Astral event becoming part of your body, because once it's in the Etheric it's part of your body. Of course, these condensations also happen at the next level too.

Here's the deal: When you have an emotion that you're in resistance to, it becomes a picture. And if that picture sits in your aura at a resistance level for thirty-six hours, according to Lewis Bostwick, it starts going down in frequency until it becomes part of your body. He didn't use the term Etheric body, but that's what it is.

That's quite amazing. This is how you create events. As a Causal soul, you're engaged in physical reality. You create reality and you even create your body in a sense.

Beliefs are shared. You may think you have a belief all of your own, but they're shared. So you look into certain belief areas, and you have emotions, and those beliefs mix with your emotions and with your breathing and they become individualized. And they sit in the Astral plane as an individualized emotion. Then if you're in resistance to that emotion, it becomes part of your permanent world by becoming part of your Etheric body. And that Etheric body is essentially what you create your reality with. The instructions flow through your Etheric body into dream space where the world is put together, and so your instructions go off into dream space and interact with other instructions and with the Buddhic plane itself. And then you wake up the next morning and here you are. You put today together by the instruction set that you took into the dream state.

I think that's just beyond cool. And you can't manipulate it. Well, you can. Some people can use their will power to do a powerful, willed magical act and send an instruction set into their Etheric body where they will get that event even if there are lots of obstructions in their overall personality. I think that's a disaster.

Now what happens more often—and it's just part of the way the world works—is that someone, their soul, focuses on some characteristics, and so those characteristics get imbedded into the Etheric body and they'll express themselves there. You can never have everything express at once. You may have a lot of money at one point. Or, say, you'd like to have a lot of money and someone else has far more than you, and so you ask, "How can that be? I have so much richer, integrated emotions. My Astral body is so much clearer. My Physical body is clearer. My Mental body is clearer." But that's not the agreement that you have with the planet, to focus on those narrow aspects that the other person is using to create a lot of money. Your agreement is to take a much bigger piece of you, and in that much bigger piece of you there will be sufficient contradictions so that you experience at least part of your life with less money than you want.

Go back in time to some emotion you were in resistance to. It can be big or it can be small. I can feel right now a bunch of pictures physicalized into my Etheric body because I was not out of resistance to an experience within thirty-six hours. It sat there long enough and gathered some other things, and they all became physicalized in my heart after a particular event.

As I look at that, energy starts running through that system and the embodied parts become rehydrated as pictures, and I clear them—most of them. It's really that easy when you get lit up. Let's say something, say impatience, physicalized into my Etheric long ago, and then today I'm watching a television show and seeing someone being really impatient. That might light up my impatience pictures or my humiliation pictures or whatever, encountering the imprints in the Etheric. That encounter, triggered by the TV show, energizes the imprints and raises their frequency to the Astral so they become pictures I can explode. We call this lighting up the pictures. If I take advantage of that lighting up, I'll explode those pictures, and they're no longer part of my Etheric or Astral body. I have cleared the underlying resistance to my earlier experience, thus assimilating it, and now my energy is open to new experience with more awareness than I had before.

There are some things that you'll be in resistance to, but your resistance will dissipate over time even without your conscious attention, because you just didn't have that big of a charge on it. Also things can become part of your body when you're attracted to an experience for positive reasons, without significant resistance.

What I'd like each of you to do for this exercise is go to a time when you were in resistance—it doesn't have to be dramatic or it *can be* dramatic. In resistance to means you were not entirely able to let it be as exactly what it was. You were pushing against it. You were trying to stifle it, because your experience was in the way of what you wanted. You were resisting your experience rather than trying to communicate with the other people in the experience. If instead you had been really centered and neutral—even if you don't like what another person is about to do—you will assimilate the entire experience and be ready to move to your next experience with openness and more wisdom than you had before. But if I do go into resistance to an experience, that energy memory, or in other words a picture, will sit in my space. If I were in enough resistance for that to sit in my space for thirty-six hours, it will become part of my Etheric body.

I will try to put it differently: Every experience that you have some resistance to will go into some other time. That resistance is a personal-aura phenomenon, an Astral phenomenon, and it will form a picture from your resistance. When a picture drops out of the Astral into the Etheric, it's no longer a picture. It's more like the flesh of your

Etheric Body. It might drop right on down through the Etheric into the Physical where it's *dis*-ease.

Within about thirty-six hours, an Astral picture, if you keep your resistance to it, drops out of the personal aura and into your Etheric body as a denser energy. Then the energies you want are less able to move smoothly through your Etheric body. The new Etheric inputs are almost like stonework they become so physical; it's like calcification, they become calcifications in your Etheric body. And that's not good. It's good from the big perspective in that, as it becomes part of your body and your unresolved issues will come through and manifest, you'll work through them and eventually gain spiritual freedom. But from the more conventional perspective, that's not good because it's likely to cause unpleasant events, and most of us prefer pleasant events to unpleasant events. Densification can also work to create pleasant events. You can open up to their manifestation and they then move smoothly into the etheric and physical.

So, you might create a picture in your aura and keep it energized because it's a goal of yours. And that picture can then become denser and part of your Etheric body, and the Etheric body is where things manifest from. That's why in a kind of paradoxical way the Etheric chakras can more powerfully open up your psychic ability than the higher-plane chakras.

So, there are Astral pictures that become stuck and become denser and move into the energy range of the Etheric. Remember, Astral pictures that get stuck become Etheric obscurations. They become little etchings. They become condensations or clumpings. I see it like something from a higher plane coming down and congealing into the chakra there. It's like they're enmeshed. It's useful and powerful to notice them as utterly distinct energies, but they're always changing. An Astral energy becomes an Etheric energy, and when you have experience, very often the Etheric clumpings will be reconstituted and rehydrated and will pop back up as Astral energy, as an Astral picture.

You'll look at your aura and say, "Well, I don't have a lot of pictures here." That's because many of them are so stuck they're condensed into Etheric matter. It's like you have them on your Etheric hard drive, and when the proper experience to light them up happens, they'll pop back up and become hard copy. They'll become a document floating around in your Astral space.

What you resist you become, so what you resist at an emotional level becomes part of your Etheric body, which you could call your inner physical body as opposed to your outer or observable body. And it profoundly affects your health and what events manifest.

Then there's the reverse process. As you have life experience, energy runs through your aura. There's calcification in the Etheric body, there's still some resistance in the Astral body. As that energy newly triggered by your experience runs through the Astral body, it will kick up obstructions wherever you have resistance to current experience. That resistance will show up in the Astral or personal aura as pictures and other obstructions. Let's say you're a neat control freak and you go into someone's house that's messy, or someone messes up your house. That's going to stir up your Astral body. There's communication between your Astral and your Etheric and that's going to do what I call rehydrate the Etheric. They once were pictures, after thirty-six hours they turned to Etheric calcifications. You experience these watery emotions, and all of a sudden, the calcifications pop back up into the Astral. And then you have the opportunity to clear them as pictures in the faster realm of the Astral, rather than calcifications in the slower realm of the Etheric. If you don't clear the newly-hydrated pictures, and most people don't, they start to dehydrate and go back into the Etheric and continue to create your experience in a less conscious Etheric way.

Emotions literally become part of your body, and part of your body literally becomes part of your emotions. I think of it as like lakes and oceans: it condenses up and becomes clouds and the clouds then become water again.

The reason exploding pictures works is that it's a technique to trick yourself into letting go of your resistance to that experience. A better word is support. It supports you into letting go of your resistance. And if you find that you can't explode a particular picture, the first place to look is, Whose energy is it? It's probably someone else's picture. It also might be that you're not able or willing to let go of your resistance to the underlying experience.

The only reason exploding pictures works is because it changes you. Consequently, exploding pictures will only work if you allow yourself to be changed. And that's by letting go of your resistance to whatever it is you're resisting.

Here's what happens: A bunch of pictures hydrate, but there's a whole level underneath this, and they sort of pressurize and hold down pictures that would also be hydrating were it not for the pictures on top of them. Once you clear those top pictures, the pictures that couldn't be hydrated, that didn't have the space to be hydrated, now have the space. They hydrate. That's why in intense experiences you can fully engage a bunch of pictures and think, "I've completely cleared these," and the next day, there are all these next pictures, and the next day these next, and so on. That's why, when you have intense experiences, it takes a while to clear through it. While that process goes on, it can even seem as if the energy difficulty is getting worse because you have all these new pictures. Of course, these new pictures were in some part of your full aura all the time, they were just tamped down by pictures that needed to be addressed first.

Now this has been going on forever, so don't all of a sudden get paranoid. You were doing fine yesterday. People grow without ever hearing of exploding pictures, without ever hearing about cords. They go through profound changes, they release contracts, without ever hearing about them. These are additional tools, not a thing to obsess about. You can have fun with these—*our* kind of fun. When you're psychic, you get to call everything work. Don't make it work, though. Make it play.

Be in the center of your head and look at an experience you had in the past that you had resistance to. Now track that experience, that picture, over the next thirty-six hours. Do a kind of time-lapse photography. See what happened to it. If it became part of your Etheric body, that's fine. If it didn't become part of your Etheric body, find something else that you were in resistance to until you find something that became part of your Etheric body. Where you see it become part of your Etheric body, where it calcified, run a white light, not a milky light but a clear, clean, lightly-Etheric light through that space. And you will see that Etheric calcification go into a picture in the Astral. Now sometimes that picture will explode immediately because you're out of resistance to it, but sometimes it will just become a picture that you're still in resistance to. Then work with that picture. See how it works into beliefs or delusions that you haven't been aware of. As you do, those pictures start exploding, and you begin to feel a difference in your heart. I think all judgments reside in the heart.

Is that a way to do a change history? Absolutely. A change history is replaying an event in your mind and making changes in your energy so that you behave in a way that you want to behave. You do that by moving to neutrality and engaging experience. In a sense, a successful explosion of a picture is a kind of change history. It's a quick way of becoming neutral.

You might ask, "Why not just do exploding pictures?" There's nothing intrinsically wrong with just doing exploding pictures, it's just that changing history gets you to engage with a real-life event in a rich way. This engagement gives you an enriched self-reflective experience of your own energy and reactions as you practice different approaches in that real-life situation. You know it's a real-life situation because it actually happened.

Go slowly so that you can assimilate these things.

There are pictures in your Astral body—pain pictures, fear pictures— that will generate a kind of repulsion between your lower and upper Etheric and between your Etheric and Physical body; it may repel large parts of the Etheric all the way out so that it's just kind of hanging around or going off in the middle of the day. It's occasionally okay if the Etheric's going off in the middle of the day. You may feel spacy, but there also may be something important for it to leave and engage experience in other planes. Most of the time, however, you'll want your Etheric energy present. See if you can create and destroy roses so that instead of repulsion, there's almost a kind of magnetic enticement for the upper Etheric to engage the lower Etheric and the lower Etheric to engage the Physical. They do it in slightly different ways. The upper Etheric becomes a bridge, so that the body is supported by larger groups of consciousnesses. The lower Etheric supports more individuation, more separateness or apparent separateness of your Physical body. And there's just enough magnetic attraction for your upper Etheric to be engaged with your lower Etheric, to be engaged with the Physical while you're awake.

Feel what that feels like to the body, to have your dream Etheric—your traveling Etheric—be aligned with it. And in between your Physical body and upper Etheric is the fixed Etheric, running the meridians and most of the nadis, just enjoying the productiveness of that relationship in the middle.

Remember, the Etheric moves much more slowly and changes and improves and deteriorates much more slowly than the Astral. So if you're in current time in the Astral, your Etheric is going to come into the current time. If you're kind of in current time with the Etheric, it might take a week, a month, a year, or a decade to change. It's going to take longer to change. They all affect the other. I've slowly become aware that there're some people whose Etheric bodies are so injured, so disrupted by pain, as a practical matter—not as a theoretical but as a practical matter—they're unable to work through their Astral stuff. They're just not able to find seniority in that area. The energy collapses out of them before they can gather it up and work on their habits and rules. These people can't fix their traumas without Etheric work. They have too much terror, too much pain, whatever it is, at a deeper level in the Astral body. This can be profound, imbedded, and unconscious.

The concept of current time is going to be much more relevant Astrally than it is Etherically. I'm not sure that there's anyone on the planet who can just come into present time at an Etheric level the way you can at an Astral level.

32

Creating Reality

The downside, and the upside, of Etheric work is that it really lights up your Astral space. That's fantastic if you clear it and an essential part of the humanity of your journey, as my teachers taught it, which is your connection with your personal self. Not individual self. Everyone, dual or nondual, has an individual self. When I use the word *personal*, I'm meaning a genuine encounter with the Astral plane. I used to say that it was important to do three times as much personal aura or Astral clearing as Etheric work. I don't think that's absolutely true, but it would have behooved us to do a lot more Astral clearing in this class.

There's plenty of room to practice Etheric work. However, Etheric work is so powerful that if you don't work through that Astral stuff and get less attached to your story—fascinated by your story is great; get more fascinated by your story, less attached—you can't get to the Etheric in a way that maintains and builds your personal engagement. Only after doing Astral work can you have the freedom that Etheric work has the possibility to bring, not just at the Etheric level, but also throughout the Astral or personal aura.

I use Astral aura and personal clearing often interchangeably, but they're not. Pictures are complex and involve Astral, Mental, and other plane phenomena. Pictures actually communicate all the way to the personal soul and they're very much part of the personal aura, but in Lewis Bostwick's system we really deal with pictures in an Astral kind of way. I'm not going to try to explain what I mean by that; I'm just going to forge right ahead. The Mental plane is really more about choices of an entire story rather than choices of a particular emotion in the Astral plane. And it's a group story. So, when you change probabilities, what you're really doing is changing a story in a very profound way.

This reality is created in the dream state and it's created at multiple levels in the dream state. It's both a premonition and a creation process. If you could see how rich, even though painful, this experience is, you'd begin to get it.

Beethoven started to become deaf in the 1790s. He didn't become fully deaf until 1818. In 1802 he was suicidal, which is completely understandable. And his music marked an epoch in human history about dealing with conflicting emotions. It's pretty clear that the particular glories that we get from Beethoven happen in large part because he was becoming deaf—and it was excruciating, he had to hide it from people, he had lots of people who hated him and would have used it against him. His ability to meet that powerfully, at least in the area of his music, changed the nature of music historically. Yes, he was a nasty, awful person, but you can begin to understand why, if you understand his history. It's easy to say Beethoven's life was awful—and it was—and it was glorious, not just for us but for him.

We only track part of the story while we're alive. You can easily say, "Well, that's not fair." But if you could track all of the causes and inputs into your experience, your experience wouldn't have the necessary surprises and drama for the full experience. I mean, Beethoven couldn't have had that experience of being deaf if he saw the really big picture while he was alive.

A more intense example is Nadia Murad. She was only sixteen, I think, when she was kidnapped by ISIS and taken with other girls from her home in Iraq. She was Yazidi; she had never been far from her village of Kojo. In a bus filled with girls being taken to Mosul to be sold as slaves, she had an inkling of what was coming, maybe not a complete picture of the actual occurrences because they were beyond her comprehension and her sense of what humans were capable of. She was afraid. She looked out the window at the night and thought of two figures from a Yazidi myth, tragic lovers who, only after dying, got to be together in the sky. She stared at them as two stars and prayed to be taken out of the bus up into the sky beside them.

At later times in her ordeal, she wanted to be killed or to die, and she imagined ways that could happen. She was sold from jihadist to jihadist and suffered violations and tortures. Even her imprisonment in these circumstances was almost unbearable, and she had already watched the male members of her family be shot and killed; she was alone in the world.

If she had died and escaped this horrible situation, as she wished, she never would have had the poignancy and terror of her escape, of barely making it to freedom through streets filled with terrorists. She never would have testified before the UN and borne witness to the crimes of ISIS, or Daesh as she called them. She never would have received the Nobel Peace Prize, as she did in 2018. A village girl from Kojo never would have addressed the Swedish academic and international community.

Imagine how powerful that experience was for her soul. It is not an exaggeration to suggest that it may have advanced her several lifetimes. Yet it is not a fate she would have chosen under any circumstances. But her soul and the planet benefited immeasurably.

What's different about a Sethian approach is it isn't just your soul that gets the advantage of this, but what you think of as yourself. That is also eternal. Death doesn't obliterate your sense of Morgan-ness or Ed-ness or Jane-ness as part of where you go. You go in multiple directions, but at least one of the directions you go in retains your Morgan-ness and sooner or later Morgan says, "Wow, that was fabulous."

Now I can see your frustration right now, and if I were having the same experience, I'd be as frustrated as you. It helps, though, to set an understanding that always and already your life is fabulous. You're always and already fabulous. Even in the midst of suicidal pain, you're still fabulous.

If you can just leave some space open—and there's something fabulous about that—that will help you relax a little more, be more open to yourself as you are, and be able to reconcile these contradictions, not right away, but in the most effective way you're capable of. Instead of being like someone else who might have committed suicide because he was going deaf, you can become Beethoven in your own life.

One of the ways in which everybody's reality is put together so that there's enough overlap that we seem to be in the same level is the coordination process that goes on in the Buddhic plane, where everyone's individual instructions are all played out in a single world, an *apparently* single world, that works for everyone's mapping. It's an incredible process.

So that part is done in the Buddhic or higher planes, but details are added in the Mental, Astral, and Etheric levels. The instruction set, the set of instructions for what you are congruent with, is placed there by your Etheric body. You have this sort of credit-card-like chip loaded, and you take it with you into the Etheric dreams, and that dream state reads all that information and feeds it up into the Buddhic plane where it's figured how to have a single reality for everyone—you, me, the Dalai Lama, a soldier in ISIS.

How you put all that together in one world, that part is processed up in the Buddhic plane, but the details—a room where you can meditate, some chairs, a sound system, how to work, and everyone's skills—that's put together in the Etheric and all of it comes off something like a chip-reading of your Etheric body. When you genuinely harmonize your Etheric and, preferably, your Astral and Mental body also, then you will have more flow that's uploaded into the dream state and then downloaded into your conscious waking life.

The time frame depends to a great extent on how congruent you are and how much congruent desire you have. Desire is sort of the petroleum, the gasoline; but a lot of people, as a consequence of that, try to rev up the gasoline part of it. That can really be disastrous. You think, "Oh, this is not going fast enough. I'm going to light a match to it." Well, you have to have the gear system in to be able to use that desire as part of the motive.

Every year, probably since I was born but at least since I went to the Seth classes, I have had the idea that it would be really great if I became famous and people studied what I had to say. Looking back on it, I'm really glad that fame hasn't happened so far. Looking back on what I was so sure of then, I am glad few people were listening to me. Probably I could have chosen different probabilities where the things that worry me now didn't bother me in those probabilities. Nobody, however famous, does a perfect job. Maybe the job I could've done then would have been good enough.

At least one incongruency that I had then is that I didn't want to do a job that would embarrass me two years later. Now that may be a really limiting belief on my part. If I didn't have that belief, maybe I would be more famous. It's surely not the only reason I'm not more famous. And of course, the older I get, the less important having a large audience becomes to me and the more I'm simply *curious* whether my ideas will ever have a large audience. If you had asked me in 1976 if I really wanted a large audience, I would have said, "Yes, I really, really, really want this." There was enough gasoline on the fire that is emotional desire; there just wasn't enough congruence for fame. As time goes by, there's less and less gasoline.

One of the most remarkable experiences I ever had was back in the 1990s when the Dalai Lama came to Ann Arbor. The Dalai Lama put an energy out that filled the entire basketball arena of fifteen thousand people, just filled it. He used a thimble full of gasoline and an ocean of congruence. I mean, a featherweight of his intent was able to fill that arena because it was so congruent. So beautiful.

People can get very, very frustrated that they are incongruent, and they don't feel their incongruence. If they did, they wouldn't be as incongruent. Realized experience adds information. It doesn't add it as specifically as you would like, but if you don't have what you want, then you can be sure that you are incongruent.

Everybody I know wishes their growth were faster, wishes they became more psychic, more grounded, less conflicted. Here's a little prayer you can use: "God grant me patience and give it to me right now."

33

Coordinate Points

In Einstein's general relativity, gravity is a bending of space. So the Earth kind of bends space. That's how the Moon travels around the Earth. Because space itself is curved. To the Moon, that circle looks like a straight line. Well, these sorts of spatial bends happen all over, and in the Etheric, where more stuff is bent, each bend is what Seth calls a coordinate point. A coordinate point is any place where your manifestations are more turbo-charged. There are bigger coordinate points and smaller coordinate points. Mountains and other natural phenomena have coordinate points. Most cities have more coordinate points than other places. Jerusalem has a huge group of coordinate points; it is one of the most powerful places on the planet. Unfortunately all kinds of hatred and fear gets poured through there.

Let's all go visit a place in the former Yugoslavia called Medjugorje. This space has this divine feminine energy. Back in the eighties, five or six young people there began having visions of Mother Mary, and it became a site of pilgrimage. They generated all these warnings of terrible things that would happen if people didn't get their act together. Then there was tremendous violence in the early nineties around Croatia with the breakup of Yugoslavia. But it still is a place of pilgrimage.

When I look at Medjugorje, I experience its divine feminine energy. I can feel it in my imagination when I hook up to it. I can feel it palpably in my imagination healing me. Now you can call that Mother Mary healing you, and there's no reason not to call it Mother Mary, but it's not Mother Mary in the sense that we think of identity. This is a crinkling of space and time in such a way that the area itself is empowered. Just the space. That is a kind of consciousness, a different kind of consciousness, a consciousness in the fabric of space itself.

Instead of thinking of a black hole as just a bunch of physical equations and something not alive, think of all of space as being alive and a black hole as being a kind of consciousness in space.

There are many little bits of space that are particularly empowered in this way, like the vortexes in Sedona or Mount Shasta.

You can make a goal for yourself and put it in one of these magical spaces. Or go to Niagara Falls. It has all these ugly little souvenir stores, but there really is an intense energy of love there. People know that, and it is an ideal place to go to kick off a marriage. They're bringing their hopes and depositing them in this incredible coordinate point.

So consciousness is not what we think it is. Medjugorje is a form of consciousness.

The crinkling of space around Mount Shasta is a form of consciousness, a dramatically different kind of consciousness. The love vibe of Niagara Falls is a form of consciousness. You could call it a deva if you wanted to. You could see it as a deva. Nothing wrong with seeing it as a deva. You could not have a Physical or Etheric body without elementals and devas holding them together. Yet that's not where we put our concepts of what consciousness is.

The ground of manifestation itself is biased in your favor. It will do what you tell it to do. But it's biased in your favor. It's easier for it to manifest the things that are good for you than the things that are bad for you. Medjugorje or Mount Shasta are enormously biased in our favor. Even Jerusalem is enormously biased in our favor, but there's so much hatred and anxiety that gets dumped in there that it has a hard time manifesting positively. Each of these power points reaches in its own way through the Etheric into each cell in your body. Maybe your cells are reaching out to it; maybe it's reaching out to you. Space itself is transforming. The larger thoughtforms, like the power spot in Medjugorje, are fully capable of helping your manifestation goals separately and in collaboration with everything else that's going on. The

power spot is alive with its own kind of intent and interest and kindness and generosity.

The programming that you carry in your body and in your aura
loosens as you become more playful, kinder, and more generous. It's
completely mutual even though you're tiny compared to it. That is
because its intention for you is particular and unique, and then you
bring your own intention to it. You can let go of your own desire and
manifestation and turn it over to this power point and let it decide how
best to aid you. You still make choices, as that manifestation energy
comes back to you over time. For now, you are letting go of consciously
calculating out every aspect. You're open to letting the power point
have its initiative and continue in the dream state and elsewhere so that
you resourcefully open and change in relation to that manifestation or
whatever is your next step.

Why does it befuddle you if you get well in two days? It's because you
have programming in there that says, "This isn't the way things go."
Now that's not evil programming. That's a system that's set in place so
that you really deal with issues more deeply. It's a good thing for it to
be in place until you're able to deal with issues with *less* structure. We
are in a system that has three dimensions of space and one dimension
of time, and that gives us a certain speed of information, certain natural
ways of organizing information. If you were all of a sudden thrown into
a system that had three dimensions of space and four dimensions of
time, you wouldn't be able to handle it.

One story you can tell around miracles is that you simply add a
dimension of time, or two, but our stories just won't handle that. And
the reason they won't handle that is we bind ourselves into stories of
self-esteem: I did such-and-such and therefore I'm a worthy person. I'm
good at this. I'm good at that. And therefore I'm a worthy person.

I don't mean flipping to the polarity of that, which is: I'm a worthy person better than others just because I know I'm a worthy person
better than others. The opposite of no self-esteem is not self-esteem in
its usual understanding. The opposite of no self-esteem is getting over

self-esteem, getting over telling yourself a continuous story. It's like in golf: you commit to a shot, you hit it. If it's a great shot, you're pleased. If it's a bad shot, you're disappointed. And then you move to your next shot. You don't tell yourself, "I'm having a seventy-two this round." You tell yourself, "I'm having a great walk," or some such. What spoils it is that story, that self-esteem story, the sense of humiliation when you hit a shot you're disappointed in. What gives golf the capacity to make a miracle is to step up to each shot, both as part of a story and as something entirely outside, with this thought: This is the first and only event in the world. I'm standing next to this little white ball, the sun is shining and the birds are chirping, and I'm having fun with my friends and being in the moment.

The approach we're on—and it's very hard for me to articulate it—is a both/and approach where we tell the story but we don't get attached to the story, and we're also in the moment, which for us is not a clock-time moment. You can be in the moment thinking about an argument you had thirty years ago if your energy is moving. If you're thinking about an argument you had thirty years ago and you're going over the same scratched record groove, then you're not in the moment. But also, even if you're in the moment in clock time, perfectly present in clock time, and your energy isn't moving, then you're not in the real moment.

34

Prophecy and Miracles

You probably all know about the reported significance of 2012 and that something huge was going to happen on December 21. People were going off and moving to Oregon—yet one more group of end-of-the-worlders planning to survive the end of the world by going to the *one* place that's not going to be destroyed. It's useful to understand that there's a play in time even when you're predicting time.

Other people said, we're going to shift to the fifth dimension even though it's a long time since that group had a hit. Some people had it that 144,000 people would shift and everyone else would suffer. Some people had it that everyone will shift. My guides had an interesting and unique take on it. They didn't even have the end of the Mayan calendar as the biggest event in 2012 or 2012 as the most intense year. In fact, 2011 was more intense than 2012; 2013 and 2014 will each be more intense and transformative than the years before. But since our lives have meaning, you don't usually make these huge quantum leaps. Our lives are also sacred as they are. There's a lot of discord going on, but it's still sacred. Jumping to some divine external resolution of that discord that has nothing really to do with growth and change on our individual parts, that's just not going to happen.

I remember in the sixties Edgar Cayce's predictions that the whole world was going to be flooded except for pretty much Myrtle Beach. Well, that was right in a certain way. Any of us who lived through the sixties saw a sort of Astral, emotional flood. All around the world you had the youth revolting when Uranus went over Pluto, or something like that. Some very heavy transits happened in the sixties. You had all the stuff happening on American college campuses; you had almost a successful revolution in France led by the students. You had the horrors of the Cultural Revolution in China. The whole world was covered in that, but not a literal flood.

They found another Mayan calendar by the way that goes well beyond 2012. It does not end at 2012. My guides say you can't have a period of time that long stay exact, and inner time and calendar time depart, notwithstanding the preciseness with which you're measuring astronomical functions. According to my guides, that particular Mayan cycle people dramatized ended in inner planes around 2001 or 2002. The cycle wasn't actually ending in 2012; it had already ended in internal time and we were already in the future by the time we got to 2012. It's just how time plays. How could you expect time to move by calendar time? Even the stars change in ways that you can't tell because you're inside, not outside, the system. That kind of literalness of clock and even astronomical time, that's a human invention. That isn't the way the inner universe really works.

In one of the *Oversoul Seven* books that Jane Roberts wrote, she was talking about a miracle happening with a dentist's patient, and Oversoul Seven was genuinely puzzled at how upset the dentist got, how upset at the idea of a miracle. Because it's really disruptive.

Now everyone in here believes in miracles, but that's said at a Puritan level. There's a set of steps that each of you thinks a miracle has to follow—let me change that: there's a set of steps that each of us thinks is involved in a miracle, and the main reason that that's so much of our personality is because we are so tied in to outcomes. So if you suddenly get a new easy outcome, what does that do to your sense of self when each of us has built up our sense of self with the plaster of saying things like, "It's her fault. It's his fault. *I* deserve this. She doesn't deserve that"?

I don't know if you can track that, but I'd like everyone to spend some time noticing how you justify yourself to yourself. This is in preparation to start moving out of justification. Put a rose out in front of you for what you think your good qualities are and another for what you think your bad qualities are. And as you're doing that, ask how you put up with yourself. *Do you* put up with yourself? What sort of bargains do you make with yourself to put up with yourself? When you encounter something about yourself that you find painful, do you start comparing yourself to other people? How much of your story about yourself comes from pain and the story is a way to cover up that pain? Once you notice that, you might start noticing how much of that pain is other people's energy and not something that you need to be pained by at all. Or the pain can be one-tenth or one-twentieth as much, but instead you cover it up with a story.

If you explore that and take that attitude, you *will* have space to go into these Etheric zones.

I think it's really cool to explore the question, Can we do miracles? Maybe thirty years from now we'll be able to walk on water. I'm not suggesting that as a serious goal. I'm just sort of playing with whether we can engage miracles in a way that makes us more engaged with everyday life, more welcoming of the contextuality that is intrinsic in our relationships, more making life a conversation. On the other hand, it would be very damaging to try to create miracles to impose your will on the world.

When Sri Aurobindo said that he and his collaborator The Mother knew how to live eternally but decided not to because they thought it would generate too much envy in people, now it's plausible to me that at the very least he could have lived another twenty, fifty, or one hundred years. Forever is a long time. But I think the real reason is, again, that to do it with the techniques that he was using, transcendent energies, would be imposing your will on the situation. On the other hand, for those of us who are genuinely, deeply engaged at a personal aura level and also utilizing more transcendent energies, it will be interesting to see just what we *can* do.

We tap into the energies that create this world. We may be okay with climate change when we think new energies will emerge that will deal with it. We still have to live through the time and participate in the creation and acceptance of those new energies. It's still important for us to work with the old energies and do our best to deal with climate change, but not from the sense that we have to save the world but, with what we know right now, to do our best because that's how we'll learn and bring the new energies in. They're not just going to come in and solve all our problems. It's incumbent upon us to do stuff like recycling even though eventually the answer might be more flowing.

To get into this miracle space, you have to, I think, not get so attached to your story. The story is fascinating, but when you get too attached to your story, you make everything too rigid. Paradoxically if you're too attached to your story, then the things you don't like about your story become necessary. You need them to hold everything together. If all of a sudden someone stole what you don't like about your story, you wouldn't know who you were.

There's a lot of civilizational programming, but that's not the real problem. The real problem is that the way we order our self-esteem requires that it be a big deal if we do a miracle. And that making a big deal out of a miracle is going to put a miracle in entirely the wrong context. It actually misses the loveliness and the elegance of a miracle. A miracle isn't that it rescues our self-esteem. If we need to have perfect teeth to have self-esteem, or if we need not to have a heart condition to have self-esteem, then it's a lot harder to have perfect teeth or that or to not have a heart condition. Because that heart condition is there for a purpose, to help you work through stuff. The climate of Mother Earth adjusts to our condition and is there to help us work through stuff.

We tend to think of miracles in the way we think of science or penicillin, as something that solves the problem. But you know the old saying: When the teacher is ready, the pupil appears. When you've learned and grown and taken the nourishment from your heart condition, or bad teeth or whatever, then a miracle can happen. It may be that it doesn't have to happen at that point. You can get yourself more conventionally healed. But the real miracle happened when you got the nourishment out of the issue. When we focus too much on our limitations, we're missing the point that, to me, is, I don't want to win the lottery to become wealthy—part of me does—but if I truly grok, if I truly understand issues of wealth, then freedom grows as we try to make money and learn things about ourselves and society, not because we have the money. To *not* need to win the lottery is the way to win the lottery, any lottery. We put the cart before the horse.

I would suggest that it's not in anyone's best interest to have a miracle that doesn't untie the knot that was there in the first place.

When I was taking the Seth classes, I always thought of changing probabilities as this neat workaround of the problem, so I would no longer have to deal with the problem. But you always have to deal with the problem until you have eaten it up and digested it and made it yours. Probabilities are not escape hatches.

Begin to get a sense of this as an agreement. As you withdraw so totally from the ordinary physical agreement—and ultimately All That Is *is* an agreement, a divinely wonderful agreement—you increase your body's capacity to heal itself in ways that don't fit with the Western scientific model. Even more importantly, you begin to support its health in ways that don't fit the model. And that's true whether you consciously track this or not.

Let's use gravity as an illustration of agreement and reciprocity. Say a refrigerator falls on a kid, and the mother is able to pick it up off him. Her kundalini really clicks on, and she does that. It's conceivable, in that case, that gravity is an agreement, and it's also useful to understand it that way. I'm using gravity as an illustration of agreement and reciprocity.

People choose certain states at a genetic level. That's an agreement too. Just like a probability wave in quantum physics that can be in a number of places at once, your genes and genealogy can be in a number of places. Every physical and psychological and even spiritual characteristic is the outcome of multiple draws at the same site, in genetic circumstances they're called alleles. Even identical twins are not identical identities; ordinary siblings represent different probabilities from the same blending of genomes.

Your health begins in the probability of genes and continues in the probability of cells and mitochondria and other organelles programmed by those genes. Those are agreements, unconscious agreements, and you continue to make choices and agreements and participate in reciprocities at every moment, sometimes consciously, mostly unconsciously, and certainly in the dream state.

You can sit down and explore an unhealthy cell and look at where it comes from emotionally and where it's coming from mentally and spiritually, and then you blow pictures so that the cell just naturally wants to move toward health with that neutrality. It will move toward being a regular healthy cell.

Walking on water is not very important, but getting over the idea that your genetics are fixed destiny—that's *very* important. It doesn't mean that genetics doesn't have to do with anything. Jane Roberts took these kinds of ideas to a ridiculous extreme, and it was part of her strength. She chain-smoked. Seth discouraged it for a while. But she became proud of her smoking. She would write how trying to get people to stop smoking was causing more damage than smoking itself. That's not true. Smoking, nicotine, is a powerful drug.

I could have but didn't engage in the following conversation. "Jane, if I drove a coffin nail into you, would that hurt?"

"Yes."

"But cigarettes are just a belief?"

She could believe in the reality of nails but not of the chemicals in processed tobacco.

Cigarettes harm you in all sorts of ways, especially taken out of the ritual context in which they arose among Native Americans. Tobacco was a ceremonial and symbolic drug. Natural organic tobacco used ceremonially occasionally could be very good for you, but the stuff you buy at the 7-Eleven is awful for you.

I'm not saying these things don't matter at all. I'm just saying they don't matter in the way we imagine. If you don't have any beliefs to speak of that predispose you to cancer, you can probably smoke cigarettes and not get cancer but, even so, why smoke cigarettes?

I say this because I was in a class where Jane was going on about the dangers of *not* smoking, and one after another people who had given up cigarettes started smoking again. I used to say I wouldn't smoke cigarettes even if they *cured* cancer. Sitting in that class with all that cigarette smoke, my wife and I always found spots in the back by the window.

In your Etheric body, there are tracks, Etheric predispositions. Those tracks can change quite substantially based on your beliefs. Choosing is a little bit misleading because you can't just say, I'm going to choose not to have a genetic predisposition to diabetes; but what you can do over time, consciously or unconsciously, is try to find pleasure in life in a skillful way. Then you can see the genetic code kind of shift or float as a clairvoyant state and almost flutter between predispositions, even after your time developing in the womb and birth, almost deciding again where it's going to land for a period of the next few months.

Those genetic decisions can be revisited by behavioral and mental changes that go very deep. They're not easy to do, but if you get to the very bottom of them, they will even change your genetic code. Unexpressed alternate genes and genetic potentials remain dormant in the body's cells, even though the cells have supposedly chosen their fates and lost all their morphogenetic flexibility, to use a million-dollar word. Then the medical profession will say, "Oh, the test was wrong."

Given that you've changed probabilities, even if you have original test materials and you re-run the test, you can't actually re-run the test because everything has changed, past and future.

Now you don't have to believe what I'm saying. You're welcome in these classes to believe some things, to disbelieve other things, and reserve judgment on the rest. I don't even believe everything I say in the sense that I know that my own opinions and even paradigms change. There are infinite options, and there is no highest and best, ever. You will always leave stuff on the table, as it were.

If you change your genetic code this way, you're going to miss doing something else, more that way or more this way. Plus, everything that *could* happen *does* happen, so at an inner level your relationship to success and failure changes dramatically anyway but over time.

To a surprising extent we are all subconsciously checking our experience against the human race's inner psychic understanding, and that helps us keep our mooring, keep our sense of where we are. For instance, Seth talked about how we wouldn't have learned how to speak if it weren't for the amount of unconscious telepathy that goes back and forth. The way you learn what words mean is not that the meaning of each word is physically pointed out to you; you grow into awareness of how to use the language in this sea of inner telepathy, together with the external training. You clairaudiently enter into the vast conversations and dialogues of the human race before you are even born. Then you specify that in a particular language.

Noam Chomsky is an MIT linguist, and he points out how all languages arise from the same logic strings in the brain. At a deep level Finnish and Navaho and Gaelic and Zulu are the same language. At a telepathic Etheric level, in the aura, they don't even sound different because they don't operate by sound. There are no separate languages in the aura. I think that *Star Trek,* without actually spelling this out, counts on the fact that all language is originally telepathic, so all intelligent races across the galaxies speak English. It's not really English, it just sounds like English to us because we translate it into a dialect. Our genes and our languages are speaking to the same clairsentient, clairaudient probabilities and using each other to do it.

When you're learning about chakras and planes of consciousness, there's this sea of inner telepathy and clairvoyance that you're checking that with. Even if you don't know what you're doing, that information is there and it provides guidance and a sense of, "Oh, okay, I'm getting this right." An unconscious feedback gives you reassurance. That's why you can receive the right note or frequency from me and just match it.

There's a lot of stuff that we do that takes time for your neurological system to adjust. Ancient Buddhist thought and modern Sethian thought talk about time being an illusion. Seth used to say, "It doesn't take time to make changes." That's good as far as it goes, but it's only one half of a dichotomy. I mean, theoretically you could fly, and some people do, not many, but there are reports of various Christian saints— or at least one guy—who got so enthralled that when he'd meditate, he'd levitate up to the statue of Jesus in the front of the building. So, you can do that, but most of the time you walk, and there's a lot of cool things that happen by walking, like building muscles or burning calories.

Most of the changes you make will take time. A lot of people get so obsessed with the idea that change doesn't need time, so they don't allow themselves time and the ebb and flow of life experience to engage what they're relating to. Time is the way we almost always engage events. Time is non-intrinsic; it's an energy just like anything else. Nothing is intrinsically true about time, but we've incarnated into a realm with one dimension of time so that we can have a certain kind of experience where things are separated from one another. And that creates a certain kind of experience. Part of the opening to life as a human being is opening to the fact most things take time. As you meet things over and over, you start to assimilate them. You meet them in one context, you meet them in another context, and they start to make sense and you start to figure out how to do things.

The next exercise we are going to do is tap into your cellular consciousness, into the fact that each cell has its own consciousness, then shift to the fact that each cell is part of your body's consciousness, and then shift to the fact that each human body is part of one big human body consciousness—I think this is referred to in Kabbalistic studies as Adam Qadmon. That's why, by the way, your body has an eternal consciousness. Whether you give birth to a child or not, your body's consciousness is eternal. Obviously this particular body dies, but its participation in this web of human bodies makes it eternal.

Then we're going to look at the fact that each cell's consciousness is part of you, the personality, so what we're noticing is that each cell is utterly itself and is simultaneously a part of other consciousnesses. Now you may have run into this idea before in the idea that every smaller consciousness is nested in a larger consciousness. You're getting that but you're also getting that these nests, these participations, don't just go up a vertical chain or down a vertical chain, but they go other directions also.

First say hello to the body with its sensations and imagine that you can tap into one or several cells in your body. And just notice that it has its own consciousness, not a self-reflective consciousness but nevertheless has its own consciousness, a kind of intentionality or directionality to it. You may be able to notice that the cell's consciousness perceives in multiple directions. When you think of it as a cell you probably imagine it has a certain kind of limited awareness and consciousness, but it actually tracks all kinds of things, by itself and together with the other cells in your body.

As you home in on its individual consciousness, scale up so you have a sense of the body's consciousness. Let's take an intermediate step and just notice your liver. Notice that it has a consciousness much larger than an individual cell's. Say hello to your heart. Notice that it has a different consciousness, a different kind of intentionality. Now scale up to the whole-body consciousness. Notice that is how it has its own consciousness, its own organization. You might even notice how it has its own joy, and joy is not dependent upon the evaluations that you make as a self-reflective human being. You might even notice that it has its own agenda that it brings to this collaboration called a human life. It's a very open agenda, but it's a different kind of consciousness than the emergent consciousness that you give a name to, whatever you call yourself—John, Gloria, Patty, whatever.

Now see if you can track how that consciousness, that body consciousness, is part of a larger human body consciousness. You can't find your body's contributions, but you can tell that all bodies fit into this larger human body consciousness. In that human body consciousness, home in to a smaller ethnic community that you're a part of, whatever your ethnicity is. Though if you really lost your connection with that ethnicity, your body might be more affiliated with a kind of American consciousness. Go back to your own personal body consciousness and just try to sense that that's not something *else* than the larger shared body consciousness. Your individual body consciousness is both its own center of consciousness and a vital part of larger group body consciousnesses. Move from your single body consciousness to the global human body consciousness, and to all living creatures' body consciousnesses, and to Mother Earth herself, back to your single body consciousness, jumping all the way back to Mother Earth.

Now imagine that Mother Earth homes in to your body consciousness in time as you experience time, and she finds herself as you. There's some sense that, from her point of view, your body is part of her. From your human self-reflective-ego point of view, your body is *your* body. Each of those points of view is divinely true, non-exclusive, though for my human ego it seems to be more one than the other. Notice how your body supports your human consciousness and collaborates with your emotions and ideas and soul to form you. Notice when you think "I" or "me" or "mine" that your body just folds right into that assigning of identity. The body becomes *your* body. But then notice how, from Mother Earth's point of view, your body is part of her. It's not that she's in resistance to your claiming sole ownership of your body, I imagine she is amused.

PART FOUR

PICTURES

35

Difficult Conversations

Every single piece of your reality is created according to your conscious beliefs or—more appropriately for our purposes—according to your pictures. Your beliefs come from your consciousness and your consciousness comes from your beliefs. This gets us closer to understanding what a matching picture is. A matching picture is any picture in your space that is in resistance to your experience at that moment. You will experience that resistance almost always as discomfort. It might be so little discomfort that you don't notice it consciously or, in certain situations, it might be substantial. But any resistance that you have to your experience will light up as a break in the smooth flow of energy in your aura.

Other people's criticisms stick in your space because it's not your energy. If you didn't catch each one of those criticisms—and you need about one thousand psychic arms to do it—they wouldn't stick in your space, they'd just go right through. Any painful energy that you have in your space is in some ways doing its best to get out of your space, but you're holding onto it with one of those thousand arms. I don't want to overdramatize that because you may be cursing and screaming at that energy and wondering how it got there.

We cannot track all of our energy. If you spend ten years working on tracking more and more of your energy, you will in fact track more and more of your energy, but you will also have increased the scope of your awareness. At the edges of your now expanded awareness, you will have an even larger outskirts of your awareness that is close enough to affect you, but it is beyond your ability to track. So, at the new larger edges of your awareness, there is a larger outskirts, a larger relevant area you can't track. You will get better at tracking your energy, but there will never come a time, nor is there ever meant to be a time, when everything is fully conscious and under your control.

Now I know there are a lot of systems that claim perfection as their goal and then claim examples of perfection, but in my tradition, there is no such thing. One of my favorite moments in the Seth classes was a bit of an anomaly because Seth was so awesome. If you go on the internet and hear Jane channeling Seth, it is a really charismatic presentation. Seth seemed to know everything and be perfectly assured and brilliant. In the classes he would pop into Jane and then he'd pop out. One night he talked to us for a while, popped out, and immediately popped back in and said, "Oh, I forgot something," and the whole class went, "You *forgot* something!"

There is no perfection anywhere, and that's the great perfection of it all. Creativity is intrinsic in it. When I said the whole universe wraps around you at every moment and every change, that's logically equivalent—I won't take you *through* the logic because it would take too long—but it's logically equivalent to saying, "Everything you do creates more unknowns and so every breath is to take what you know into an encounter with the unknown, and you automatically do that." Now you may do that skillfully or you may do that kicking and screaming, but you automatically do that.

And people can get really down on themselves. It's not that you're stupid. It's that you, me, and all of us are constantly engaging the unknown. One of the ways in which humans engage the unknown is by resisting and holding onto other people's energy in their space. Our own energy is our authentic way at a personality level. Another person's energy, even if it's the Dalai Lama's, is not our energy at the personality level.

Notice who you are, not just your strengths and weaknesses, but who you are. Your being moment by moment *is* the universe's exploration. The universe has no interest in your being perfect, it has an interest in your being who you are. It has an interest in your being unique.

Now we're going to play with and explore how our personalities are wrapped in the universe. And that makes a really nice pun: I meant it as wrap, like Christmas wrapping, but rapt, as in rapture, also fits. We are *rapt* in All That Is.

What is other people's energy doing there in your space?

At the center of my spiritual journey is the developing ability to have a difficult conversation. You can become enlightened without ever learning how to have a difficult conversation. If you're a guru, you'll have people around you and, since you'll have all this charisma, any time you get irritated, they'll think it's their fault. You never have to learn how to deal with irritation, yet in principle you're enlightened.

This is a place where I think Lewis Bostwick went awry, where his reading line is not fully engaged in everyday life. You can clear a lot of pain out of your space by doing readings—that's one reason we learn to be psychic readers. Most of you are not that interested in being professional psychics; yet doing ordinary daily readings, if you're blowing pictures, can speed up the clearing of pain out of your space.

If someone wanted to have a difficult conversation with Lewis, he'd essentially say, "I'm not interested, go set up your own school. Go do something else. Here, this is what we're doing."

There is nothing wrong with committing to what you're doing and setting boundaries, but you're not really engaging the world if you surround yourself only with people who agree with you. And, I think, you're not really clearing pain out of your space until you can have a difficult conversation.

We're not about creating a world in which you never get aggravated, like the princess and the pea, where you have to protect yourself from all bruises. We're talking about learning how to embrace life as it is.

So many of you are scrupulous about getting the right answer. There *is* no right answer. It's just a bunch of stories, and that's the meaning of it, to tell some really great stories. As time goes on, you get to where your stories have some real panache to them—more style, they're more beautiful, they hang together better—but they're still just a story. It's not like you need to be Leonardo da Vinci, one of the greatest artists of all time. Those notions of comparing greatness have a place, but not in validating your or anyone else's life.

The point is to use the techniques to create movement and meaning in your life, not to have the right answer or paint the *Mona Lisa*.

Sometimes when I work with people, I'll suggest, "Blow some pictures," and I worry that they won't know when to blow pictures when I'm not there. But that's just my suggestion of how I would do it. You can always come at these things from multiple directions. There's never just one right answer for when to blow pictures or any other technique.

One of the biggest problems I see in people doing clearings is that they often think they can only move forward if they have the right answer. The wrong answer can move you forward too. You can think that an energy is your mother's, for instance, even though that's not quite right. So you work on your mother's energy, and it turns out that it's some family thoughtforms that came in off of your mother. That attempt to work with your mother's energy still moves you forward.

Sometimes when you work with an energy, a chakra or picture, it will expand and transform. It breaks and the energy is in a bigger form but without the old picture anymore. There are all sorts of variations within a fully interdependent reality.

When you have experience, pictures become available to you to explode and clear. And that's what makes everyday experience so important for those of us who are committed to everyday experience on its own terms and for its own purposes.

For example, dealing with irritation is an exciting, valuable process that works for ourselves and psychic ecology, and also moves the human race toward group consciousness.

Even if you are enlightened, you cannot engage in group consciousness without being able to have a difficult conversation when the need for one occurs within the energy framework of your humanity, which is essentially the personal aura. There is no away to avoid it or transcend it through perfect love.

Where and what is the edge of your aura? In the Astral or personal aura, there is a difference between what is and isn't you. Ideally and theoretically, though this is a perfect picture and unachievable, and it wouldn't be desirable to achieve it, all of what's inside the edge of your aura could be only your energy and what's outside the edge of your aura is someone else or something else. Of course, no matter how accurately you use your personal awareness, at least some of your personal energy will still be on the outside, and some of others on the inside, but you can use the theoretical ideal on perfect separation into you and not you. There is an inside that is you and an outside that is not you. Everything that is inside that aura, whether it's you or not, is your responsibility. Everything that is outside of that aura is not your responsibility except wherever you have any of your personal energy.

You don't get to say what does or doesn't happen outside. It doesn't mean you have no preferences for what goes on. You can affect what goes on outside through communication that is nonmanipulative and noncoercive.

Thus, setting a boundary is very different from most people's picture of it. Basically, setting a boundary is knowing what the edge of your aura is and being responsible for what's inside, which is your emotions, and communicating to what's outside.

Most people think, "That person's treating me badly, so I'm going to set a boundary and tell them what to do." That's not setting a boundary; that's getting enmeshed. Setting a boundary is being grounded and owning your space and communicating, "When you do such-and-such, I feel such-and-such, and I'd like you to do such-and-such." They may or may not do it, but then you get to decide what to do in response. Setting a boundary has nothing to do with doing a tap dance on the other person, or telling them the truth. Telling them, "You're a selfish so and so" is not setting a boundary. That's also getting more enmeshed with them.

Clearing pictures doesn't disengage you. It unenmeshes you and gives you the opportunity to be profoundly more engaged.

Most people have a lot of pictures in their aura. You feel a lot clearer than you actually are, for those pictures have a way of hiding themselves, but they will still affect you. If there's a lot of pictures lit up in your space, that will make you tired. If you suddenly find yourself really tired, check how many dozens of people you have allowed to fill your space. Ask, "How many pictures do I have lit up in in my space?"

You come here to be senior in your space. A lot of people think they're being senior in their space by feeling free to disagree. But sometimes their disagreement is not their own energy. It's like that bumper sticker that says, "Oppose authority." My response to that is, "Says who?" A kind of obligatory freedom to oppose authority doesn't seem to be a genuinely autonomous stance. Your best response to someone's opposition is just to say hello and recognize any matching pictures, decide what you want to do, and respond wisely.

Recently I've met some people who seem to be cultivating wisdom, but when you look deeper, they've learned a lot of words and concepts of wisdom, but they haven't connected it with the soul and they've stayed just as blaming and just as unwilling to take unconditional responsibility. They can't have a difficult conversation and grow from it.

36

Boundaries and Matching Pictures

Your personal aura is made up of two aspects, space and desire-information. Most people tend to focus on the energy and desires in their aura and are insufficiently aware of their space. The space is from your boundaries—if you have them. Until you start practicing, there's a good chance you won't have boundaries, the personal aura will just sort of peter out. As you start practicing, you start to get clearer, cleaner boundaries. What happens inside those boundaries is like your psychic womb. That's what you're creating. Whatever is in that aura is what you're creating. If it's someone else's energy in your aura, then it's their life, at least in part, that you're creating with your aura. You may think it's your life, and in a sense it is, because you're living it—but if it's with their energy, it's their life. It's imbued with their kind of awareness, but not their *focused* awareness.

Information is kind of an abstract concept, but all experience is information. Unassimilated information is pictures. The reason that we clear our aura is so that we're in current time and operating off of our own energy, not perfectly, but basically. You can make this practice simple by being senior in your own space. What does it mean to be senior to an energy in your space?

As you walk through the world, you're constantly reading the world clairvoyantly, though most people are not aware of it. If somebody has an energy in their space that you're in resistance to, that's what we call a matching picture. It can be confusing because a lot of matching pictures are apparent opposites. Conservative political views will often be matching pictures to liberals because each party is in resistance to the other. In fact, it's probably the case that pictures where you are totally in agreement with another person and not in resistance to yours or theirs isn't a matching picture, because it won't light up.

Matching pictures has nothing to do with whether they're identical. Matching pictures has to do with an underlying weakness, fear, anger, or resistance, even though the expression may be opposite. There doesn't have to be any sense of culpability in matching pictures.

Matching pictures create a large part of your reality. If you're a victim of terrorism, you have matching pictures with the terrorist, even though the terrorist is culpable and guilty in a sense that you aren't. It's all experience. It's just hard to track with logic; the logic is several layers beneath the surface. They do match in a logic at those deeper layers.

We're going to focus on one particular way of defining a matching picture. There will be others, but, this, I hope, will be the simplest and most powerful.

When you interact with any experience, energy runs through your system. When you're in theoretical perfect flow, the energy that runs through your system is at a perfect flow. Every deviation from that smooth comfortable flow in your aura is the result of a resistance. As you're listening to me right now, you can't help but have some places where you're in resistance to my presentation: "Gee, I'm bored." "How about getting to the point." "I've been struggling a bit." "I'm about to lose my female grounding." "Gee, I don't understand this." These are among any number of pictures you might have in your experience of my presenting these ideas right now.

Now, theoretically, you could say, "Gee, I wonder when he's going to get to the point?" and not be in resistance to that question. If that's the case, then you won't have any matching pictures by the definition that I'm about to give you.

We use the phrase lights up for a picture or resistance because it literally lights up in the aura. If you think back to the incandescent light bulb that was used in the late 1800s to just a few years ago, perhaps you know they each have a filament inside the vacuum of the bulb called a resistor. As current goes through that resistor, energy is released by the resistance, and that energy is released as heat and light. The light bulb glows and also gets hot.

Likewise, it is usually the case that the portion of an experience to which you have resistance will generate inflammation, and that is heat. But that's not our subject for today. Our subject for today is the energy that is generated and lights up as you interact. You have certain emotions, sensations, and ideas that generate a flow through your aura. Every place they bump up against a resistance, that resistance or picture lights up.

If you're paying attention to your aura, you'll experience that resistance usually as a feeling, a sensation in your aura or sometimes as a sound, but most often as a lighting up. It's a funny kind of lighting up because the picture itself won't let energy flow through it. The energy runs around the picture, so that if you look inside of a picture when you're getting lit up, it's darker on the inside and the light getting disrupted on the outside lights up. That's where that darkness is. A picture is disruptive to the flow of that energy.

When you're running energy, fear and pain will often light up in your space. That's an important part of why we do this work, to clear those barriers. It's not the only reason we do it, but it's a very important part.

GLORIA: We find that one of the best ways to *address* our judgmentalness is to recognize our humanness in judgment, to allow that we may not be perfectly nonjudgmental, but we can be in *flow* about the fact that we have judgment.

When we are in flow, we are naturally in a healing mode. An easy way to be in flow is to simply be exploding our judgmental pictures.

JOHN: A reminder that matching pictures are your pictures that light up where you are in resistance to whatever you are giving your attention. Most of our matching pictures are going to be well hidden from ourselves. But one of the most visible pictures in most of us is our self-righteousness. If we are being self-righteous, we simply are in resistance.

So, for almost everyone, self-righteous will probably be one of our matching pictures. Not for everyone, but for most. It doesn't matter if one is right or wrong; if we are being self-righteous, we are in resistance and not in flow.

When you find someone else's energy in your space you want to move it out, and when you find energies that aren't in current time, you want to bring them into current time. It really is amazing how those events are vibrating now essentially the same way they were vibrating ten, thirty, forty, fifty years ago, which means that you are literally not in current time. You can't ever be perfect, so it's important to it to let go of the idea of having an aura that is entirely in current time.

There are people who do certain kinds of exercises where they would tell you they are entirely in the moment or nearly entirely in the moment, but if you look at their aura, that's not true; it's just that they're not communicating with those parts that aren't vibrating in current time. In this system, current time doesn't mean in the moment. Current time means not being in resistance to time. In this system, daydreaming is often fine because ours is a very psychological system, and so you may be very productively daydreaming about something that happened forty years ago, making new connections, assimilating something that you hadn't assimilated before, and gaining new understandings. There may be times when a daydream is pleasant and you just want to step into the daydream. There's nothing wrong with that as long as you have alternatives to daydreaming too.

And you can be with your awareness in the moment in a highly resistant sort of way, and that wouldn't, for us, be current time even though you *are* in the moment.

If you have just suffered a tragedy and then tomorrow afternoon, if your mind isn't going to the tragedy, you're not in current time. A day later your mind is still going to be on that tragedy. There could be someone who is having so much will power and force that they're right there on what they're eating and drinking and not thinking about what happened yesterday, but that's rare. Our sense of current time is in some ways like a concept Seth had in *The Seth Material,* which was the first book that had a large circulation; he called it psychological time. Psychological time would be psychologically flowing time.

As you explode resentment pictures, you'll come into current time. As you explode even pleasant pictures, you come into current time. Any picture you explode will stop fixedly vibrating in your aura and it'll become just information that you can, from time to time, revibrate in your aura as you experience it. Any experience, pleasant or unpleasant, that's vibrating in your aura has not been fully assimilated; assimilation only occurs when they're no longer actively vibrating in your aura but they're stored as information. They often don't get stored as information and continue to vibrate in your aura because you haven't finished assimilating them. And assimilating them is not something that happens once and for all. You'll have an experience and then ten years later you'll have another experience that will cause you to re-evaluate the earlier experience. You bring it back as information in your aura as you assimilate it from your new fuller understanding.

If all you do is work on chakras without exploding pictures, then you generate enormous power but you don't generate a real encounter with your personal life. You're not likely to explode pictures until you have cultivated more perception of your aura as a whole. Then you'll become more aware of it not vibrating in current time.

You step into a picture by matching your crown to that color, and that picture becomes your world of attention. A lot of people don't think they have dealt with their pain until they have stepped into their pain in that sort of way, that they've stepped into their pain pictures. That kind of catharsis type of approach, research shows, is not actually very effective at freeing you from your emotional traumas, even though it is the psychic description of what Freudian catharsis was expected to do. We almost never work at that level.

We do our work *not* stepped into a picture. We put the picture out in front of us, move out of resistance to the experience, and assimilate the experience in part by exploding the picture. Look at the most horrible experience. You're going to get sucked into that picture a little bit, but you don't have to go full bore *into* the picture. In fact, what you'll do is intentionally set your crown at a different color so that you can stay out of the picture. If it's a really toxic picture, probably just exploding it won't do, but you can put it out in front of you and see what it lights up in your space. You can see what keeps tugging your crown to match the principal color of that picture and tries to pull you into that picture. You keep creating and destroying roses and you keep clearing until you can look at that picture without getting sucked into it. Then you can explode it.

When I change history, I do step inside the picture, or maybe partially step inside the picture. That is because, in change history, or resourcing history, we associate back into the experience, but keep enough neutrality to be able to re-experience the original event. But we experience it with changed energy and changed imagined actions that we use to become more resourceful.

In the dream state, things tend not to be as clearly segregated between inside and outside, but I would imagine it would depend upon what you were doing in that particular dream. You could be more inside it or more outside it; there may be no one answer for that.

One of the principal things you do in the dream state is compare experience across time. So it may be that you had temporarily assimilated that experience, but with new experience, you pulled it back out to compare it to all the rest of your life experience, particularly what's happening now, and to put it in a different kind of framework base based upon who you are now. An event is not done and over at any one time. You're always rewriting your understanding of your past. If you aren't, you're in serious trouble.

You can be fine with your aura being in chaos, which is a good skill to have because there will be life experiences where your aura is in chaos, and you can't say, "Everybody stop, I need to meditate."

You can't fully appreciate even beginner's concepts as a beginner, so for a beginner, we just keep it simple. We say if you see a picture, you zap a picture, but you don't really start to appreciate that something's vibrating in my aura, and isn't that cool? I think people are getting it and over time you might get it more: it is extraordinary that your aura can be vibrating in multiple times and multiple people.

What *is* your attention? Where is it? Where does it come from? Where do you get your attention from? It's a really tricky question because we don't naturally or normally ask ourselves questions like that.

For some of you, there is a source of attention that seemed to come from up above, and I'm going to substitute the word *soul,* but, depending upon what your attention is turning to, different parts of your aura will capture that attention and direct it.

If you get the concept of hello, you've essentially gotten the system; this is another one of those linchpins. It's really core as we look at concepts around the personal aura and being able to engage life. Wherever you've turned your attention, it's because something in your aura has become senior and captured your attention. Now you want your aura to be able to invoke your attention; you want to be able you know something's going on. It's sort of like, something's going on in your body, you want to have a sense of touch. You want to be responsive to what's going on in your aura. There's a kind of perfect picture you can have where you never lose your seniority to what's going on in your aura. Now that's a perfect picture. Perfect pictures, by definition, can never be achieved, and I don't even know if that would be a particularly good outcome.

You can experience your attention as like a fly flying around and, from time to time, it will get enticed by a picture in your aura, and then you will become that until that sort of burst of energy is discharged for a bit. Now that fly is actually your I that, instead of being in the center of your head, is just sort of going from one place to another. Our attention moves and our attention gets broken up. You can't have a picture without having some of your attention, in this sense of attention, locked into that picture.

Every picture that's in your space has taken some of what you would put in the center of your head and has locked that up, and it's taken some of your will, and some of your will is continuing to vibrate that picture. This isn't exactly the same thing as will power. This is your will in the sense of it being a kind of momentum to life and an ability to direct your choices, to make choices. Just provisionally, you might think that your will is necessary for there to be a personal form.

A picture is another word for form. Your will stamped out that picture; not stamped out in the sense of destroyed, stamped out in the sense of there being a die, a cast. Your will takes emotional energy and space and gives it a form and, as such, it is a kind of instruction set to the universe, "This is the world I want," even when you really, really, really also don't want it. Words are tricky here. But what's in your aura is what gets created in your world. Whatever pictures you're creating in your aura, they become part of the overall energy field, out of which your reality gets created.

Now the problem with pointing this out—that your attention gets focused into pictures that, with other energies, create your reality—is that people get afraid of their own mind. Being afraid of your own mind just doesn't work, folks. You can't trick your mind; you can't yell at your mind or punish your mind to make it create the picture that you think you want so that you get the reality that you want. Your mind will always contain tensions and contradictions, and rather than being afraid of that fact, it's best to be open to it. In one important respect this whole system is to help you not be afraid of your own mind. Essentially everything in there is trying to help you consider the possibility that all life expands in all directions, all experience is sacred. It is true that pain is a part of human life, and sometimes pain can be overwhelming. It's also true that that life goes on, that everything is ultimately redeemed.

The more courage you can bring to life, the more pleasure and happiness you're going to have and the more you're going to be open to joy. And that's the only reliable way of becoming happy. Remember, the universe is what is actually biased in your direction. If everything you created was the pictures and energies that you created personally, life would be a lot harder than it is.

It's like you always have All That Is in your soul. You always have a little hand under your elbow, helping you, not pushing here but just sort of supporting you. No matter what you think, they are always there, along with the Earth and the Sun and all kinds of other consciousnesses. In that sea of support, all of those are in partnership, and they are just as excited to figure out what's going to happen in your life as you are. Consider that. Really consider it.

The idea of matching pictures is a deceptively tricky one, but it's very powerful. It begins to help you understand how you create your reality. Every pleasant or unpleasant experience will involve matching pictures. As you're clearing pictures and other people's energy out of your space, you're releasing resistance to the world as it is. And, ideally, you're becoming more open.

As soon as you come into this system you start hearing about matching pictures. And yet matching pictures is a very hard concept to really own. I suspect that many people who have been with us ten or fifteen years still don't really have a clear sense of what a matching picture is. I realized this when one of my long-term students said to me, "I can't possibly have matching pictures with Donald Trump, can I?"

You can substitute whoever you want. The question is: "How can you have a matching picture with someone that you think and feel you dislike with every cell in your body, that you're in complete disagreement with?" The answer brings you into a deep and fundamental understanding of how we create our reality. There is no portion of reality in any universe where you haven't created your relationship, and that includes Donald Trump or whomever.

This doesn't mean that you are literally and hegemonically creating your own reality and the reality of everyone else around you. No, you're creating or choosing a reality in the Buddhic plane where it is put together in synchronicity, moment by moment, with everyone else's reality. It is also put together so that every little bit of it fits with your beliefs—there are no exceptions to this. It doesn't matter how unskillful or skillful you are. It doesn't matter whether you're Donald Trump or the Dalai Lama. People you're around are, by definition, people that fit your belief system. By definition. You can't pick and choose to alter that fact.

Theoretically, you can disagree with someone with all your heart and soul and not be in resistance to them, and then you wouldn't have a matching picture. That's only theoretical. If they are unattractive to you in a portion of your reality, then you have matching pictures. So we can also say, by definition, if there's anything in your reality that you don't like, you created it by your matching pictures. By saying, "You created it," I don't mean that you causally created it, that you made them behave in that way; I mean that you dove into one of the infinite universes where they behaved in that way. You matched it.

A matching picture is any picture that gets lit up when you're interacting, consciously or unconsciously, with an event or person. The point is not about who's right or who's wrong. The point is, every time that you have resistance, you light up; and what you resist, you become. So, it is really useful for you to find your resistances to people and events. And if you have huge resistances, it becomes even more important if you get particularly lit up by things. Even with people and events that you agree with, you will find resistances. If you are a Donald Trump supporter, then you're going to share his resistance to immigrants coming across our southern border from Mexico or Central America.

Let's find something that will light you up so that we can have this experience. Let's start with the politician that you most support, and look at the energies that oppose him or her because that's going to light you up.

Create a rose for your preferred candidate. Create another rose for all of the things that could go wrong. Look at that second rose and you will feel, hear, or see personal aura blocks that could be one foot by two feet. You could call that a matching picture. It could be a conglomeration of pictures, one tiny picture in your sixth chakra, or one thousand pictures in your sixth chakra.

Let's start off by creating and destroying roses for those pictures that light up in resistance to the goal that you have for your candidate. If you're for Donald Trump, you'll have matching pictures for anyone who *opposes* a border wall. Of course, you can have matching pictures for anything that gets lit up, a cord, an energy that's not yours, karma. Anything that gets lit up, anything that is in resistance to your experience at the moment we will call a matching picture. We'll use our tools to assimilate and process them. It might help to bring your crown to gold. It might also be a good idea to replenish your energy, cut off your grounding cord, and create a new male or female grounding from time to time.

Exploding matching pictures is the most important and powerful thing that you can do in the political arena.

Hand in glove with this concept, that I'm good and the other person is bad or I'm right and the other person is wrong, is the concept of punishment. A lot of the alienation that we see is driven by a deep belief that we need to punish error. Most of us have beliefs that we are aware of or not that the most effective way to make someone better who is currently in error, our self or other people, is to make them behave.

Please be in the center of your head. Cut off your grounding cord and create new male or female grounding. What I'd like you to do now is to create a rose for a politician that you have the most resistance to. Take the person whose politics you dislike most, put that person out in front of you, and work on finding your matching pictures—the resistances you have to that being.

Then start to clear the pictures that light up. Now, create a second rose between you and that person who you most resist. Let that second rose fill with the energy that you spontaneously start using to oppose that other person or even to wish that that he or she would change.

You might be able, as you do that, to find some of that energy that opposes or wishes to heal or change the person of whom you are most disapproving. You might be able to find that some or even a lot of that energy imagines it is inflicting pain. You might not think of it as inflicting pain; you might think of it as making them pay attention to what you think is important, making them understand the truth. But if you look carefully, you will also find in that "making them" energy a piece that, if it got to them, would inflict pain on them.

I'm not saying you can never do something that people find painful. But you can simply act on your own preferences, after you consider the situation, without jumping into the person's space.

❦

I will describe the two easiest ways of doing focused meditation. One is to do a mantra or use your breathing. There're some downsides to those way of focusing your mind, but if you're having a hard time, that can work. The mantra for the first chakra is lam. It is a really good approximation of the natural vibration of the chakra, but it's not exact. If you do that for a long time, it'll groove the energy, maybe a bit too much so you would have that mantra always vibrating in the chakra. You can do the mantra meditation and then, as you get more psychic, you'll be able to see that tape loop of sound going over and over; the one that you've laid on top of the chakra.

The other technique I use is like surfing. Your surfboard to get into the chakra is any picture or cord or knot in the chakra itself. Because how do they stay there in the chakra? Well, they stay there on a wave of energy. So you can repurpose that very energy that holds the obstruction at the chakra; use it to hold your attention on the chakra.

This is a tricky technique because when you kind of surf on a picture stuck in the chakra, three things can happen that can interfere with your surfing the energy toward your chakra. One is when you home into a picture or a cord that's near the chakra, it will tend to light up other pictures and cords, and you'll have monkey mind; you'll go from picture to picture, hopping like a monkey.

The second thing that can happen is you'll lose your seniority to that picture and you'll match your crown to the picture or to the cord; you'll fall into someone else's energy and you'll fall asleep. So if you can stay senior to your surfboard by having your crown not match it, you'll stay awake. Easier said than done.

The third thing that will happen is not a problem at all, it's great. That picture will just dissipate. You'll have to find another picture, but there'll always be other pictures or cords or knots in your chakra.

None of this is easy, but none of this has to be done perfectly either. I mean none of it will be done even close to perfectly. You don't have to be able to sit and meditate for a day-and-a-half without ever thinking of anything other than your first chakra. If you can do it for fifteen seconds at a time, that's very powerful.

It's impossible to be cordless. What is possible is for you to clear the cords that are lit up in any situation. As you clear more and more cords, you gain more and more neutrality and more and more openness to life as it is. It may even be true that you have an infinite number of cords. There will always be cords, there will always be pictures, there will always be other people's energy in your space. It's not our goal to get perfectly clear. It is impossible to be perfectly clear because we arise interdependently. Since we're not completely separate beings, we can never actually get all of the energy separate; but what we *can* do is be engaged in this drama as if we *were* separate beings exploring what it is like to be separate beings and have good boundaries and an authentic kindness and generosity. And the way we learn how to do this is by clearing enough space in our aura that we can engage others and still have our energy running fairly smoothly.

All of us go through our day unconsciously reading the environment and our self and, when we see something we're in resistance to, we match a crown to it and then we become what we are resisting. That's why learning how to read becomes a spiritual journey at a personal level, because you learn how to go through your day and communicate with people without matching your crown to them or resisting them. Whatever your crown vibrates at, that becomes senior in your space and that becomes the predominant energy. So when you learn how to be senior to what you're looking at, then you can communicate to it, you can value it, you can let go of resisting it. This is an idea that will become richer over the years; it is one of those that's not just an intellectual thing. It's a long-term goal. When you get where you can stay senior to all these various things—I'm not saying do it perfectly—but when you can become more and more senior in your own space so that you are who you are and you are in communication with what's going on outside you without getting enmeshed in it, a new form of intimacy arises.

Have a regular daily clearing. It can be two minutes or twenty minutes or, if you have time, forty minutes on the weekend or sometimes twice a day; no matter the length or timing, always do some clearing. You will also have things that are lit up throughout the day. You might come home from work and your boss treated you in a certain way, and you think, "This is an example of how men get away with murder and women are mistreated and I'd better do something." Your meditation is a good time to clear your energy around the interaction with the boss, and figure out a skillful response given the probable tensions and conflicting goals you face in this difficult interaction.

Back when I was growing up Dinah Shore had this television show and it was advertising Coca-Cola, and she would sing, "Twenty million times a day, at home, at work, or on the way, there's nothing like a Coke." Well for you, twenty million times a day, at home, at work, or at play, there's nothing like a meditation clearing.

When you really bring your skills to an unpleasant situation, it will be less unpleasant because you will find it interesting and fascinating in developing your skills to deal with it. You will do what's called going meta in the situation, as in meta-physical. You go to a different level so that your concern is no longer primarily about that person or the energy you hate. It becomes a slightly different thing: "How do I deal with the energy that I'm hating?"

You're trying to flow through your barriers. The external situation expresses your barriers, and prompts you to assimilate those inner areas where you have set up barriers. Then your barrier will dissipate, no longer generating the external obstruction. The barrier is a bunch of pictures. Those pictures are the way you have packaged your experience. They structure the stories you tell yourself and through which you create subsequent experience. Where your story is off, rigid, or undigested, you try to protect yourself by holding on to those pictures that compose the story. But you want to flow through that barrier those stories generate. Part of your own energy is composing that barrier. You can flow through the barrier by assimilating the experience that has those pictures stuck.

Pictures are like knots in a musical instrument's strings. That energy that you're bumping into is a knot, your own knot. Because that knot is there, it makes your aura clunk. You don't want to put tone-deafening material around that sound so that you can't hear the unpleasantness anymore; you want to assimilate the experience and untie that knot so that the string makes a full and easy flow. After exploding the pictures, the next time you come through that part of your aura, you will flow smoothly through it. You flow through the unknotted energy. The obstruction won't be there anymore.

If you're revisiting a past experience where you got really, really angry and furious, matching your crown in the same way you did the original time means there's a good chance you'll get every bit as furious again as you're redoing it. But once you get the hang of it—it may take you a while—you can relatively easily revisit the experience half- instead of fully-associated with it. Instead of matching your crown to what someone said, because you were already off-balance in the original situation so it just took this one little thing to cause you to tumble, you go into it a bit more slowly, a little more carefully.

Put a rose between you and what the person said so that you can maintain some neutrality and set your crown at a different color. Now you may think, "What a nasty thing to say," rather than rolling into fury.

You may find this very hard to do, but keep practicing.

All healing involves growth, but all growth doesn't necessarily involve healing, because healing is for places where you're stuck. And some growth involves growth where you haven't been stuck. It's a kind of effortless flowing.

When your kundalini kicks off, there's a couple of things that you can do. I think the most effective thing is to say, "I know my kundalini is kicking off," and then use the kundalini to heal whatever problem the kundalini was kicked off to heal. You say hello to the kundalini energy and ask, "What triggered your kicking off?" Light that up and find a way to move out of survival.

You might as well set a thief to catch a thief. Your kundalini initially got kicked up because you went into survival when you probably didn't need to go into survival. You can ask it to help you find why you thought you needed to go into survival, and either clear that or make some adjustments. Possibly you had an either-or belief in there, that you're either a unity or an individual, so touching in the unity of the Atman might have kicked it off. Survival pictures are usually triggered by some conditioning in the body where the body says, "Wait, I don't feel safe here." So you might male- or female-ground it and reassure the body that you're going to come back as yourself, but you're exploring something more transcendent right now, not to abandon but to enhance your persona.

It is useful to know that a given pain is going on all the time underneath your awareness; it's also a nice understanding to have that you couldn't exist without some sense of alienation. It's not necessarily a bad thing. It may be that your boundaries aren't clean enough yet for you to open up into more expanded states comfortably, but if you can develop some amusement and blow pictures and just say hello to those other pain energies and ask yourself how you can feel more comfortable, I think the answers will emerge.

Begin to appreciate the space that you have to explore human emotions. We have an aura, a personal aura. Yet that aura in some sense is your Astral body, and it is a space in which emotions occur. They occur as energies, as vibrations, or as lack of flow in a kind of emotion, as blockages in the aura or Astral body. And that occurs within a much, much larger space that is itself conscious. For now we will call it the Astral plane.

I find it helpful to have a sense of the whole Astral plane collaborating, creating the space for me—creating the conference hall in which simultaneous performances are always going on. Sometimes you're conscious and awake, sometimes you're more conscious in your sleep or in other dimensions. *All* of that is supported by the Astral plane.

Have a sense of your experience moving in your aura as a whole. Perhaps you can become aware of your aura creating the space and material for an experience to take place. The aura becomes the mother of the experience. The aura becomes an instrument in which the experience vibrates.

The aura is a live, conscious intentionality instrument, but not exactly in the way that you think about your human intentionality. Even as that experience vibrates, create and destroy roses, meaning pictures, so you assimilate your experience. Then, in your aura, the experience becomes saved as information. Your aura is once again ready for the next experience, for the next moment. It can vibrate in whatever way is appropriate to that next experience, to that next moment.

We only focus on pictures when they stay around too long. The capacity to form a picture is a peculiar human ability. Well, I don't know. Maybe cats and dogs and trees, for all I know, form pictures. But our capacity as humans to form pictures is what gives an experiential particularity to our aura. It's what allows us to focus our attention on the story that we're creating. You make up a story by pictures.

Take a moment. Imagine that you have a beautiful, pinkish red color. Let's make it a rose color that emerges from the heart. How did you get that to happen? You formed a picture. And the picture activated and organized the space of your personal aura. I don't mean empty space but the space and substance of your personal aura. You can call it the space and strings of your personal aura. You vibrate with the capacity to create a picture and what allows it to self-organize.

Spend some time appreciating your capacity to create a picture and have it affect your aura, the space and strings of your aura.

Remember, no matter how many pictures you explode, there's still more pictures there.

A picture is your capacity to mold, activate, or vibrate in a coherent fashion the hundred million strings of your aura, even the ten quadrillion strings of your aura. What holds them? What coordinates them so they stay in a certain pattern, or move in a certain pattern, or develop in a certain pattern?

The strings are organized with shape and coordination by something in the center of each of our heads. And that something goes through a little structure in the center of my head that I can locate by putting my finger on each of my temples. Lewis called that the picture-making machine.

All of this takes place within the larger context of the global Astral plane. In some ways this is how our dreams are worked out within a larger structure with seven billion other human beings currently alive, and more than a few on inner planes that aren't alive, plus all kinds of animals and plants, devas and elementals, stars, and planets together in a vibrant symphony.

Find a picture, or several pictures, somewhere in your aura. Can you get any sense of what is holding that picture together? What energy? Where is that energy coming from?

Your ability to make a picture is a vital part of the uniquely human experience of having emotions and creating stories. The way that humans create pictures and make stories out of them is fabulous. I want to encourage your ability to do that. The issue becomes when you hold on to your stories. Whenever you find pictures floating in your aura, it's probably because you held on to a story. The issue with an old picture is not whether it's a pleasant picture or an unpleasant picture; the question is whether the picture is applicable to your current experience. If it's currently applicable, it's what helps coordinate what I was calling metaphorically the myriad or millions of little strings in your aura that come to vibrate together and create complex emotional systems. When they continue to vibrate within the same picture, but you're no longer having that experience, the picture becomes very limiting.

You'll know a picture that's active because you probably won't see it as a picture. You'll be *in* it. You'll be in the story of that moment. But a picture that you find is almost always a picture you're holding on to. If it's an unpleasant picture, you're holding on to it because you're in resistance to it. If it's a pleasant picture, you're holding on to it because you're in resistance to moving to the next experience; you're holding on to the old pleasant experience.

Most of your pictures—most of the energy—will be closer into the body. But it will extend all of the way on out to the edge of your aura.

Dealing with death pictures that are lighting up in your space is the core of real queasiness. A death picture will vibrate in a very scary way in your aura, notwithstanding the fact that many deaths are beautiful. There are many parts of your brain that are just set up to be afraid of death.

There are ways to use your kundalini to take that death picture into a bigger perspective, and it no longer frightens you. Plus, you've already died successfully many times.

37

Evil

When you think of all life expanding in all directions, the concept of evil is only the result of the self-reflective ego. There's no sense at all to the term evil without the particular narrow focus of the self-reflective ego. If evil existed, it would be something that makes the universe less than it was before and, since all consciousness expands in all directions, there is no such thing as real evil in an absolute objective sense, only apparent evil.

Perhaps it's easier to understand from this point of view: If you think of yourself as having an essence and arising from this essence, then the concept of absolute or real evil would be a being that had an essence whose objective it was to make the universe, or any part of it, less than it was before. And that simply doesn't exist. Only human beings within their own subjectivity could be said to be trying to make the universe less. Evil arises out of ignorance and not out of an essential quality.

Obviously there are people who do evil things, but this is evil only within the terms of the self-reflective ego. It's impossible for an animal to do something evil. An animal can't act with the motivation of a human doing something evil. Larger consciousnesses certainly can't. So evil is really a kind of human insult. It isn't an actual state of being. It's a characterization.

I suppose there could be evil if all punishment were imposed by some Father God, but all punishment is imposed by your self to give yourself a healing, even if you don't realize that's what you are doing. In that way there is goodness, but there is no fundamental evil. There's relative evil, of course there is. But there's no fundamental evil; there's only temporary delusion.

There are certainly evil actions, if you want to use evil in that sense. But the distinction is a profound one, because even Bernie Madoff, who intentionally stole money from huge numbers of people, cannot intend at his essence, in an absolute way, to genuinely steal.

In the long run, Bernie Madoff will work through what he did as Bernie Madoff, though it could be a long while, and be redeemed. And he may suffer, but the suffering is not imposed by some mean paternalistic god; it's imposed by Bernie Madoff himself, with the deep intention to heal the brokenness that led him to such relatively evil actions. That's why Bernie Madoff is not fundamentally evil. Bernie Madoff needs to get out of his delusion that he is better off stealing from people. He's gotten started by going to jail.

I'm using this rather than stuff that people have more shock and horror about, but it applies to everyone, even to people who commit acts far, far, far worse than theft.

You can't have one emotion at a time and you can't have an emotion all by yourself, even though the core of the basic set of techniques we teach uses the story that there is something called my energy and there is something called other people's energy. In Nazi Germany, everyone, including the victims of the Third Reich, had matching pictures with the Nazis. The Nazis' actions were evil in the ordinary and useful way that we use language to characterize heinous actions, but not in an absolute sense. For evil to be absolute, it would have to arise out of the true nature of the actor, not out of ignorance of the actor. Seth and numerous other teachers for thousands of years assert that the relative evil we do is actually a violation of our true nature. Evil actions always arise out of ignorance rather than our nature.

Everyone has a concept of right or wrong, which is a useful thing to have. The downside is that it puts you in resistance; it makes you imagine that a dichotomy exists between self and a person you're rejecting. But there are no limits to the self, no limits to what we can create. There are no exceptions to the proposition that we create our own reality. You create your own reality in the womb, you create your own reality at birth, you create your own reality at nine days old, you create your own reality at nine years old, you create your own reality at ninety years old. And everywhere in between. Awake or asleep, you create your own reality.

That evil action that we're treating as not ourselves *is* our self, that is our creation. When we create out of ignorance, we can create relative evil. Eventually experience will carry us out of our ignorance, and sooner or later, each of us individually will learn and fulfill our true nature. The good action that we do is also our self. Everything is us. Pogo's saying, "We've met the enemy and it is us," is a deep metaphysical principle.

Let's say you have a report that there's a ghost in my house and it's really angry, it's doing this, it's doing that. It's easy to see that as an actual person who's dead. I do not believe that those are actual beings with essences. I believe they're debris from beings who have died with unresolved stuff. They're thoughtforms. They don't have their own mobility. All their mobility is derivative. It's generated by someone who *was* a being. It came from a once-live being, but it is an empty thoughtform without essence.

Certain things get detached. The example I use in my mind is a rocket ship with multiple stages. And these things that we call ghosts are just a stage. They're not the real mission. They're part of the overall body, not the essence. So, can they generate harm? Yeah, they can. But they can only do it if someone in that house is feeding them energy.

These thoughtforms will very often have a rudimentary consciousness. So you'll say, "Get out of my house!" and it will say, "I'm here to make you miserable!" If you engage it, all the conversation will be in that general range. That thoughtform doesn't have a real intellect. So it may seem like it has animosity toward you; it just has leftover animosity. And you can send it to the light if you want to. I'd just pull my energy out of it because that's part of what's giving it energy, your energy *in* it. I'd pull my energy out of it, blow my matching pictures, and send it back to whoever it belonged to.

Now there are huge thoughtforms that create powerful and awful situations. There are still major thoughtforms over the Middle East that arose out of the Crusades where the Christian Europeans decided that they could go "liberate" Jerusalem from the infidels.

Those thoughtforms are still there. If you go to the Middle East, you can get caught up in those thoughtforms. And you're not going to be able to send everybody's energy back to them from such a large thoughtform. But what you *can* do is pull your energy, from whatever lifetime it got in there, out of those thoughtforms.

By the way, if you want to try to promote peace in the Middle East, you might sit down and see if you can find some of those thoughtforms from other centuries and pull your energy out of them and blow pictures and clear karma.

In the case of concentration camps, people have dealt with so much more of that energy. If you go to Buchenwald, you'd think there'd be a much bigger thoughtform than over the Middle East, but no way, not even close.

38

Further Relationships between the Astral and Etheric

Your Physical-Etheric collaborates with your personal aura. In some ways there's an intrinsic tension between your Physical-Etheric and your Astral because they vibrate in a different energy range—just like there's an intrinsic tension between men and women. There are attractions between men and women and there are tensions between men and women.

So there's an intrinsic tension between your Physical-Etheric and your Astral, but by grounding, you help your Physical-Etheric context find itself; grounding gives it a reference. To go a little more abstract, your Physical-Etheric is always part of the Earth, and when you ground, you're always making that a little bit more explicit.

As twenty-first-century humans we tend to think of us and Earth as separate, but that's a delusion. Just because you can walk around and it doesn't seem like Mother Earth's walking around—it seems like you're walking around *on* Mother Earth—but your body *is* Mother Earth walking around *in* Mother Earth, as Mother Earth.

Given that we ground, why do we male- or female-ground? We male- or female-ground to stay neutral. Both being male and being female come with a lot of genetic programming, and you could mistakenly wipe that genetic programming out. I've seen advanced meditations do that, and that's one way of becoming neutral. We don't do that in this system. For instance, if you just wipe out the energy of your uterus or ovaries, then you're nice and neutral; but then you've lost the energy of your uterus and ovaries, which is this wonderful, complex, maddening matrix that you get to deal with if you're female on this planet. In our system, and in the Berkeley Psychic Institutes, as they encounter this, we develop the concept of female- and male-grounding to leave that genetic programming in there so that you can have access to it and ground it so that you can also be senior to it.

Most healers who work directly in the Etheric do not adequately clear the Astral level, and that's a problem. You can heal someone. They can even feel emotionally better because, remember, when you clear something at an Etheric level, if you're not connecting your Etheric with the Astral, you can break that emotional connection and you can feel perfectly friendly and loving while your Astral body is still all gooped up.

What happens to many people is that their Astral body kind of shrivels up and it moves into the background. It's possible to get to where you're very loving out of a mechanical Etheric level and also bring in a lot of Buddhic-plane energy, so it is a profoundly loving energy, but it hasn't addressed what I would argue is your fundamental humanity in the Astral plane. A lot of people say your whole purpose here is to transcend the Astral plane. I don't agree with that.

Whenever you do Etheric work, follow it with some personal aura clearing. You can also do it simultaneously, but when it's new to you, it's a little bit like juggling and you may not be able to do these simultaneously. Distinguishing between Astral and Etheric chakras isn't easy or straightforward, even for an accomplished psychic. You may think you're noticing a difference, and in a month you'll be noticing a *different* difference. Each level of difference you notice gives you more skill to be able to do a wider range of things.

There are also two ways to work on the Etheric. One is to get stagnant Etheric energy to flow. The other is to clear Etheric energy that doesn't look or feel very good. You can just clear it and throw it away. That's different from Astral energy. If it's Astral, the question is, Is it my energy or someone else's?

Your own pictures tend to be more compact; they're more concrete in some ways. If it's yours, you want it so that you can assimilate it. Someone else's energy in your space will always be a little more spread out. It's never that clean because you'll always have pictures and conglomerations of other people's energy sort of hanging around like a Halloween decoration in your aura. Sometimes I'll start with clearing other people's energy because their energy forms a cloud through a larger portion of my aura, but sometimes I'll just go straight to the picture because it's a compact way to address energy.

The Etheric is the polarity of that. There's no such thing as your Etheric energy or not your Etheric energy. The only reason I would say that Etheric energy isn't yours is because of some complementary process going on in your Astral that isn't your energy. While strictly speaking, it's nonsense to say that that's not your Etheric energy, but etheric energy can be entangled with Astral energy that's not yours. Clearing the Astral will help clear the lower-quality Etheric energy.

If it's your energy, your authentic process, but not in current time, it will be balled up into a picture. It doesn't matter if that picture is a happy experience or an unhappy experience; it limits the freedom of your aura to expand and be open to new experience. At the deepest level, if you clear pictures, it will clear other people's energy out of your space. If you clear other people's energy out of your space, it will clear pictures. So really each technique leads to the same outcome, a clearer you who is more open to new experience.

What's new about the New Age is each of us, individually, dealing with Astral emotions in the Astral plane. So, while we're doing this Etheric work, we're trying not to get too neutral too fast and miss the Astral stuff. Clearing the Etheric will give you a more solid foundation to engage your emotions. And it will improve your physical health and help you manifest things. The danger is clearing the Etheric without also engaging the Astral at approximately the same time. Without being careful to validate both the Etheric and Astral level, you could just override those emotions.

Running energy through your aura tends to light stuff up and make it easier to find. Focusing in on a chakra or a layer of the aura is like looking through a microscope. Focusing allows you to home in more narrowly and see the area you're focused in on more clearly, with more detail. If you're focused on the third chakra, you're going to find a lot more pictures and cords there than if you look at the aura as a whole. On the other hand, if you can learn to look at the aura as a whole, you can start to see whole systems better. That can be better for life problem solving because often a problem in your life involves more than one focused area of your aura.

You can clear your personal aura by running energy through a layer. A layer is not the same as a sub-plane. Those are entirely different concepts. A sub-plane is a specific energy frequency. A layer is a narrower frequency *range* than the aura as a whole. In that respect they have some similarity. The layers of your personal aura arise out of a function of the chakra. The fourth layer arises out of a function of the fourth chakra throughout your entire aura. Any pictures dealing with your social identity will be in that fourth layer. Why not just focus on the fourth chakra itself? There are good reasons. As you become more clairvoyant, you start to home in on the layers more, and as you home in on the layers, it facilitates your becoming more clairvoyant.

Let's say you have a picture stuck in your crown in the fourth layer of your aura. That picture would partake of both the fourth layer and the seventh chakra. So it might be, for example, how you situate yourself socially, how you want to appear to the world, that's a fourth-layer issue. Instead of being around your heart, it might be around your crown because it deals with past lives, with a past-life setup of this lifetime. Or it might have to do with channeling your mother's idea of what your social persona should be.

Pictures won't be evenly distributed. There will be more pictures closer in to the body, although this is just a tendency, not a rule. And they will tend to congregate around one or more of the chakras. Each chakra exists in all seven layers of the aura, so, for example, if I go into the fourth layer of the aura I can choose to look at the fourth layer, one chakra at a time.

If you do a chakra just by itself, you are focusing narrowly in on one thing. When you do a layer and a chakra at the same time, you're narrowing it in two ways. If I limit it to anything that vibrates in the rough frequency range of the fourth layer of my aura, I'm ignoring all other six layers of the aura. It's like a filter at an eye doctor, you're only looking at the fourth layer of your aura. It's a way of focusing your attention, and you see details and you feel details that you don't notice when you're paying attention to your whole aura. By honing your attention to the second chakra in the fourth layer, you're putting your attention on something very small. You get a very thorough clearing.

Gloria has this really lovely image. When she is not focused, her attention is like a bunch of trick-or-treaters, little children running from house to house in anticipation of what they're going to get. Portions of her personality will pull her attention hither and yon like the expectation of the trick-or-treaters. When she's calm and centered, then the center of her head opens up in this kind of calm observant clarity that is her soul, and that's like the parent standing back and sort of helping the children avoid danger while they go trick-or-treating. That's a really lovely image.

When I did this exercise, I initially found my attention getting pulled or driven, mostly from stories I would tell myself. When I'd get lost, it would be in subvocalized stories that I was telling myself, though it would also get pulled from other aspects of the aura. I noticed that it would kind of feed in through my crown. I kept looking to see where it was going, and it was going to the reticular formation. It turns out that the reticular formation is that part of the brain that directs attention, and it is inside the brain, a little behind the ear, going up to about midpoint on the ear, extending about two inches vertically. The part that is most involved in attention seems to be toward the top of it. It's in the brainstem, in the medulla and the pons, and one of its functions is the state wakefulness.

The brain is really complex, and any time you try to have a simple description of what one part of the brain does, it turns out that it does a lot more and it's more interactive with other parts of the brain. I eventually found that my attention was in the reticular formation, but that it would get these little pings on it where my story would redirect my attention, or this picture or that picture would redirect my attention.

You don't really have to track what your attention is. Wherever it seems to come from, what you want to be able to do is to sustain it and to keep it from getting knocked around. There are going to be two major sources, which are really the same thing but it is useful to distinguish them. The first major source of getting knocked off your attention into monkey mind is the things in your aura as a whole that are lighting up and dragging your attention away, maybe a to-do list, maybe something that happened on your way to get here, something you might do next week, anything like that. Then the other thing—it's essentially the same phenomenon—is whatever lights up between you and your energy focus. So if you turn your focus to the third chakra, you're going to have stuff light up in the third chakra area, and that will tend to knock you off your focus.

Now one of the things that we've started doing last year is kind of a psychic jiu-jitsu. If there's a picture disrupting your focus, some energy is holding that picture in that place, instead of resisting that picture you can use it like a surfboard; you can look at that picture and find where its energy source is to move toward. Let's say the source is your third chakra. If there's a picture near your third chakra, there's some energy that places that picture there, and you can just kind of ride that energy to carry your focus toward the third chakra. If you do that, after a while, that picture will explode. Exploding a stuck picture is good, but you'll have to find something else to hold your focus.

Now it doesn't have to be a picture, it could be a cord. Again, if there's a cord into your third chakra, there's some energy in that cord that is moving it there. If you can find that energy, you can use it to help you sustain your attention on the third chakra. I often find little knots in my third chakra. I'll often use those distortions and knots as the energy that directs me toward the third chakra.

Energies that aren't yours will be around the chakra, and some portion of those is going toward it. You could use that, but I tend not to use it as my surfboard because it's someone else's energy. Actually, my favorite is the knots in the chakra itself, because something is tying the knot right there that is hooking into the chakra itself.

You can use a picture. It could be that this energy isn't yours and you could use it anyway, but there's a good chance that the energy will be yours, just not in current time, but again, call it psychic jiu-jitsu. Whatever obstruction is there can't be there without some energy holding it there. If we had a choice, we'd have no obstructions, but if they're there you might as well use them for your own benefit.

Observe what is messing with your focus. The answer will be things in your aura. But there are two aspects of things in your aura. There are those that mess with your attention and take it elsewhere; they are anywhere in your aura. Then there are things that your attention kind of bounces off of as it homes in on the third chakra. Essentially it's the same thing, but they're in different locales.

You cannot climb into your life without your first three chakras; you can't climb into your personal life without access to them. You can't directly encounter your physical body without accessing it through the third chakra. Those chakras aren't better or worse; they're all part of this divine universe, and the higher energies are cool too. It isn't that we don't use the higher energy, it's that we don't exclude the lower energies. All consciousness expands in all directions and every piece of it is sacred.

You can have odious energy come through the sixth chakra or the seventh chakra and you can have lovely, wonderful energy come through the first, second, or third chakras. It will be a higher energy when it's through a higher chakra. It's complex, but just to simplify, it'll be a higher energy when it comes through a higher chakra, though it won't necessarily be better.

The old theosophical literature contains a lot of that bias, so they talk about having all of your energy in the highest sub-plane of a particular plane, but the sixth and seventh sub-planes of various planes are very important for structure. You couldn't really have a physical body without energy in the sixth and seventh sub-planes of the Astral. You would not be better off if all of your Astral energy was in the first sub-plane, which is what the old theosophical or Alice Bailey literature implies. It is true that your nastiest emotions hang out in the sixth and seventh sub-planes of the Astral, but one of the most spiritual things you can do is learn how to be in sub-planes with clarity and kindness and generosity.

The old yoga literature says that if your third chakra is clear, you will have perfect health. That's probably an idealized picture, but it is a really cool chakra to work on your physical health and, as you clear that chakra. you are likely to improve your health. It is also true that this is the chakra that people run anger and impermissible aggression through, so it requires some discrimination. But people run spaciness and non-engagement through their seventh chakra, thinking that they're getting nonattachment when they're really getting nonengagement. Every energy can be done skillfully or unskillfully. Every frequency range can be done skillfully or unskillfully.

You could hit a picture in your third chakra that was relevant to certain conversations, and you would bounce into your fifth and get lost in the conversation. And again, you can have a kind of delight as you notice the things that go wrong in your aura because you begin to get a sense of how alive and how magical it is.

Every chakra goes through every other chakra, and so when you do focus on one chakra, sometimes you'll find that what you really need to do is go to another chakra and address those issues because they're so interwoven. You want to learn how to weave in energies together; they really will interact. Sometimes you'll do that by looking at weaving energies and sometimes you'll just focus in primarily, say, on your third chakra.

After a while you'll stop getting pulled away quite as much to the first chakra or to the seventh chakra and you'll start to home in more specifically on the third chakra. It's a really boisterous world, all kinds of stuff going on all the time.

Focused meditation in and of itself can improve your physical health. When you start to turn your attention to focused meditation, you'll almost immediately move out of the center of your head and into the analyzer and start responding to all the requests that are in your telepathics. As you go back into the center of your head, you'll find it very healing through your sinuses and you'll feel immediately younger. Understand, this is very real. This reality exists because of a set of telepathic agreements. You wouldn't see what you see but for the telepathic agreement. So, as you clear your telepathic agreements, you actually open the capacity to fundamentally change things.

Now again you can drive yourself crazy over this stuff and get too urgent; you can go chasing after yet one more solution to solve whatever problem seems so significant. We give these techniques because we hope that, by developing skills, you'll get better outcomes. If you grasp onto those techniques too much, you'll be supplying your own resistance. Ideally you relax into it in a kind of exploration.

When I talk about physical health, I'm also talking about mental health. The whole thing is a system. The very definition of a system is that when you operate on one piece of it, it affects the whole system. There are aspects of mental health that are directly addressed through the third chakra. The belly-button field is particularly at that portion of the third chakra system that most directly addresses physical health. Now you can't really validly have physical health without mental health, not reliably. In a particular lifetime you can, because things are kind of set up that way, but for reliability you want to work on the whole system, though at any one point it may be better to work on one part of the system or another part of the system.

People often come and say, "Well, I want to explore past lives." And

I say, "I don't normally go hunting for past lives." Past lives light up in a reading whenever they're relevant. So sometimes it's appropriate to explore past lives and that's the place in the system where you're going to get your maximum benefit. Another time you might say, "My spouse is dangerous. Can I explore my past lives with him?" My answer is, "If your spouse is dangerous, let's get you into a safe place and then decide what to do." Now theoretically you could do it by just dealing with your past lives; that's just not a particularly wise place to address it, at least at that moment.

A large part of what we're going to do this week is help you find a safe place to look at what is scary and dangerous. It isn't really dangerous and it just seems scary. There are times in my life where things were so bad, and I would think of Albert Ellis who would say, "Well, what's the worst that could happen?" And then I would run a dialogue with myself like the following.

"I could lose my job."

"Okay, I lose my job. Then maybe Pamela would divorce me? Is that the worst that could happen?"

"Well then maybe I'd be homeless on the street and maybe I'd starve to death."

"Is that the worst that could happen?"

"Probably."

"Could you live with that?"

"Being a psychic, I guess I could. Because I would just move into the afterlife."

When you drill down to those places and say, "What if this happened?" and you imagine it would really be awful, the real question is, "Could you live with it?"

I certainly wouldn't *want* to live with it, but I could live with it. I've drawn great comfort through the decades from that. I highly recommend it.

I came into this system through Lewis and Jane, and there are certain things I imbibed that I haven't addressed. I remember the first time I met Lewis, him telling me about his system of spiritual practices; he said, "What I do is I line people up in a row and I have them do a reading and, as they do that reading, they're clearing, and because they're sitting in front of people who have various pain pictures, *they* will get lit up and that will help them access their own pain and at least start to move that pain." Then he said, "What we found out is there are places where pain and pictures get so wrapped up tight that you could meditate for a century and never get to those pain pictures."

Now you could transcend that pain, but you would never actually get to the pain pictures.

Lewis said, "I figured out a way to clear pain."

Well, he did, and it *does* work and we're going to explore why it works throughout the week and we'll explore it from a number of different directions. The reason it works is that the pain that you're avoiding that seems so powerful to you is part of a system and, as I've been saying, the definition of a system is if you activate the system at any point, you involve the whole system. Every part of the system is interconnected or it wouldn't be a system. Now what happens is that we take the system called our humanity, which is part of the Earth, part of the Sun, and part of the cosmos and we put these little moats around our pain to protect ourselves. That might be temporarily expedient, but the moats, the barriers, change your system, making you artificially separated in your personal aura, unable to use it to engage this life in its own terms and for its own purposes.

We're going to look at some safe places. By places, I mean psychic states, and then what we want to do is use those safe places as a resource state and take the pain a little bit at a time and clear it. You never clear all your pain, but when you begin to find that, "Oh yes, I have safe places," then climbing in and getting lost in your pain isn't quite as scary because you know, at some point, you're likely to find your way out long enough to be able to find one of those resource stations.

Pain occurs in the system because of your blockages. You can lose the system aspect of it, and it can be an island of pain that's physical or emotional or mental or spiritual even. But pain anywhere affects the whole system. Ideally if you're operating in a system when you address the pain anywhere, you heal the whole system even if you're not paying conscious attention to the whole system. Sometimes it's easier to address the pain in one location or another. Sometimes it might be easier to address the pain by looking at past lives. Sometimes it might be easier to address it by crossing probabilities. Sometimes it might be easier to address it by getting a massage. I find that the day after I get a massage, I'll very often have insights about my emotional armoring that's been triggering the pain, a tightness in one place or another. I encourage people to have flexibility in dealing with pain, sometimes working in one way, other times in another way.

Grounding is absolutely pivotal to this system, so what I'm about to say might be surprising. There's a lot of times when your pain is overwhelming that maybe grounding is not the way to go. You may want to have some stability before you start grounding because, once you start coming into the body, you're going to find some of that pain.

The first technique we'll do is going out of your body as a point of light. I'll describe it briefly now and, in a moment, lead you through it. First, you go to the top of your head. Then you go three feet above your head. Then you go five hundred feet above. Go to the edge of the atmosphere, the edge of the solar system, which has moved out considerably in the last twenty years. It used to be Pluto, now it goes three times as far out into the Kuiper Belt beyond Pluto, but you can go to Pluto if you want to. At each place, look at something painful and see how you react to it.

To start off, create a rose for something mild to moderately painful, just one thing, don't throw in everything. Create a rose for something that's moderately painful, put it out in front of you, and just sort of notice how you feel when you look at that. Does your heart tighten up? What happens to your feet? What happens to your breath? What happens to your jaw? What happens to your emotions? What are your thoughts? How strong or weak is it?

Now be in the center of your head. Go up as a point of light up to your crown. I am saying we are leaving the body. We're not talking here about fully leaving the body with your awareness. Just use the image of a point of light to represent your attention, and you can imaginatively place enough of your attention and energy to do the job. Then go up three feet as a point of light. From there, look at that rose that was moderately painful and, without looking for what you think the right answer is, ask yourself how you respond to that pain now. Create and destroy roses, use your tools from out there. Can you see the pain as part of something bigger that's not all black and white?

Okay now go up five hundred feet above your head. Look out at the whole universe and then look back at that rose and see how you feel about it now. As you start to get farther out of your body like that, the pain, stress, and anxiety hormones that are rushing through it when you think of painful events recede from your awareness as your body awareness gently recedes.

From up there, look at that mildly painful thing. How is it looking now? As you move each step, again create and destroy roses and use your tools. If you get to neutrality, then move step by step back into your body, checking your neutrality at each step, using your tools if you lose your neutrality. If you can't find neutrality at one location, move your attention further out of body as a point of light and try using your tools from further out. Right now, we are only dealing with a mildly painful incident. You may not need to go very far. But more difficult issues trigger your stress, pain, and anxiety hormones so strongly that they can overwhelm your ability to focus. By leaving the body behind, you get enough space to clear the issue, and then you can re-enter the body with enough neutrality to deal with and eventually to clear the stress hormones.

Go up to the edge of the atmosphere. How does that pain look now? Go up to the moon's orbit and look at it now. Go to the orbit of Pluto and look at it from there. Go to Alpha Centauri, the nearest star that is not our sun, look away from the pain, and dig the freedom that you feel there. Then look back at the pain and see if you can keep any of that freedom.

Go to the edge of the Milky Way Galaxy and look back. Go to the edge of the universe even if, strictly speaking, it may not have an edge.

Some energies, when I was working with them, would require me to go *beyond* the edge of the universe, which I guess is plausible for psychics, even though it's not clear what "beyond" would mean in that case. But get a sense of the vastness of your existence out there and, with that vastness, look back at your pain, that rose. See how you feel about it. And then come back to the edge of the galaxy. Let your body adjust as you come back to the Galaxy because your body keeps track of you no matter where you go to. See if you can bring more of that resourcefulness back. Come back to the closest star to our solar system, then to the orbit of Pluto, and again look at the pain and let your body adjust. See how you can let it be part of something bigger. You have that good feeling in addition to whatever else you're feeling.

Come back to the orbit of the moon. Back to the edge of the atmosphere. Come back as a point of light, as a golden, white, or blue point of light five hundred feet above your head, whatever feels best. Again look at it. Come back three feet above your head. Let your body adjust. Now come into your crown and as a gold, white, blue, or pink point of light, take a look at the thing that was bothering you. Create and destroy roses. Explode the rose of the issue. Fill your aura with lots of golden sands and just the right amount of Earth energy for your body this time. And, when you're ready, stand up, stretch, and reverse polarity. Take a minute or so to write down your experience.

VIVIAN: Talk about golden crowns. I have all this pain, all this old survival energy. The blockage is there and it hurts. And man, I just pushed all that shit out. But this hurts too much. I've got so much will power you wouldn't believe. I say, "Don't bug me now!" I know it's one layer at a time. I say, "Don't kill me now. Just back off." That's not cool. I get so irritated. Like where am I leaking? How do I pluck this? I have worked with this a long time and I am really unhappy, and I don't know what to do with this problem.

JOHN: Put it in a rose, give the rose a grounding cord, blow pictures, and clear out the energy that isn't yours. Then you will be able to look at the problem with relatively little agitation. But you'll actually be starting to clear the problem. Just because you are not consciously aware of an emotion doesn't mean it isn't there. Just because you don't know it's there doesn't mean that it isn't there and, if it's there, the whole flow isn't going naturally.

For you, this is one of those issues that come up in life that you've poured lots of things into. But that's part of the cure and also part of the issue. Seth said many times, "You can't make a flower grow faster by pulling its leaves." We have the issues we have. From time to time you're going to run into something that's harder and going to last longer than you think it ought to.

VIVIAN: It's been a year. I have so much patience you wouldn't believe. It's just lingering, and I've been very kind to and patient with it.

JOHN: You don't get the choice of how much patience. You don't get to say, "Okay I've been patient. Now damn it, do it now." You don't develop patience that way. It doesn't work that way just because you have this wonderful will. But use it. Don't set yourself up, that because I have this wonderful will, I can will it away all the time. You may be able to, but you may not be able to. Explore using your will, but don't bully it into going away. It won't work. What you have is a dialogue with life, nothing more.

VIVIAN: Tears come down my face. *I want it to go away.*

JOHN: Stop for a moment and break this trance and hear this. Odds are that you will get through this. But you can't demand, "Beyond this line, life cannot go." You can say, "I really really, really want to be able to get through this and be happy." But you cannot say, "Because I have a strong will power, I will always be able to do this." You have to engage that as a real experience, and the odds are overwhelming that you will be able to do it, but it will take however long it takes and, if you insist on it going faster, sometimes that will work because you have a strong enough will power. But if you don't deal with the underlying issues, sooner or later, the issues will get more powerful than your will power, no matter how powerful your will power is. Because your will power is set up to help you engage the world, not to put up a dam between you and what you consider to be unacceptable.

VIVIAN: I just wanted to have a gentle flow, one thing at a time, not jamming it so hard.

JOHN: Of course you want it, but that doesn't mean that's the way it's going to happen. *You* don't get to say, "I'm willing for the world to be chaotic but only *this* chaotic." A channeled being once said to three of us—that included the channel—"Everybody wants to be spontaneous; they just don't want to be surprised." You don't get that choice. Now I'm pretty confident that you're going to get better, but I'm even more confident that *you* don't get to say how many issues are connected. So, it behooves you to use your will power and brain power skillfully, and then you not only increase the likelihood that your healing will proceed smoothly, but you can also stop treating your problem as something happening to you. You can also treat this as part of the adventure of being alive. And if you insist that it be what you're willing to put up with—I put up with fifteen different things, I shouldn't have to put up with a sixteenth—you don't get to engage this with a curiosity that leads to a kind of enjoyment.

You don't know the big picture. You may be saving yourself twenty or thirty lifetimes.

VIVIAN: I have so much shit in my life. I feel like three lifetimes of shit. And I'm finally getting to the point where I can breathe, and then this fucking shit had to happen on my way home. And I can tell you about curiosity and all that. I'm full of nothing but curiosity. And I have courage, because if I don't, I'd have died a million times already. And with all this work, I get ambushed. Wow! That's not good. This is very problematic. I'm being yanked around by a force I don't understand. And I have to reexamine everything I know. I don't even tell my husband about this because it's going to freak him out. He loves me a lot, and I don't want him to know how painful this is.

JOHN: Crying is allowed. There's no crying in baseball, but crying is fine here. My heart goes out to you; it really does. And you will deal with this as best you can. I have some advice, but you will deal with this as best you can. And that's what you're doing.

GLORIA: I suggest people let her have that space. A lot of people have gone into responsibility, including on the phone. Let her have that space.

JOHN: Blow your matching pictures and if you feel compassion toward Vivian, and I think we all do, you can acknowledge that you feel compassion toward her, and you can blow your matching pictures. That maximizes Vivian's possibility of dealing with the disappointment, the anger, and the challenge. Take a breath. Fill your aura with lots of golden suns.

The intention of this seminar is to have enough repetition and yet come at things from slightly different directions so that people get a firmer and firmer grasp on how you change yourself using these powerful energy techniques. You may not get it right away, but realize that you can deal with issues that seem too big to deal with by raising your psychic awareness just enough that you stay engaged with the issue.

Again, particularly in Hindu approaches, there are many systems that will raise you so far above the issue that it doesn't seem to bother you anymore. That's a very narrow understanding. Instead, you can raise your frequency just enough to really be engaged with whatever's lighting you up.

The reason you engage with it, rather than transcending it, is because every bit of your experience is sacred. You have the opportunity to take your experience with you, and that experience provides a core for you for the rest of eternity.

When you think of the rest of eternity, please stop thinking of it as a train track that goes down one direction. The rest of eternity is like popcorn popping all over the place, and each time it pops it becomes a center and pops in multiple directions, so each kernel then pops into a whole box, so you have boxes of popcorn coming out from all over. That's what eternity is, and many of those boxes will be full of the tritest, seemingly insignificant thing that happened. When you start to look at it, you say, "But this was so insignificant. How does it turn out so amazing, how does it expand it all directions?" Gloria, would you please share your experience, which is a perfect example of how our experience expands in all directions?

GLORIA: When Todd and I were in here getting things ready, I saw a cigarette butt on the ground and I picked it up and I was like, "Oh, this is one of those things that really, annoy me." I thought, "I'm going to look at the cigarette butt," and so I was giving it the universe, and it was very simple for about ten seconds, and then I realized, "People are unconscious, they're throwing trash on the ground, it's a boundary issue, blah, blah." And then I let go of that and thought about what it *really* meant to me.

JOHN: Wait, wait, slow down a little bit because this is actually so big I think people are having trouble tracking it. Even after Gloria has worked on this, there is quite a lot of pain connected with this, and I see people kind of checking out. The objective is for each of us to get a sense of how one seemingly utterly insignificant event that Gloria chose because it was easy, turned out to be a gold mine of stuff. Male- or female-ground and close your first and second chakra down to ten percent. I noticed that Gloria is trying to go through this quickly so she doesn't take up too much time. Let's give it enough time so that people get it.

GLORIA: I haven't actually gotten to the point yet.

JOHN: And notice how, because she's throwing this picture out of thinking, "I haven't gotten to the point yet," most of you stopped paying attention to her, because she was telling you, "This isn't the point yet."

That's the kind of thing you learn to track, even if you can't track it consciously, so that you can pay attention to what happens in life even if there's this big energy that says, "Don't pay attention to this," because then you can really engage it.

GLORIA: It's really easy to go unconscious with where I'm going to go next. Some of you know that all of my immediate family have crossed over, and four of the six died of lung cancer. So that's an immediate flash for me—like there it is again, there's lung cancer. And what I have been looking at lately for the last five months is how lung cancer or cancer in general is a chosen exit strategy for a lot of people, and there's a certain amount of creativity in that. I've been looking and giving it space to be what it is for how it moves through our lives.

I was looking at that and then recognizing the richness in which we've engaged that as a family. They got to play out certain dharmas with us. We got to learn about neutrality. We got to learn how to be caring and respectful. We got to explore *so* many issues around that chosen disease, so its richness just keeps going and building and it comes full circle, that something as destructive as that, and unconscious, comes back in and really creates meaning in my life.

Now I'm not suggesting lung cancer as an exit strategy for any of my friends here. But it *is* a strategy. Something I'm coming to appreciate is how we choose to move through and explore our challenges in our life, and how it happens to touch all of our relationships. So that was my cigarette butt this morning.

JOHN: That was great, and when you said that I suddenly got something about lung cancer: It comes from people trying to be unconscious, and yet it forces them, because it takes a month or two or three or longer. It forces them to pay attention to the days of their lives. It circles around. That unconsciousness, in turn, forces them to pay very specific attention for a good little bit of time to their symptoms and to their interactions with their daughter or their sister. It's just excruciating to think about because it's painful and horrible, but every portion of life is grounded in and surrounded by an ecstatic joy that we can't track in ordinary consciousness, but it's there. And since all consciousness expands in all directions, ultimately each and every action is redeemed and experienced in this exquisite joy that arises out of the particularity of the experience.

The major reason I wanted Gloria to share this is, when you're making changes, there will be layers and layers and layers that you never imagined and you will get more and more out of anything you pay attention to and really metabolize than you could ever have expected.

And it's really strange that there will be these particular events that you'll hit upon at times and you'll say, "How could something as unimportant as that be so incredibly important?" Yet it happens again and again and again. It's a hint about the nature of the universe itself. Everything, every event, has universes of meaning. When we're physical we can only track one direction, but my friend Will, who's been dead now for thirty-seven years, continues to have experiences. One of the places he's exploring life is exactly that: he's taking apart probable lives and rearranging them by exploring a moment in a way that could take a century, because when you really explore it, it opens up into universes.

Ed and Ann were talking about what you do with the universe you created in your mind when you're done with it. You can probably do other things. The best idea as far as I'm concerned is to put it in a rose and explode it. That has two beneficial effects. One is, it begins to teach you what kind of creativity you have. Physical reality is set up to put training wheels on your creativity; it's like a like a go-cart designed for four-year-olds. It can only go about two miles an hour and can't hurt anything, rather than setting you up in a Ferrari, which would not be a great idea.

Being alive in this four-dimensional world is in many ways like riding a bike with training wheels. There's a gap between your experience and your interpretation of that experience, and my guides say, "That's why you're here. There's something very valuable that occurs in that gap between your experience and your interpretation that's uniquely human. Humans are the only beings who tell themselves stories in the particular way that we do, a story that vibrates in the Astral plane with its apparent gap."

And what we're learning to do is to tell ourselves more skillful stories, but those stories are part of the spiritual ecology. Humans' capacity to tell those stories is part of what we contribute to the world like trees contribute shade and all kinds of things.

Creativity happens slowly because, if it happened any faster, you and I would really lose control. And that slowness allows us to take our time and explore little details in depth.

And so by creating and destroying universes, you get a sense of your *un*obstructed creativity. You get a sense of what it means to create a picture and explode it—that each picture has its own little universe.

And the second thing is, if there was someone else's energy in that picture or thoughtform or whatever you're exploring in that universe, when you explode the universe, their energy will naturally go back to them.

One of the aspects of our exquisite focusedness is the often charming, often disturbing tension between men and women. That's one of the cool things about being human in this era. And a lot of our work in the personal aura is directed at becoming more aware of those intrinsic differences. But nothing stays the same and, as we move into the Aquarian Age and group consciousness, there will be ebbs and flows. When you start looking in a more multidimensional way, and when you start looking at the Sethian Etheric body, the hard difference between men and women starts to disappear.

I think everyone here knows that we're ideologically committed to how important and helpful it is to have many different sexual orientations. Without that multiplicity, it actually would be much, much harder in this world to deal with the intrinsic tension between men and women, if it weren't for the connections that gay, lesbian, bi, transgender, and queer people make. They make heterosexual relationships much easier; they would be far harder if there weren't some people sort of holding the ecology of sexuality all together—if there were only the two isolated camps—but when people start to fill in these gaps in the middle, then the overall global energy allows for more communication. It facilitates the communication back and forth.

That's why it's so important that hard differences start to disappear from our culture. It doesn't mean that your identification now doesn't matter, but it's only part of something much bigger. Your essence might be very male and, in this life, you might be female and vice versa. Your body, which is obviously separate from anyone else's body, is also interdependent. Remember, it's just this one part of reality that we focus on in this period of human history so that we can develop a self-reflective ego as preparation for group consciousness.

There are plenty of other tensions. If you're gay and a couple or lesbian and a couple or transgender, you have tension with the society at large unless you are lucky enough to live in the Netherlands or something. There's quite a gap or polarity between the biological programming between straight men and women. The programming that makes someone LGBTQ+ often falls in between those polarities. Each of us unconsciously has roots into the group foundations of human consciousness. LGBTQ+ people, by filling in that foundation between the starker gap between straight men and women, give us all a more secure inner foundation. Now, of course, there is a large part of society that is scared of that because they're scared of ambiguity. They want strict rules. They want it to be the way it was when, as Archie Bunker said, "Girls were girls and men were men." But that's part of the transition. We're moving from seeing everything in black and white to seeing things in color. So if you are heterosexual, you ought to be very appreciative of everyone who's LGBTQ+.

We're at a place where the differences between men and women are starker, though they're at a different octave. Back in the fifties it was almost as though what made someone a woman was the clothes, and now we have a very different idea of what makes someone a woman or what makes someone a man. That reminds me, here is the first postmodern philosophy joke: Two philosophers were walking by a fence with a sign that said, "Nudist colony." There is a knothole in one of the wooden boards, so the first guy looks in and says, "Joe, there are people here without their clothes on!" Joe says, "Are they men or women?" And the first guy says, "I can't tell. They don't have their clothes on."

So today we are experiencing the differences between men and women as being really stark, and that large difference is useful for where we are as a culture because it's a very deep exploration, I would suggest, in respect to difference based on communication. We're coming back to this huge difference between men and women, but instead of it being based upon prohibitions and rules, ideally we're moving to something based upon appreciation and communication.

In the fifties you might have respect for differences based upon rules and prohibitions. There were just men and women. Of course, there were gay people, but they were all in the closet—well, maybe not all of them. But now we have maybe five or six different genders, so maybe fifty years from now we'll have 150 different kinds and more flexibility and flow. I would expect our sense of identity to be so profoundly extended that in some ways there will be less starkness in men and women. There'll be more recognition of not merely a continuum but multidirectionality and multiple interactions and tensions. We're not moving toward eliminating tensions. We're moving toward ever more subtle engagement and appreciation of tensions. A life without tension would be unlivable.

People often talk about kundalini as being a sexual energy. Kundalini is a sexual energy only when it's activating the second chakra. It's not the same as sexual energy. However a lot of systems, particularly male-oriented ones, use celibacy to build-up or gather up that kind of energy to trigger or kick off that kundalini. They don't run kundalini at a clairvoyant level the way we do. When you're not running kundalini at a clairvoyant level, it is easy for kundalini to do a lot of mischief. If you *are* running kundalini at a clairvoyant level and being playful about it, then there's lots of stuff you can do with it. Still, it's wise to be playful and conservative with kundalini.

Hormonally a lot of it comes from testosterone, for both men and women. Psychically it comes from lots of places including the second chakra. That second chakra energy is everywhere. I mean, in a sense, the whole Earth is full of a sexual energy that's involved in growth and reproduction. What we call sex is just one small part of what this sexual energy does.

There's an indirect connection between female sexual energy and female grounding. If you're not female-grounded, your energy is chaotically going all around, so if you're running a lot of sexual energy that's going to be chaotically flying all around too and easily misread.

I'm hoping that part of what we will learn tonight is how to cut the other sex some slack and appreciate that the tension is not guilt, it's an intrinsic tension. It's not that men are insensitive or that women are flirts. It's that a man's energy and a woman's energy around sex are, not surprisingly, quite different.

I'm sure that if you're in a culture where there's more playful flirting then it probably is okay to do more flirting. Let's say fifty years ago, or sixty, seventy years ago, when there were more strict social mores, you might have been able to flirt a little bit more without it being interpreted as a come-hither.

This exercise is intended to help you gain some sensitivity as to how different sexual energy is for the other sex.

The energy that drives a man to have sex, that is involved in his excitement and that is engaged in it, is really different from a woman having sex and her excitement. I'm not sure how easy this will be to see, but here's my suggestion: Go back to a time when you were having sex with someone of the other sex. As a psychic, see if you can feel the energy of their excitement, and contrast that with the energy of your excitement. If you look at the energy, it's really, really different. When a man is sexually excited, there's this huge energy to do something, to do something and finish—to do something toward a specific goal and then close down. For women, it's an energy that just sort of opens up without any particular goal in mind. This is my experience and my description, yours may be different. I'm hoping that each of you can see how different those energies are.

Even when it's recreational sex for women, it is still not this kind of closing-down energy that I experience when I look at a man being sexually excited.

Okay, so please be in the center of your head. Remember sometime when you were having sex with someone of the opposite sex. First, you might just look at your own sexual energy as that's happening, your own excitement, and then just put a grounding cord on that energy so that you can look at his or her sexual excitement. If this works for you, I think you will be impressed at how different it is, but I'm not sure this will be easy. Just do the best you can.

If you're female and you're running somebody's male grief—I call that the male grief racket—give it back to him because he can use it, he knows what to do with it. In a body operating well, he can turn that male grief into male clarity, male simplicity. That thing that feels so awful in your space if you're a woman, that becomes female grief, is actually an asset, it's just an asset in a different kind of body.

PART FIVE

THE SEVEN PLANES OF
CONSCIOUSNESS AND
PERMANENT SEEDS

39

Planes of Consciousness

7TH PLANE—ADI: Emptiness

6TH PLANE—MONADIC: Unity

5TH PLANE—ATMIC: Laws of Physics

4TH PLANE—BUDDHIC: Gestalts

3RD PLANE—MENTAL-CAUSAL: Soul in Causal, Thinking in Mental

2ND PLANE—ASTRAL: Emotional or Personal Aura

1ST PLANE—PHYSICAL-ETHERIC: Physical Body and Energy Underpinning

The Monadic Plane gives birth to the Mental-Causal Plane.
The Mental-Causal plane gives experience to the Monadic Plane.

The Atmic Plane gives birth to the Physical-Etheric Plane.
The Physical-Etheric plane gives experience to the Atmic Plane.

The Buddhic Plane gives birth to the Astral Plane.
The Astral plane gives experience to the Buddhic Plane.

Notice or allow how the Buddhic participates and undergirds and supports the Astral. The Astral feeds back into the Buddhic, making it more than it was, each interpenetrating and supporting each other—enhancing, making possible.

We have this vertical description of the Seven Planes that is very useful and functional, but there are all these rabbit holes that bring one plane or sub-plane into relationship and interaction with and interdependence with others. That's because the whole universe is interdependent.

Higher and lower cease to have a lot of meaning. Higher and lower put you into a kind of effort and a sort of comparison of higher and lower. Maybe a better way to think about a higher plane is as a more complex plane. It's like Google: the more links that you have, the higher on the Google rank you get. That's also how consciousness works. The more interconnections you have with more rich dimensions, the more complex and fuller the consciousness is.

Remember, the universe is a divine play of phenomena. To humans those phenomena appear to be separate; we seem to have the experience that there's a me and a not-me. That's an illusion. Everything is interdependent with everything else. Everything arises in oneness, and every apparently discrete package is merely that: *apparently discrete.*

Likewise, we think of planes as being objective energies in the sense that we think of physics as describing objective energies, but it's much more accurate to think of planes as consciousnesses. The particular focus of a lot of our psychic work is the Physical-Etheric Body, the Astral Body, the Mental Body, and the Causal Body. Each of those has its own consciousness and is arising out of interwoven consciousnesses. The Etheric plane is itself conscious. All of it is conscious—it's huge— and smaller segments of the etheric have their own consciousness even while participating in the greater whole.

Get a sense of the life, the different kind of life, that flows through the Etheric—its own life.

The Astral plane as a consciousness is a being inside of whom humans have their emotional lives as part of the Astral plane's innards. When you're having an emotion, you're maybe the vagus nerve of some being or something like that, not you alone the human race all together. So the Seven Planes are not a description, like a so-called scientific description, they're a map of relationships.

Most of you are comfortable being in the Astral plane. There's recognition in Astral energy. You get a sense of your Astral body. You notice how it's always in communication, how it's always unfinished. You appreciate it in the present moment. Get a sense of your Astral body. As you feel your Astral body, see if you can turn your attention to the larger Astral plane itself. See if maybe the Astral plane, or at least the Astral plane for five hundred feet around you, is at the same energy frequency. Compare the Astral plane to the Earth and its atmosphere. You don't tend to think of those that way, it's just a space. But notice that the Astral plane is alive everywhere. It is a consciousness. First of all, it's alive as a space with its own forms in its space and entities such as yourself.

You can experience the peculiar type of consciousness that is the Astral plane, which for human beings has a great deal of individuality. This may not make any sense at all—or perhaps you can sort of get a sense—that the Astral plane really cares for beings such as yourself and other animals that have Astral bodies and Astral lives.

You might begin to appreciate the peculiar limits on the Astral plane when you're conscious or when you're dreaming. You might get a sense of the reciprocity, your emotional life in its space and capacity, yours and everyone else's that you interact with.

The old Western mystics used to have guardians that you'd encounter as you entered into a plane. Instead of imaging guardians, imagine a god or goddess who lovingly attends to your Astral life. Notice how you have been living all of this life in the universe as if it were entirely by your effort. Notice that every emotion that you have is within that sea of capacity, of options. And yet the limits are only there to provide a kind of focus or clarity that your adventures and contradictions can play out, like a fabulous art gallery that supports seven billion artists at a time on the planet, each of whom have their own little exhibition that's changing all the time. Can you get a sense of that light behind, within, and around your emotional life that curates and supports you, like a fabulous movie studio producing your work?

Years ago, I was saying to this channeled being, "I want to Astral travel." And it said to me, "The Astral plane wants you to travel through it." Until that moment, I had never thought of it like that, the Astral plane being alive with its own intentions and there to help me.

There are multiple causes or origins of our lives as humans; it is a grand collaboration. For instance, the laws of physics are set up in the Atmic. The raw material from which the emotions emerge is created in the Buddhic. And a lower self-reflective energy comes from the Astral.

There is some powerful way in which the shape of events, including your body itself, is created by your soul in collaboration with other souls. Your soul's consciousness is multidirectional, not individuated.* So, tonight, we're going to say hello to how the Causal causes things.

Just imagine that you can feel the shape of your body emerge out of that Causal soul. That shape doesn't fully determine you because something unique in your personality gives a certain magic and newness to your body as well as to your emotions and gives your thoughts a solidity of experience. And yet all these things—your body, your emotions, your thoughts, your experiences—emerge out of the matrix of the Causal, your soul in collaboration with other souls.

What we're going to try to do here is get a sense of how two different kinds of consciousnesses collaborate. We're going to look at your Physical-Etheric body and note how it grows out of the Earth, how it's constantly in communication with Earth and the solar system, how it crosses probabilities, and how it doesn't use the kind of reasoning that we do at a personality level but uses an incredible network intelligence that's constantly evaluating all kinds of things. It joyfully collaborates with your emotions in the Astral.

Your Astral is your most individuated part of consciousness maybe on this planet—at least where we talk about energy in terms of yours versus not yours. All of this takes place within *your* Astral body, which is given space and nurtured and supported by the *global* Astral body.

---

*This is true in the understanding of individuation that humans have in linear time.

Say hello to the global Astral plane. Imagine that you can see the sun shining through, pervading this entire Astral body and everything in it. That means you, your neighbor, your family, your parents, people in incarnation, people out of incarnation, people awake, people asleep. And, in particular, feel the sun shining into this ball of neutral engagement in the sixth and seventh sub-planes of the Astral.

So now you have the soul diving down, the Atman diving down, and the sun shining into and through and becoming part of this ball of fluid energy. And again, just enjoy it: the sun, the Atman, and the soul.

Become aware of the moon, the moon's inner light pervading the entire Earth Astral, and in particular your aura and the sixth and seventh sub-planes of the Astral, this ball of fluid, neutral engagement, passionate engagement and openness to what is. Feel the moon join the sun, feel your particular Hindu Atman and your personal soul.

Let all of those mix. And let that fluid have its passionate embrace of experience with a complete openness of what is. And let the Earth and the animals and the stars and guides, let every appropriate energy join in and dance to a passionate embrace of experience.

While you have a complete openness to what is, take a moment and realize that part of the strength of this ball of openness, this neutral fluid, is that it brings wisdom from many, many, many different consciousnesses. It creates something that is larger than the sum of its parts, and yet it is uniquely you in this incarnation, and yet eternal.

Perhaps you've noticed that all of these consciousnesses rolled up in one gestalt that is you, at least this part of you, cherishes everything that ever happened and partakes deeply in the beauty of even the ugliest of phenomena.

Spend some time creating and destroying roses. Destroy some red roses; then see what happens if you create a red rose and don't destroy it. Some of the fluid stays with the rose. It's what holds it together, coordinates it, makes it cohere. If you create a hundred roses and don't explode them, you might even be able to notice a little bit that part of you is no longer in the center of your head. Explode all of those roses. I always find it very comforting to create and destroy some roses, bring that fluid back into the center of my head, and spend time just resting in that fluid, gathering more fluid as pictures that we've created in the past explode.

Not everyone necessarily will be able to do this, but everyone can participate and it can start to build an emerging possibility. When you're ready, you will become more aware of it.

Where do you suppose that fluid comes from? Nothing is composed only of itself.

When I talk about there being a fluid in the center of the head, I wasn't referring to a physical fluid; I was talking about energy that feels like a fluid to me. I was using a metaphor. I think this fluid, the very personal center of the head, tends to vibrate more in the sixth and seventh sub-plane of the Astral. So let's spend some time enjoying it and appreciating it. Just be with it, be it, the neutrality of that fluid in the center of the head. It is where you gain neutrality and more narrow focus. It isn't exactly what I've been calling the personal aura, but it is the center of neutrality for sixth and seventh sub-plane pictures. And the sixth and seventh sub-planes are really the most individualistic emotions. They are transitional into the physicality of the Etheric/Physical. As issues become Physical-Etheric and you run energy through the Physical-Etheric, the pictures pop back out into the Astral. You run energy through the Etheric and it lights up those Astral things you can clear: lots and lots of thoughtforms, lots of family forms, stuff like that. Certain energies are sped up and they transition back into the Astral where they're much easier to clear.

I'd like you to start thinking about waking human consciousness as your home signal. And imagine then that you're a traveler and, as you go into these foreign lands like the Causal and the Buddhic, not only will the food you eat change and the hotels you stay at and the museums you go to change, but *you* change. When you go into the Buddhic, try to feel yourself as emerging group consciousness, not instead of your being human but in addition. For the time being your body has a tendency to hold you into the form of your waking human consciousness. What I'm hoping you'll begin to get is you are also a group consciousness right now. Perhaps looking at it, you could imagine yourself as becoming a group consciousness ten thousand years in the future. That's one true way of seeing it. But you're also right now a group consciousness.

The purpose of this practice is to simultaneously increase your ability to commit to your humanity even as you recognize that that isn't all that you are, that these other things are equally meaningful. They're not as relevant to your waking consciousness, but they're every bit as real and every bit as relevant in the long run to who you are.

Let's start at the third sub-plane of the Astral. Just try to match, in the same way as if a choir were singing and you were trying to match the pitch. I'm going to radiate out this energy, you can let it come to you. Now go up to the second sub-plane of the Astral.

Go up one more sub-plane to the first sub-plane of the Astral. This is the third person you've been in this exercise. And in this first sub-plane of the Astral, you may be able to feel your soul peeking in here. But instead of thinking of it as your soul peeking in, think of it as changing your gestalt. So you, in the first sub-plane of the Astral, are a being whose emotional reality is in some ways directly connected to the soul, here is where the soul's awareness and your personal emotional reality, in some ways, blend. You can think of this "you" and the soul as two separate entities, but for this exercise, see if you can think of yourself as a blended awareness. You're moving away from your home station and you're over in Paris now, but instead of the external scenery changing, you yourself are a different entity, you're a human-slash-soul. This is every bit as real as any other version of you.

Go up one more step. You're at the seventh and lowest sub-plane of the Mental. As you step into that Mental plane, you can bring your home waking consciousness with you, but you can also notice yourself becoming a portion of all the thoughts on the planet, centered in your own individuality and yet you. In the seventh sub-plane of the Mental, you *are* a being of thoughts. See if you can stretch a little bit more and take pleasure in being a being of thoughts. This being of thoughts participates in the thinking. It's what this being does, and this being is you, a version of you every bit as real as any other version of you.

Move now to the sixth sub-plane of the Mental and you change again, it's a little more abstract. To the fifth sub-plane. The body that you've associated yourself with becomes less and less what you are. More and more, it's this kind of thinking, not brain thinking, but this kind of solar-system thinking. And the fourth sub-plane. You go up one more. Become the fourth sub-plane. Just as Seth comes into us—Seth is like a whole sub-plane or plane or tier of planes—the fourth sub-plane has its own consciousness. It can greet you as an individual or you can become a participant in it. Even in the fourth sub-plane of the Mental, there isn't just one you. There's kind of you associating with your individuality, interacting with the sub-plane. There's you *as* the fourth sub-plane. There's you as a being native to this fourth sub-plane. You could think of it as an aura floating in the fourth sub-plane that's every bit as real as any other you.

See if you can check out its life. It has a kind of openness and comfort. This isn't something *other* than you, this is you, and yet part of this you on the fourth sub-plane is who it is because of what other versions of you do. Part of its experience is fed by what you were doing, the down-in-physical-reality you.

Let's say hello to how the Physical is born out of the Atmic; that is, how Atmic participates in the physicality of your body and the Earth, how it finds joy in your physicality, and how your physicality is supported by the Atmic.

And, in a similar way, say hello to your entire Astral. And say hello to the Buddhic; notice how your individuality and uniqueness grow out of the Buddhic, out of group consciousness and synchronicity in the Buddhic. Notice how the particularity, self-reflection, and even the alienation of the Astral answer questions and clarify confrontations. The Buddhic gives birth to our emotionality because you wouldn't have emotions without *everyone* having them.

The Mental-Causal grows out of the Monadic, out of your Atman. The Monadic gives birth to the individuation of the unity in the Causal. The Mental-Causal gives support and experience to the Monadic.

40

Permanent Seeds

What we're going to cover now are the permanent seeds. In the old literature they were called permanent atoms. The old theosophists called them permanent atoms back before anyone really knew what an atom was, much less what subatomic particles were. Choa Kok Sui called them seeds, I don't know if he invented that or not, but that's where I saw the term and that says more of what they are.

The old idea was that unfinished physical business didn't get assimilated into the soul and just hung around and became the first sub-plane of the Etheric. Unfinished Astral business hung around at the first sub-plane of the Astral, and unfinished Mental business hung around at the highest sub-plane of the Mental, which is the fourth sub-plane of the Mental-Causal. And this unfinished business became the seed for issues the soul would work out for its next incarnation. And so when the soul moved down into incarnation it would pick these seeds up and they would, again, become the core of the soul's expression and orientation throughout the next incarnation. That's the traditional understanding of what a permanent atom or a permanent seed is, it is your leftover unfinished business from your last incarnation. And that business, because it was unfinished, couldn't be assimilated into the soul, so it got left over there and it became what was next, the agenda for your next lifetime.

It was very mechanical and fixed and determined. Of course, that assumes linear incarnation and doesn't understand the interdependence of all things or begin to express the dynamism of all information or incarnation.

Every description is a simplification. It's one of the reasons one wants to be careful not to buy in too rigidly to what you think you're seeing and then try to make it true. You can make it a kind of working description and let that working description change over the years as your abilities grow and as your familiarity grows.

The permanent atoms or seeds play a pivotal role in your awareness. They are terminals where higher energies intersect and interact with lower-plane energies.

The way we slice it up, there are three permanent seeds. The lowest one in the body is a couple of inches above the belly-button in the liver, and this is the Astral or Emotional permanent seed. That's at the first sub-plane of the Astral.*

The next permanent seed up vibrates at a lower frequency, at the first sub-plane of the Etheric, and that's the Physical-Etheric permanent seed. That's in the center of the chest. Some schools place the Physical permanent seed in the heart chakra.

The Mental permanent seed will be at the fourth sub-plane of the Mental. After that, you get the Causal, which is your own individuated soul. It is in the center of the head. You can encounter the blue pearl of the Mental permanent seed in the center of your head or in your crown. It doesn't have to be in just one place; you can use either place for it, or both places.

Now you might think of permanent seeds a little more broadly, as the soul's investment in the next incarnation, where the soul at the Causal level would put an instruction set of things hopefully to be accomplished. For instance, it would put the Physical instruction set at the heart level, vibrating at the first sub-plane of the Etheric. At least that's the access point for it.

From a Sethian point of view, the permanent seeds are much more dynamic than a one-time deposit of information. Also from a Sethian

---

*The permanent seed is always on the highest sub-plane of what it is seeding.

point of view, it's not so much an instruction set as a dynamic model with innumerable possibilities.

A permanent seed is also a bit like the Bermuda triangle. It's sort of Etheric, but it's neither really fish nor fowl, it's really a hybrid phenomenon. So instead of the intellectual image of the permanent atom or seed being leftover unassimilated information or being a one-time deposit, I'd like to suggest that you imagine that the permanent seed is more active, like the way a computer works: that certain amount of information that you are likely to be using is shuttled into the active memory and other things that you're not likely to be using stay on the hard drive but, if you need them, they'll be shuttled into the active memory. If you change your habitual pattern, you'll start leaving them in the active memory and moving other things out of the active memory; I think that's more what the permanent seeds are.

A Sethian explanation of permanent seeds—though Seth never talked about permanent seeds by name that I know of—is more beautiful: the permanent seed is your soul's moment-by-moment participation in your life. It is a warehouse of possibilities. It is a warehouse and it is a model of a somewhat ideal incarnation, but it is never a single model, there is never only one choice.

The Physical permanent seed would be the Physical-soul communication exchange point and supply depot. You can use the Physical permanent seed as a resource and get a healing from it. Everything emerges, or apparently emerges, out of the Physical permanent seed. In a sense, this is all like a sort of soap-bubble dream, and the whole dream exists at once. What, for your body, is a sense of a self traveling through time happens for the soul simultaneously. It is within and without simultaneously.

Look at, feel, see the energy of the permanent Physical seed, that access point, and get a sense of all the resources that are available there from your soul for running your body. See if you can get a sense of how, through that portal, the soul is always already engaged with every single cell in your body. I imagine it as a kind of soul buzz that the cell rides on. The soul buzz stays in the background; it allows the cell to vibrate at a physical rate, but somehow or other the cell, in an important way, emerges from the information and support of the soul. The cell communicates back through that portal in the heart area to the Causal soul. There's constantly a two-way communication that allows the soul to stay at its vibration and the cell to stay at its vibration, and yet in a profound way, each to mix with and empower the other. This communication and mixing and empowering all happen at the permanent seed.

Let's say you have some issue physically. You can contact your physical seed and say, "What's up here? What do you suggest?" And that energy can just pulsate out, through your body and through the extended body. Let there be communication back and forth between your body and your permanent seed.

Each permanent seed is a separate consciousness and each comes together for the gestalt consciousness, and they become the primary components of your personality. There have to be many, many, many other energies that play and dance through this also. In the final analysis, these things are not physical things, so location is fluid.

Say hello to every cell in your body and attend to this forever constant resource state—not something once and done and some abstraction, but something closer than any distance that you can name, and yet each in its own sphere, simultaneously and paradoxically.

You might just pick one improvement that you would like for your body. As an ego-self, communicate that to each cell and to your soul, and allow that request to be processed so that each of those three aspects—the self-reflective ego, the set of cellular consciousnesses, and the soul—are in constant conversation. Hopefully your self-reflective ego has some neutrality and playfulness in this.

Now become aware of your Astral or Emotional permanent seed between your belly button and the xiphoid process, which is a little round bone where the ribs come together. That would put the Astral instruction set in the middle, side to side, of the liver, about two inches below the xiphoid process at the first sub-plane of the Astral. I'm projecting that energy now. Other energies in that sub-plane form the Earth, the sun, the stars, the moon, and other consciousnesses.

See the soul joyfully, with infinite capacity, standing outside and yet giving birth to your Astral self with its apparent limitations, diving through the looking glass of the Emotional permanent seed, and becoming a primary constituent of your emotional life. Be aware that it has the capacity to play with that identity from the opposite side of that looking glass.

This is your access point for the conversation with your emotional aura, which itself is a kind of body, and your Causal soul. Notice how the Emotional permanent seed is a resource bank for every Astral energy in your Astral body. Notice how the soul, through the permanent seed, participates in everything the Astral body does. The permanent seed, and thus the soul through the permanent seed, participates in every moment of every cell in the Astral body without intruding. It has a fundamental vibration that supports and allows the Astral body to continue and offers a wide range of options from which it itself must choose.

Every cell in the Astral body—there aren't actually cells—communicates back through this portal, moment by moment, with the Causal soul. This is how the soul participates in each and every action that the Astral body undertakes. The soul receives the outcome without controlling the behavior. Your self-reflective ego can jump into this dialogue, making decisions and making requests

If you're lost or, as they say in the South, feeling puny, beaten up, and you wonder how you can go on, or even if you just had a bad day, get in touch with your Emotional permanent seed. You can learn to feel its confidence, its resilience, its playfulness, its sense of meaning and joy; you can use your Emotional permanent seed as a resource to start to figure how you can experience this moment of this day as meaningful.

You wouldn't want to sit around all day monitoring your Emotional permanent seed, but what you can do is give yourself more space, at least subconsciously, to that communication and support, which is there every moment of your life. From time to time, sit down and look at it in a more focused way.

Allow your self-reflective ego to choose one improvement that you would like emotionally and to communicate to your Astral body, every corner of it, and to your soul through the emotional-permanent-seed communication center.

Turn your attention to your Mental permanent seed in the fourth sub-plane of the Mental plane. The access point is in the center of your head. Say hello to your Mental body. Notice how, through the Mental permanent seed, the Causal soul establishes a ground of being out of which your Mental self arises. Allow each cell in your Mental body to be healed, supported, nourished, and encouraged by the wisdom and security of your personal soul. Notice how each such cell constantly engages in conversation with the soul and vice versa. Your self-reflective ego enters into the conversation with requests and decisions and, if it's open, gets feedback from the soul, consciously or unconsciously, and from the bits and pieces of the Mental body, which I'm calling cells.

Pick one improvement you would like for your Mental body and make that request; throw that request into your Mental body and the conversation it's engaged in through the Mental permanent seed with the soul. Remember that for any change to occur, your self-reflective ego will also have to change.

I prefer to think of the seeds as multidimensional living interfaces, or transformational energy organisms, that set up the basic trinity of Eastern mysticism: creation, sustaining, and assimilation at the end of the cycle. That's the Hindu trinity of Brahma, Shiva, and Vishnu. You have similar trinities in Buddhism.

In Western terms, the soul transforms itself through a dynamic energy organism; these are gigantic consciousnesses living and exploring in multiple times and probabilities in ways that human can't even imagine, all kinds of realms of consciousness, only one of which is you. That big, big, incredibly conscious and utterly nondual energy transforms itself into the more constrained and restricted energy that is operative in a human being at a physical-emotional-mental level. It becomes three-dimensional, or four-dimensional, or five-dimensional, rather than infinite. It camouflages itself, to use a Sethian term, in a slightly different context: it forgets itself. It forgets its freedom, or it temporarily sacrifices its freedom, for the specificity that comes from human experience.

A large part of your Physical Etheric body is made up of soul energy that has hypnotized itself into fewer dimensions, more constraints, and more specific sets of experiences. When you die and the soul takes in your experience, it's mostly just taking in itself. It was always and already itself.

You can communicate with all three seeds simultaneously. I think this is what Alice Bailey meant by the chord. She describes a sound ringing forth: the vibrations of the permanent seeds aligning with one another and, in their chord, forming a consciousness.

These three working together are your personality as we commonly understand it. Yours will be different from anyone else's before, after, and during your life. And there will be a difference in your permanent seeds as time goes on. They're sort of like those electronic maps when you're driving. If you take a certain turn and go in a certain way, you can re-set your course, or how to get to your old course will change.

For those alive three hundred years from now, the nature of the permanent seeds will surely have changed.

Get a sense of the riotous creativity of the soul. It is easier to understand that the soul chooses to incarnate as you if you understand that it incarnates in all kinds of directions that are completely outside our human imagination. Through the permanent seeds, the soul is both and simultaneously inside and outside your experience. It offers a vast wisdom, stability, and joy. It's a passionate desire, sustaining an utter openness to your experience, whatever it may be, providing the raw material and impetus for what you think of as you, your personality.

41

The Etheric

Our fixed, or lower, Etheric body is the template or blueprint for our physical body, our physical health, and the chakras. It is the lowest frequency and densest two sub-planes of the Etheric Plane. The third and fourth Etheric are denser than the first and second. Unless you're ill, they stay with your body. I call that the lower Etheric body or the fixed Etheric. The first and second sub-plane of the Etheric body are the upper Etheric body, and that travels. That's what leaves and starts the dream space.

The first Etheric is the highest frequency and least dense sub-plane of the Etheric. The Physical permanent seed sits there in the heart-sternum area of Brahma Nadi, which is a very thin shining nadi in the center of the sushumna central channel, vibrating at the first sub-plane of the Etheric. It sends out a sound to harmonize with the other permanent seeds. That's where your soul intersects time and space and physical reality, outside of time and space, or at least half in and half out, and supports and generates your physical body in collaboration with other energies. It is multidimensional and, in fact, includes all seven planes.

Also inside the sushumna are the Chitra Nadi, which is interconnected with other nadis into and through the Earth, and the Vajrini Nadi,* which is the color of fire and part of our traveling Etheric or

---

*Sometimes called Vajra Nadi

379

upper Etheric body. If you were out dreaming, you would be in this traveling Etheric and it is what you would feel as yourself.*

The fourth sub-plane is where acupuncture takes place. This is so dense an energy that you can affect it with a physical needle. In the two circuits that form the Microcosmic Orbit, you can connect the governing and conception meridians by placing the tip of your tongue to the roof of your mouth, an exercise in Chi Gong.

The third sub-plane is where your nadis are; nadis are not the same as meridians. Yogis say, "Clear nadis equal perfect heath"; that's the basis of yogic breathing exercises. I don't know if that's true, but it certainly will move you toward good health. Remember that each petal of a chakra is a nadi; each chakra is the intersection of nadis.

The blueprint and structure of the Etheric body set up the structure of your body. The Earth weaves itself into your energy system, at least the upper three sub-planes of the Etheric, as the nadis. It doesn't weave itself in as some sort of external force. It weaves itself in as an innate part of your life force through devas.

There are certain nadis that carry Etheric energy beyond our bodies, like lei lines, as they go out to one another and across the planet. We can reach that energy at the second Etheric. Instead of thinking of these as something outside you, you can image them as your extended Etheric body, how you reach out into the world. When you run into various nature spirits in those lei lines, you understand them to be part of yourself. That will change what you can do with them.

We call nadis at the first and second sub-plane of the Etheric global nadis instead of lei lines because there's a lot of misunderstanding attached to the concept of lei lines, these energy channels that go around the world and are particularly strong in certain places like Stonehenge.

Our first step will be to calibrate these different sub-planes of the Etheric. You're building neurological flexibility, and if it doesn't come to you today, it will come sooner or later. It will set the ground. That is, if it doesn't come to you today *consciously,* it will still change your relationship to the planet and to nature spirits.

---

*Unless you were dreaming in one of the higher planes like the Mental or Atmic

Not only is your fixed Etheric integrated with every molecule of your physical self, but so is your upper Etheric by its very alignment and clicked-in-ness with the lower Etheric and integration with the body. Notice that there's a joy and playfulness that's always present from the natural-ness of the upper Etheric. It is part of the background of how you engage every moment. Can you feel the soul's joy in just engaging physicality? That is in your entire upper Etheric, your traveling Etheric. It's part of the joy that people feel when their heart is open, and it's part of your essential physical nature that you can miss

Now a lot of very psychic people will have a hard time aligning the traveling Etheric body with the fixed Etheric body, and a lot of psychic teachings that tell people how to be psychic say to push that traveling Etheric body out far enough that it sets up a kind of gap.

My guides say that there are some advantages and disadvantages to that. In the Aquarian Age, we'll build on an extended Etheric body. For now, though, we would encourage you to be dreaming or not. Your upper Etheric is either here and aligned and *in* the body or out traveling. Most of the time when you're awake here, that's where you want your Etheric body to be. At another time we will learn how to do Etheric traveling.

Robert Monroe has an extensive method he has developed to dislodge his upper Etheric and travel in the Etheric body. A lot of times when people are doing past-life work, they'll extend the Etheric body three inches below their feet and then three inches above their head and then three inches simultaneously above and below. You can stretch the Etheric body in a way that allows it to dislodge and start traveling.

What we're going to attempt is the opposite of that: to really try to get your upper Etheric and lower Etheric aligned. Allow yourself to become aware of the first sub-plane of the Etheric, now the second sub-plane, then the third sub-plane, and the fourth. In the fourth sub-plane, feel your acupuncture body around and in your physical body. Keeping that feeling, extend your awareness to the third sub-plane, the nadi body. Notice how the nadi body and the acupuncture body form a unit together. Those are probably aligned with your physical body, and you want them aligned with it.

Turn your attention up to the second sub-plane and see where your Etheric body is in that second sub-plane. Is it off to the side someplace, or is it floating above you? See if it's nicely in alignment with your body. Or is some of it in and some of it out? Keeping that awareness, extend it to the first sub-plane. Then you have the whole traveling Etheric body.

Etheric roots are quite palpable; it's not just an image, the way your Astral grounding is. I'm not really sure that the Etheric roots will extend down to the Earth if you're, say, flying in an airplane. But there's no reason you can't bring up Earth energy through them.

There's an Etheric grounding that you're doing with the Etheric roots out of the soles of the feet, and then there's the Astral or personal-aura grounding, though, theoretically, if you do one well, everything will align because that's the definition of a system. Since everything is part of everything else, if you did any one thing in the universe really well, it would be in alignment with everything in the universe

Those people who ground with tentacles through their feet are grounding at an Etheric level, down into the Earth. It usually goes ten to twenty feet. Imagine the Earth. Imagine its energy flowing into your feet as tentacles. Your body is picking up important Etheric energy all of the time: earth, air, the food you eat.

Remember, asking, "Whose energy is it?" is not applicable to the Etheric. In Etheric energy, there isn't *my* energy or *your* energy. There's high-quality energy and not-so-high-quality Etheric energy; there is appropriate energy or not-appropriate energy. That's why when you eat something it becomes part of your body—your Etheric body.

One of the ways we get Etheric energy is from the sun. We all breathe the same air; it comes indirectly from sunlight, the sun vitalizes the air with prana. C. W. Leadbeater, the turn-of-the-nineteenth-into-the-twentieth-century clairvoyant, called them "vitality globules." Etheric energy is made up of these particles.

If you go out in the sunlight and look in the air, you'll see these things that you'll probably think are floaters or your eyes playing tricks on you. They are even easier to see at the beach. Don't look at the sun; look at the air that is filled in with vitality from the sun.

These globules are taken in by breathing and sent to the spleen under the left lower ribs. The spleen has two important chakras, one facing front, the other facing back. They have six petals each. The globules come in as white light, which is broken into various colors and distributed to various parts of the body, both from the petals and the center of the chakra. Feel your spleen chakras at an Etheric level breaking down that white light and sending red energy down to your first chakra—and by that I mean your first Etheric chakra—a lower frequency than its Astral counterpart.

It has no emotional energy. If you feel emotional energy associated with it, that comes from the Astral and not the Etheric. They vibrate in the same vicinity but not in the same energy.

There's also a purple energy radiating down from the spleen to the first Etheric chakra.

The Etheric body is constantly taking in energy and expelling energy. It's a living part of the ecosystem like trees. In a sense it's part of the trees and the rest of the Earth. Through your Etheric Body you are part of everything on this planet. Also, through your emotional body, you're part of all the meaning produced on this planet. And you become part of the meaning of lakes and mountains and trees because you're here today and they are already a part of your meaning. It's not separate from the ups and downs, the wisdom and delusions. Remember, you engage the outside world because it *is* you.

Sometimes when you're doing the Etheric work, pictures, which are always an astral phenomena, will explode without your being aware of them. Other Astral energies will also be leaving and going back to the persons they belong to, leaving gaps you will want to fill with golden cosmic energy vibrating at a personal aura level. That red and purple energy is still flowing into the perineal chakra, while a lovely orange energy is flowing into the pubic or second chakra.

Turn your attention to the green and red vital energy going from the spleen to the belly button chakra. Notice the yellow and blue going into the heart from the spleen. Chakras, auras, and energy from nature, from the Earth and sun, are part of one system; they don't create the system, they *are* the system. Notice how that blue stream continues up, giving a kind of light blue to the throat chakras and then indigo to the pituitary chakra and your sixth chakra. Some people will have more of that yellow turned into a gold in that pituitary chakra, some people will have more blue, and some people will have white or other colors.

Notice blue going on up and creating the violet in the crown chakra and that yellow-gold going into the very center of the crown and creating gold, again at an Etheric level. Feel the entire energy coursing through your Etheric body, which is in the same space as your Physical body, maybe an inch or two beyond. Of course, the health rays go further out. Be aware of the pinkish energy that leaves the center of the spleen chakras and travels throughout the nerves, vitalizing them, cleansing them, healing them. This Etheric vitality is constantly running, whether you're attending to it or not.

You can really chill out in the Etheric and you can repair your system. I mean, you can drive around in a Lexus, but if the roads are horrible, you're not going to be that comfortable. This is doing that roadwork, all the bridges and the roadwork. Even if the Republican-controlled legislature won't pass taxes to repair the roads, you can.

There are lots of sources of Etheric energy. One of the cool places that you pick up energy is from the planets. That is why astrology works. Planetary energy is cyclical and patterned.

The chakras *are*, in fact, consciousnesses. They are not just mechanical vortices or filters. Chakras are real, but they are not a hard, fixed structure. Each chakra is a consciousness made up of innumerable consciousnesses. Even the tiny parts of a chakra themselves are huge, extending interdependently into other consciousnesses. Tiny parts are much huger than most people imagine their *whole* chakras.

There aren't any actual walls of a chakra, but they have the appearance of there being a wall because there are various spins. A chakra's spinning is not a thing spinning like a pinwheel, because a pinwheel has solid material that spins in a single solid mass. It isn't really that the chakra spins. It's the energy that belongs to the system of the chakra that spins. There's no psychic tissue to form a boundary. The chakra self-constructs itself out of energy.

A chakra is not a piece of land that's a structure; it's energy that self-referentially goes into a discernible state, not unlike your identity itself. There is no place where there's a riverbank on your identity. There seems to be because bodies seem to be individualized. But even bodies are not. There is no Noel, there is no Kathy, there's just a kind of flow that we identify, and it's an interdependent flow. It's got all kinds of other things flowing into it. And in the Sethian world, that's not a problem, that's really, really cool. Just because you're changing all the time is not a reason to think you don't exist forever both inside and outside of time.

According to my guides, the spin to watch is the one that goes clockwise. It's not clockwise as if you were inside your chest looking; it's clockwise as if you were standing out in front of yourself looking at the clock face of the chakra. Getting in touch with that spin will allow you to get a deeper bead on the chakra. When the chakras interact and come into harmony with one another, this spin is an additional harmony.

If you notice the spin, help it spin smoothly. Intend that it spin more smoothly so that, in spinning, it removes impediments to its spinning, sort of like a self-cleaning oven. Let each chakra develop the spin most appropriate to that chakra. Let all the Etheric chakras you've worked on vibrate in harmony; each is self-correcting and, to an extent, each helps the other chakras align. Attend to a general sense of the spin of all the chakras you've been meditating on: knees, hips, perineum, pubic, lower third at the belly button, upper third, heart, lower fifth at the notch of the neck, upper fifth, jaws, armpits, elbows, palms of your hand, ears, between the eyebrows, center of the forehead, back of the head, crown. Just get a sense of them all vibrating in a chorus. The more accurate one chakra gets, the more accurate the others get, even though they're not the same.

Turn your attention to the Astral, the personal aura. Notice how much faster the Astral vibrates, even while the Etheric continues to vibrate slower and more accurately spinning and aligned. The Etheric doesn't have any emotions in it. Emotions from the Astral may go down and touch the Etheric in vibration, but the Etheric is just this clean, uncomplicated energy.

There's an implicit American can-do attitude when we start working in the Etheric. To an extent that's fine. Lots of us would like to be healthy, rich with great relationships, and there is nothing wrong with that. But there is a kind of structure that we are trying to put on the Etheric that is unnatural, as if we are treating *Hamlet* as an action flick. We have been treating our Etheric as an action movie.

There's a lot of action there. I mean, there's an argument to be made that *Hamlet*'s an action flick like *Diehard with a Vengeance* or whatever. But I don't think that's a particularly subtle reading of *Hamlet*. If that's the way you go into it, I don't think you're really going to get it. Yet that's what we've been doing as a culture; we've been treating the Etheric as an action movie.

We are going to untether the Etheric as an instrument merely to be controlled. Time runs differently in the Etheric, so we will untether time a little bit. A lot of the really good stuff in the Etheric is also happening here, but it's clearer there, like the difference between a high school play and Broadway. There are bright lights going on as part of our experience that we're not tracking. We're just getting the high school theater version of it.

The physical body, with its three sub-planes, has an energy. Can you feel it, how your head is different from your armpit or knee? Can you smell your skin? Where the physical body vibrates, we don't consider it a vibration at all, but it is. The Physical-Etheric as a whole is an energy plane; it isn't just the Etheric that is energetic. The Physical is the denser portion of the same energy, its densest three sub-planes. Our senses are set to register that as our world, and it's solid to us, but it isn't solid to other consciousnesses that don't experience it with our time and space.

The fourth and third Etheric sub-planes form the stable part of the

Etheric that stays with your Physical body. Just feel that part of your Etheric Body. See if you can feel that it's a higher frequency than your Physical body but not by much. Now go back down to the Physical. Experience that as a vibration and how, even as a vibration, it's lower than the Etheric.

Move your awareness up into the upper Etheric, leaving the lower Etheric and the Physical body. Feel that part of your overall Etheric body that's vibrating in that higher level. All of these are in the same space; they're just different frequencies. The Etheric body may go out slightly farther than the physical body, but ever so slightly. Notice how when you are falling asleep, the upper Etheric sort of pops out of the body.

42

Soul and Atman Consciousness

The Causal soul is not limited by time, but it still is happening now to incarnate as you, to be born as you, to live as you, to die as you. See if you can find its intention to be born as you. Why would it leave its nondual, non-suffering space, its permanent ecstasy, and be born as you? Perhaps you can just feel that sense. It doesn't depend upon time or space but a clear and perpetual intent that is revalidated each moment of your experience in time.

Reach out to some frequency in the first, second, or third Causal, and you'll start to have contact with your personal soul—that is, the soul that is incarnating as you even while it does other things. The soul is really quite a magnificent being, unconstrained in time and space. Its consciousness flows across time and multiple spaces, in various times and even in no time. It knows you as a baby; it knows you as other incarnations. In some ways you were always part of it and in some ways you were always separate of it as a personality. Feel this soul and let this soul beam down into your crown.

Now the soul's energy is multidimensional and it engages this first sub-plane of the Etheric in a multidimensional way. It moves through time and space effortlessly—that is, it is not limited by time or space—and, as it flows through, up and down your Brahma Nadi. It integrates all your experiences that you're having today, all your experience that you've had in other lifetimes, and across probabilities, even while it gives exquisite support and nurturing to you in your experience of linear time.

Your soul doesn't shove you out the door and then say, "How did you do?" when you die. It is there moment by moment. The soul communicates to you in the way it can at each moment. To your soul and to your Atman, you're more fun than a whole bunch of the cutest puppies and kittens you ever saw.

Most of us go through life unable to update the soul on our own terms. But your soul is participating, in its own multidimensional way, every moment and in many more dimensions than your personality can track. It is exploring your life through you. It can always provide more alternatives than you can explore in any one lifetime. The truth is that everything that *can* happen *does* happen, but only some things happen *physically* in this probablity. There are a lot of yous that are every bit as physical as you are. To them *you* are the probable self. You are the unreal self or the not-quite-real self. *It* is what's happening. He or she is what's happening. And that's part of how the soul explores *both* paths. Robert Frost's wildest fantasy of roads traveled and less traveled doesn't begin to match your soul's experience.

Your soul experiences your life moment by moment, though it doesn't have moments in the same way you do. It explores it moment by moment and also all at once. This sort of playing with words is necessary to develop neurological flexibility, to start to get a greater appreciation of how all things expand in all directions.

Embodiment is like a creative dream that you awaken from, from time to time. And what you awaken to during sleep is the uncamouflaged you. When you die, eventually you find and learn how to inhabit the uncamouflaged you.

The soul doesn't just know itself just as your soul; it also knows itself as the Atman. You *can't leave* the Atman in a sense that we might talk about. As a human, you have to have this artificial sense of separateness to think that you've left something. That's what human beings have been culturing. But your cat doesn't think, "Oh gee I wonder what my soul is doing tonight while I'm stuck here prowling for mice."

It's a cat when it's a cat, but it isn't just a cat. When it goes to sleep and its tail is twitching, there are other things going on there. Your cat has never left the Atman. Only *you* think you've left the Atman. And that's intentional.

The soul is always playful in its own space, always nurturing, always sees the sense of humor in everything, even as it has a vast appreciation for the struggles that occur in human awareness—and even as it co-participates in those through your Physical permanent seeds.

Allow the brilliance and multidimensionality of your soul to flow through this fine stream called Brahma Nadi. Let the soul flow in and through all those energy points where you have hardened and blocked. It's okay to be hardened and blocked in certain places. They'll free in their own time in their own way. The soul provides a big framework in which you can open up to all of your experience.

Feel how the personal soul has a passionate desire, direction, and intent. In its own realm this intent is to experience everything that could possibly happen. One of the things that it experiences, out of that intent, is the specific experience of you as a human being in a place something seems to happen or doesn't happen. You either married this person or you didn't. See if you can feel that drop of an octave or octave-and-a-half to where the soul in its own plane passionately explores *everything*. And one of those everythings is dropping down into the camouflage reality of your personal self.

Now, here's the tricky part: Can you feel the soul dropping down into the sixth and seventh sub-planes of the Astral? There it passionately engages the particular, the limited, the doing-one-thing-means-that-you-can't-do-another-thing that is its opposite. And yet the soul is completely and utterly passionately open to the opposite of what seems to be the one and only outcome.

As it moves on up to the first sub-plane of the Buddhic, the soul knows itself as all of the consciousnesses of and all the wisdom you will have at the end of a full reincarnational cycle. All the kindness and generosity resides here. Time, as you understand it, and causality, as you understand it, are not operative. Though the Buddhic may seem like a very different time-space, you can still interact with your soul there as it knows itself here.

Buddhic energy is a group consciousness, synchronistic energy; connections are made by meaning not by mechanics or causality. In the upper realms of the Buddhic, you share consciousness with every other human of this time.

Start off at the sixth sub-plane of the Buddhic being a part of a group consciousness. Your soul is no longer focused on one narrow set of reincarnations that seem to be you. There's a group of people reincarnating—you might think of it as a group soul at this point. It includes the same soul that you knew in the Causal, but now it's not just your soul, but includes three or ten or even fifteen others. Some of them may be currently incarnated; others are not. When you meet them here, you may love them or you may hate them. The sixth sub-plane can be quite intimate, and it's kind of amusing that some of the people who dislike each other the most are actually kind of co-beings. They share a soul very intimately, not a personal soul but a very small group soul.

The Buddhic plane starts to create chaos with your idea of identity because past lives of yours begin to mix and match. An inner neighbor of yours that shares a group soul with you has its own incarnation; it might be your spouse, or it might be someone on the other side of the planet that you never meet in this lifetime. It might be someone who doesn't incarnate while you're incarnated. You literally share experiences with them, and you can even divvy up karma amongst you.

People travel in meaning exploration groups. Certain meanings and themes get developed and enhanced through lifetimes.

The group with whom you share a soul grows larger and larger the higher up you go. At the fifth sub-plane it starts to go wider. At the fourth it goes even wider. In the first sub-plane you share a soul with every human being and even with every nature spirit and deva, every animal.

In earlier or later incarnations of a group soul, your portion may come two-thirds from you and one-third from your neighbor. That can be kind of frightening if you think about it: from one lifetime to another, I'm not even coherent with myself. But this wild creativity is what sustains your subjectivity.

You can get over trying to sacrifice for the next incarnation, though it behooves you to work to develop as much authentic kindness and generosity as you can. After all, you and someone else may have been one person in an earlier lifetime. Or you may become one person in a later lifetime. All those little pieces of the oversoul that got together and made Magic Johnson in this lifetime may break up into fifteen different individuals in the next lifetime. And the lifetime after that he may come back together into two different individuals only.

The Atmic is a full octave higher than the Buddhic and works by the same principle, but there you touch an incomprehensible energy that not only covers our solar system but interacts with other star systems, especially Sirius, and other galaxies. Allow something incomprehensible but wonderful through the very definition of physicality at the Atmic level. The laws of physicality have more room for brightness.

Allow an emanation, a beam of light, to shine down into the third sub-plane of the Etheric and whoosh through all of your nadis, changing and improving the light-filledness of them, the flow of flexibility and love, and allow that healing to proceed both at the Atmic level and at the third sub-plane of the Etheric.

The third sub-plane of the Etheric sets up the structure of physicality. The second sub-plane is where Vajrayana and certain mystical tantric practices take place, though Vajrayana can't take you all the way to emptiness, which is at the first sub-plane of the Adi.

The fourth sub-plane of the Etheric—I can't justify this but it makes perfect sense—is kind of the equivalent to the heart, which is the fourth chakra and also reciprocal to the Buddhic plane, where you have the group consciousness that underlies and creates the space for our having personal emotions.

The fifth sub-plane of the Atmic is where the laws of physics are established for the planet as we experience it.

How are the laws of physics established? How does a law like gravity originate in the fifth sub-plane of the Atmic and become physical law? Find it for yourself. From the fifth sub-plane of the Atmic, look down into the cells of your body and let the programming that makes it susceptible to gravity light up. Notice that there's some reciprocation in that programming. The programming doesn't actually reside in your body or in the cells of your body only. You may think of bits and pieces of it in each cell or each molecule in your body, but it somehow or other is in communication with that same kind of programming in every other person's body in this world, and even in the sea, the air, and going through the whole planet, maybe the whole solar system.

Sense that programming, not in a literal but a metaphorical way, in the cells and atoms and quarks of your body. If it were just in your body, it wouldn't be gravity, but it extends beyond your body and is mutually dependent in its being in every other physical body on this planet, whether it's an atom or a person. See if you can appreciate what a cool gift gravity is, all the interesting dramas that play out in this portion of the universe because of that collaboration between the Atmic plane and your body and every other body on this planet and beyond.

Go up to the fourth sub-plane of the Atmic and begin to look at something that is analogous but different between the fourth sub-plane and your Etheric body. There's a kind of Etheric physics we are already acquainted with. Remember, the densest part of your Etheric body is the acupuncture meridians and the next Etheric layer up is the yogic breathing nadis. The next level up is where Tibetan tantra occurs. The next level up from that is where your Physical permanent seed is. All of those have different sorts of rules and relationships that are analogous to gravity but not identical to gravity. Become aware of how they're interrelated with every aspect of Etheric reality. This doesn't necessarily come from the fourth sub-plane but from the whole Atmic plane. It's what allows the Etheric to have coherent forms, somewhat stable forms. It's very analogous to gravity—Etheric gravity—though in your Etheric body you can float or walk through walls, at least some portions of your Etheric body can do that.

The Atmic is probably the plane that is involved in learning how to exit life in the Rainbow Body.

See if you get any sense of how your emotions feed into the Etheric body so that they color and give quality to your Etheric body. They don't quite set the laws of physics for your Etheric body, as that's set up in the Atmic, but they do set up qualities and tendencies for your personal Etheric body, and the whole Astral plane sets up tendencies for any human Etheric body.

Let a light shine down from the Atmic, down through the Etheric and into the Physical. See if you sense the nature spirits moderate and modulate this energy Physically and Etherically, without which you couldn't really have gravity or structure of the Etheric. See if you can sense that in some manner those nature spirits are part of you. Otherwise, there would be no recognizable you. Now there are big spirits that help gravity exist through large parts of the planet. You can let those light up. See if you can see smaller ones that are interconnected with your body; interconnect your body with other bodies so that gravity works at a Physical level and something similar, but less restrictively, at an Etheric level.

The Atmic plane is curiously not where we find the Atman; that's in the Monadic. The Monadic is where I start to see the Hindu Atman, which is at once unified with everything and yet particularly me. At the beginning of the fifth plane of the Monadic I recognize that Atman that is everything and yet is simultaneously, uniquely, the source of me and my eternal dance. In whatever dimension I dance, the Atman is always there and making sense. And by me I don't mean this particular incarnation. It knows itself as lots of different things simultaneously and yet it has a unique affinity from this incarnation's point of view. It's kind of the core that makes each incarnation eternal, whether or not it's your last incarnation. It dives into all of your experiences as a human being and, in particular, operates through the neutral fluid at the center of the head at the sixth and seventh sub-planes of the Astral. That is where it contributes to creating you, together with the personal soul.

In the Monadic, all the apparent contradictions—any tensions between polarities that are not spontaneously resolving and flowing into harmony and playfully back into tension, any place where that play of polarities has gotten clogged—are propelled into healing.

Step through the looking glass into your Atman's perception of you—in your humanity as you usually understand it; in your humanity as being part of a weather system or an election; in the increasing, though sadly not without setbacks, movement toward World Peace; you as a six-year-old and you as a sixty-year-old; you in this probability and you in other probabilities; you as you existed before this planet existed and you as you will exist again after it no longer exists—all these at once. Your Atman fully participates in every moment, simultaneously fully conscious in every moment and every presentation of yourself at every level, experiencing them all together and yet exquisitely separately. Notice how joyous and open the Atman is compared to your personality. Enjoy the interplay of all those aspects, yet let each be utterly separate.

As you move up—though I don't know that up continues to make sense in the Monadic or Adi—at each sub-plane, distinctions disappear, categories disappear. Sense the fullness and the emptiness at the Adi, the disappearance of all categories.

Let's go on a field trip together. You don't need your parents. Let's just go visit my friend Will at in the Monadic plane. Hopefully this will be a very attractive plane ride, no TSA even.

We're going to go up to Monadic and try to hook up with your Atman, that spark that's at the ground, at the beginning, the end, and middle, of your consciousness. And from that spark I'm going to try to help you find Will's spark. Then see what you can see as you feel or see or intuit Will's spark. Perhaps you will see his Multipersonhood—his or her or its Multipersonhood.

It's quite possible that you won't consciously get large parts of this seminar, but you're developing neurological flexibility and you're making connections at inner levels, and this takes time. I'm teaching it and we're zipping through it in a weekend, but this sort of growing awareness, for example, of what the Atman is, that took place over a year or two for me, and a growing awareness of what that ribbon of violet light was, that took place over fifteen or twenty years until I could recognize Will with confidence

Let's start at the sixth sub-plane of the Mental. I'm radiating that energy out if you want to match it. And the fifth sub-plane of the Mental, fourth, third sub-plane of the Causal, second and first. Moving on up to the seventh sub-plane of the Buddhic, then sixth, fifth, fourth, third, second, and first. Moving on up to the Atmic, a change in frequency, seventh, sixth, fifth, fourth, third, second, and first. Moving on up to the Monadic, seventh, sixth, fifth, fourth, third, second, and first. Find where that Unity consciousness turns to spark you. It is an eternal always-and-already spark and yet it is also changing. It changes in a way that it doesn't change. This is a Unity level with All That Is, and in that Unity, nevertheless, it is also emerging as a spark that is Will. Say hello to it.

As you have observed this spark of Will or of the Multipersonhood of Will, it may dawn on you that there's no resistance to experience here. In a very real way, there's no inside or outside, even though there's newness and growth. This is a very subtle perception, but it's one that grows in your heart and your mind over the coming days and weeks and months. What would it be like to have no resistance to experience, to have clarity and differentiation and preferences, but no resistance?

Just let yourself observe whatever you observe, whatever you intuit or feel.

At the same level, turn your attention to Seth as he-it-they exist at this level. You may hook into his energy, and after you've done it for a while, see if you can become aware of how it has no resistance to experience. It goes off in all directions, and in all of them there's no resistance. It isn't that nondual awareness is a frequency that you find in the Monadic plane, it's that the beings you find here tend to have nondual awareness.

The highest plane of the seven planes that are mostly relevant to human consciousness we call the Adi—other books give it other names—and that is related to and reciprocates with the first sub-plane of the Etheric.

The Monadic, which is the next full plane down, will be related to the second sub-plane of the Etheric. The Atmic, which is the third sub-plane down, is related to the third sub-plane of the Etheric, and the Buddhic, which is the fourth sub-plane down, is related to the fourth sub-plane of the Etheric and the acupuncture meridians, and so on.

I want to emphasize: the seven planes we study are those relevant to human consciousness. Planes themselves go on indefinitely through different experiences and relevances, most of them incomprehensible to humans, though some energy from higher planes than the Adi is starting to be relevant now as we approach the Aquarian Age.

What we experience of this planet is just one point of view. The planet and its consciousness go in all kinds of directions. Not every aspect of the planet has gravity as we understand it; every aspect that we can *see* does. That's *our* version of the planet, but this is like a huge multiplex with all kinds of films going on. The film that we're looking at has gravity in it.

The Adi plane as a whole is where distinctions cease to be barriers. Any distinctions are completely permeable with changes in a sea of play. They are rising and falling without any constraints, empty of any permanence or reality.

CONCLUSION

End of Class

Hopefully, you have made some progress. Put your present situation on a rose. Give that rose a grounding cord. Put it off to your left and tell that rose you'll come back to it and work on it. For now, you are setting it aside so you can blow pictures. You can even hand the rose off to your dream-self to let it and your guides cue that in your lesson plan, as it were, so that you can be ready to work on it. Or you might just say, "Okay, next Tuesday, I'm going to work on it." You're setting it aside for now and promising yourself that you'll do practice with it.

Once an inner decision has been made, the guides will often take that as the operative event; but in our terms, the operative event is when it manifests externally, which might be a decade later.

Put up the class on a rose and pull your energy out. As you explode it, know that the class has ended. Pull your energy out of each other, the people you had talks with, and send their energy back to them. When you send energy back, you send it permissively, you don't jam it in someone else's space. Don't say, "Here, this belongs to you! Take it!" If they don't want it, you can give it to their guides or the Sun or the Earth. Or if they really don't want it, they'll find someone else to put it in, someone who is in agreement at an energy level for it be in their space until they're ready to change.

Please pull your energy out of Gloria and send her energy back to her. Pull your energy out of me or Mataji and send our energy back to us.

Create a rose for where you were before this class as an energy being, and now create a rose for where you are now. Just announce to everybody on the planet, on or off the planet, anyone who's interested, that you've changed and that you're going to continue to change. They don't have to accept or acknowledge that you've changed, you're just letting them know: change of psychic address. See if you can find a smile somewhere.

Create a rose for all the spiritual information that has come in over the last week—this seminar started in the dream state—and let that rose divide into three parts. One is the energy that you're ready to assimilate as a waking human being now. Hand that part up to your Akashic Record Keeper; put it above your crown. Let it file that information, harmonize it with all your other information. Like a computer, it can keep information on a hard drive; it can also download it into something else. Let it download that information that is useful for you now as a human with a body.

Let the second part of that spiritual information rose be information that's relevant to you as a human with a body but that you may not be ready to assimilate now. Hand that information up to your Akashic Record Keeper up above your crown and let the record keeper queue your rose up as a program of experience to come in a productive way: in the dream state, as a matter of doing your work without any conscious attention, as part of the seminar—however it comes in when it's queued up and ready to come in when appropriate. It doesn't have to come in any one particular way, it's queued up flexibly.

Finally the third part of the spiritual information is not particularly relevant to you as a human when you're awake and in your body. Hand that up to The Akashic Record Keeper. The Akashic Record Keeper forwards it to other aspects of yourself who can use that information. Please fill your aura with lots of golden suns and just the right amount of Earth energy for your body at this time.

Glossary

Angelic Realm: A separate range of consciousness on Earth that is not physical. Beings of the Angelic Realm move through their lives and toward the good naturally, the way a plant moves toward the sun. They do not suffer.

Baby being: A new baby being is created for each new incarnation by the Causal Soul and Atman well before the decisions are made about your new incarnation. It has a full voice in creating and the right to veto any pre-birth decision. It ceases making sense to call it a baby being as you grow up. By that time, it is essentially who you think of as yourself.

Calcification: The act of an energy becoming rigid through resistance or stagnation. Of course, this is a metaphor.

Camouflage: Humans are set up neurologically to perceive experiences in limited ways. Seth called those neurological limits camouflage. His point was that human experience occurs in a realm where the fundamental nature of reality is camouflaged. While you can alter your neurological system to lessen the extent that the fundamental nature of reality is camouflaged, Seth makes it clear that the camouflage is supportive of the human drama, and therefore altering your neurological circuits to see through the camouflage permanently is counterproductive from the Sethian point of view.

Cellular consciousness: Everything has its own consciousness, including single or groups of cells.

Chaos systems: A chaos system is any phenomena that can be analyzed by Chaos theory. Chaos theory is a field of mathematics that studies dynamic systems that are very sensitive to small changes and are not predictable despite the clear rules governing them. Mathematicians have discovered many patterns in the seeming random disorder or chaos of those systems.

Circuit: The word *circuit* as used here is a metaphor taken from an electric circuit. We use it to evoke what makes something your past as opposed to something that merely could have happened. Our normal understanding of the past is that it no longer exists. The Sethian understanding is that all of the past, as well as the future and anything that could have happened or that could happen in the future, exists in just as much reality as the present moment. What makes a particular moment in the past *your* past is analogous to an electric wire forming a circuit between your present and that particular past.

Clear: As in, to clear something. The two basic clearing techniques in this system are exploding pictures and returning energy that isn't yours. Both pictures and other people's energy in your personal aura obstruct the free flow of energy through your aura, and thus limit your ability to respond fully and authentically to your experience.

Coordinate points: Locations on, in, or above the Earth with particular power to intensify the manifestation of inner energies.

Crown: The crown is an important chakra on the top of the head, usually enumerated as the seventh chakra. While there will always be many colors of energy in the crown, in our system, we find that the color of the dominant energy of the crown in the personal aura sets a strong direction to your behavior, thoughts, and feelings. Unconsciously, everyone changes their crown color frequently to match the energy color of whatever they are reacting to. When you match what you are responding to, then your new crown color strongly pushes your behavior. If you can learn to monitor your crown color, and set it at a color of your choosing, then you can decide what color directs your behavior.

Current time: Current time in this system isn't about being in this moment of clock time, or even a description of time at all; instead, it's a description of what your aura is doing. If a part of your aura is able to vibrate freely wherever you want to turn your attention, then that part of your aura is in current time, even if you are placing your attention on the past or the future. Current time is the ability to turn your attention where you want it. This definition arises from the fact that whenever we hold onto a stuck picture, that part of our aura is not able to respond freely to new experience or a new focus of our attention.

Densification: The process of energy moving lower in frequency. Densification is a necessary part of any energy moving from a higher plane to a lower one; for example, emotional energy moving into physical manifestation.

Devas: Beings of the Angelic Realm who help create all physical forms and events. There are also Devas who help create forms and events in higher planes.

The Driver: The part of our brain that is set up to move us to take action to escape pain.

Enmeshment: Energetically entangled.

Female grounding: Female grounding is a grounding technique that addresses the unique energies of women. It involves adding small cords from female parts of your body after creating a grounding cord; from the ovaries, uterus, the two branches of the sciatic nerve at the sacrum, and the female creative space (which is in front of the body in front of the uterus) to the grounded first chakra. These organs are whole and operative at the Etheric, regardless of any surgeries that may have taken place.

Hello: To greet something and allow it to be as it is, exactly as we find it or experience it. Hello is not about approving or disapproving. You can say hello even if you approve or disapprove, but your hello doesn't include your opinions. You acknowledge to yourself whatever feelings you have, but the hello is just a neutral acknowledgement of what you perceive.

Gestalt: A unified whole that is more than the sum of its parts.

Grace: Flowing; moving within your life reasonably well.

Grounding cord: An extension of Earth energy from your first chakra down into the center of the Earth. This is used to ground your emotions while working with energy in your aura. *See also the Grounding Cords exercise.*

Guides: Multidimensional entities who work in inner realities to help you according to their best understanding. You do not have to take your understanding of any guide's communication as truth; it is important to make your own evaluation and to continue testing your understanding against your growing experience.

Impermanence: The fact that no phenomenon is eternally unchanged. Without ever mentioning the word, Seth flips the normal way mystics use that understanding. In Seth, it resolves, with other principles, into the optimistic implication that all consciousness expands in all directions and therefore each subjectivity is eternal, within and outside of time, and forever sacredly creative.

Interdependent origination: Neither you nor anything else exists separately as an island unto itself. Everything is interwoven with everything else, though each part of any gestalt is interwoven in its own unique way. While Seth may never have used this technical term, in his teachings it was central and when combined with impermanence, and other ideas in his teachings, implies that all consciousness expands in all directions. Every subjectivity, even though it is always changing, continues to grow in all directions eternally, both within and outside of time.

Karma disc: Clairvoyantly, you can see karma in anyone's aura present as a disk of light. There are psychic ways of clearing these karma disks.

Linear time: Sequential time, clock time.

Male grounding: Male grounding is a grounding technique that addresses the unique energies of men. It involves adding a small cord from the top of your grounding cord to the prostate.

Moving energy: Willing energy to move. Any time you do or think anything, you move energy, consciously or unconsciously. The Will automatically directs energy. As you become consciously aware of energy, you can consciously direct it, though if the energy is someone else's, it often won't cooperate; even if it is your own, you may have tensions and contradictions that limit your ability to move it in the way you desire.

Neutrality: Openness to the experience of the moment as it is. Neutrality doesn't mean that you like an experience. You can be in neutrality even as you might also try to change yourself and/or the external world. But in neutrality, your aura energy stays open to the experience and your sensations, feelings, and ideas about the experience.

Nadis: The circuits of energy flowing in the Etheric body that are a major center of attention for many yogis. By clearing blockages in particular nadis, one can generate power to transform the Etheric body.

Octave: We use this word as a metaphor for one energy vibrating at a higher frequency than another. Drawing from music theory, we might say that the next higher subplane is one note higher than its predecessor, while the next plane is one octave higher than its predecessor.

Permanent seeds: Permanent seeds is a phrase popularized by healer Choa Kok Sui as a more accurate descriptor of the old Theosophist concept of permanent atoms. From a Sethian perspective, John and Gloria's system sees permanent seeds as the core of the soul's expression and orientation throughout this incarnation. Your soul's participation, moment by moment, in your life is largely through the permanent seeds.

Pictures: A psychic structure that vibrates in your aura, holding intentions, feelings, or beliefs. A picture, by holding some aura energy in a sustained vibrational pattern, tends to generate an external event or hold and sustain sensations, emotions, and beliefs. Ideally, when the experience that the picture is holding ends, the picture dissolves and the energy that was being held vibrating in a specific and limited pattern is again free to vibrate throughout its entire natural range. Then the energy is free to respond to new experience. When pictures do not dissolve on their own, we call them stuck. *See also the Pictures exercise.*

Plane/sub-plane: The nineteenth and early twentieth century Theosophists developed a belief system that gives an orderly way to study the frequency of mystical energies. They divided the whole universe into seven frequency ranges that they called planes, perhaps because each can be explored as a separate universe with its own laws and interests. They further subdivided each plane into seven sub-planes, and even further subdivided sub-planes into sub-sub-planes. The plane/sub-plane system is an elegant and easy way to develop your technical prowess. In reality, all the energies are interdependent so the Theosophical plane system is a simplification of the rich interconnectedness of all energies.

Polarity: An intrinsic part of consciousness that manifests as apparent opposites. Each side of a polarity penetrates all aspects of the other.

Power spot: A large coordinate point that is fully capable of empowering and speeding up the manifestation of your energy separately and in collaboration with everything else that's going on. The power spot is alive with its own kind of intent, interest, kindness, and generosity.

Rainbow body: When we use the term, we mean the new Etheric transformation that occurs when you raise the vibration of every living cell in your physical body from the physical plane up to the Etheric plane, permanently leaving physical incarnation. Instead of dying, you merely transition to living in the Etheric world.

Resource state: A psychological or energy state that helps you be resourceful.

Roses: A visualization used to hold energy and perform psychic actions on the energy such as explode pictures or read the energy. *See also the Roses exercise.*

Spark: That which gives rise to you.

Strange attractors: A pattern of order within chaos. While you can never circumscribe where a dynamic chaos system will go, the strange attractors give it something akin to a center of gravity and serve as a metaphor for an identity in the midst of dynamic and unbounded actions.

Survival: going into survival; a mode of thinking and aura energy that arises out of the first chakra. Usually, we are too much in survival, treating wants and wishes that are really preferences as necessities.

Sample Exercises

The following passages explain some the basic components that are used in many of the exercises in *Recentering Seth*:

Roses

A rose is a powerful tool used to hold psychic energy of any kind. Roses are an important symbol in Western mysticism, analogous to the lotus in Eastern mysticism, and act as a focal point for working with energy. To create a rose, imagine one in front of you of any size that appeals to you. Your visualization does not need to be clear; you can even just "feel" the rose if you are kinesthetic rather than visual. Then, imbue it with energy from your aura or from any psychic phenomenon that you are exploring.

Pictures

The vibration of your aura can create a psychic structure called a picture. Pictures represent events you experience or imagine, emotions, or beliefs. They are created and destroyed spontaneously and regularly as you go through life, but sometimes they become stuck in your aura when they represent an experience you react to with resistance. Exploding stuck pictures is a way of freeing your aura. When you explode a picture, the energy that was being held in a single repeating pattern is free to vibrate through its full natural range, thus returning that energy to be free to respond to new experience.

To explode a picture and free its energy to vibrate anew for new experiences, you will first create a rose. This rose will hold your picture outside of your aura so you can perceive it more clearly. Once you have created this rose, visualize moving your picture out from your aura and onto your rose. Imagine a ball of golden cosmic energy enveloping the rose that holds your picture. Next, visualize that both the picture and rose explode, freeing the restriction on that energy's ability to open to new experience.

Grounding Cords

Grounding is a practice that helps to stabilize your body and separate it from emotional fluctuations while you work with your energy. In order to ground, you use an energy tool called a grounding cord. One method of creating a grounding cord is to imagine a ball of earth-green energy at the base of your spine. Visualize that ball dropping down, falling all the way to the center of the Earth, where the Earth energy is neutral. As the sphere of energy falls, imagine a cord connecting it to you, and neutral energy flowing through it between you and the center of the Earth.

Being in the Center of your Head

Bringing your awareness to the center of your head helps you to achieve neutrality. The center of your head is very near your sixth chakra. It's two inches behind and two inches above your pineal gland. The practice of noticing where your awareness is located can help you to bring your awareness to the center of your head. Invite your consciousness to rest at the center of your head. Alternatively, you can measure the distance between your awareness and the center of your head. This act of measuring brings your attention to both in such a way that your awareness tends to naturally move back into the center of the head.

Practice moving your awareness outside of the center of your head and then back in so that you become comfortable noticing the difference.

Index

About the Author

John Friedlander began his meditation practice early in 1970 and traveled to India in 1971 and 1973. While living in a yoga ashram, John was introduced to the Jane Roberts' Seth channelings and, together with Jane's non-Seth writings, they have been the basis of John's studies and understandings of the world ever since. John had the great good fortune to study personally with both Lewis Bostwick, founder of the Berkeley Psychic Institute, and Jane. In August 1973 John traveled to Berkeley, California, to study with Lewis. His system was the starting point for and is still the vital underpinning of John's psychic practice and teachings. John and his co-author Gloria Hemsher's interpretation of Lewis's system, modified by Seth's understanding of consciousness, is developed in their books *Basic Psychic Development* and *Psychic Psychology*. In January of 1974 John moved to Ithaca, New York, to study in Jane's Seth classes. In his fifty-plus years of study, John has also focused at times on Buddhist meditation and theory, the ideas of Aurobindo, Theosophical belief systems, communication skills, the Michael channelings, and other systems.

John graduated from Duke University and Harvard Law school. He began practicing law in 1974, first in a couple of small general practice law firms, then in highly sophisticated plaintiff's business torts,

419

securities and antitrust litigation practice, and finally as a sole practitioner with a general practice.

In 1989 John moved to Ann Arbor, Michigan, with his wife who was starting her career as a professor at the University of Michigan. This gave John the freedom to be a full-time psychic, teacher, and writer.

Currently, John teaches, writes, and does psychic readings. John and Gloria have a website, Psychicpsychology.org, that contains trainings and calendar information.